SLAVERY ATTACKED

SLAVERY ATTACKED

SOUTHERN SLAVES AND THEIR ALLIES 1619 – 1865

Merton L. Dillon

LOUISIANA STATE UNIVERSITY PRESS
BATON ROUGE AND LONDON

Designer: Diane Batten Didier
Typeface: Aster
Typesetter: G & S Typesetters, Inc.
Printer and binder: Thomson-Shore, Inc.

Library of Congress Cataloging-in-Publication Data

Dillon, Merton Lynn, 1924–
   Slavery attacked : Southern slaves and their allies, 1619–1865 /
Merton L. Dillon.
      p. cm.
   Includes bibliographical references (p.   ) and index.
   ISBN 0-8071-1614-9 (alk. paper)   ISBN 0-8071-1653 (pbk.; alk. paper)
      1. Slavery—Southern States—History. 2. Slavery—United States—
Anti-slavery movements. 3. Southern States—History—Colonial
period, ca. 1600–1775. 4. Southern States—History—1775–1865.
I. Title.
E441.D55   1990
975'.03—dc20   90-6067
                                                                        CIP

The paper in this book meets the guidelines for permanence and durability of th
Committee on Production Guidelines for Book Longevity of the Council on Librar
Resources. ∞

Contents

Acknowledgments

A book as long in the making as this one inevitably incurs heavy obligations on the part of its author. The greatest of these is to the many persons, past and contemporary, whose work has made possible my own. I hope that the footnotes and bibliography adequately convey the extent of my debt to them. Other obligations come to mind. The Graduate School, the College of Humanities, and the Department of History of the Ohio State University provided a grant-in-aid and allowed me time that facilitated my research and writing. A senior fellowship from the National Endowment for the Humanities, awarded some years ago for a different project, contributed in important, unforeseen ways to this one. I am grateful to all the staff at Louisiana State University Press for their courtesies, but especially to Margaret Dalrymple, editor-in-chief, for encouraging my project from the time she first learned of it, and to John Easterly, production editor, for his exceptional competence in editing my earlier book and coordinating the editing of this one. I am also grateful to Joan Seward, my copy editor, for planing rough places in the manuscript. Finally, my appreciation goes to Marjorie Haffner and Janice Gulker, valued members of the office staff of the Ohio State University's history department. Their cheerful assistance helped me through many a crisis during the final stages of preparing the manuscript for this book.

SLAVERY ATTACKED

Introduction

North American slaveholders strove for the absolute submission of their labor force and also its isolation from any group with which it might make common cause. But those were goals difficult if not impossible to attain, and probably few truly expected to do so. An approximation must suffice. With some success, slaves contrived to resist demands for submission and, despite all precautions, succeeded in finding people who welcomed and even encouraged their resistance. For generations such subversion proved manageable, but with nearly every passing decade it became more troublesome and more ominous. Eventually, after many years of vigilance, slaveholders faced in the slaves and their allies a combination too powerful to be overcome. The result was the fall of their regime.

From one point of view, this outcome seems surprising, for though West Indian and Latin American slaves challenged their owners with devastating rebellions and extensive, long-lasting maroon settlements, slaves in North America appeared comparatively docile and reconciled to bondage. Never throughout their long history did they carry out a large-scale insurrection. The three major rebellions that did occur—in South Carolina (1739), in Louisiana (1811), and in Virginia (1831)—had relatively few participants (a few hundred at most), were confined to small areas, and were of short duration. It is true that some conspiracies to rebel, particularly in New York (1741), in Virginia (1800), and in South Carolina (1822), purportedly gained more adherents—thousands, it was said—and thus may have had greater potential. But we shall never know, for each was exposed and its leaders were tried and executed before their plans could be carried out. Slaveholders seemed to have met every challenge successfully.

Yet the apparent stability of the North American slave system masks the danger contemporaries saw in it and belied its vulnerability. Slavery contained within itself the seeds of its own destruction. Few owners could fail to know that their labor system rested ultimately on force—the threat of reprisal—and the willingness of slaves, however extorted, to remain in bondage. Slaveholders must have realized that slaves continued to work at their assigned tasks, finally, because coercion—and the absence of formidable allies—compelled them to do so. And the owners also must have known that it was to secure that labor and to preserve their own dominion that they kept the slave population under steady surveillance and ruthlessly punished transgression. It was similarly obvious that on the day their power to dominate disappeared, their regime would fall.

The necessity for force was not theoretical. Only with unremitting effort could slaves be kept at work on the masters' terms. Many ran away, and everywhere owners were faced with workers who malingered, ignored orders, and otherwise resisted exploitation—even to the point of violence. Although such subversive behavior was far from universal, it occurred often enough to make the potential for massive disorder and consequent ruin a constant dread.

Overwhelming evidence shows that slaves sought not so much advantage within the system as escape from it, even its destruction. However, their own energies might not be enough to achieve those ends. In this conflict, as in any other, outside aid would be useful, if not essential. Accordingly, slaves welcomed allies in their struggle for autonomy. Likewise, enemies and rivals of the owners, whatever their attitudes toward blacks or toward slavery itself might be, repeatedly made use of the slaves as a means of attaining their own ends.

For many years, circumstances allowed slaveholders to keep their slaves adequately in check and to counter the menacing outside forces. But, eventually, the two sources of opposition—the slaves themselves and the owners' rivals and enemies—joined forces to bring ruin to the slaveholding South.

This book, then, is about the slaveholders' long travail and their ltimate failure. It is about the changing relationship of slaves to ther groups within the South and beyond it. It is about the ways in which slave resistance was linked to foreign relations, war, and invasion, and to internal social and political conflict.

1

$\infty\infty\infty\infty\infty\infty\infty\infty\infty\infty\infty\infty\infty\infty\infty\infty\infty\infty\infty$

A Worrisome People

The English who settled at Jamestown in 1609 faced a hostile environment. Hunger, disease, and early death were the fate of most of them. Indians and Spaniards threatened the colony. Factionalism plagued it. To these misfortunes (each of them arguably unavoidable) the Virginians soon chose to add slavery. This eventually proved to be a source of disorder and insecurity fully as grave as any of the other ills that beset them.

Sometime in the summer of 1619, a Dutch man-of-war landed "20. and odd Negroes" at Point Comfort, where the James River empties into the Chesapeake. So reported John Rolfe, future husband of Pocahontas, shortly after the ship had sailed away. If, as has been argued, the white settlers wavered for a while between holding the new arrivals as slaves and treating them as indentured servants, the indecision did not last long. By 1640 some, perhaps most, of the Africans in Virginia undoubtedly had been enslaved, and just as quickly as more became available, those white proprietors who could afford to do so added to their numbers.[1]

Practice and custom soon were codified in law. During the 1660s,

1. Susan M. Klingburg (ed.), *Records of the Virginia Company of London* (Washington, D.C., 1906–35), III, 241–48; Wesley Frank Craven, *White, Red, and Black: The Seventeenth-Century Virginian* (Charlottesville, Va., 1971), 73–103; Wesley Frank Craven, "Twenty Negroes to Jamestown in 1619?" *Virginia Quarterly Review*, LVII (1971), 416–20; Robert McColley, "Slavery in Virginia, 1619–1660: A Reexamination," in Robert H. Abzug and Stephen E. Maizlish (eds.), *New Perspectives on Race and Slavery in America: Essays in Honor of Kenneth M. Stampp* (Lexington, Ky., 1986), 11–24.

he colonial assemblies of both Virginia and Maryland defined slav-
·ry as a lifelong, inheritable condition and provided legislation de-
.igned to protect it. In South Carolina, founded in the 1670s by pro-
)rietors familiar with the slave-labor system of both the Barbados
ind the Chesapeake area, no period of indecision was evident. There
he institution unquestionably existed from the first settlement. And
n Georgia, where the trustees had planned to keep slavery out,
)opular demand soon led to its introduction. In the New England
:olonies, as well as in New York, Pennsylvania, and New Jersey,
)lacks were introduced at an early date with little if any controversy
·egarding their slave status.[2]

Nowhere in the English colonies did any effective counterforce
:xist to prevent white settlers who could afford to do so from taking
·ull advantage of the alluring economic opportunities offered by the
:xploitation of blacks. The Europeans were free to do with them as
.hey liked. It is hardly surprising, then, to find that well before the
:nd of the seventeenth century, the great majority of blacks in En-
5lish America were slaves in law as well as in practice and that
:ontinued importation steadily increased their numbers. At the
;ame time, the supply of indentured white servants diminished.
There were only about three hundred blacks in Virginia in 1648, out
)f a total population of fifteen thousand, and only two thousand (or
5 percent of the population) in 1670, but by 1710, about one-quarter
)f the population of Virginia and Maryland were black slaves. In
South Carolina in 1720, they made up 40 percent of the population,
ind importation continued undiminished.[3]

We can be reasonably sure of the motives that led profit-seeking
:olonists up and down the Atlantic coast to hold blacks as slaves
ind to import more of them. Equally important for understanding
.he southern past are the anxieties and dangers that resulted from
.hose decisions. The profits and convenience of slave labor never
:ntirely disappeared, but neither did its constantly unfolding haz-

2. Paul C. Palmer, "Servant into Slave: The Evolution of the Legal Servitude of
.he Negro Laborer in Colonial Virginia," *South Atlantic Quarterly*, LXV (1966), 355–
70; James Curtis Ballagh, *A History of Slavery in Virginia* (Baltimore, 1902), 31;
James H. Brewer, "Negro Property Owners in Seventeenth-Century Virginia," *Wil-
iam and Mary Quarterly*, 3rd ser., XII (1955), 575–80; Carl N. Degler, "Slavery and
.he Genesis of American Race Prejudice," *Comparative Studies in Society and History*,
II (October, 1959), 49–66; Edgar J. McManus, *Black Bondage in the North* (Syracuse,
N.Y., 1973); Lorenzo J. Greene, *The Negro in Colonial New England, 1620–1776* (New
York, 1942).
3. David W. Galenson, *White Servitude in Colonial America: An Economic Analysis*
(Cambridge, Eng., 1981), 118–68; U.S. Bureau of the Census, *Historical Statistics of
·he United States, Colonial Times to 1970* (2 vols.; 1975), II, 1168.

ards. At no time could American slaveholding society be called se
cure. Efforts to eliminate threats to its survival failed. No soone
had challenges in one form been dealt with than they reappeared i
different shape. Never for long could slaveholders escape the nee
to defend their interests from both internal and external foes. Th
constant need to be on guard helped set the course of southern his
tory and in that manner influenced the development of the nation
  An internal threat appeared almost as soon as slavery was insti
tuted. Native Americans, attempting to defend themselves agains
relentless European encroachment, might use dissident black
within the European settlements as military instruments to destro
the invader; likewise, blacks might view Indians as allies in thei
own struggles for freedom. Even if no such political connection
were made, backcountry Indians still might harbor runaway slave
and thereby add another element of insecurity to a valuable bu
unstable institution. Those possibilities—absent nowhere—seemec
most alive in the Southeast, where potent Indian tribes lived clos
to large concentrations of slaves. Accordingly, authorities there took
steps designed to prevent the unthinkable—an Indian attack coor
dinated with a slave uprising. Everything possible was done to
prevent the two threatening groups from recognizing and taking ad
vantage of their common interest. Indians and blacks were encour
aged to view each other as enemies, and Indians were rewardec
for returning runaways. For example, in South Carolina, Indian
helped round up insurgents after the great rebellion at Stono ir
1739. But these efforts were not completely successful, for in Geor
gia and South Carolina in particular, runaway slaves continued tc
find refuge in the Indian country. In South Carolina, the point o
greatest danger, officials decided—though their efforts proved fu
tile—to encourage the importation of indentured servants rather
than black slaves on the ground that white servants would help
guard the frontiers against Indian attack while also defending against
slave insurrection.[4]
  Potential danger appeared within the white settlements as well
Living among the ambitious importers of black labor was a mi-

  4. William S. Willis, Jr., "Divide and Rule: Red, White, and Black in the Southeast," *Journal of Negro History*, XLVIII (1963), 157–76; William S. Willis, Jr., "Anthropology and Negroes on the Southern Colonial Frontier," in James C. Curtis and Lewis
L. Gould (eds.), *The Black Experience in America: Selected Essays* (Austin, 1970)
42–46; Robert L. Meriwether, *The Expansion of South Carolina, 1729–1765* (Kings-
port, Tenn., 1940), 17, 18, 27; Lathan A. Windley (comp.), *Runaway Slave Advertisements: A Documentary History from the 1730s to 1790* (Westport, Conn., 1983), IV, 36
40, 43, 102, 104; III, 94, 265, 638.

rity of whites who, though seldom openly opposed to slavery, were
t committed to it either. They were exasperatingly slow to adopt
e attitudes essential to maintain it. Their hesitancy posed a prob-
m for ambitious planters, for a persistent absence of internal con-
nsus would threaten the masters' control of increasingly valuable
operty. The disciplining of slaves—always a challenge—would be
ade even more difficult if part of the white population failed to
eat them as members of a base class or—still worse—if they
lped them escape or in less drastic ways encouraged them to rest the owners' authority.

In the seventeenth century, especially, there were signs that these
ings were happening. Instead of quickly developing closed soci-
ies, the southern colonies for a long time left room for much diver-
ty in attitude and practice with respect to slavery, and whites re-
ained far from united in resolve to debase the growing black
pulation. So long as this situation continued, the owners' social
sition and their property would be problematic.

Race consciousness, with its attendant bias, developed more
owly than is sometimes supposed. Whatever degree of prejudice
e colonial elite felt against blackness—and Winthrop Jordan has
oved that the bias was deep and of long standing—the white in-
entured servants, who supplied most of the labor in seventeenth-
ntury Virginia and Maryland, were less quick to interpret their
vn color as a badge of superiority over their black fellow bonds-
en. Although in outward appearance and cultural traits the two
oups markedly differed from each other, this finally mattered less
an a later generation might expect. And in any case, until late in
e seventeenth century, blacks in the Chesapeake Bay area and
ven in the Carolinas remained too few to be perceived as a threat
 white cultural dominance. Under such circumstances, lower-
ass white colonists—servants and even small farmers—could ig-
ore racial barriers without feeling they courted danger or violated
boo. The blacks' condition as slaves unquestionably was wretched,
ut so was that of many white servants. The burdens and griefs of
ondage were not confined to blacks alone.[5]
Relationships between members of the two oppressed groups

5. Winthrop D. Jordan, *White over Black: American Attitudes Toward the Negro,*
50–1812 (Chapel Hill, N.C., 1968), passim, but esp. x–xi, 91–98, 110; Gerald W.
ullin, *Flight and Rebellion: Slave Resistance in Eighteenth-Century Virginia* (New
rk, 1972), 187n, 191n, 192n; Warren Billings (ed.), *The Old Dominion in the Seven-
nth Century: A Documentary History of Virginia, 1606–1689* (Chapel Hill, N.C.,
75), 145, 151–59; Peter H. Wood, *Black Majority: Blacks in Colonial South Carolina
m 1670 Through the Stono Rebellion* (New York, 1974), 54–55, 97–98.

were sometimes close, even intimate. Blacks and lower-class whit
who worked together at their masters' tasks did not in every i
stance end their association when they left the fields at day's en
Apparently they enjoyed each other's company, for, we are told, th
drank together, slept together, ran away together—all with mo
awareness of shared predicament than of racial difference.[6]]
breaching the wall of racial solidarity, such waywardness threa
ened the masters' control over their black property and thereby in
periled development of a slaveholding society.

But the gradual decline of white servitude in the eighteenth ce
tury and the improving economic lot of small farmers lessened tl
likelihood of such collusion, while the rapid increase in the numbe
of blacks, many of them newly arrived from Africa, sharpene
awareness of cultural differences and, in some instances, of ec
nomic competition. Yet some free white persons, especially those
the lower orders—David Brion Davis has called them "independe
and irreverent fraternizers"—long continued to relate to blacks
ways suggesting either ignorance of the racist implications of pr
slavery laws and customs, disagreement with them, or outright d
fiance. Testimony of slaves implicated in an alleged conspiracy
South Carolina in 1739 revealed that white agitators—all of the
lower-class and some of them itinerants—understood the slave
grievances and had encouraged them to revolt.[7] Slavery obvious
did not serve the interests of all white persons equally. Not everyor
could grasp its purported social and political necessity, and eve
fewer persons were in a position to reap its economic benefits.

The area in which early lower-class white colonists most cor
spicuously evidenced their lack of concern for the proscriptions
slavery was that of sex. While in principle the races from an ear
day may have been expected to remain biologically apart, in pra
tice whites and blacks appraised each other from the beginning a
potential sexual partners. One of the earliest pieces of evidence te
tifying to the presence of blacks in Virginia is the record of the pur

6. Ira Berlin, "Time, Space, and the Evolution of Afro-American Society in Briti
Mainland North America," *American Historical Review*, LXXXV (1980), 44–78; E
mund S. Morgan, *American Slavery, American Freedom: The Ordeal of Colonial V
ginia* (New York, 1975), 325–27; Billings (ed.), *Old Dominion*, 159.
7. Timothy H. Breen, "A Changing Labor Force and Race Relations in Virgin
1660–1710," *Journal of Social History*, VII (1973), 3–25; David Brion Davis, *The Pro
lem of Slavery in the Age of Revolution, 1770–1823* (Ithaca, N.Y., 1975), 279n.; Phil
D. Morgan and George D. Terry, "Slavery in Microcosm: A Conspiracy Scare in C
lonial South Carolina," *Southern Studies*, XXI (1982), 120–23, 138–41.

ıment assessed a white man named Hugh Davis for the offense of
ʻing with a negro."[8]
Some legal interracial marriages took place in seventeenth- and
ʒhteenth-century America, though so subversive of social order
d economic interest did the ruling classes think these to be that
e colonial legislatures soon outlawed them. Not surprisingly, a
ınsiderably higher incidence of irregular sexual activity character-
ːd relations between the races. This did not in every instance in-
·lve white men and black women and thus cannot reasonably be
cribed to the aggressive, brute force of the master class. In 1681,
ʳ instance, Mary Williamson of Norfolk County, Virginia, commit-
d the "filthy sin" of fornication with William Bassett's slave
ımed William, for which offense she was assessed a heavy fine.
illiam, in his turn, refusing to display either shame or contrition
ʳ his deed (on the contrary, he "very arrogantly behaved himself
Linhaven Church in the face of the Congregation"), was punished
ith thirty lashes.[9]
An incident that occurred in late summer of the same year in
ɛnrico County provides a still more revealing illustration of re-
xed racial barriers in early Virginia. There, several white men and
omen, presumably from the class of small farmers, gathered at
ıomas Cocke's farm, where the slaves were clearing the orchard of
ɛeds. No thought of maintaining distance between the races was
·ident when, as the afternoon wore on, all adjourned to drink to-
ːther in Cocke's house. The conviviality of the occasion led a
ıuaker woman named Katherine Walker to fling aside every consid-
ʳation of racial distance as well as of propriety. She embraced and
·ssed the slave Jacke while reproving him for not more often visit-
ıg her and her husband's home. She became much more familiar
ith the slave Dirke, even lifting his shirt and commenting admir-
ıgly on the dimensions of what she saw there. Then when Jacke,
ʰo clearly was her favorite, passed near her on his way to draw
ıore cider, she "putt her hand on his codpiece, at which he smiled."
ɔon after, having retired to a bedroom, she was seen behaving in a
ke, but still more brazen manner, with a slave named Mingo. How-
ɹer one explains this episode—if only by reference to cider imbibed
ʏ a motley gathering in August heat—the sociability manifested

8. Jordan, *White over Black*, 78.
9. *Ibid.*, 161. The theme is explored in James Hugo Johnston, *Race Relations in
ʳginia and Miscegenation in the South, 1776–1860* (Amherst, Mass., 1970), esp.
ʳ5–76, 179–81.

by the entire company, not by a wanton Quaker woman alone, de**m**
onstrated a degree of interracial comity perilous to slavery a**n**
nearly unthinkable in a later time.[10]

In seventeenth-century Maryland, a similar laxity evidently p**r**
vailed. There, some white people who were well advanced on t**h**
social scale evidently saw nothing wrong with intimate relatio**n**
ships between their female white servants and male black sla**v**
and may even have encouraged them, a practice the colonial asse**r**
bly took outraged note of and felt obliged to prohibit.[11]

If interracial liaisons of this and more conventional kinds had re
resented simply one more means to exploit a subject people, th**e**
would have been seen as strengthening the bonds of slavery rath
than as weakening them, but they were not so regarded. Instea**d**
such relationships were viewed as a major threat, because notio**n**
of caste did not accompany them. They demonstrated that so**me**
white persons considered racial differences irrelevant. In a socie**ty**
in which slavery was based on race, such disregard obviously wou
prove fatal. Interracial sex, which in another setting might ha**ve**
been seen as a matter of personal choice, of instinct, of pleasure,
a slave society early acquired a political aspect from which it nev
could be free.

In an effort to strengthen the white colonists' sense of racial excl**u**
siveness, the Virginia House of Burgesses in 1661 imposed a fine **o**
interracial fornication; other colonial legislatures in due course e**n**
acted similar laws, and children of slave women, however "whit**e**
they might appear, were ruled to be "black" and enslaved. Whe
lawmakers placed the stamp of illegality on interracial sex, it b**e**
came disgraceful as well as risky. The shame attending mixed-ra**c**
liaisons, especially those between black men and white women, b**e**
came so overpowering that eventually such activity came to be a
sociated only with the very lowest class of white women, althoug**h**
in the nature of things, others sometimes indulged as well. And, **a**
is well known, the sexual exploitation of slave women by free whi**te**
men continued unabated, almost as though prohibitory laws did n**o**
exist.[12]

10. Billings (ed.), *Old Dominion*, 161–63.

11. Johnston, *Race Relations*, 165–90; Helen T. Catterall (ed.), *Judicial Cases Co**n**cerning American Slavery and the Negro* (Washington, D.C., 1924–26), IV, 28, 49, 5
61–62, 370; *Archives of Maryland: Proceedings and Acts of the General Assembly
Maryland, October 1678–March 1683* (Baltimore, 1889), 204.

12. John Codman Hurd, *The Law of Freedom and Bondage in the United States* (Bo
ton, 1858), I, 236–37, 242, 249, 250, 251, 253, 263, 290, 292, 295, 298, 301, 302; Joh**n**ston, *Race Relations*, 187–88; Jordan, *White over Black*, 137–42, 473.

'erhaps more indicative of the depth of interracial sympathy, be-
ıse it occurred outside the tangled thicket of sexual expression,
s the frequency with which blacks found among colonial whites
dy accomplices in their resistance to slavery. Here, too, indi-
ual desires and calculation took precedence over the demands of
te and society. As we have seen, slaves and white indentures
rking together at the planters' tasks found racial differences easy
ignore. Not surprisingly, their shared predicament sometimes led
·m to join forces to resist intolerable treatment, as in 1663 in Vir-
ıia, where a reported plot in Gloucester County involved both
ite servants and black slaves, and in 1711 when a colonist com-
ıined that "the negroes and other servants grow so intolerant that
m afraid what the issue will be." The danger was judged espe-
lly great in Maryland, where in the first half of the eighteenth
ıtury Catholics fell under suspicion of such intent.[13]

Worrisome as were the racial attitudes of dissidents and lower-
ss whites, the day-to-day response of blacks to their enslavement
derstandably more immediately concerned the owners. To no
e's surprise, newly arrived Africans were slow to be reconciled to
ife of captivity. "Seasoning" and acculturation failed to elimi-
te—may even have increased—their desire for personal au-
ıomy. One of the most common and most nearly complete forms
resistance by both "new" and acculturated blacks was to declare
ımselves free by simply running away, a practice that would
ıgue owners as long as bondage lasted. Almost as soon as they
ived in America, blacks began fleeing the places their owners
ınted them to be. To the planters' dismay, white settlers some-
ıes helped them do this, thereby adding a political dimension to
ıersistent problem.

Often runaways absconded only to satisfy some transitory pur-
se—perhaps to escape punishment—and then, having found no
tter place to be, soon returned. But others fully intended to make
e parting permanent. Some of them retreated in groups separate
t only from the master but from all white society. Evidence of
ch maroonage is abundant, especially in the Carolinas and Geor-
ı, but in Virginia as well. Runaways, when gathered in numbers
maroon settlements, constituted a grave social problem and

13. John Cotton to Rowland Cotton, October 27, 1711, in Miscellaneous Manu-
ipts, New-York Historical Society, New York, N.Y.; Herbert Aptheker, *American
gro Slave Revolts* (New York, 1943), 164–65; Ulrich B. Phillips, *American Negro
·very: A Survey of the Supply, Employment and Control of Negro Labor as Determined
the Plantation Regime* (New York, 1918), 472; Billings (ed.), *Old Dominion*, 159.

sometimes a military threat, for armed as they often were, th
were likely to menace white settlers and their property. In the 16{
the slave Mingo fled from his master in Virginia to take up a se;
rate existence and then together with several followers lived by r.
aging the plantations of Rappahonic County. In 1729 Governor W
liam Gooch reported to the Board of Trade that another band
fugitives, apparently intending to become self-sufficient and se'
all connection with white society, had retreated into the Blue Ric
Mountains with arms and farm tools, but that pursuing coloni
had attacked them and reenslaved the survivors. A few years lat
in Virginia, six slaves in Accomac County fled their owners: "Tl
are armed with Guns, &c and have broke open several Houses.
committed Felonies, have taken a Canoe." With the spread of wh
settlement into the West, the isolation upon which maroonage (
pended lessened and its incidence, accordingly, declined. Yet, as l;
as 1830, a group of thirty or forty such persons was found in t
Dover Swamp in North Carolina, and in Florida the allied Ser
noles and blacks managed to resist white encroachment :
decades.[14]

Such fugitives, who in the eyes of white colonists were band;
constituted a drain on the white economy as well as a source of d
order. They also undermined slavery itself, for they were livi
proof of the enmity of the blacks and of their daring, skill, a,
strength. Further, they sometimes enticed other slaves to join the
In Georgia in 1767, a slave named York was thought to have be
decoyed from his master by members of a maroon settlement. So
afterward, three newly imported blacks were "supposed to be c;
ried away from the bluff (where they were fishing) by some runaw
negroes in a canoe." And when, in 1774, six "new" blacks dis;
peared from a Georgia plantation, their owner took for granted th
they "got in with a parcel of Mr. Elliot's negroes who have been r
away for some time."[15]

As colonial society matured and its economy became more co;
plex, runaways, especially those with marketable skills and th
less likely to be inclined toward maroonage, could reasonably cou
on making a living in the developing market economy, free from
master's supervision. The prospective cooperation of white perso;

14. Aptheker, *American Negro Slave Revolts*, 167, 179; Windley (comp.), *Runav
Slave Advertisements*, I, 21; J. Burgwyn to the Governor, November 15, 1830, in G
ernor John Owens Letter Book, 1828–30, in Governors' Papers, North Carolina D;
sion of Archives and History, Raleigh.
    15. Windley (comp.), *Runaway Slave Advertisements*, IV, 23, 37, 58–59.

implicit in slaves' calculations as they planned their escape.
as, when Will fled, he took with him the tools he used for making
oden bowls. Sandy, who, though much addicted to drink and
en to profanity, nonetheless had served Thomas Jefferson as shoe-
ker, carpenter, and horse jockey, carried off his shoemaker's tools
en he quit Jefferson's plantation, and Cudjoe, age eighteen and
gola-born, took his bricklaying tools with him. Such skilled
ves probably intended to blend into the growing free black city
oulation as independent workmen or, perhaps, to attach them-
ves to white craftsmen who would pay them for their skills. In
ner event, if they made good their escape, they and the whites
o connived with them would have established a relationship in-
npatible with slavery as southern planters knew it. The political
ential of such a development was incalculable.[16]

When fugitives took to woods and swamps, whether as solitaries
maroons, they had little need to seek help from anyone except
haps potential fellow runaways. But if they chose a less isolated
, aid would be welcome—and it was not impossible to come by.
re, too, the planters discovered, racial solidarity was incomplete.
ubtless, other slaves and free blacks were the first persons a fu-
ive ordinarily appealed to, for they were innately subversive, but
ves also found that some whites were willing to ignore what the
ders of society insisted was their racial interest. White colonists,
en though living in emerging slaveholding societies, wrote passes
help runaways satisfy challenges from the suspicious and the
jilant; they hid them from pursuers; they arranged passage on
ips bound for faraway places.[17]

The master of Tom Flute, a slave who was fond of cards and even
bondage somehow had accumulated cash, supposed that "he has
a forged Pass, as he has been concerned with some white People
the same Stampe." Flora was thought "to be harboured under the
uff by sailors." William Wood, a former sailor, helped Betty and
r white servant friend escape. Davy's master suspected that he
as had dealings with a woman of infamous character in this
ighbourhood, named Anne Ashwell, and that she has advised him
run away." Sall Cooper, "for some Time past much in the Com-
ny of a white man," presumably followed him to Norfolk. A white
an named Peter Gossigon, recently a sailor on board a man-of-
r's tender, was said to make a practice of trying to persuade

16. *Ibid.*, IV, 38; I, 73; III, 126.
17. Wood, *Black Majority*, 243–44; Julia Floyd Smith, *Slavery and Rice Culture in
w Country Georgia, 1750–1860* (Knoxville, Tenn., 1985), 187.

slaves to go off with him on the promise of freedom; the slave J
evidently accepted his offer. Tom was seen working on board a s
bound for Liverpool. A white oysterman in Virginia used his boa
help a slave and a white servant escape.[18]

The circumstances of abandonments such as these suggest t
the motives for extending aid often were not purely altruistic.
cities in particular, where slavery early displayed a flexibility a
variety rare in rural settings, whites secreted runaways and hel
them ply their crafts, expecting to profit from the transgressi
Bob's master, knowing he was a very good blacksmith, suppo
someone of that trade harbored him. The owner of the shoema
Tom speculated that he "may probably be concealed and kept at
trade in Annapolis . . . by some white people, who make too famil
with my slaves to my great prejudice." In South Carolina, Januar
master supposed "some evil white person" employed and concea
him. And in that colony Barnaba, too, was thought to be "harbou
by some evil disposed white Persons being a remarkable fine Sea
stress, and easily kept at her Work, without Discovery."[19]

The small farmers of colonial North Carolina made themsel
notorious by harboring fugitives from the plantations of their ricl
neighbors to the north and to the south. But even in the heart
Virginia and South Carolina—bastions of slavery—white propr
tors sometimes employed black laborers whom they must ha
known to be fugitives, and helped them elude their lawful owne
Here, as in the cities, the display of generosity may have been
large part self-serving, for the slaves' labor skills tempted enterpr
ing whites, almost always in need of extra hands, not to ask t
many questions about the past of the men and women who arriv
at their door seeking asylum and work. In South Carolina, Her
Laurens found that his runaway Sampson had been harbored by
poor worthless fellow," who, nonetheless, taught him to process
digo and "to speak tolerable good English."[20] Another South Ca

18. Windley (comp.), *Runaway Slave Advertisements*, II, 63; IV, 53; I, 4, 84, 1
107; III, 504.
19. *Ibid.*, I, 305; II, 112; III, 205, 328.
20. Jeffrey J. Crow, *The Black Experience in Revolutionary North Carolina* (Ralei
N.C., 1973), 40–42; William M. Wiecek, "The Statutory Law of Slavery and Rac
the Thirteen Mainland Colonies of British America," *William and Mary Quarterly*,
ser., XXXIV (1977), 277; Gerald W. Mullin, *Flight and Rebellion*, 110–15, 190n, 19
Wood, *Black Majority*, 243, 245, 253n, 264. See the case of Sampson in Henry Laur
to Joseph Brown, June 28, 1765, in Philip M. Hamer *et al.* (eds.), *The Papers of He
Laurens* (Columbia, S.C., 1968–), IV, 645. For a like incident in New York, see Ed
J. McManus, *A History of Negro Slavery in New York* (Syracuse, N.Y., 1966), 113–

planter complained, "It is a customary thing for the back set-
s of this province, to take up new negroes, and keep them
ployed privately."As early as 1763 this had become a "pernicious
tom."[21]
uch illicit activity probably contributed to the immediate wel-
of individuals and, in a small way, aided the development of the
onial economy. But this made the practice no less damaging to
masters' interests and no less subversive of slavery. Blacks and
ites were partners in deception, and their deception was at the
ense of the master-slave relationship.
Parallel events occurred at the subterranean level of colonial so-
ty. There in the American underground, whites joined blacks in a
of crime, with thievery being the most common activity. Blacks,
ve or free, generally did the stealing, and whites, less likely to be
pected, arranged to receive and sell the stolen goods, though
es might be shared or reversed. In any event the biracial broth-
ood of thieves forged in colonial America enjoyed a long and
grant life. Suspicions concerning interracial thievery weighed
vily in the trials growing out of the New York slave conspiracy
1741. In 1759 in Charleston, an exasperated John Paul Grimké
rged that his slave boys Cuffee and Sharper made a practice of
bing him and then running away, "being harboured and enter-
ned by some evil-disposed persons in this town while their money
ts." The practice did not stop. More than a half century later,
uth Carolina citizens still complained that "fugitive slaves are
rboured . . . by unscrupulous people who encourage them to rob
d steal from their industrious neighbors." Corruption entered
en the machinery authorities devised to maintain the slave sys-
n. Members of the slave patrols, a black refugee reported many
rs later, sometimes struck deals with the persons they were sup-
sed to discipline, agreeing to "take whatever the slaves steal pay-
; in money, whisky, or whatever the slaves want." Slaveowners
dom were allowed to forget that white persons who lived on the
nge of society could not be trusted to maintain the behavioral
tterns that were required to preserve slavery. They always were
en as potential allies of the blacks, and the blacks, it is clear,
wed them that way as well.[22]

1. Windley (comp.), *Runaway Slave Advertisements*, III, 151–52, 227, 604.
2. *Ibid.*, III, 170; Gerald W. Mullin, *Flight and Rebellion*, 60–61; Wood, *Black
iority*, 243; Catterall (ed.), *Judicial Cases*, III, 20; IV, 27, 34, 36, 38; Ferenc M. Szasz,
ie New York Slave Revolt of 1741: A Re-examination," *New York History*, XLVIII

The variety of collusive and wayward activities indulged jointly by blacks and whites, free persons and slaves, suggests t neither slavery nor freedom in early America had developed the meaning those words eventually would acquire. It also suggests t the concept of race as yet exercised only limited prescriptive po⟨ and that slavery as an institution was slow to manifest the do neering quality that later would emerge as perhaps its most tell characteristic.

This fluid circumstance—when much in interracial relationsh was still unsettled—would not last long. As eighteenth-cent white southerners committed themselves to plantation agricultu the black element in America came to constitute an increasin valuable economic asset whose possibilities would be fully ploited. White farmers in ever increasing numbers joined the sla owners' ranks. This meant increasing importation of blacks as v as more efficient use of them.[23] The result for many white colon was wealth and expanded opportunity. Yet, the ever-growing ser⟨ population generated anxieties even as it created fortunes and lidified the social position of the white proprietors. This was so cause, quite apart from such disquiet as the slaves' distinctive ra⟨ and cultural characteristics produced, it was obvious that their terests clashed with those of their oppressors. No special gift prophecy was needed to foresee the probable result. Slaves did accept the restrictions and brutalities to which they were subj without resisting, sometimes to the extreme of violence agai owners and overseers. Accordingly, the society that grew and pr pered as a result of the exploitation of slave labor produced indiv uals who warned of the disaster that awaited a people who rel upon such an explosive labor system.[24]

Although white colonists found their slave property virtually dispensable, they also distrusted it. They had no difficulty in see that blacks shared the common human desire to be free of restrai

(1967), 217, 227; Grand Jury Presentment from Georgetown District, Novembe 1799, in Grand Jury Presentments, South Carolina Department of Archives and ⟨ tory, Columbia; Benjamin Drew, *A North-Side View of Slavery: The Refugee; or, Narratives of Free Slaves in Canada* . . . (Boston, 1856), 157; [George Ball], *Fifty Y⟨ in Chains; or, The Life of an American Slave* (New York, 1858), 220–24; John Bro⟨ *Slave Life in Georgia: A Narrative of the Life, Sufferings, and Escape of John Brow⟨ Fugitive Slave, Now in England* (London, 1855), 57–58.
   23. These changes and their profound implications are discussed in Michael ⟨ lin (ed.), *American Negro Slavery: A Documentary History* (New York, 1976), 10–2⟨
   24. Jordan, *White over Black*, 111–15.

l to pursue their own welfare. Colonial masters may have been
ially prejudiced, but they seldom contended, as their descend-
s often did, that slaves willingly accepted their lot or that
cks as a race possessed inborn traits peculiarly fitting them for
dage.
Little in their experience could have led them to such a con-
sion. In the pioneering stage of colonial development, before a
ernalistic plantation society evolved, slaves regularly displayed—
l were valued for displaying—unslavelike qualities of independ-
:e and resourcefulness. But the time soon passed when the slaves'
.onomous behavior could be used to work to the benefit of the
ster. Directors of more settled slave-staffed enterprises under-
od that such characteristics, if channeled in the wrong direc-
n, might subvert the slave-labor economy and destroy white-
ninated plantation society.[25] And the subversion certainly would
hastened if the slaves found allies among the white population.
Some entertained the frightening possibility of a massive, coor-
ated slave uprising. Others judged this event unlikely, noting
t slaves in America were not intimately bound together by cul-
al ties, since they came from a variety of African backgrounds
l for a time lacked even a common language. But as astute colo-
ts understood, this diversity provided no guarantee against slaves
nbining to resist an increasingly oppressive bondage: "Freedom
ars a Cap which Can Without a Tongue, Call Togather all Those
o long to Shake of the fetters of Slavery," warned Governor
xander Spotswood in 1710 as he urged the Virginia assembly to
ct stern laws to control the colony's slaves. The governor of
uth Carolina in 1711 expressed similar misgivings about the
rse of that colony's development. And in 1732 the trustees of
orgia, perhaps mindful of unsettled social conditions elsewhere
America, prohibited slavery in their new colony, partly on the
und that an enslaved population would imperil it.[26]
Danger of rebellion could not be eliminated by strict laws of the
t Spotswood proposed for Virginia. On the contrary, as colonial

25. Peter Wood makes this point for South Carolina (Wood, *Black Majority*,
-103). Gerald W. Mullin finds Virginia planters almost from the beginning "patri-
hal" and thus unsympathetic with slave autonomy (Mullin, *Flight and Rebellion*,
33). See the suggestive comments in Duncan J. MacLeod, "Toward Caste," in Ira
lin and Ronald Hoffman (eds.), *Slavery and Freedom in the Age of Revolution* (Char-
esville, Va., 1983), 225.
26. Alexander Spotswood quoted in Jordan, *White over Black*, 111; Allen D. Candler
.), *The Colonial Records of Georgia* (1904; rpr. New York, 1970), I, 50–51.

society became more cohesive and the bonds of slavery correspo
ingly tightened, resistance gained the focus it previously had lack
and the possibility of slave combination grew. Continued expans
of the black population throughout the eighteenth century addec
the danger. The facts were unsettling. After the 1730s, blacks con:
tently made up between 40 and 50 percent of the population of
lonial Virginia. In South Carolina, from an even earlier date, t
constituted an absolute majority.[27]

With white dominance so precarious and distrust of slaves so
tense, a white colonist need not have been unnaturally timid or
flicted with morbid imagination to experience doubts about the
curity of life and property and the stability of the American soc
order. No slave upheaval occurred in the mainland colonies on a:
thing like the scale of racial disorders that enflamed the Caribbe
islands, but white Americans learning of them shuddered at the p
ils faced by societies that resembled their own. Knowledge of sl;
rebellions reached American slaves as well. It could not have be
otherwise, for slaves continued to be imported from the West Indi
where turbulence was endemic. In some instances, participants
the island revolts were sold to the mainland colonies rather th
executed.[28]

The importation of a radical tradition was only one source of i
planters' concern for the stability of their labor force. Most of i
Africans adapted with remarkable facility to the new country, b
instead of assuring subordination, acculturation was itself a sou;
of instability. Acceptance by blacks of ideas and institutions co
mon to white Americans threatened to undermine their slave stat

Almost as soon as they learned English, many slaves beca;
Christian, a process encouraged by pious planters as well as by t
Anglican church. However, this achievement sometimes increas
discontent, for seventeenth-century Americans—both black a
white naïvely supposed that by accepting Christian baptis
slaves automatically became free. So alarmed were slaveholders
this notion that by the end of the seventeenth century, Marylar
New York, Virginia, the Carolinas, and New Jersey had passed la

27. Gerald W. Mullin, *Flight and Rebellion*, 16; Jordan, *White over Black*, 102–1
Wood, *Black Majority*, 36; U.S. Bureau of the Census, *Historical Statistics*, II, 1168
28. Wood, *Black Majority*, 221–24; Daniel Horsmanden, *The New York Conspire
or, A History of the Negro Plot, with the Journal of the Proceedings Against the Consp
tors at New York in the Years 1741–42* . . . (2nd ed.; New York, 1810), 73, 128, 170, 2
226.

uring masters—and advising slaves—that conversion did not re-
se slaves from bondage.[29]
Slaves, nonetheless, only reluctantly gave up the notion that bap-
m made them brothers in Christ with the white population and
itled them to freedom.[30] They persisted in believing they had
n wronged—a belief Christian doctrine did nothing to dis-
—and that justice rendered by a far-off authority someday would
rrule their oppressors and set the grievance right. Thus, when
xander Spotswood came to Virginia as royal governor, slaves
agined he brought with him the king's order "to sett all those free
t were Christians" and to free those who afterward accepted bap-
m. When nothing of the sort happened, they held "unlawful meet-
;s" and engaged in "loose discourses" aimed, some whites feared,
rebellion. Shortly afterward, in New Jersey, slaves expressed the
ne complaint: In defiance of the king's edict of emancipation
ir masters refused to free them.[31] Slavery, these incidents sug-
st, was felt by at least some slaves to be a temporary state and
e that defied a just ordering of society. Somewhere there must
st a power sympathetic to their welfare. Whether they sought
t ally in earthly or supernatural form, they never abandoned
ir search. It naturally followed that as long as the Old South
ted, southern whites would be preoccupied with preventing that
y from being found.
n becoming more like white Americans, blacks made slavery
rder to maintain and to justify. At no time could colonial masters
unt on slaves to accept bondage willingly or to behave in slavelike
nner. No one could be surprised when unbroken, unseasoned
cks fresh from Africa disobeyed their owners and tried to run
ay, but it was more troubling to find that some of the most accul-
ated slaves proved to be unruly, violent, and willful property.
en the ablest and most valued of them might stubbornly insist on
rcising an independence of judgment that did not reconcile with
subordination demanded by both the evolving rigid concept of
very and the developing paternalistic ideal of the planter. Lan-
n Carter's slaves regularly behaved in ways he found exasperat-

29. Edmund S. Morgan, *American Slavery*, 331–32; Jordan, *White over Black*,
–93, 180–87, 190–93.
30. White colonists considered this belief a major source of unrest; thus the evan-
ist George Whitefield was accused of being the "cause of all the disturbance"
ong New York slaves in 1741 (Horsmanden, *New York Conspiracy*, 360).
31. Aptheker, *American Negro Slave Revolts*, 79–80.

ing, but one of their most curious transgressions—from his poin
view—was their practice of performing tasks in a better and m
thorough fashion than he had intended.[32]

These problems were vexing and likely to make persons short
patience regret their dependence on slave labor, but even had pla
ers not been surrounded by "outlandish" and intractable bla
restless under the yoke of slavery, they might still have had misg
ings about the direction in which their society was moving. C
tainly, many deplored the presence of allegedly inferior beings
ward whom they felt prejudice, but more important, they w
apprehensive about what the future might bring from them. 1
slave upheavals that periodically disrupted the West Indies ga
ample cause for alarm, but the reflective found still other grour
for concern that had little to do with passing events.

Americans who read the Bible were familiar with the bondage
the Israelites and the fate that befell their Egyptian captors. The
whose education extended to the history of Greece and Rome kn
that in antiquity, as in modern times, slaves constituted a ma
element in the population. They also could not forget that the a
cient world had been wracked by slave rebellion. Americans und
stood that however harmless and compliant their bondsmen at a
given moment appeared, they nonetheless *were* slaves. And slaves
all times and in all places had a historically defined part to pl
Obedience and unrequited lifelong labor ideally characterized tl
role, but it might also be punctuated by rebellion. Greek and Rom
writers had told the dreadful story.[33]

We know now that such fears were groundless, but white colon
Americans had no reason to be confident they would be spared t
fate suffered by slaveholding peoples in the remote past. There w
enough evidence of slave discontent on any plantation to sugge
that the experience of antiquity might be repeated in colonial Nor
America. And above all, mainland colonists could not ignore the
volts that punctuated the history of the West Indies. Comforting, b
largely irrelevant, was the impression that the vast majority
slaves were faithful if sometimes exasperating workers, harmle
and loyal to their owners. The fact remained that the explosive m
terial long ago introduced into America constantly grew in quant
and thus in potential danger.

32. Jack P. Greene (ed.), *The Diary of Colonel Landon Carter of Sabine H
1752–1778* (Charlottesville, Va., 1965), I, 369, 568.
33. For William Byrd's awareness of the classical precedent, see Jordan, *WI
over Black*, 111.

Another disturbing prospect must also have occurred to thought-
persons. Slaves constituted not only a military threat but also a
itical one that might be manipulated to overthrow the social or-
·. The Virginia slavemaster William Byrd in 1736 alluded to the
ۨger as he looked back at the factional political and social strife
t in earlier decades had afflicted his colony. Especially pertinent
s the record of the great rebellion of 1676, when Nathaniel Bacon,
ۨ desperate moment in his dispute with Governor William Berke-
, had sought new recruits by offering freedom to the servants and
ۨves owned by Berkeley's followers. Such events gained in perti-
ۨce when it was recalled that absolute unity among the white
ۨulation in support of slavery had not been achieved. Poorer
ites—or any other disaffected group—their racial pride not yet
ۨy developed, might forge an alliance with slaves based on com-
ۨn interest.[34]
ۨet all such threats were prospective only. These horrors had not
ۨpened in mainland America, and they might never happen. Of
ۨre pressing concern to officials and to the majority alike were
ۨmediate dangers looming from beyond colonial borders. English
tlers lived alone in a perilous world. While internal factionalism
ۨeatened to shatter their still fragile societies, external enemies—
ۨians, Dutch, French, Spanish—might encroach upon their fron-
ۨs at any moment. If that happened, then enslaved blacks likely
ۨuld respond in ways fatal to their English masters.[35]
ۨn time of war, persons not fully incorporated into society and
ۨt out from its benefits could not be counted on to come to its
ۨense; they might even join its enemies. The English colonists'
ۨnerability in this respect was no secret. Thus, enterprising for-
ۨn foes could be expected to exploit the opportunity of making
ۨnmon cause with slaves, their natural allies living in the very
ۨart of the English colonies. "Insurrections against us have been
ۨen attempted," said the council of South Carolina in 1734, "and
ۨuld at any time prove fatal if the French should instigate them
ۨe negroes) by artfully giving them an expectation of freedom."[36]
ۨventually white southerners would conclude that the chief
ۨrce of danger to their institutions was not to be found in the slave

ۨ4. Stephen Saunders Webb, 1676: The End of American Independence (New York,
ۨ4), 6–7, 66, 86, 110, 121, 123.
ۨ5. Ballagh, History of Slavery, 79.
ۨ6. Quoted in William A. Schaper, "Sectionalism and Representation in South
ۨolina," in Vol. I of American Historical Association, Annual Report . . . for the Year
ۨ0 (Washington, D.C., 1901), 310.

dissatisfation that was inevitably generated by bondage—in fa
they came to deny that such discontent existed—but rather in h
tile outside forces seeking to bring them down by inciting rac
discord. In the nineteenth century, northern abolitionists would
identified as the great external fomenters of slave rebellion. But d
ing most of the colonial period, it was the Spanish located to
south of the English colonies who appeared to be the instigator
slave resistance.

The English had planted their settlements overseas in part a
challenge to Spanish dominion in the New World. In the West Ind
and on the southeastern shores of North America—places wh
slavery was a key factor in economic growth—the persistent Ang
Spanish rivalry found its focus. Spanish Florida was a long-sta
ing irritant to the English settlers, a source of hope to slaves, an
drain on the resources of the South Carolinians, who for a long ti
were its nearest neighbors. The perilous circumstance in wh
southerners thus found themselves hampered whites in Georgia
their campaign for permission to acquire slaves, an effort Jan
Oglethorpe suspected the Spanish of encouraging precisely beca
slavery would weaken the colony. One Captain Dempsy predicted
1738 that if Georgians realized their ambition to become slaveho
ers, in two months time not fifty of five hundred slaves would
main, "for they would fly to the Spaniards, wherefore it would
be fit to allow of them until all Florida be in our hands for then th
would have no place to retreat to."[37] It was a lesson all southern
eventually would learn: No slave region could be secure if a host
state bordered it.

Two years later, a great slave rebellion having erupted in Sou
Carolina, objection to introducing slavery in Georgia seemed s
more compelling. In conversation with a Charleston mercha
Georgia's governor revealed his concern that "Negroes might
the throats of our people and run to the Spaniards." Ignoring e
dence offered by his own colony's recent experience, the South Ca
linian answered that "if Negroes are well used, they never ru
Such unjustified confidence was too much for the governor. He he
edly contradicted his guest: "Liberty, protection & lands which t
Spaniards have proclaym'd to all Negroes that run to them, a
the nearness of Augustine to Georgia would prove a great temp
tion . . . and . . . in Carolina some who were thought so faithfull
to be made Overseers of others . . . had made their escape to Aug

37. Candler (ed.), *Colonial Records of Georgia*, V, 315.

ie, and headed rebellions, & this very lately." The taunt silenced
e Charleston merchant, and he "reply'd nothing."[38]
For generations, Anglo-Americans regarded the Spanish fort at St.
ıgustine as an extreme peril to their own settlements. Slaves could
•t be kept ignorant of the significance to themselves of the Spanish
esence. White South Carolinians often worried about the possibil-
ɩ of their slaves absconding to the refuge of Spanish Florida, and
distressingly large number did so. As early as the 1680s, a group
"diverse negro slaves" ran away from their South Carolina mas-
rs to St. Augustine. The exodus continued, an Underground Rail-
ad toward the South. The Spanish lure extended even to New En-
 land, where in 1741 five slaves stole a boat in Boston harbor,
anning, so it was said, to make their way to Florida.[39]
The danger appeared to increase, and anything might be believed.
aves became pawns in the Anglo-Spanish struggle for empire. In
'33 an edict of the Spanish king promised freedom and protection
all fugitive slaves arriving in St. Augustine from the English colo-
es. When one such group eluded their pursuers and reached Flor-
a, so the English ruefully noted, "They were received with great
ɔnour, one of them had a Commission given to him, and a Coat
ced with Velvet." In 1737 reports reached Charleston that the
ɔanish planned a full-scale assault against their English neigh-
ɔrs, intended, in the words of South Carolina's lieutenant gover-
ɔr, to "unsettle the colony of Georgia, and to excite an Insurrection
the Negroes of this province." The governor alerted the colonial
ilitia, and the General Assembly established patrols to keep the
aves in order.[40]
In February, 1739, rumors spread through Georgia that large
ımbers of South Carolina slaves were about to escape to Florida.
ıter in the year—on the very weekend when news reached Charles-
•n that war between England and Spain finally had begun—the
ng-feared uprising materialized. Early Sunday morning, Septem-
ɛr 9, in St. Paul's Parish, near Charleston, the slaves began to
ıther. Reportedly of Angolan origin, the rebels also were said to
ɔeak Portuguese and to be Roman Catholic converts, factors which,
true, suggest possible exposure to revolutionary experience un-
ıown to most North American slaves. Some twenty of them, led by

38. Ibid., 476.
39. Wood, Black Majority, 51, 239, 305; Lorenzo J. Greene, Negro in Colonial New
ɪgland, 150.
40. Wood, Black Majority, 305; Candler (ed.), Colonial Records of Georgia,
ɔl. XXIII, Pt. 2, pp. 232–33.

the slave Jemmy, started their march. At Stono Bridge they b
headed the keepers of a store—the means of death typically er
ployed by warriors lacking firearms—and seized small arms ar
powder. Then they made their way southward toward the road th
led to St. Augustine, gathering recruits and plundering, burnin
and killing as they went. A wholesale desertion to the Spanish w
under way. Late in the afternoon the rebels, then numbering fifty
more, halted in a field near the ferry on the Edisto River. There the
danced and beat drums while they awaited the arrival of more r
cruits. By that time, alarm having been raised throughout the cou
tryside, armed and mounted white men prepared to move again
the rebels. Against such odds the blacks' main force was scattere
and the flight was stopped, though remnants of the band remain
unsubdued and at large for many weeks afterward. Nearby India
helped round up the survivors, thereby testifying to the colonist
success in preventing an Indian-slave alliance.[41]

   Not surprisingly, in view of that close call, rumors of conspiraci
periodically swept the colony for years afterward, eventually ma
ing antebellum South Carolinians perhaps the most sensitive of a
Americans to the safety of their institutions, the most resentful
criticism, and the most ready to resist external threats. They ha
learned that as long as outside enemies existed and as long as slav
had allies, not even the most repressive regime could make slave
secure.

   English settlements farther north shared the southern concern fe
slave loyalty, though their greater distance from Spanish Floric
made the danger less acute. In the late 1730s, informers in Marylar
exposed a purported conspiracy by blacks to seize control of th
colony. Officials charged Roman Catholics—allies of the Spanis
crown—with inciting slave unrest and masterminding the plot. N
even New York escaped the Spanish fear. In the spring of 174
while the Anglo-Spanish war still raged and New Yorkers lived i
dread of attack by a Spanish fleet, about 150 slaves and 25 allege
white accomplices were arrested and charged with setting fire to
number of buildings in the city, the first stage, authorities su
pected, of a full-scale uprising that would be coordinated with

---

41. Wood, *Black Majority*, 308–20; Aptheker, *American Negro Slave Revolt*
187–89; Michael Mullin (ed.), *American Negro Slavery*, 84–86. Oral tradition of t
revolt evidently persisted among blacks in South Carolina, for in the 1930s a form
slave claimed to be descended from the revolt's leader. George P. Rawick *et al.* (eds
The American Slave: A Composite Autobiography: Supplement, Series I (Westpo
Conn., 1977), XI, 98–100.

anish invasion. The courts accepted the reality of the charges. In
:ious retribution thirteen slaves were burned alive, eighteen were
nged, and seventy were banished. Four of the accused whites, in-
1ding one woman and a man reputed to be a Spanish priest, also
:re executed.[42]

A degree of hysteria no doubt accompanied these and similar
:idents, and the extent of the conspiracies may have been exag-
rated. Yet there could be no denying the presence of revolution-
y material in American society, nor could one dismiss the possi-
lity that an impulse from either within the colonies or outside
em might at any moment produce upheaval. The dread of slave
iances with an outside power or with an internal faction persisted
long as slavery itself endured. It would have momentous conse-
ences. It encouraged American expansionist policy and Indian
moval, it generated fear of northern abolitionists, and it served
ally as a principal ground for southern withdrawal from the
iion.

The Spanish threat that loomed so large in the minds of Ameri-
ns early in the eighteenth century gradually subsided as political
nditions in Europe changed. Still, slavery in English America was
enjoy no respite from outside interference, for the French menace
ew as the Spanish threat declined. Northern colonists had clashed
.th the French and their Indian allies on several previous occa-
ons, but those faraway battles, most of them fought in Canada,
.d brought little disruption to the South. In 1754, however, war
.th France broke out again, with inescapable effect. This time the
nflict started in the Ohio valley, so near to concentration of blacks
at its impact on southern society was immediate and severe.
irly the next year, a white servant named James Francis and the
ive Toby ran away from a Maryland plantation, taking with them
gun, powder, and shot. Their master drew the appropriate conclu-
on: "It seems to be the Interest, at least of every Gentleman that
is Slaves, to be active in the beginning of these Attempts, for
hilst we have the French such near Neighbours, we shall not have
e least Security in that kind of Property."[43]

In the summer of 1755, General Edward Braddock, commander-
-chief of the British army in America, marched his troops from
:adquarters in Maryland toward French-held Fort Duquesne at the

---

42. Thomas J. Davis, *A Rumor of Revolt: The "Great Negro Plot" in Colonial New
rk* (New York, 1985), *passim*. The trial records are in Horsmanden, *New York
nspiracy*.
43. Windley (comp.), *Runaway Slave Advertisements*, II, 23.

fork of the Ohio River, site of the present city of Pittsburgh. Wh
his splendid force of regulars and Virginia militiamen neared t
fort, they ran into an ambush of French and Indians sent to del
the British advance. In the ensuing battle, Braddock and many
his men were killed, leaving only a remnant of battered survivors
return in disarray to the security of Fort Cumberland in Maryland

Persons who had seen the proud army march off to engage t
French now witnessed its humiliating retreat. The implication
that sudden change in fortune, whites suspected, would not be l
on the blacks who observed it. Although the maintenance of slave
rested ultimately on force, it depended in its day-to-day functioni
on the slave's recognition and acceptance of the master's position
power. There could be little doubt that when the English and col
nial forces experienced defeat, their own self-esteem suffered. H
much more grievously, then, must they have been wounded in t
eyes of blacks? Colonial officials believed they must expect disside
elements within their borders to take advantage of the changed b
ance of power resulting from military disaster.

In the wake of Braddock's defeat, officials in both Maryland a
Virginia prepared to resist the expected slave uprising. Marylan
governor, Horatio Sharpe, wrote "Circularly Letters to have t
Slave, convicts &c well observed & watched & [gave] Orders for t
militia . . . to be prepared to quell it in case any Insurrection shou
be occasioned by the Stroke." In Virginia the possibility of sla
unrest was judged grave enough even to affect deployment of t
colony's military forces. The number of militiamen who could
spared to fight the French must be limited, said Governor Robe
Dinwiddie, on account of the necessity to leave troops in ea
county "to protect it from the combinations of the negro slaves, w
have been very audacious on the defeat on the Ohio." The govern
explained why this was so. "Those poor creatures," he told the Ea
of Halifax, "imagine the French will give them their freedom." [45]

Concern for the effect of war on the slaves even reached across t
Atlantic Ocean to trouble the composure of Englishmen. As soon

44. Stanley M. Pargellis, "Braddock's Defeat," *American Historical Review*, X
(1936), 253–69.
45. Jeffrey R. Brackett, *The Negro in Maryland: A Study of the Institution of Slave*
(Baltimore, 1889), 94–95; *Archives of Maryland*, VI, 251; Robert Dinwiddie to t
Earl of Halifax, July 23, 1755, in John C. Fitzpatrick (ed.), *The Writings of Geor*
Washington (Washington, D.C., 1931–44), I, 151n. See also Dinwiddie to Charles C
ter, July 18, 1755, in R. A. Brock (ed.), *Official Records of Robert Dinwiddie, Lt. Gov.*
the Colony of Virginia, 1751–1758. Virginia Historical Society Collection, n.s., III a
IV (2 vols.; Richmond, 1883–84), II, 102.

ord of Braddock's defeat arrived, the Reverend Benjamin Fawcett, prominent dissenting clergyman, prepared *A Compassionate Address to the Christian Negroes in Virginia*, in which he appealed for ιe blacks' continued loyalty: "At one Time or other it will probably ε suggested to you that the *French* will make better Masters than ιe English. But I beseech you to consider, that your Happiness as *Ien* and *Christians* exceedingly depends upon your doing all in ɔur Power to support the *British Government.*"[46]

As it turned out, concern for slave allegiance was less necessary ιan Fawcett and the colonial governors supposed. Whatever poten-al for social disruption existed in the war with France was not to ε realized. The French exerted little military effort in southern re-ions, and the extensive campaigns that finally brought their re-ɔunding defeat were fought in Europe, India, and Canada rather ιan in the American South. After 1763, English power in North merica faced no serious challenge from any European rival; thus ɔlonial slaveholders temporarily were freed from imminent out-.de danger.

But while revolts, conspiracies, and foreign threats had been dis--acting mid-eighteenth-century Americans, new ideas about hu-ιan rights had begun to transform attitudes toward slavery itself ιd quietly to erode its legitimacy. The spread to America of En-ghtenment theories shattered the ideological innocence of slave-olders. Experience already had taught that slavery was a fragile ιd unstable institution with unavoidable political implications. Iow, in the 1750s, some began to suspect that it also was wrong. A εw force had appeared whose effect could only be subversive. The ιght of individuals to autonomy, to independence, became a widely ccepted principle as Americans developed arguments to justify ιeir rejection of British control over the economic and political as-ects of their lives. When these arguments gained currency as truth, became hard to believe that independence and personal au-ɔnomy were rightfully the monopoly of a master race. White mericans questioned slavery as never before. The new ideas also ιanged the attitude of slaves toward their bondage. Even to the ₂ast reflective of them, freedom, however it was defined, always ad been desirable. For some, it now became a right. And in the ope of enjoying that right, some slaves, like their white country-ιen, would accept the use of force.

46. Benjamin Fawcett, *A Compassionate Address to the Christian Negroes in Virinia* (London, 1756), 17–18.

2

☙☙☙☙☙☙☙☙☙☙☙☙☙☙☙☙☙☙☙☙☙☙☙☙☙

The Disruptive Power of Ideology

Creation of a natural-rights ideology forever altered perspective toward slavery on the part of Americans, both slave and free. Whit colonists long had viewed the growing black population with mi giving. Now, with increasing concern for the welfare of individua and for the proper limits of power, whites begain to doubt the ju tice of their actions and to question even the moral basis of the society. The effect of the new ideas on the slaves was as profoun Slaves, who always had found subjugation and forced labor painfu to bear, now learned that bondage was wrong and that they, to held claims on the newly discovered store of human rights. Whe resistance became linked to ideology, it took on new meaning an led to a prolonged period when slavery was subjected as never be fore to questioning, challenge, and disruption.[1]

Slaves saw the connection between their hopes for freedom an colonial claims for autonomy about as soon as their masters di Parliament's passage of the Stamp Act in 1765 awakened white colc nists' concern for their political rights, which they acted in concer to defend. Resistance to tyranny proved contagious. With littl prompting from whites, slaves, too, learned the language of th Revolution and understood that their long-standing desire for lib erty harmonized with the spirit of the new age. The sight of black parading through the streets of Charleston in January, 1766, an

1. David Brion Davis, *Problem of Slavery*, 488–89.

outing "Liberty!" must have been unsettling indeed, for white
outh Carolinians surely knew that if such sentiments spread, if
lantation slaves self-consciously linked the new ideology to their
ay-to-day resistance, the result would be disastrous.[2]
  While colonial statesmen drafted petitions to King George III as-
erting American rights within the empire, slaves appealed to simi-
ir doctrine to justify their own claims to freedom. A few in New
ngland did this by presenting formal petitions to governing bod-
es. "The divine spirit of freedom, seems to fire every *humane* heart
n the continent," observed certain Boston slaves in 1773 as they
eseeched the General Court for emancipation. A year later, other
lacks in Massachusetts pursued the logic of equal rights in the rhe-
orical conclusion of an appeal to Governor Thomas Gage and the
ieneral Court "Shewing That your Petitioners apprehend we have
n common with all other men a natural right to our freedoms."[3]
  Blacks in the 1770s were as unwilling as other Americans to limit
efense of personal liberty to the mere drafting of formal appeals to
n abstract system of rights. A few of them tried to forge a political
ntislavery strategy that would implement liberal ideology. In the
ill of 1774, when Boston appeared to be approaching a state of in-
urrection, slaves corresponded with the royal governor of Massa-
husetts. If Governor Gage gave them arms, they wrote, they would
in the British in putting down the impending rebellion. Their
rice? Freedom.[4]
  Although nothing apparently came from the proposal, its signifi-
ance should not be underestimated. The overture to Gage was one
f the earliest and most politically innovative efforts by slaves to
articipate in the revolutionary movement. Above all, it evidenced
wareness of the part they might play in any struggle between com-
eting groups of whites, a possibility that had long troubled south-
rn slaveholders.
  At almost the same time—November, 1774—rumors spread that
laves in Virginia also saw in the political turmoil a chance to better
heir condition. The planter and revolutionary war leader James

2. Pauline Maier, "The Charleston Mob and the Evolution of Popular Politics in
evolutionary South Carolina, 1765–1784," *Perspectives in American History*, IV
1970), 176; Henry Laurens to John Lewis Gervais, January 29, 1766, in Hamer *et al.*
ds.), *Papers of Henry Laurens*, V, 53–54.
  3. Herbert Aptheker (ed.), *A Documentary History of the Negro People in the United
tates* (New York, 1951), I, 8.
  4. Charles Francis Adams (ed.), *Letters of Mrs. Adams . . .* , (4th ed; Boston, 1848),
0. The difficulties inherent in such efforts are discussed in Phillips, *American Negro
lavery*, 117.

Madison outlined the contour of their expectation by noting that "
America and Britain should come to an hostile rupture, I am afrai
an insurrection among the slaves may and will be promoted." A
ready, Madison believed, blacks had laid their plans: "In one of ov
Counties lately a few of those unhappy wretches met together an
chose a leader who was to conduct them when the British Troop
should arrive."⁵ Again in the 1770s as in the days of the Spanish an
French wars, an external enemy offered slaves an opportunity fc
freedom.

Planters soon discovered that political and social divisions amon
whites at home also might encourage slave unrest. In May, 1775,
grand jury in Dorchester County, Maryland, found that disaffecte
whites had talked of forming coalitions with slaves to promote
revolt against the great landlords. Some months later, a count
committee complained of the growing "insolence of the Negroes
and reported on efforts to disarm them. "The malicious and impru
dent speeches of some among the lower classes of whites," the con
mittee explained, "have induced them to believe, that their freedor
depended on the success of the King's troops." White solidarity wit
respect to slavery and the subordination of blacks may have bee
stronger in the 1770s than a century earlier, but it still could not b
taken for granted.⁶

In the developing imperial crisis, the slaveholders' vulnerabilit
fascinated the makers of English policy as much as it alarmed whit
Americans. When overt warfare began to loom as a distinct possibi
ity in 1773, a British observer assessed as minor the role the Sout
would be able to play in the mounting resistance. "The Souther
Provinces may be entirely thrown out of the Question," he ex
plained, "not only as being thinly peopled & enervated. But fror
the great Majority of Negroes intermixed, which exposes them t
immediate ruin whenever we detach a small Corps to support a
insurrection." Early in 1775, while colonial leaders debated mean
to resist British policy, Governor Gage, from his post in Boston, ol
fered advice and warning to South Carolinians: The colony shoul
make sure it sent only moderates to the forthcoming Second Conti
nental Congress, for "it is well known that if a Serious Oppositio
takes place, you can do but little—You have too much to take car

5. James Madison to William Bradford, November 27, 1774, in William T. Hutcl
inson and William M. E. Rachal (eds.), *The Papers of James Madison* (Chicago, 1962–
I, 129–30.

6. Ronald Hoffman, *A Spirit of Dissension: Economics, Politics, and the Revolutio
in Maryland* (Baltimore, 1973), 147–48.

nd think of, but should you proceed [to] much greater lengths it
ay happen that your Rice and Indigo will be brought to market by
egroes instead of white People." In Virginia, too, as the revolution-
ry movement proceeded, the slave population continued to evoke
pprehension and was considered an obstacle to effective colonial
esistance. James Madison, who a year earlier had expressed fear of
ave revolt, now, in June, 1775, considered incitement of slaves by
n enemy to be "the only part in which this Colony is vulnerable; &
' we should be subdued, we shall fall like Achilles by the hand of
ne that knows the secret."[7]
  Already rumors had reached America suggesting that the British
lanned to enlist both Indians and blacks to help subdue dissi-
ent white colonists. Lord Dunmore, the Virginian William Lee be-
eved, had informed the ministry of an impending slave uprising.
laves, Dunmore allegedly reported, looked favorably on the Brit-
sh, for they believed the king intended to free them. Whether Dun-
ore actually had so informed his government or not, it was true
hat he boasted to the Earl of Dartmouth of his ability to "collect
om among the Indians, negroes and other persons" a force suffi-
iently large to quell the brewing white rebellion. In England such
uggestions encouraged confidence in British ability to cope with
olonial resistance. On his visit to the House of Commons in October,
775, Ralph Izard, the South Carolina rice magnate, listened to a
peaker who "was particularly rancorous against Americans and
lumed himself much on the expedient of encouraging the Negroes
n the Southern colonies, to drench themselves in the blood of their
nasters."[8]
  American suspicions of British objectives account for the section
f the Continental Congress' Declaration of the Causes and Neces-
ity of Taking up Arms (July 5, 1775) that cites General Guy Carle-
on's effort to provoke the Canadians "and the Indians, to fall upon
s," and adds, "We have but too much reason to apprehend that
chemes have been found to excite domestick enemies against us." A
ear later, Thomas Jefferson immortalized that charge in the Decla-

7. Hugh F. Rankin, *The North Carolina Continentals* (Chapel Hill, N.C., 1971), 29;
ohn R. Alden, "John Stuart Accuses William Bull," *William and Mary Quarterly*, 3rd
er., II (1945), 318; James Madison to William Bradford, June 19, 1775, in Hutchinson
nd Rachal (eds.), *Papers of James Madison*, I, 153.
  8. Worthington C. Ford (ed.), *Letters of William Lee* (Brooklyn, 1891), I, 143, 144;
Ralph Izard to a Friend in Bath, October 27, 1775, in *Correspondence of Mr. Ralph
zard of South Carolina, from the Year 1774 to 1804* (New York, 1844), 58, 125; Robert
. Olwell, "'Domestick Enemies': Slavery and Political Independence in South Caro-
ina, May 1775–March 1776," *Journal of Southern History*, LV (1989), 21–48.

ration of Independence by including in his catalog of George III
crimes the allegation that "he has excited domestic insurrection
amongst us." More than likely, their dread of British intentions to
ward Indians and slaves persuaded some otherwise reluctant south
erners to support the Patriot cause.[9]

Despite British expectation and American concern, slaves prove
less than unanimous in support of the British cause. When fightin
finally broke out between rebellious colonists and imperial forces i
1775, blacks could be found on both sides of the conflict, as painfull
divided in allegiance as were their white Patriot and Loyalist cour
trymen. For slaves, the British occupied an ambiguous position. A
Americans, they were likely to fear the British as invaders and op
pressors; as slaves, they welcomed them as liberators.

In numerous instances slaves aided, sometimes even served in
the Patriot armies and in other ways contributed significantly t
the revolutionary war effort, for which service they customaril
were rewarded with emancipation. But wherever British armies ap
peared in plantation country, nearby slaves were tempted to joi
them. Owners were distressed by such desertions, but they were no
surprised. Scarcely twenty years earlier, the war with France ha
disclosed wavering slave loyalties, and memories of still earlie
Spanish intrigue could not yet have totally faded. Now a new gen
eration of white Americans prepared to confront a like situation.

In April, 1775, after news of the battles of Lexington and Concor
reached Maryland, "six gentlemen of respectable characters" calle
on Governor Robert Eden to report their "great apprehensions o
some attempt being made by the servants or slaves for their liberty.
With some show of reluctance, the governor agreed to supply "arm
and ammunition to keep the servants and negroes in order." A fev
months later, two delegates from Georgia to the Continental Con
gress revealed a similar concern to John Adams: If the British
should land on the coast of South Carolina and Georgia and pro
claim freedom to the slaves, twenty thousand blacks would fle
their owners and join the invaders. As a Massachusetts resident who
never had lived among a large slave population, Adams had troubl
crediting such a grim forecast. How could slaves located far in the

9. Sidney Kaplan, "The 'Domestic Insurrections' of the Declaration of Independ
ence," *Journal of Negro History*, LXI (1976), 243–55; Olwell, "'Domestick Enemies,'
21–48.

10. For the slaves' response to the Revolution, see Benjamin Quarles, *The Negro i
the American Revolution* (Chapel Hill, N.C., 1961), and Gerald W. Mullin, *Flight an
Rebellion*, 130–36.

nterior learn about the British presence and coordinate their flight? The negroes have a wonderful art of communicating intelligence among themselves," he was told. "It will run several hundred of miles in a week or fortnight." Still direr prophecies of black disaffection were voiced in those anxious days. Some whites in Georgia in July, 1776, confessed that they feared much worse at the hands of slaves than mere bloodless abandonment.[11]

Nowhere on the continent did slave flight occur on the scale predicted by the Georgians; still less did slaves rise up and slaughter their masters. But as white Americans had feared, ruinously large numbers of them chose to seek sanctuary within British lines. Defections along the South Carolina and Georgia coasts were especially large, with one owner reporting the loss of three dozen slaves in a single day. No place or person was exempt. When General Cornwallis left Thomas Jefferson's plantation after using it as headquarters for ten days, some twenty of Jefferson's slaves accompanied him. (Three of these returned, Jefferson remembered, only to die of "camp fever.") A report from a woman in North Carolina suggests the British attraction for slaves of every age and condition: All but two of those owned by her brother were "determined to go to them—even old Affra." And in South Carolina in May, 1779, with a British army operating nearby, Eliza Lucas Pinckney found she could no longer control the blacks at Belmont. If the slaves decided to join the enemy, she concluded, there was no use whatever in trying to stop them, "for they all do now as they please everywhere." The appearance of a force not amenable to planter control disrupted the slave-master relationship and sometimes destroyed it. A slaveowner in Charleston reported his discomfiting exchange with seventeen-year-old Quamerin shortly after British armies had won notable successes in the South: He "told me to my face, 'he can go when he pleases, and I can do nothing to him, nor shall I ever get a copper for him.'"[12]

11. Hoffman, Spirit of Dissension, 146–47; Charles Francis Adams (ed.), The Works of John Adams, Second President of the United States, with a Life of the Author (Boston, 1856), II, 428; The Lee Papers . . . 1754–1800, New-York Historical Society Collections, 1871–74 (4 vols.; New York, 1872–75), II, 115.
12. Julian P. Boyd (ed.), The Papers of Thomas Jefferson (Princeton, N.J., 1950–), VI, 224; XIII, 363–64; Jean Blair to Hannah Iredell, May 10, 1781, in Don Higginbotham (ed.), The Papers of James Iredell (Raleigh, N.C., 1976), II, 239; Mary Beth Norton, "'What an Alarming Crisis Is This': Southern Women and the American Revolution," in Jeffrey J. Crow and Larry E. Tise (eds.), The Southern Experience in the American Revolution (Chapel Hill, N.C., 1978), 214; Windley (comp.), Runaway Slave Advertisements, III, 577; IV, 84, 85.

The mass desertion brought financial disaster to some planter but not to be omitted in tallying cost was the anguish owners fe when they saw close associates whom they had imagined to b grateful and loyal abscond to the enemy. Surely it was more tha the red ink in their ledgers that caused the sleep of the great Vi ginia planter Landon Carter and his daughter Judy to be trouble night after night by dreams of their lost slaves. The blow to the a sumptions of paternalism was in itself a painful incident of war.[13]

The British would have been unenterprising indeed had they no capitalized on the military advantage offered them by the slave much as the Spanish had done a generation earlier. In Novembe 1775, Lord Dunmore, the last royal governor of Virginia, pro claimed freedom to all adult males who would flee their master and come under his protection. The exact number who responded— mostly from the Chesapeake Bay area—remains a matter of dis pute, but whatever its magnitude, the loss was large enough to brin their owners all the distress the British intended, and to demon strate again that the slave population offered an enemy easy mean to derange the American society and economy.[14]

But that was not the whole of it. Slavery also weakened the Pa triots' war effort by requiring diversion of troops and supplies to protect the home front. In April, 1776, Charles Lee, writing from Williamsburg, warned of an imminent "piratical war" and slave in surrection. He called upon northern states to dispatch immediat military aid to Virginia, not to drive back the British but to main tain domestic order. Lee explained why this must be done: "An inf nite number of slaves are to be watched over." Shortly afterward officials in Maryland found that men on the Eastern Shore "reluc tantly leave their own neighborhoods unhappily full of Negroes whe might, it is likely, on any misfortune to our militia become very dan gerous." In September, 1777, the Patriot lawyer William Pace of fered advice: Maryland's forces on the Eastern Shore should remain there in order to control both the white Loyalists and the slaves whe came down from the interior hoping to make contact with the Brit ish. In Hartford County, too, the militia was employed not to figh the British but "to prevent the Negroes, servants, and disaffectec peoples from going to the enemy." Again as in earlier times slave

13. Jack P. Greene (ed.), *Diary of Colonel Landon Carter*, II, 1064.
14. Benjamin Quarles, "Lord Dunmore as Liberator," *William and Mary Quarterl* 3rd ser., XV (1958), 494–507.

ned with marginal persons in recognition of a common interest
at was at odds with the dominant part of society.[15]
The emergency seemed as great in states farther south. In Febru-
y, 1777, General Robert Howe urged the president of Congress to
ation a large body of troops in South Carolina expressly to coun-
ract the slaves' temptation to join the British. In 1778, when the
·itish increased their influence on slaves by moving their military
·erations to the South, the Georgia legislature ordered one-third
the troops in each county to remain where they were as a per-
anent slave patrol. In March of the next year, a committee of the
·ntinental Congress found that South Carolina was "unable to
·ake any effectual efforts with militia, by reason of the great pro-
·rtion of citizens necessary to remain at home to prevent insurrec-
·ns among the negroes, and to prevent the desertion of them to the
·emy." The problem persisted. In early 1782 the South Carolina
gislature required each militia company in the state to organize a
·-man patrol whose sole duty would be to maintain order on the
antations.[16]
Even though insurrection in the bloody and destructive form
·hite Americans most dreaded failed to materialize during the war,
·e close watch they placed on slaves did not prevent a species of
volt. When slaves joined the British forces, served as spies and
·formers, bore arms, and fought the Americans, as some did, they
·ere in effect engaged in armed rebellion against their former mas-
·rs. One example of such activity, which understandably horrified
·aveholders, also illustrates the danger of generalizing about slave
·sponse to the conflict. In the winter of 1781 a unit of some 150
·hite and black soldiers swept into the interior of South Carolina.
·nly "by the intervention of their own slaves," the governor was
·ld, were some whites saved.[17]
In time of war, with the balance of power among whites drasti-
·lly changed, slaves simply could not be controlled, and the loyalty
· none could be taken for granted. White Virginians later suspected

15. Charles Lee to Robert Morris, April 16, 1776, in Lee Papers, I, 425–26; Hoff-
an, Spirit of Dissension, 185, 204.
16. Quarles, Negro in the Revolution, 125–26; Worthington C. Ford et al. (eds.),
·urnals of the Continental Congress, 1774–1789 (Washington, D.C., 1904–37), XIII,
·6.
17. Judge Burk to Governor Guerard, December 14, 1785, in Governors' Message
· the Senate, January 24, 1786, in Governors' Messages, 1791–1800, South Carolina
·epartment of Archives and History, Columbia.

that even some who from outward appearance remained faithful
their masters secretly had aided the British by committing acts
sabotage. Some of those who fled to the British and then returne
were thought to be principals in later conspiracies to revolt.[18] Mu
of the difficulty Americans experienced in these respects result
from their loss of mastery in the eyes of slaves. Although slave
ultimately rested on brute force, it also depended to large degree
the slaves' acceptance of its legitimacy, on their acknowledgeme
of the "right"—even though extorted by coercion—of the whites
rule. But such compliance was fragile. Evidence that the owner
power had declined could destroy the institution of slavery t
crumbling its foundation of legitimacy.

The British were able to land on the coast at almost any poi
they chose and to occupy almost any territory. White America
thus appeared weak, their soil at the mercy of an invader. Son
planters who had closely identified themselves with the Patri
cause—Thomas Jefferson among them—fled at the approach of tl
British. Others, even though less tainted in British eyes, tried to sa
themselves and their slave property by avoiding the routes armi
were likely to take. Such behavior severely tested slave faithfulnes
Through inability to hurl back the invader, planters lost their con
manding air, and slaves responded accordingly. The import of tl
phenomenon was not lost on American strategists. Charles Lee, fc
one, warned of the stunning effect the fall of Charleston would ha
on slavery throughout the South Carolina low country. The ci
must be defended, he explained, not only for its own sake but b
cause its loss would signal to slaves the impotence of their master
When the city finally was taken, reports of slave flight by owners i
the region proved the prediction accurate.[19]

As the war progressed and British armies campaigned throug
the southern counties of Virginia, perhaps as many as 30,000 slave
were lost to their owners. The story was repeated elsewhere. On
estimate places the number of blacks throughout the colonies wh

18. John Clarke to James Monroe, June 12, 1801, in William Palmer, Sherw
McRae, and H. W. Flournoy (eds.), *Calendar of Virginia State Papers and Other Man
scripts, 1652–1869, Preserved at the Capitol in Richmond* (Richmond, 1875–93), I
201; John B. Scott to James Monroe, April 22, 1802, in Executive Papers, Virgin
State Library, Richmond.

19. Charles Lee to Richard Henry Lee, April 5, 1776, in *Lee Papers*, I, 379, 4
Windley (comp.), *Runaway Slave Advertisements*, III, 584.

ade good their escape at 100,000.[20] The statistic, even if accurate,
not entirely satisfactory, however; for by no means can all slaves
ho fell into British hands be presumed to have acted voluntarily
- to have accepted willingly the British disposition of them. An
ndetermined number of those captured were sold elsewhere as
ooty of war. The British, slaves learned, in some instances proved
s careless of their welfare and desires as their American masters.
ı early July, 1776, Landon Carter reported, the British commander
ı Virginia sent a load of blacks "to one of the Islands which so
armed the rest that the County of Gloster [sic] was disturbed by
ıeir howlings."[21] It does not seem likely that the 2,500 whom the
ritish took from Charleston to Jamaica or the 2,000 sent to East
lorida, whether sold as slaves or not, found their circumstance sig-
ificantly bettered by the change. Despite such perfidy, the oppor-
ınity offered by the British presence was tempting to slaves, and
othing owners did could prevent the venturesome from taking ad-
antage of it. The slaves' response to warfare strikingly demon-
rated both southern vulnerability and their own urge to escape
om bondage.
The fate of the many thousands of blacks who cast their lot with
ıe British no doubt varied greatly and in most cases cannot be dermined. But the fortunes of some are matters of record. When the
ories fled Boston after the Battle of Bunker Hill, their own slaves
ıd some others accompanied them to Canada. Probably a few of
ıese eventually found themselves in England; later, following in-
ependence, some who had remained in Canada, or their descend-
ıts, returned to Boston to swell that city's already sizable free-
lack community. An uncertain number of absconding southern
lacks also found a haven in the northern states.[22]
Some blacks voluntarily returned to their owners after a season
ith the British, but sojourn in the British camps was likely to
rengthen the self-confidence that had inspired flight in the first

20. Herbert Aptheker, *The American Revolution, 1763–1783* (New York, 1980), 218.
uarles, *Negro in the Revolution*, p. 172, tallies some 19,000 slaves evacuated with
ıe British.
21. Quarles, *Negro in the Revolution*, 167; Jack P. Greene (ed.), *Diary of Colonel
ındon Carter*, II, 1056. The sufferings of slaves who escaped to the British are de-
iled in Sylvia R. Frey, "Between Slavery and Freedom: Virginia Blacks in the
merican Revolution," *Journal of Southern History*, XLIX (1983), 388–97.
22. James Oliver Horton and Lois E. Horton, *Black Bostonians: Family Life and
ommunity Struggle in the Antebellum North* (New York, 1979), viii, 137n.

place. Probably the transformation that his master noted in St
phen was not unique: "He affects to be free . . . he is very specio
and knowing, having been some time with the British." Others, fin
ing themselves emancipated by their flight, left the British cam
and managed to blend into the growing free-black population th
flourished in such cities as Savannah, Charleston, and Richmon
The experience of freedom predictably led to the resolve never to t
enslaved again. Nanny, who ran to the British in May, 1779, and
the end of the war accompanied them to St. Augustine, managed
escape from her master's agent while he was trying to bring h
back to South Carolina. Stepney, who went with the British forc
from South Carolina to Virginia, was somehow returned to h
owner, only to flee again. A family of five slaves left James Islar
with the British in 1779. After being in Savannah for a while, th
disappeared from white society altogether, probably retreating in
Indian country.[23]

To the chagrin of patriotic slaveholders, many blacks chose to r
main with the British after military victory at Yorktown confirme
independence. Others left with the French. Perhaps as many as t
thousand blacks crowded aboard British ships as they sailed fro
Savannah and Charleston in 1782. When British armies withdre
from Virginia after their defeat at Yorktown in October, 1781, thre
thousand former slaves left with them. With their anguished owne
vainly protesting and seeking intercession from every available a
thority, the blacks were taken first to New York, and then, in viol
tion of the Treaty of Paris, to Halifax, where they were lost to the
Patriot masters forever.[24]

The revolutionary experience gave white Americans new reaso
to understand that the loyalty and docility of the slave populatio
could not be taken for granted. "In a time of war, slaves rendere
a country more vulnerable," was the painfully learned lesson Wi
liam C. Davies of North Carolina conveyed to his countrymen i
1788. While the Patriot soldier surely knew that in regions dista
from British armies the great majority of slaves remained with the
owners throughout the war and that impressive numbers supporte
the American cause even to the extent of serving in the Continent

23. Windley (comp.), *Runaway Slave Advertisements*, III, 380, 408, 712, 713, 7
735, 740; IV, 104–105.
24. Their saga is told in James W. St. G. Walker, *The Black Loyalists: The Sear
for a Promised Land in Nova Scotia and Sierra Leone, 1783–1870* (London, 1975), 1–
and *passim*.

mies, this knowledge inspired little confidence for the future. As
rly as 1785, Charles Thomson, secretary of the Continental Con-
ess, remarked to Jefferson that he feared America's slaves more
an Algerine pirates or potential European foes. If slavery were not
ded by "religion, reason and philosophy," he predicted, it would
meday end "by blood."[25] The commonly held opinion that even-
ally a slave-inspired disaster was inevitably going to happen was
powerful incentive for the several gradual emancipation schemes
it forward following the Revolution, including that of Jefferson. In
hostile world, American national security would be imperiled by
s slave population. And no slaveholder, as events soon proved,
uld be certain that any quarter, even within his own country, was
nmune to subversion.

British wartime policies designed to disrupt slavery were pre-
ctable. Such timeworn tactics were regarded as an unavoidable,
odious, technique of war. Far more startling to southern slave-
lders and ominous for their future security was an incident occur-
ng in Massachusetts during the Revolution. When some thirty-
ur slaves from South Carolina were carried off by the British and
en recaptured by two Massachusetts vessels, the *Hazard* and the
yrannicide, the Massachusetts Supreme Court refused to order
em returned to their owners and eventually set them free. The
dges' decision infuriated South Carolina's Governor Benjamin
uerard: "No act of British Tyranny could exceed the encouraging
e negroes . . . to desert their owners to be emancipated." The de-
sion, added the governor, "seems arbitrary and domination [*sic*]."
e found in religious differences between North and South an ex-
lanation for the court's perverse judgment. But understanding did
ot bring forgiveness: "The liberation of our negroes disclosed a
ecimen of Puritanism I should not have expected from gentlemen
f my Profession."[26]

The incident bore alarming implications for white southerners.
o have defeated one enemy, it appeared, was only to have acquired
nother. The British were unlikely soon to renew their interference
vith American slaves, the Spanish menace had lessened, the French
vere gone. But what if revolutionary and religious ideology, rein-

25. Jonathan Elliot (ed.), *The Debates in the Several State Conventions, on the Adop-
on of the Federal Constitution . . .* (Philadelphia, 1907), V, 31; Charles Thomson to
homas Jefferson, November 2, 1785, in Boyd (ed.), *Papers of Thomas Jefferson*, IX, 9.
26. Benjamin Guerard to John Hancock, October 6, 1782, in George Henry Moore,
otes on the History of Slavery in Massachusetts (New York, 1866), 173.

forced by sectional political ambition, should someday lead nort
erners to assume the liberating role recently played by Europe;
powers? The prospect for the South in that event would be omino
indeed.

Some leading southerners, aware that in parts of the North at
tudes toward slavery conflicted with slaveholding interests, felt u
easy at the prospect of creating a stronger union in 1787. Northe:
and southern economic interests had already clashed in the Con
nental Congress. Some individuals, still relishing their shedding
British restrictions, wished to remain free to carry out private pu
suits without interference by others through the instrumentality
the state. On that account they found the decentralized governme:
created by the Articles of Confederation ideal and might be expect
to resist proposals to expand the power and efficiency of gover
ment. Yet in the 1780s, despite such sentiment, the need for a mo:
effective union to replace the Confederation was widely acknow
edged by public-spirited Americans of all sections.

Thus Southerners, including great slaveholders, joined in in
tiating the movement that led to the Constitutional Convention i
Philadelphia in 1787. But even while some of them were concedir
the necessity for stronger government, others opposed the ne
political creation, which under hostile leadership might disregar
southern interests and use its augmented power to doom their p
culiar institution.

A taste of things to come was provided in 1787 when represent;
tives from all parts of the country met in deliberation at Philade
phia, where the issue of slavery, in the words of Abraham Baldwi:
delegate from Georgia, caused the Constitutional Convention "pai
and difficulty." Its power to irritate, slaveholders must have rea
ized, would be no less in the new union. Delegates to the conventio
managed to compromise their large differences on slavery, but the
could not hide them. They accepted its existence, agreed to cour
three-fifths of the slaves for both apportioning representation i
Congress and levying direct taxes, authorized a fugitive slave lav
prohibited restriction on importation of slaves for twenty years, an
gave the new government power to aid in putting down insurrec
tions. Yet to the slaveholders' dismay, some northerners insisted o
viewing the new constitution as an antislavery document.[27]

27. *Annals of Congress*, 1st Cong., 2nd Sess., 1200; Staughton Lynd, *Class Conflic
Slavery, and the United States Constitution* (Indianapolis, 1967), 153–54.

Apprehension that an antislavery majority eventually would con-
ol the new government and turn its power against the South ex-
ained some of the widespread reluctance among southerners to
tify the Constitution. Their fears were not without foundation.
1at slavery violated human rights was no longer a novel or eccen-
ic opinion, even in the South. In a national government, such an-
slavery sentiment would find a larger and more effective sphere of
fluence than ever would have been available under the decentral-
ed Confederation. Creation of a national forum promised to inten-
y the clash of sectional interests and give opponents of slavery
hanced opportunity for expression. There, in a strong Congress,
itislavery sentiment and sectional interest might someday com-
ne to ruin the slaveholding class.

In northern states, some Federalists assured voters that in form-
g the new government the Founding Fathers had arranged for the
ventual end of slavery. Or, as William Dawes explained to the Mas-
chusetts ratifying convention, "We may say, that although slavery
not smitten by an apoplexy, yet it has received a mortal wound,
id will die of a consumption." James Wilson of Pennsylvania tried
be less figurative. By making possible the end of the slave trade
1808, he told voters, the Constitution had laid "the foundation for
anishing slavery out of the country." It was not simply, as some
elieved, that by halting slave importation Congress would unleash
l-defined forces that eventually would destroy slavery; instead,
Vilson promised direct antislavery action: "Yet the lapse of a few
ears, and Congress will have power to exterminate slavery from
ithin our borders."[28]

Suspicion that this was exactly what some northern interests
itended gave southern delegates pause as they prepared to hold
1e ratifying conventions that would determine whether they joined
1e new union or went their separate ways. Southern proponents
f ratification found it necessary to overcome grave misgivings.
harles Cotesworth Pinckney acknowledged that the "religious and
olitical prejudices of the Eastern and Middle States" turned the
eople of those sections against southern institutions; but, he as-
ired South Carolinians, the disagreeable northern antipathies
ould have little practical significance. The powers of Congress
vere strictly limited to those enumerated in the Constitution. Con-
ress could not intervene in southern local affairs or interfere

28. Elliot (ed.), *Debates*, II, 41, 452, 484.

with local institutions. Further, observed Pinckney, the new gover
ment offered slaveholders a most desirable advantage. The Cons
tution guaranteed the return of fugitive slaves, an obligation tl
Confederation had neglected to place on its members. With that pr
vision, a grievance suffered for a century and a half—the escape
blacks to areas beyond their owners' reach—now promised to l
remedied.[29]

But not all were convinced. Patrick Henry, steadfast again
ratification, felt nearly as confident as did antislavery northerne
that Congress someday, somehow, would find in the new docume:
power to end slavery. It would be led to such action, Henry pr
dicted, by "urbanity" and, he added—perhaps recalling the difficu
ties slavery caused the South during the Revolution—by "the nece
sity of national defence."[30]

James Madison, a leading participant in the Philadelphia conver
tion, discounted Henry's forecast. Just as Pinckney argued in Sout
Carolina, Madison assured doubters in Virginia that the powers
Congress were confined solely to those specified in the documen
Thus, he promised, Congress never could trespass on slavery. D
spite reassurance from such prestigious figures, skeptics still foun
grounds for questioning the efficacy of a mere document to foresta
the will of a politically and religiously aroused North. "I apprehen
it means to bring forward manumission," insisted James Gallowa
of North Carolina. Though his colleague James Iredell worked har
to persuade him of his mistake, Galloway still could not bring hin
self to vote for ratification.[31]

Such persistent doubters failed to dissuade the southern pr
union majority. Southern apprehensions, though strong, were cour
teracted by the still more compelling reasons for accepting the ne
government. While most of the proratification arguments bore n
direct relation to slavery, one of the most persuasive clearly did. Th
new, stronger union, southern advocates argued, provided an i
valuable assurance—it would help suppress slave rebellions. "Ou
negroes are numerous, and are daily becoming more so," observe
Governor Edmund Randolph at the ratifying convention in Vir
ginia. "When I reflect on their comparative number, and compara
tive condition, I am the more persuaded of the great fitness of be
coming more formidable than ever."[32]

29. *Ibid.*, IV, 285, 286. See also James Madison's comments, *ibid.*, III, 453.
30. *Ibid.*, III, 590. See also p. 623. George Mason argued similarly, *ibid.*, III, 270.
31. *Ibid.*, III, 621–22; IV, 101–102.
32. *Ibid.*, III, 192.

Madison agreed with Randolph's assessment of both the danger
d the means of security: "The Southern States are, from their
1ation and circumstances, most interested in giving the national
vernment the power of protecting its members." George Nicholas,
o had little patience with indirection, spelled out for Virginians
e exact meaning of Madison's observation: The new Constitution
ovided "an additional securing" against slave insurrections, "for,
sides the power in the state governments to use their militia; it
ll be the duty of the general government to aid them with the
ength of the Union when called for." The Confederation, as Nich-
s knew, had been charged with no such obligation, and during
e Revolution, southern states had been forced somewhat igno-
niously to appeal to the North for military aid. Slaveowners long
uld value the Union, despite its irritating aspects, partly because
ey believed it provided them with an essential safeguard. The na-
nal government would preserve the peace in South Carolina, a
arleston newspaper assured its readers following revelation of
nmark Vesey's conspiracy in 1822: "It was established expressly
ensure domestic tranquility and suppress insurrection."[33]

The southerners' deeply rooted misgivings about the new govern-
nt were effectively countered in the 1790s, if not quite elimi-
ted, by the unmistakable advantages a stronger union offered.
utherners also believed that they would dominate the new gov-
iment.[34] Slavery as a local institution presumably lay forever be-
nd national jurisdiction. Yielding to that benign interpretation,
e slaveholding states joined in ratifying the Constitution. In so
ing, however, southern leaders committed themselves to constant
;ilance lest the new government, at the bidding of antisouthern or
tislavery groups, overstep its bounds, usurp power, and interfere
matters properly outside its province. From the day the new gov-
iment became operative, slaveholders assumed the role of per-
tual guardians of state sovereignty.

Though fearful of centralized power, slaveholders could take com-
t in the knowledge that however menacing to some southern in-
ests the newly operative government potentially might be, it still
ered protection against slave insurrection. Almost any sacrifice
uld be worth making in order to guard against that horror.

Such an emergency soon loomed. When the French Revolution of
89 threw Europe into tumult, the United States possessed no coin

33. *Ibid.*, 415, 427; Charleston *City Gazette and Daily Advertiser*, September 27,
22.
34. Lynd, *Class Conflict*, 202–203.

with which to purchase certain exemption. Revolutions, it becai
clear, were not to be relegated to the heroic past, nor would futu
upheavals always be as limited in social impact as the war
American independence had been. No sooner did evidence for th
disquieting generalizations appear in Europe than events in t
French colony of Saint-Domingue taught a third shattering tru
Revolution could not be held as a monopoly in the hands of whit
The expanding revolutionary impulse had led to race war on an
land near the United States, and there was no assurance that t
upheaval could be stopped at the American shore. Thus, in t
1790s, southerners faced special strains as the possibility grew tl
slavery would be subverted either by blacks themselves or by wh
dissidents mobilizing nonslaveholders against it.

3

e̶e̶e̶e̶e̶e̶e̶e̶e̶e̶e̶e̶e̶e̶e̶e̶e̶e̶e̶e̶e̶e̶e̶e̶e̶e̶e̶e̶e̶e̶e̶e̶e̶

Another Kind of Revolution

1788, in a mood of enthusiastic patriotism, Charles Cotesworth
ıckney contrasted for his fellow South Carolinians the fortunate
ndition of postrevolutionary America with the Old World's deca-
nce. "To the liberal and enlightened mind," said Pinckney, most
Europe afforded "a melancholy picture of the depravity of human
ture, and of the total subversion of . . . rights." But happier days
/ ahead, because young America had put ancient Europe to
ıool. According to Pinckney, the people of Ireland, the Nether-
ıds, and France recently had added to their freedoms under Amer-
ı's tutelage, and he hoped the process would continue: "Let it be
ır prayer that the effects of the revolution may never cease until
ey have unshackled all the nations that have firmness to resist the
ters of despotism."[1]

But how, from what, and by whom would nations be freed? Pinck-
y, a member of South Carolina's planter class, could not have
·eseen the consequences of his answered prayer. His self-congratu-
ory words were spoken before mobs in Paris stormed the Bastille,
fore the rise of the Jacobins, before the Terror, and—to him most
sconcerting of all—before blacks in the French colony of Saint-
ɔmingue, echoing slogans of revolutionary Europe, overthrew and
ıughtered their white masters.

---

1. Elliot (ed.), *Debates*, IV, 319–20.

In 1791, revolution convulsed Saint-Domingue. There, in the
lantic Ocean southeast of the United States, free mulattoes, bl;
slaves, white settlers, and French, English, and Spanish armies
into a desperate, confused struggle that drenched the island w
blood. Led first by Toussaint L'Ouverture and then by Jean-Jacq•
Dessalines, the once-captive blacks gained the upper hand. They
feated all European efforts to subdue them and eventually est
lished their own dominion. The creation of the Republic of Haiti
1804 as the second independent nation in the Western Hemisph
was a triumph of revolutionary theory and of black military pr•
ess. As such, few white Americans and almost no white southern•
could welcome the event. President Jefferson observed to the Frer
chargé d'affaires in Washington that the example of Haiti thre•
ened white rule in every slaveholding state.[2]

Once again, as in the days of the Spanish menace a half centu
earlier, the large American slave population (approximately one c
of every five Americans in 1800 was black) sharpened southerne
awareness of their vulnerability to external threats. Slavery thus
had managed to survive war and the challenge of liberating i•
ology, but those stresses had left the institution temporarily we;
ened in parts of the South and had even brought emancipation
much of the North. Now the interests of American slaveholders w•
threatened as never before by a manifestation of the French Re•
lution occurring in the West Indies dangerously close to Americ
shores.

The close trade relations Americans enjoyed with Saint-Doming
allowed them easily to follow its turbulent affairs, and when, in t
summer of 1793, a French fleet brought thousands of refugees
southern coastal cities, their tales of horror gave immediacy to t
awful impact of black revolt. With some of them came ostensit
still-loyal household slaves whom white southerners suspected
being contaminated with revolutionary intent.[3]

The uprising appalled South Carolinians in particular. The situ
tion of planters in the low country and those in Saint-Doming
were too similar for Carolinians to regard revolt in the island w
anything but alarm. White officials there, recognizing the bonds

2. Alexander De Conde, *This Affair of Louisiana* (New York, 1976), 101. Detai
accounts of the revolt are in T. Lothrop Stoddard, *The French Revolution in San ₊
mingo* (Boston, 1914), and C. L. R. James, *The Black Jacobins: Toussaint L'Ouvert*
and the San Domingo Revolution (Rev. ed.; New York, 1963).
3. Frances S. Childs, *French Refugee Life in the United States, 1790–1800:*
American Chapter of the French Revolution (Baltimore, 1940), *passim.*

ıpathy that united the two societies, dispatched anguished ap-
ls for aid: "This rich country will soon be nothing more than
eap of ashes" was the message sent Governor Charles Pinckney
the island assembly in its plea for troops, ammunition, and pro-
ions. Soon afterward, an emissary appeared before the South
·olina legislature to plead the slaveowners' cause. The law-
kers, readily conceding their interest in suppressing the rebel-
ıs blacks, eventually authorized up to three thousand pounds to
the French.[4]
·he slaveowners' concern was not the preoccupation of a mo-
nt. The shock of successful black rebellion never ceased reverber-
ng through the antebellum South. For decades it called forth ra-
l fears and insecurities. As long as slavery existed, the island's
ne symbolized how extensive racial disorder might be and served
·ally whites to defense of their race and institutions.[5]
·he United States government early displayed official concern for
· insurrection, with George Washington's administration advanc-
money to aid whites fleeing the island. As partial payment of the
·olutionary war debt owed France, the French minister, Jean
ptiste de Ternant, also received American funds to help supply
·nch military forces in Saint-Domingue. However, these tokens
l little to deflect the course of the insurrection. The United States
the most part refrained from interfering in the confused internal
ıirs of the French colony.[6]
l more aggressive antirevolutionary policy might have won pub-
support, but it could have done so only by overriding opposi-
n from those white Americans who, to the distress of slaveown-
, continued to defend the right of the oppressed, whatever their
·or, to resist tyranny. Echoes of the American Revolution sounded
·ough public discussion of the issue. "Is not their cause as just as
·s?" asked Abraham Bishop of Connecticut, a question certain

. Colonial Assembly of Saint-Domingue to Governor of South Carolina, August
1791, in Enclosures, Governor's Message to the House, December 5, 1791, in Gov-
ɔrs' Messages, 1791–1800, South Carolina Department of Archives and History;
·rge Terry, "A Study of the Impact of the French Revolution and the Insurrection
·Saint-Domingue upon South Carolina, 1790–1805" (M.A. thesis, University of
th Carolina, 1975), 42–43.
. Monroe Fordham, "Nineteenth-Century Black Thought in the United States:
ıe Influences of the Santo Domingan Revolution," *Journal of Black Studies*, VI
·5), 115–26; Alfred N. Hunt, *Haiti's Influence on Antebellum America. Slumbering
·ano in the Caribbean* (Baton Rouge, 1988).
. Harry Ammon, *The Gênet Mission* (New York, 1973), 21; Rayford W. Logan, *The
ɪomatic Relations of the United States with Haiti, 1776–1891* (Chapel Hill, N.C.,
1), 100–107, 179, 301–303.

to disconcert any planter who heard it. In 1791, when the Penns
vania legislature debated supplying aid to the besieged whites
member pointed out the inconsistency "on the part of a free nat
to take measures against a people who had availed themselves
the only means they had to throw off the yoke of the most atroci
slavery."[7]

To the consternation of southerners, exploits of the black ret
found still more outspoken admirers. The Connecticut Federa
Theodore Dwight saw in the fate that had overtaken the isla
planters "a dispensation of Providence which Humanity must
plaud." Jabez Bowen, Jr., a Rhode Island native then living in Ge
gia, risked a public declaration of sympathy for "the brave sons
nature," and in Kentucky, David Rice, a Presbyterian preacher a
politician, defied the values of the slave society developing arou
him by praising the black rebels as "brave sons of Africa . . . sacri
ing their lives on the altar of liberty." The cleavage in Americ
opinion and the deep hostility to slavery revealed by such sta
ments could only compound southern insecurities.[8]

Antislavery radicals, sharing southern apprehension that Ame
can slaves might at any moment follow the Saint-Dominguan
ample, speculated on their own course of action should this h
pen. When slaveholders faced servile rebellion, predicted Thom
Branagan of Philadelphia, God would not come to the aid of
oppressors, nor, he suggested, should God-fearing men. Dwig
too, thought no help would be forthcoming from earthly sourc
"Surely, no friend to freedom and justice will dare to lend them
aid." The Reverend Charles Nisbet, British-born principal of Di
inson College in Pennsylvania, welcomed the prospect of an Ame
can slave insurrection for its political value. "A Negro war, wh
may probably break out soon," he wrote, was just what was neec
to further the antislavery cause. A rebellion would convince Ame
cans that their own survival required emancipation. In 1796, in
early statement of the Higher Law doctrine, a northern abolitior

    7. [Abraham Bishop], "Rights of Black Men," *American Museum*, XII (1792), 2
Jean de Ternant to Armand de Montmorin, September 30, 1791, in Frederick Jack
Turner (ed.), *Correspondence of the French Ministers to the United States, 1791–17*
Vol. II of American Historical Association, *Annual Report . . . for the Year 1903* (Wa
ington, D.C., 1904), 53.
    8. Timothy Dwight, *An Oration Spoken Before the Connecticut Society for the F
motion of Freedom and the Relief of Persons Unlawfully Holden in Bondage* (Hartfc
1794), 19; Walter G. Charlton, "A Judge and a Grand Jury," in *Papers of the .
Annual Session of the Georgia Bar Association . . . 1914* (Macon, Ga., 1914), 210; Da
Rice, *Slavery Inconsistent with Justice and Good Policy . . .* (Philadelphia, 1792), 9.

:lared that if slaves rose against their masters, the "political
ims" slaveholders had upon the North would "be opposed by the
ims and the remonstrances of conscience."⁹
▸uch sentiments understandably both offended and alarmed white
₁therners. Only a few years earlier, they had been persuaded to
▸port the new Union, in part because of its promise to assist in
▸pressing slave revolts. Now they had reason to doubt that the
▸mise would be fulfilled. If they felt themselves misled, even
▸ated, who could be surprised?

⅃orthern expressions of sympathy for the black Saint-Domin-
ıns—they were actually taunts addressed to slaveholders—sup-
ɟd an additional source of anxiety for the safety of southern insti-
ions. These scattered antislavery, antisouthern statements made
private citizens in unofficial capacities were rendered still more
rming by attacks mounted during the same years in the United
ıtes Congress. As southern opponents of the Constitution had
rned might happen, antislavery voices made themselves heard in
national government almost from its inception. Persons hostile
the interests of slaveholders attempted to use federal power
ıinst them. In particular, those veterans of antislavery thought
ɟ action, the Quakers, repeatedly petitioned Congress to end
: slave trade. The resulting debates produced strong antislavery
tements from northern legislators and correspondingly strong
.enses from southerners.¹⁰
℃ongressmen from Virginia, where doubts about slavery were
nmon, remained for the most part silent while they listened to
·thern colleagues assail their institutions. Not so the Georgians
₁ South Carolinians. Untroubled by conscience, representatives
m the Deep South had determined to acknowledge their interests
thout apology and to defend them. They responded in angry de-
ᴅe by condemning all antislavery petitions and by entering mo-
ns aimed at silencing any discussion of slavery. Many reasons
re offered to justify such policy, but preeminent was the charge
ₐt public controversy would reach the ears of slaves. Knowledge
ₐt they had white partisans and potential allies would undermine
: slave-master relationship; it might even incite insurrection.

▸. Thomas Branagan, *The Penitential Tyrant; or, Slave Trader Reformed . . .* (2nd ed.;
ᴠ York, 1807), 147–48; Dwight, *Oration*, 19–20; Charles Nisbet to William Rog-
August 17, 1792, in Pennsylvania Abolition Society Papers, Historical Society of
₁nsylvania, Philadelphia; *Connecticut Courant* (Hartford), December 12, 1796.
0. Thomas E. Drake, *Quakers and Slavery in America* (New Haven, Conn., 1950),
–107.

Slave resistance easily could be linked to politics. Although up
ings would be put down, they explained, the necessary result wo
be increasingly severe repression of the slaves rather than the ar
lioration the petitioners claimed to seek.

Congressmen from Georgia and South Carolina refused to toler
even petitions that called only for ending the slave trade, a meas
supported by a broad spectrum of humanitarians, not by antisl
ery advocates alone. However philanthropic the measure mi
seem, southern congressmen explained, it would serve as the f
step toward destroying slavery itself, and that was unacceptal
They first made their views explicit in February, 1790, when
House of Representatives heard a petition from the Pennsylva
Abolition Society, signed by Benjamin Franklin, calling upon C
gress to "step to the very verge of [its] power" to act against slave
Southern statesmen did not underestimate the significance of
document. Did the Pennsylvanians "expect a general emancipati
of slaves by law?" asked Representative Thomas Tucker of Sou
Carolina. If so, they were much deluded: "This would never be s
mitted to by the Southern States without a civil war." James Ja
son of Georgia concurred. A federal effort to end slavery, he warn
would "light up the flame of civil discord; for the people of
Southern States will resist one tyranny as soon as another." Slav
never would end peacefully, he predicted. Southerners already h
taken their stand on the issue. "The other parts of the Continent n
bear them down by force of arms, but they will never suffer the
selves to be divested of their property without a struggle."[11]

Later, in response to yet another antislavery petition from f
blacks, John Rutledge, Jr., of South Carolina, put forward a peace
but ominous defense of slaveholders' interests. There need be n
ther abolition nor civil war. Many northerners and even a few p
sons in the South, Rutledge conceded, thought abolition "reasc
able and unavoidable," but they were mistaken. "Sir, it never w
take place. There is one alternative which will save us from it;
that is, that we are able to take care of ourselves, and if driven to
we will take care of ourselves." Secession and the creation of a sep
rate southern nation was the defense Rutledge proposed against
menace of abolitionism. Further speculation about so drastic a
course proved unnecessary, at least for the moment, for Congr
already had adopted the report of a special committee headed

11. *Annals of Congress*, lst Cong., 2nd Sess., 1197–98, 1200.

iel Foster of New Hampshire, which accepted the southern posi-
n that Congress had no authority over slavery within a state.[12]
Although the Foster report was a substantial and long-lasting
ithern victory, it could not altogether remove concern. Antislav-
' sentiment was not likely to wither away, and there was no rea-
1 to believe that a mere committee report would cause its advo-
.es to cease agitation or abandon their efforts to gain political
wer. The flurry of antislavery petitions that reached Congress in
: 1790s might make a slaveholder uncertain whether the more
mediate threat to property and social order arose from antislav-
' groups and their potential influence in the national government
from the black revolutionary forces in Saint-Domingue. There
.s one important difference, however. The slave rebellion in the
2nch colony posed danger to southern interests against which
2toric and parliamentary maneuver offered no defense.

If American slaves did not spontaneously rise against their mas-
's in imitation of the island revolt, blacks on the island, enthusi-
:ic and doctrinaire, might themselves take the initiative and try
transport their revolution to the mainland. In 1793, Secretary of
ate Thomas Jefferson relayed to the governor of South Carolina
orts (though he said he himself did not believe them) that Saint-
minguan agents had been dispatched to the southern states to
:ite insurrection. Some years later, when relations with France
d drastically deteriorated, the South was swept by rumors of a
ojected French invasion to be launched from the island. In April,
97, Alexander Hamilton, assuming that American slaves would be
robable auxiliaries of France," recommended increasing the artil-
·y and providing two thousand cavalrymen as "guards against in-
rrection." Shortly afterward, on the eve of the undeclared naval
ir with France, former Secretary of War Henry Knox urged Presi-
nt John Adams to prepare for an attack by ten thousand French-
:ruited blacks. If this force should land in a "defenceless part" of
e Carolinas or Virginia, he warned, the slaves would "instantly
n them." At about the same time, Robert Goodloe Harper of
uth Carolina disclosed his belief that the French expected the in-
sion to be followed by an insurrection whose groundwork already
d been laid by "missionaries previously sent." Suspicion per-
ted that foreign agents had infiltrated the South. In March, 1799,

12. *Ibid.*, 6th Cong., 1st Sess., 242; Howard A. Ohline, "Slavery, Economics, and
ngressional Politics, 1790," *Journal of Southern History*, XLVI (1980), 335–60.

South Carolina's Senator Jacob Read warned that the danger of s
version did not lie in a distant future: "Emissaries are now actua
in the Southern States at *their pious work*. They may be of all co
plexions & not known to each other." Representative John Rutled
Jr., also of South Carolina, shared Read's belief in the reality of s
version. In his opinion South Carolina slaves were no longer
ideological innocents masters hoped for. French agents had be
sent to America to incite slaves, he charged, "to feel the pulse of tl
country, to know whether these are the proper engines to make
of: these people have been talked to; they have been tamper
with." Similar apprehension also was voiced in the North. Sai
Domingue could be expected to serve as a springboard for invasic
warned the antislavery Pennsylvanian David Bard in 1804. "Eu
pean powers have armed the Indians against us, and why may th
not arm the negroes?" was Bard's nervous question.[13]

Invasion, of course, did not materialize, but this good fortune c
not allay suspicion that American slaves had taken courage from t
success of the black revolt. White southerners did not suppose th
slaves were immune to the libertarian ideas that aroused the hof
of oppressed people everywhere. They recognized that slaves, as
tently as whites, sought to be masters of their own lives and wou
seize on any model that proved freedom could be attained. Thus
may not have been nervousness alone that led white southerners
the 1790s to interpret overheard slave conversations as evidence
slave plots. Masters in Richmond, Norfolk, Charleston, Savann
and other cities where French refugees had settled suspected th
slaves of conspiring to follow the Saint-Dominguan example. "V
dread the future & are fearful that our feelings for the unfortun
inhabitants of the wretched island . . . may be our own destructior
wrote a self-pitying resident of Charleston. "How hard upon o
poor citizens to be always patrolling and guarding."[14]

Deteriorating foreign relations contributed to domestic alarm.

13. Andrew A. Lipscomb (ed.), *The Writings of Thomas Jefferson* (Washington, D
1903–1904), IX, 275; Alexander De Conde, *The Quasi-War: The Politics and Diplom*
of the Undeclared War with France, 1797–1801 (New York, 1966), 84; Elizabeth D
nan (ed.), *Papers of James A. Bayard, 1796–1815*, Vol. II of American Historical As
ciation, *Annual Report . . . for the Year 1913* (Washington, D.C., 1915), 90; Jacob R
to James P. Jackson, March 23, 1799, in Jacob Read Papers, South Caroliniana
brary, University of South Carolina, Columbia; *Annals of Congress*, 6th Cong.,
Sess., 242; 8th Cong., 1st Sess., 996.
14. Aptheker, *American Negro Slave Revolts*, 96–97; Mrs. Pinckney to Mrs. Ma
gault, February 5, 1798, in Manigault Family Papers, South Caroliniana Library, U
versity of South Carolina, Columbia.

ıe, 1798, when war with France was expected hourly, word
.ched Georgia that a shipload of blacks from the West Indies was
ıut to land at Savannah. The governor immediately ordered "all
٠ horse companies in the state . . . held in readiness to march" and
ɔealed for federal aid. "The President," he explained, "will no
ıbt see the propriety of preventing those people from being
ded . . . where so many thousands of persons of color might be
ited to insurrection by their seditious tenets." The Georgia gov-
ıor provided South Carolina officials with an explanation of
ɔnch intent: "The political prospect is dark & the enemies of the
ɔ. may think to profit from the different classes of people among
previous to a possibility of support from, or even a knowledge of
ack by the general government." In July the governor saw danger
ɔming from yet another quarter. Fugitive slaves on Amelia Island
ght "attempt to force their way . . . into this state which must be
ɔvented by all possible means, for war now appears inevitable &
have that description of persons sowing sedition among our
ves whilst we are facing an invading army might be attended
ːh almost fatal consequences."[15]

ʌs in earlier years, white southerners viewed the blacks as poten-
lly dangerous enemies in time of war—but not in wartime only.
March, 1800, the British brig *Maria* sailed into Charleston harbor
ın Kingston, Jamaica, with black troops aboard. The ship had
ːn engaged in helping suppress the Second Maroon War in the
ɪtish colony. Under other circumstances, South Carolinians might
ʋe considered the ship's black crew "loyal," but so insistent was
٠ concern produced by the arrival of armed blacks from the
ɔolt-ridden Caribbean that the ship's arrival, reported South Caro-
a's governor, caused "some anxiety to the citizens." He shared the
ling, for he suspected "that some of the Black troops, have been,
d probably now are notorious villains; and, that as French ne-
ɔes they have been concerned in some of the mischiefs in the West
lies." The governor took every conceivable precaution to allay
ːh public fear and his own. No South Carolina black, free or slave,
s to be allowed to board the ship. He ordered the vessel to posi-
ɪn itself "under the guns of Fort Johnson" in order to guard
ɡainst the injurious consequences which . . . might come from the

5. James Jackson to Mayor John Glen, June 11, 1798, James Jackson to the Sec-
ɪry of War, June 17, 1798, James Jackson to the Governor of South Carolina, June
1798, Jackson to James Seagram, July 23, 1798, all in Executive Papers, Georgia
ɪe Archives, Atlanta.

landing of those negroes, and their consequent communication w
our Slaves." He requested the British consul in Charleston to or
the crew to use "no arms whatever while in this port."[16]

Two years later, the South Carolina governor dispatched alar
ing news to officials in neighboring states and to President Jeffers
A frigate carrying "french negro incendiary prisoners" was ab
to land somewhere along the southern coast and the prison
"turned loose upon us." So determined was the governor to prev
contamination of South Carolina slaves that he issued sanguin
instructions to the state's military commanders—"*none*, of such
cendiaries, are to be *taken prisoners*." This fear, bordering on pa
noia, would lead South Carolina and several other southern sta
in the 1820s to pass Negro seamen's acts. These laws provided t
black crewmen either could not land at all or must be confined
jail while their ships were in port. Although the United States
preme Court declared South Carolina's law unconstitutional,
state defied federal authority and enforced it anyway.[17]

Recurring perils from abroad during the Federalist period m
the divisive effects of domestic political disputes appear danger
in the extreme. The white population must present a solid fr
against both slaves and foreign foes. They must set aside sectio
and ideological differences and seek consensus. In particular, ur
southern leaders, no more antislavery petitions should be deba
in Congress. Representative James McDowell of North Carolina,
specter of Saint-Domingue still before him, entered a plaintive
peal for silence: "When thousands of people have been massacr
and thousands have fled for refuge to this country, when the p
prietors of slaves . . . could only keep them in peace with the utm
difficulty, was this a time for such inflammatory motions?"[18]

Still, the motions did not cease. In January, 1800, an especia
exasperating antislavery petition originating in Philadelp
reached the House of Representatives. Its signers Absalom Jo

16. John Drayton to Timothy Pinckney, March 26, 1800, Drayton to British Con
March 8, 1800, Drayton to Constant Freem, March 22, 1800, all in Executive Journ
John Drayton, 1800, in Governors' Papers, South Carolina Department of Arch
and History, Columbia.
17. General Orders to Brigadier Generals Horry, Vanderhorst, and McPher
September 9, 1802, and Drayton to Jefferson, September 12, 1802, both in Govern
Papers, South Carolina Department of Archives and History; Phillip M. Har
"Great Britain, the United States, and the Negro Seamen Acts, 1822–1848," *Jou*
of Southern History, I (1935), 3–28.
18. *Annals of Congress*, 3rd Cong., 2nd Sess., 2043.

d others—were free blacks, leaders of their race in Philadelphia
ɪo engaged in antislavery activity before many whites outside the
ligious Society of Friends were prepared to do so. The petition
rticularly annoyed supporters of slavery because it demonstrated
ɪt some blacks already occupied a position that theories of racial
bordination denied was possible. Harrison Gray Otis found the
cument nearly as offensive as did his southern colleagues. Politi-
l activity of the sort Philadelphia blacks engaged in "must be
schievous to America very soon," said the Massachusetts repre-
ɪtative. "It would teach them the art of assembling together, de-
ting, and the like, and would soon, if encouraged, extend from one
d of the Union to the other."[19]
Blacks throughout the country, Otis understood, were about to
sume an active political role. Perhaps even in the Deep South
few already held such aspirations. Representative Rutledge of
ɪuth Carolina observed that the Philadelphia petitioners were do-
ɡ in the North what slaves aspired to do in the South. "Already
d too much of this new-fangled French philosophy of liberty and
uality found its way and was too apparent among these *gentlemen
aves] in the Southern States, by which nothing would do but
eir liberty."[20]
Evidence of black striving and fear of contamination from abroad
ɪ to official measures aimed at security. Nearly all slave states in
e 1790s enacted laws to prevent admission of slaves from the West
dies, and state officials redoubled vigilance to detect spies and
ɪrl back invaders. Domestic carelessness needed remedy as well.
fter the scenes which St. Domingo has exhibited to the world,
ɟ cannot be too cautious," observed Postmaster General Gideon
ɾanger, himself a native of Connecticut. Granger warned southern-
ɪ of a danger arising from within the postal service. "The most
tive and intelligent" slaves, he observed, "are employed as post
ɪers. These are the most *ready* to *learn*, and the most *able* to *exe-
ɟe*. By travelling from day to day, and hourly mixing with people,
ey must, they will acquire information. They will learn that a
an's rights do not depend on his color. They will, in time, become
achers to their brethren."[21] The objectionable practice, it goes
ɪthout saying, soon was ended.

19. *Ibid.*, 6th Cong., 1st Sess., 231.
20. *Ibid.*, 230.
21. *American State Papers, Class VII: Post Office Department* (1834), 27.

That some southern whites were genuinely fearful can hardly
doubted; yet circumstances required them to continue to live a
work in intimate contact with slaves even while professing to dre
their fury. Crops had to be planted, tended, and harvested; hous
hold chores had to be done. Such necessity set practical limits
repression. The number of slave patrols in most states was i
creased in the 1790s and supervision became more vigilant. Yet
day-to-day practice, considerable freedom of action still was
lowed, and black-white relationships continued to be conducted,
with something less than complete trust, then as if trust we
possible.

The relaxed state of affairs was particularly evident in Virgin
and Maryland, the part of the South where antislavery sentime
was strongest and most freely expressed. The numbers of free blac
in the upper South increased considerably in the 1780s and 179
as many owners manumitted part or all of their slave proper
either out of pangs of conscience or because slaves had great
declined in value. There, too, the severe criticism of slavery th
accompanied the revolutionary movement and the lingering h
manitarianism it fostered had helped temper some of the harshe
aspects of the institution.[22]

Both in towns and throughout the countryside, a class of ar
san slaves had appeared—carpenters, blacksmiths, masons—who
skills assured them a measure of autonomy inconsistent with
ideal of total control. Some accumulated small amounts of mone
thus adding to their sense of independence while also gaining a
cess to a measure of the world's material pleasures. In carryi
out their duties practically free from supervision, skilled slav
moved about and consulted with other people besides their owne
Slaves who operated river boats, for instance, traveled many mil
through the interior of the states, talking and dealing with whor
ever they wished. Even plantation slaves commonly enjoyed consi
erable freedom of movement beyond their home places. They p
tronized grog shops and with no consistent interference held sizab
social gatherings and religious meetings. On occasion repressic

22. Such was the opinion of contemporaries: James Monroe to Speakers of t
General Assembly, December 5, 1800, in Stanislaus Hamilton (ed.), *The Writings
James Monroe* (New York, 1893–1903), III, 240–41; [St. George Tucker], *A Letter tc
Member of the General Assembly of Virginia on the Subject of the Late Conspiracy* .
(Baltimore, 1801), 5–6, 8–9; George Drinker to Joseph Bringhurst, December 1
1804, in Pennsylvania Abolition Society Papers.

uld be severe and reprisal for offenses could be savage; yet slave
trols operated only sporadically, and authorities often winked at
)lations.[23]
When this relative freedom was brought to their attention, white
.itherners had trouble justifying their laxity. Instead they were
ely to profess alarm at what had taken place and to predict its
imately harmful effect. As it turned out, they were not mistaken
their apprehension.

In the summer of 1800 it became clear that some of the most privi-
;ed slaves in Virginia had become intensely embittered as a result
their bondage and hostile to the whites responsible for perpetu-
ng it. The opportunities afforded them by a diversifying economy
.d a republican society taught them that even more might be
eirs. Not surprisingly, some of the "freest" of the slaves sought
rough concerted action and violence to shake off all restrictions.
In counties around Richmond, enterprising slave artisans and
eachers moved through the countryside organizing the discontent
at festered within the black population. Some who were not le-
imately supplied with passes by their owners wrote their own.
ey traveled to slave barbecues and religious meetings to seek out
low conspirators; they met like-minded slaves in taverns and
acksmith shops and at secret rendezvous. Their plan was to de-
lop a military organization and then capture Richmond, kill
any of the whites, and establish black control. They believed the
ass of disaffected but less acculturated and less committed slaves
)uld eventually come to their support.[24]

Leadership of the conspiracy, uncertain at first, eventually fell
twenty-four-year-old Gabriel, who with his brothers Solomon
d Martin (a preacher) ran a blacksmith shop for their young mas-
r Thomas Henry Prosser, one of the wealthiest men in Henrico
unty. Able and dependable though Gabriel was, he also had a
rce temper. In 1799, before his revolutionary activity made him
torious, he had been convicted of maiming his white neighbor
raham Johnson by biting off part of his ear. Although this was a
pital offense, Gabriel had been sentenced only to be branded on
e hand and confined for a month in Rose's brig, Henrico County's

23. On the relaxed conditions in Virginia, see Gerald W. Mullin, *Flight and Rebel-*
n, 127–30, and Robert McColley, *Slavery and Jeffersonian Virginia* (Urbana, Ill.,
54), 57–75.
24. The following account of the conspiracy generally follows Gerald W. Mullin,
ght and Rebellion, 140–63.

noisome jail.[25] Within a few months of his release, he was planni rebellion.

As became a skilled craftsman, Gabriel developed his plan a selected his lieutenants with studied care. He was, above all, a pra tical man. He dismissed enthusiasm alone as insufficient grour for service in his corps. A candidate's ability to command and fight was the prime qualification. Gilbert wanted to be a capta but Gabriel refused him—"He stuttered too much." Toby held ra as captain for a time, "but was turned out being undersize." Mar was too old to be a soldier, Gabriel decided. Instead, he would "r bullets and keep them in bullets."[26]

The leaders did not count on the inspiration of the moment carry them to victory. They made careful assessments of their st tegic situation, using the best information they could get. In t summer of 1800 no armed forces were available for Virginia a thorities to use against a rebel force. Since for two years the Unit States had been engaged in undeclared naval war with France French army, the rebels believed, might land to support the revc The Catawba Indians also might come to their aid. Recognizi their military limitations, the conspirators sought expert advi One Charles Quersey, a French veteran of the Battle of Yorktov and supposedly sympathetic to the slaves' cause, would help dir the first phase of military operations.

Under Gabriel's leadership, the conspiracy took secular and tional form. In spite of preacher Martin's large role the plan show few features of a religious or messianic movement. It could harc have been otherwise, for notwithstanding heavy gains recen made in Virginia by evangelical churches, this was still a secul age. Although both Baptists and Methodists were making many co verts, especially among blacks and nonslaveholding whites, the n revivalism had not yet altogether displaced the rationalistic outlo of the dominant white element, neither had it quite beaten back t influence of the Enlightenment on the blacks, especially amo such privileged craftsmen as Gabriel. But insofar as it had done s

25. Philip J. Schwarz, "Gabriel's Challenge: Slaves and Crime in Late Eighteen Century Virginia," *Virginia Magazine of History and Biography*, XC (1982), 283–3 Bert M. Mutersbaugh, "The Background of Gabriel's Conspiracy," *Journal of Ne History*, LXVIII (1983), 209–11.
26. Palmer, McRae, and Flournoy (eds.), *Calendar of Virginia State Papers*, IX, 1 153; Trial of Samuel Prosser, September 11, 1800, in Negro Insurrection File, in l ecutive Papers, Virginia State Library. The latter source contains important det omitted from the record printed in *Calendar of Virginia State Papers*.

e doctrine of spiritual freedom as preached by the revivalistic
ergy powerfully reinforced the secular justification for throwing
f bondage. Nevertheless, the conspirators proceeded to develop
eir plans with little overt recourse to religious inspiration. On
e battle flag the leaders planned to display, they would inscribe
e words "death or Liberty," a slogan transmitted to them from the
volutionary era.[27]
The conspirators had large, though limited, political goals. Their
m, said Gabriel, was "to subdue the whole of the country where
avery was permitted, but no further." The slave John testified
at Gabriel asked him "to join him to fight for his country." Al-
ough the slaughter required to attain their goals undoubtedly
ould be vast, the leaders did not intend it to be indiscriminate.
ccording to the slave Ben Woolfolk, "All the whites were to be mas-
cred, except the Quakers, the Methodists, and the Frenchmen, and
ey were to be spared on account . . . of their being friendly to lib-
ty." They intended also to spare all the "poor white women who
ad no slaves."[28] Far from providing reassurance, such discrimina-
on could only add to slaveholders' alarm, for it suggested that the
nspirators recognized a community of interest between them-
lves and antislavery advocates and, still more ominous, that they
w members of certain religious groups and the nonslaveholding
hites as their friends.
By August 30, Gabriel's plan had matured. It would be set in op-
ation at midnight. But on the afternoon of that day, Tom and Pha-
oh, two slaves privy to the conspiracy but not committed to it,
cided to end their silence. They revealed the plot to Mosley Shepard, their master. Since the uprising was scheduled to begin within
few hours, authorities had no time to prepare to meet the danger.
ut preparation proved unnecessary. A torrential rain storm began
noon and continued into the night. Bridges were washed out, and
ads became impassable. Slaves could not assemble; the revolt
ould not take place.
With Governor James Monroe in charge, a massive roundup of
spects began immediately. Authorities took scores of depositions,
ials were held, and eventually the courts condemned more than
enty slaves. The judges acquitted some twelve of the accused. An-
her seven received pardons. One of the last of the conspirators to

27. Palmer, McRae, and Flournoy (eds.), *Calendar of Virginia State Papers*, IX, 147,
1, 152.
28. *Ibid.*, 152.

be captured was Gabriel himself, who evidently had been harbor
for an extended period by whites—exactly by whom never was d
termined. When authorities conducted him from jail to the gove
nor's house for a private—and unrevealing—interview, "a gre
cloud [crowd?] of blacks as well as whites gathered around him
Whether it was hostility, admiration, or only curiosity that dre
them there, we cannot know.[29]

Revelation of Gabriel's conspiracy occurred before any part of
became operative and even before evidence of unusual slave unre
appeared. Extensive in organization and devastating in potenti
though it was, the conspiracy remained only a plan. Although son
whites were terror-struck when they realized the fate Gabriel ar
his men had designed for them, public officials went about the i
vestigation and the trials that followed with not even momenta
surrender to hysteria. Under Governor Monroe's direction, officia
made every effort to avoid exploiting the sensational aspects of tl
affair, and the jurists who gathered the evidence gave their disco
eries minimal publicity. It is evident that Monroe and his advise
hoped in this way to avoid arousing panic, but they also may ha
had political reasons for wishing to make as little as possible of tl
incident. As Jeffersonians, they were vulnerable to accusation
having spread the radical principles that evidently encouraged tl
conspirators.

Elsewhere, too, officials made sure the projected uprising was n
sensationalized. In South Carolina, where danger of imitation w
thought to be extreme, Governor John Drayton, who already ha
advised editors to refrain from discussing Jefferson's antislave
views, now urged them to ignore recent events in Virginia. Charle
ton newspapers thus printed only sketchy accounts of a "rebellior
with no hint that slaves had been involved. But such self-censorsh
did not mean that white southerners remained uninformed abo
what had happened. Even in remote Mississippi Territory, the eve
aroused concern.[30] Gabriel's conspiracy never acquired the charge
aura that would surround Nat Turner's revolt a generation later; y
its implications could not be evaded, and for years afterward, r
mors of new plots and impending rebellion troubled the South.

29. *Ibid.*, 156.
30. Charleston *City Gazette and Daily Advertiser*, October 22, 1800; Winthrop Sa
gent to "Sir," November 16, 1800, printed broadside (N.p., n.d.), in Ohio Historic
Society.

In keeping with the spirit of moderation set by Governor Monroe, e courts exercised more forbearance toward the accused than ight have been expected; nevertheless, the number of death sen- nces was large enough to trouble Monroe. He appealed to Jeffer- n for advice on how the state could punish the convicted slaves thout resorting to execution. Although he provided no clear-cut swer, Jefferson replied that even in his neighborhood, "where miliarity with slavery and a possibility of danger from that quar- r prepares the general mind for some severities," sentiment was rong "that there has been hanging enough." As usual, Jefferson as conscious of acting on a stage open to universal observation. he other states & the world at large will ever condemn us," he vised, "if we indulge a principle of revenge, or go one step beyond solute necessity." And then he proceeded to express again those miliar doubts that for so long had plagued members of Virginia's ling class. Critics outside the South, wrote Jefferson, "cannot lose ght of the rights of the two parties, & the objects of the unsuccess- l one."[31] Even slaves, Jefferson implied, possessed the right to ght for their liberty, and those who oppressed them were in the rong.

Jefferson's was an attitude that if widely held could only encour- e more attempts at rebellion. Self-doubt also would be likely to nder efforts to suppress antislavery dissent. But slavery could not ng be maintained unless apology were banished, rational de- nse—a proslavery argument—took its place, and all whites ac- pted it. Division among the white population simply could not be lerated. Ample material for such defense already existed, as state- ents by South Carolina congressmen recently had proved, but for e moment its formulation in Virginia was delayed.

In the wake of the conspiracy a northern newspaper published a t of topical verse on the subject:

> . . . remember ere too late,
> The tale of St. Domingo's fate.
> Tho *Gabriel* dies, a host remain
> Oppress'd with slavery's galling chain.

31. James Monroe to Thomas Jefferson, September 14, 1800, in Stanislaus Ham- on (ed.), *Writings of James Monroe*, III, 208–209; Jefferson to Monroe, September , 1800, in Paul Leicester Ford (ed.), *The Writings of Thomas Jefferson* (New York, 92–99), VII, 457–58.

And soon or late the hour will come
Mark'd with Virginia's dreadful doom.[32]

The taunting prophecy—written by a New England Federalist
grasped a reality that slaveholders in Virginia found hard to evac
Whites in South Carolina and Georgia, too, felt apprehensions sin
lar to those that haunted Virginians and, perhaps, experienced the
even more keenly. But in those states, unlike Virginia, fear was f
the most part uncomplicated by the doubts of rectitude that, at lea
for the moment, so clearly plagued slaveholders in the upper Sout

32. Quoted in Linda Kerber, *Federalists in Dissent: Imagery and Ideology in Jeff*
sonian America (Ithaca, N.Y., 1970), 46.

4

⛓⛓⛓⛓⛓⛓⛓⛓⛓⛓⛓⛓⛓⛓⛓⛓⛓⛓⛓⛓⛓⛓⛓⛓⛓⛓

Domestic Conspiracy and New Foreign Threats 1800–1819

Slaveholders in the upper South found themselves poorly prepared to meet the challenge that Gabriel's plot forecast. While acknowledging the gravity of their situation, they dealt with it only
halfheartedly and with no clear sense of direction. While Governor
James Monroe and his advisers remained composed, others throughout the state acted in a confused, aimless, almost distracted manner.
Fears of insurrection, no doubt reinforced by the revolt in Saint-
Domingue, were so deep and of such long standing that official efforts to promote calm could not entirely succeed. Terror-stricken
whites fled neighborhoods where danger seemed imminent.[1] Some
of the more stolid, while remaining outwardly calm, still revealed a
sense of helplessness before the prospect of an entire people rising
in rebellion. Even the wisest among them could conceive of no sure
way to resolve the crisis.

It was not simply that the white population lacked military resources adequate to put down servile rebellion, though some of the
many patrols and military units hastily formed to intimidate the
blacks indeed do seem to have been deficient in both equipment and
leadership. Yet the irresolution and apparent lack of clear direction
did not arise just from matters subject to computation and rational

1. *Hints for the Consideration of the Friends of Slavery, and Friends of Emancipation*
(Lexington, Ky., 1803), 11–12; speech of Representative Daniel Sheffey, January 11,
13, *Annals of Congress*, 12th Cong., 2nd Sess., 701.

assessment. Something of its intangible, emotional aspect was su
gested when even proposals aimed at more effective defense we
criticized on the ground that these plans contained their own fa
element of risk. For example, objections were raised when state c
ficials distributed arms to strengthen local regiments: Slaves, wi
their superior and insurmountable power, might capture the ar
nals and seize the weapons for their own use.[2]

Further, some suspected the conspiratorial slaves of benefiti
from strategically placed white friends who supported their aim
destroying the Virginia planters—perfect unity of the white pop
lation never had been achieved. Plantation disorder, in some min
was linked to larger social and political conflicts. The planters' en
mies were thought to lurk everywhere. The opposition of antislave
religious groups—Quakers, Methodists, Emancipating Baptists
and of some envious poor white people might be presumed, but pc
sons of high degree fell among the suspect as well. Thomas Jeffers
reported that his neighbors believed John Adams' administrati
deliberately encouraged slave attack by leaving federal arsen
poorly guarded. And advice reached Governor Monroe, as he w
preparing to prosecute Gabriel and his coconspirators, that t
state's deputy attorney could not be trusted to uphold the slaveho
ers' interests—he was by birth an Englishman, he associated wi
suspected abolitionists, he supported "all the measures of the E
ecutive of the United States."[3] White Virginians, fearing they we
facing a coalition of blacks, Englishmen, Federalists, and abolitio
ists, and already only too aware of the Saint-Dominguan upheav
saw themselves threatened on many fronts, with no adequate d
fense at hand.

These unsubstantiated notions reflected the profound self-dou
that by 1800 plagued members of the ruling classes in Virginia
well as ordinary citizens. They were dependent upon an instituti
that ideologically was fast becoming an anachronism. Of course,
was common knowledge that slave labor formed the base of t

2. Benjamin Oliver to James Monroe, September 23, 1800, in Executive Pape
Virginia State Library; Thomas Newton to James Monroe, December 29, 1800,
Palmer, McRae, and Flournoy (eds.), *Calendar of Virginia State Papers*, IX, 173; T.
Randolph to James Monroe, February 14, 1801, in James Monroe Papers (microfil
Manuscripts Division, Library of Congress; W. Bentley to James Monroe, Septe
ber 8, 1800, in Palmer, McRae, and Flournoy (eds.), *Calendar of Virginia State Pape*
IX, 138.

3. Thomas Jefferson to James Monroe, November 8, 1800, in James Monroe I
pers; Richard E. Lee to James Monroe, September 25, 1800, in Executive Pape
Virginia State Library.

riving economy of the sugar-rich Caribbean islands and of the
ce-indigo culture of South Carolina and Georgia. Slavery re-
ained a vital economic interest in Virginia as well. Yet Enlighten-
ent ideas and changed religious sensibilities had become so per-
sive that never again could slavery be accepted unquestioningly
part of an unchanging social order. Only if blacks were defined
being outside the rest of humanity, hopelessly incompetent and
nately savage, could their permanent subjugation be defended.
anters increasingly resorted to this solution for the contradiction
thin their society. But even if racist ideas prevailed, however
rnestly voiced, a troublesome possibility intruded to contradict
em: Some of the clearest-minded Virginians at the turn of the
ntury conceded that in America's evolving republican society,
acks could not be kept in that state of ignorance and servility that
one might assure their continued subjugation. Yet no alternative
slavery appeared feasible. A few years later, Monroe would in-
rm Jefferson of his support for gradual emancipation—if it could
accomplished "on principles consistent with humanity, without
pense or inconvenience to ourselves."[4] A proviso of such magni-
de, of course, assured the perpetuation of slavery despite wide-
read acknowledgment of its inequity and despite the insecurities
bred. Virginians were caught in a dilemma from which there was
 escape.
A society thus perplexed might be expected to shore up its foun-
tions. The Virginians tried to do this, but their efforts appeared
tful and halfhearted. Some whites believed they faced an abso-
tely overwhelming challenge against which no preparation could
ail. Here and there, vigilante groups took the offensive by waging
arfare against unarmed blacks.[5] But the success of such cam-
igns brought little assurance, for Virginians did not foresee them-
lves threatened by sporadic, localized outbreaks of a few dissident
aves whom available military units could quell. Instead, they ex-
cted large-scale, coordinated warfare. Fierce black armies shout-
g "the negro-war song" would materialize in the countryside and
ll upon helpless towns and plantations. White civilians, defended
ly by improvised, inept military forces, would be crushed by fe-

4. [Tucker], *Letter to a Member of the General Assembly of Virginia*, 5–6; Stanislaus
amilton (ed.), *Writings of James Monroe*, III, 353.
5. An account of one such foray is in Charles William Janson, *The Stranger in
merica, Containing Observations Made During a Long Residence in That Country . . .*
ondon, 1807), 395–98. See also James Fletcher to James Monroe, January 1, 1801,
Executive Papers, Virginia State Library.

rocious slave assault. Whatever the explanation, it is apparent th
the mood in parts of Virginia from 1800 to 1802 strikingly r
sembled the Great Fear that swept rural France only a dozen yea
earlier, terrorizing the populace with the delusion that "the bri
ands" were coming.[6]
A manifestation of the anxiety felt in that troubled time was t
white Virginians' belief that the generally peaceable black peop
who were their daily associates could be transformed in a day or
night into ferocious warriors. A contemporary noted "the treache
ous submission of their demeanor"—the air of harmlessness th
they affected, the better to confound the whites.[7]

Slaveowners had learned long ago to take for granted a troubl
some, irreducible amount of resistance on the part of their bond
men and a degree of resentment toward the master's authority, b
recent events in Saint-Domingue had revealed hatred extending b
yond the experience of any Virginian. Devastation of the Frenc
colony suggested that the blacks' thirst for vengeance was unlir
ited, that ordinary slaves could become terrible and warlike. Appa
ently they possessed both will and ability to combine to destrc
their oppressors. An anonymous writer contrasted the whites of Vi
ginia, panic-stricken after Gabriel's conspiracy, with the deceitf
blacks who, "tho' watched by the jealous eyes, and threatened t
the united opposition of thousands, maintain an unaccountab
cheerfulness of mind, that renders them terrible as an army wi
banners."[8] No ordinary preparation would be adequate to meet s
fearsome a confrontation. Perhaps, in fact, the challenge could ne
be met successfully at all. It was the contrast between what *was* ar
what at any moment *might be* that helped create nearly intolerab
apprehension in certain slaveholding areas.

State officials tried with little success to account for the slave
conspiratorial behavior and to prepare a policy for resisting it. Th
many trials of slaves accused of plotting insurrection "and the a
plications growing out of them for pardon or transporation ... c
those condemned" led Governor Monroe in 1802 to forgo his usu
spring visit to his plantation. He stayed at his desk in Richmor
and pondered recent events. "The spirit of revolt has taken dec
hold of the minds of the slaves," he wrote at that time, "or the symp

---

6. Janson, *Stranger in America*, 398. The standard work is Georges Lefebvre, *T*
Great Fear of 1789: Rural Panic in Revolutionary France (New York, 1973).
7. Janson, *Stranger in America*, 360.
8. *Hints for the Consideration of the Friends of Slavery*, 11–12.

ns which we see are attributable to some other cause." He con-
sed puzzlement at the widespread disaffection: "After all the at-
ntion which I have paid to the subject my mind still rests in
spense on it."[9]
But what other explanation than a desire for freedom could there
? Monroe found the evidence disagreeable and hard to accept;
vertheless, the proof lay in the official records—dozens of slaves
arged with plotting rebellion had confessed guilt. Their goal, ac-
rding to their own testimony, was freedom for themselves and
ath for the slaveholding whites.

Association of the conspiracies with the whites' own concepts of
erty made the unrest especially disquieting and hard to deal
th. The state might hang the leading conspirators, but ideas, as
rginians had reason to know, were not likely to be extinguished
the snuffing out of lives. The only just solution and the only
re means of restoring order was emancipation. Yet any attempt
end slavery would encounter so many obstacles and so much op-
sition as to make the goal all but impossible to achieve. Even if,
some means, slavery could be done away with, slaveholders be-
ved the result—the creation of a greatly enlarged population of
e blacks—would produce terrible problems, perhaps even the ra-
l conflict emancipation proposed to avert.[10] What course, then,
s left to follow? Nothing but repression, which almost certainly
uld be accompanied by continuing anxiety among whites while
inging no assurance of slave tranquillity.

In the absence of acceptable policy for dealing with slave unrest,
was tempting to search for scapegoats. Blame might take the
ace of remedy. Upon the first revelation of Gabriel's plot, a Vir-
nia newspaper confidently located its source: "This dreadful con-
iracy originates with some vile French Jacobins. . . . Liberty and
uality have brought that evil upon us." The explanation was
ought valid in other slaveholding regions as well. Although Wil-
m R. Davie of North Carolina found scant evidence of conspiracy
that state, he noted abundant signs of slave discontent, arising,
believed, from the same source as in Virginia. "It is plain," he

9. James Monroe to Thomas Jefferson, May 17, 1802, in Stanislaus Hamilton (ed.),
ritings of James Monroe, III, 348–49.
10. Robert Sutcliff, Travels in Some Parts of North America in the Years, 1804, 1805,
d 1806 (Philadelphia, 1812), 50; Jack P. Greene (ed.), Diary of Colonel Landon Carter,
1055; John Taylor, Arator; Being a Series of Agricultural Essays, Practical and Po-
cal (2nd ed.; Georgetown, 1814), 114–16.

wrote, "that the much abused terms of '*Liberty and equality*' ha
misled these wretched people as well as many others; under the
every crime is sanctified; and all feeling and reflection banished."
Governor Monroe, himself an exponent of republican ideolog
could not endorse the easy explanation, for it placed primary blar
on men and principles identified with his own political associate
Yet he did not reject the charge out of hand either. After long refle
tion he offered a slightly more complex reason for the slaves' treac
ery than his political opponents had set forth, a theory brave enou;
to locate its origin not in France but in Virginia itself.

Monroe attributed "the public danger" to the "contrast in the co
dition of the free negroes and slaves, the growing sentiment of li
erty existing in the minds of the latter, and the inadequacy of ti
existing patrol laws." But even this interpretation, for all its sugge
tion of sober, informed thought, offered no remedy. The presen
throughout Virginia of free blacks was a social fact not easily ¿
tered; neither could the slaves' ideas of liberty—ideas they shar
with the white population—be eradicated. Only more restricti
laws could be passed. But Monroe saw no benefit in subjecting bla
people to stricter controls. There was no answer to the problem
revolts short of eliminating slavery. "Unhappily while this class
people exists among us," Monroe concluded, "we can never cou
with certainty on its tranquil submission."[12]

With this statement Monroe joined critics of his own time a
earlier who also took for granted that slavery itself generated rebe
lion. However, such a verdict pointed to a fatal flaw in southe
society and thus could not generally be accepted. Few indeed we
willing to acknowledge that so fundamental a source of wealth a
position carried with it the probability of disaster. Easier, mo
comfortable explanations were sought—and found.

Despite lack of evidence that anyone except slaves themselv
were involved in the conspiracies, the search went on for culpri
Suspicions of that sort were hardly new. Well before the Revolutio
Landon Carter charged "new light" religion with making slaves i
subordinate. The continued growth of evangelicalism througho

11. Fredericksburg *Herald*, September 23, 1800, quoted in Jordan, *White o
Black*, 396; William R. Davie to Benjamin Williams, February 19, 1802, in Benjam
Williams Letter Books, Vol. III, in Governors' Papers, North Carolina Division of ,
chives and History.

12. James Monroe to the Speakers, January 16, 1802, in Stanislaus Hamilton (e
Writings of James Monroe, III, 238–39; *ibid.*, December 5, 1800, p. 243.

e South—and among both races—appeared to promote discon-
nt. Further, it threatened to unite blacks and whites in an egali-
rianism that was utterly at odds with slavery. Now even certain
ives designated themselves preachers and brought still more
acks under the sway of subversive religious fervor. Some persons
10 discounted the disruptive influence of religion nonetheless lo-
ted the source of discontent in ideas that incited the slave popu-
tion. A few years after the rash of conspiracies had subsided, the
rginia statesman John Randolph credited slave unrest to "the si-
nt but powerful change wrought by time and chance upon the
mposition and temper" of society. To this imprecise analysis Ran-
lph added a specific impetus to disorder: "The French Revolution
d polluted even them." Then he identified a particular category
villains: "Peddlers from New England and elsewhere" dissemi-
ted egalitarian ideas "throughout the Southern Country." The
uth's problem originated, then, in the idea of universal liberty.
rom the spreading of this infernal doctrine," Randolph con-
ided, "the whole Southern country has been thrown into a state
insecurity."[13]

John C. Calhoun, usually more optimistic in those years than was
e saturnine Randolph, never disputed the truth of Randolph's
arge. Calhoun took second seat to no one in suspicion of New En-
anders and of French libertarianism, but he found that slave un-
st was a problem peculiar to Virginia and not one characteristic
the entire South. Slaves in the rice-growing regions of South
rolina lived in greater isolation than those in the upper South.
us a smug Calhoun reported that none of the fears that daily
agued white Virginians were felt in his own state. Slaves in South
rolina, he declared, remained untouched by radical thought: "I
re say more than half of them never heard of the French Revolu-
n."[14] What might be expected from the other half, Calhoun did
t say.

13. Jack P. Greene (ed.), *Diary of Colonel Landon Carter*, I, 378; Jacob Read to
arles Pinckney, June 10, 1807, in Charles Pinckney Papers, South Caroliniana Li-
ary, University of South Carolina, Columbia; Elisha Dick to James Monroe, Sep-
nber 26, 1800, in Palmer, McRae, and Flournoy (eds.), *Calendar of Virginia State
pers*, IX, 178; John Scott Strickland, "The Great Revival and Insurrectionary Fears
North Carolina: An Examination of Antebellum Society and Slave Revolt Panics,"
Orville Vernon Burton and Robert C. McMath, Jr. (eds.), *Class, Conflict, and Con-
isus: Antebellum Southern Community Studies* (Westport, Conn., 1982), 57–95; *An-
ls of Congress*, 12th Cong., 1st Sess., 450–51.
14. *Annals of Congress*, 12th Cong., 1st Sess., 480.

Unlike either Calhoun or Randolph, Governor Monroe held th
the progress of liberty could neither be resisted successfully n
turned back. The liberal ideas of the age, he assumed, created sla
disaffection. One need not search for peddlers of sedition to accou
for unrest, although it was natural, he admitted, to suspect "othe
who were invisible."[15]

Minds less spacious than Monroe's found blame easy to assess ar
remedy close at hand. Since exponents of liberty and the rights
man—Jacobins, Jeffersonians, abolitionists, evangelicals, Quakers
as well as free blacks were held responsible for inciting slave disco
tent, it followed that order could be restored and the South ma
secure by adopting two drastic measures: The libertarians shou
be silenced, and the free blacks should be got rid of by colonizi
them elsewhere.

The strongest of motives—self-preservation—suggested to slav
holders the wisdom of tempering their long-standing enthusias
for universal liberty and human rights. An era of reaction and i
creased repression was about to begin throughout the slave countr
It would be marked by fear and suspicion of all influences judg
subversive of slavery. Unfortunately for the composure of whi
southerners, such hostile influences materialized at once from se
eral directions and in unmanageable forms.

At just the moment when slaveholders located in radical thoug
the source of threats to domestic security, news arrived that Franc
the reputed seat of worldwide subversion, planned to reestablish i
power in North America. By the secret Treaty of San Ildefonso n
gotiated in 1800, Spain had transferred its vast territory of Loui
ana to France. Observers in New England did not hesitate to expla
what this move might mean. "If the French once get an establis
ment upon the Spanish territory, in the vicinity of the southe
states, it will behoove the planter to look well to his own hous
hold," commented a Connecticut editor.[16] "Much evil is appr
hended . . . from the spirit of insurrection which will inevitably
infused into the slaves by their *Gallic brethren*," wrote another.
year later, the *Port Folio*, a Federalist magazine, reported with lit
sign of regret that the French were expected "(. . . soon after the
arrival in Louisiana), to deprive our southern democratic citizens
their property, by exciting their negroes to run away from them."

15. Stanislaus Hamilton (ed.), *Writings of James Monroe*, III, 241.
16. Quoted in Aptheker, *American Negro Slave Revolts*, 28.
17. Quoted in Kerber, *Federalists in Dissent*, 40.

ese prospective dangers were not, as might be supposed, taunts
t forth only by self-satisfied New Englanders bent on antagonizing
terests they opposed. The British chargé d'affaires found that
arly all politicians he met in Washington dreaded the conse-
ences the transfer of Louisiana would bring to the South. From
eir new outpost, the French would contaminate American slaves
ith a "spirit of insurrection." A Virginia planter relayed to Gover-
or Monroe his own speculations on the disturbing news that, since
e cession of Louisiana to France, importation of slaves into the
estern territory had been prohibited.[18] What would that exclusion
ean to the American South? A free area to which slaves would
cape? The loss of a potential market for excess slaves? Whatever
e answers, the transfer of Louisiana undoubtedly signified omi-
ous change. A hostile power on the border of the southern states,
iend and foe of slavery agreed, would constantly endanger south-
n institutions.

The United States, one reasonably might believe, faced a dimin-
hed and troubled future if Louisiana remained in French control.
he concern immediately was felt in diplomacy. Secretary of State
ames Madison authorized Robert Livingston to convey to French
fficials the United States' "momentous concern" over France's ac-
uisition of Louisiana. Among other baneful aspects of the transfer,
e was instructed to emphasize the unsettling effect the French
resence would have on American slaves, who, in Madison's words,
ad been "taught to regard the French as patrons of their cause."[19]

As it turned out, Livingston found no need to dwell on dire pre-
ictions. Contrary to all expectation, Napoleon abandoned plans to
reate a new American empire. His financial problems and the in-
bility of his armies to subdue the blacks in Saint-Domingue
tripped glitter from the scheme. He would sell Louisiana. The sur-
rised American agents seized the opportunity, and in 1803 Presi-
ent Jefferson cast aside every constitutional scruple in order to ac-
ept the offer.

Several powerful arguments could be advanced for buying the

18. De Conde, *This Affair of Louisiana*, 112; Richard King to Secretary of State,
ebruary 5, 1802, in U.S. Department of State, *State Papers and Correspondence Bear-
ng upon the Purchase of the Territory of Louisiana* (Washington, D.C., 1903), 13;
eorge Goosely to James Monroe, June 5, 1802, in Executive Papers, Virginia State
ibrary.
19. Department of State, *State Papers and Correspondence*, 7. For a discussion of
efferson's views on Louisiana and Saint-Domingue, see John C. Miller, *The Wolf by
he Ears* (New York, 1977), 130–41.

territory, most of them quite unrelated to slavery or exclusively
planter interest, but hardly any consideration was more compelli
than the chance to eliminate a source of slave unrest. For years aft
Louisiana became American territory, planters still found the ri
lands of Mississippi and Alabama of doubtful value because of he
tile Indians and their Spanish allies in East and West Florida.
Louisiana had remained in French hands, it seems unlikely that t
Black Belt could have been developed as a slave region at all.

The security and opportunity promised by Jefferson's diplomat
achievement would be fully enjoyed only in later years. For the pre
ent, the United States continued its constricted existence in a wor
made hazardous by the war-to-the-death in which England an
France engaged. As the war entered a desperate phase, issues grov
ing out of neutral rights on the seas threatened to engulf the natic
in conflict with first one and then the other of the great combatant
Once again southerners had special reason for concern.

With war imminent, from both North and South came appraisa
of the slave population as a source of military weakness as well as
menace in its own right: "They may be considered as a piece of a
tillery . . . which the most unskilled of our enemies may play c
against us," wrote George Tucker of Virginia. The Federalist Tim
thy Pickering's assessment was little different. "In case of foreig
war," he predicted, "Virginia must keep at home half her force
prevent an insurrection of her negroes; and if attacked in her ow
dominions her danger and imbecility would be still more manifest
The existence of an internal enemy, both Tucker and Pickering in
plied, must be considered in shaping the nation's foreign and de
mestic policy.[20]

Concerns such as these helped make possible abolition of the for
eign slave trade by Congress in 1807, near the height of the diplo
matic controversy with England over neutral rights. Perhaps th
measure would have been enacted even had fears of the blacks no
assumed new dimensions during those years. Since the slave popu
lation grew steadily by natural means, importations were found les
necessary than before. Further, the trade faced steady moral on
slaught, and British moves toward ending it within their empir
exerted powerful influence on Americans. Nevertheless the sense c
emergency generated by recent slave conspiracies and the growin

20. [Tucker], *Letter to a Member of the General Assembly of Virginia*, 14; Kerbe
Federalists in Dissent, 40.

.elihood of war helped remove whatever reluctance congressmen
.t toward supporting the measure. In the air of apprehension pre-
.iling in 1807, even defenders of slavery were likely to agree with
.e Quaker abolitionist Thomas Branagan's comment that "every
.ave ship that arrived at Charleston, is to our nation what the Gre-
.an's wooden horse was to Troy."²¹ On that issue a majority of con-
.essmen from all sections could concur. Momentarily ignoring sec-
.onal differences, northern and southern congressmen joined in
.utting an end to slave importations.

Motives in this, as in most political decisions, were mixed. Some
.presentatives from slave districts perhaps saw in the act means of
.ducing the supply of slaves and thus of increasing prices. At the
.her extreme, antislavery congressmen, more sanguine than they
.ad cause to be, welcomed the prohibition as promising an early
.ad to slavery itself. For others with humane intentions, a philan-
.tropic desire to end the notorious horrors of the slave trade was
.itical in determining votes. But threading through all these con-
.derations was fear of the blacks, a sentiment outsiders were more
.kely to feel free to express than were slaveholders themselves. "To
.mport slaves is to import enemies," was the blunt assessment of
.avid Bard, antislavery congressman from Pennsylvania. "It is this
.ade," wrote a visiting Englishman, "that has multiplied the lurk-
.ng assassins, till they swarm wherever the planter turns his eyes."²²

Abolition of the slave trade did little in the short run to lessen the
.anger whites saw in a rapidly growing black population, and the
.oming war with England appeared to magnify the menace. The
.ave of reputed conspiracies that had swept the upper South fol-
.owing Gabriel's conspiracy subsided after 1804, but awareness of
.e potential for catastrophe by no means disappeared.

A massive slave rebellion—not merely a conspiracy—in Louisi-
.na impressed this truth on all who learned of it. On the evening of
.anuary 8, 1811, slaves on the German Coast, the sugar-producing
.rea some forty miles northwest of New Orleans, rose in rebellion

21. Thomas Branagan, *The Penitential Tyrant: A Juvenile Poem* . . . (Philadelphia,
.05), 51. A group of South Carolinians complained that their state's reopening of
.e trade in 1803 was a measure "fraught with evils which may threaten our country
.ith ruin and destruction . . . from beyond the seas—or elsewhere." Petition from
.irfield District, in Slavery Petitions, 1800–30, Legislative Papers, South Carolina
.epartment of Archives and History, Columbia.
22. Betty L. Fladeland, *Men and Brothers: Anglo-American Antislavery Cooperation*
.rbana, Ill., 1972), 79, 80; *Annals of Congress*, 8th Cong., 1st Sess., 995; Janson,
.ranger in America, 360.

under the leadership of the mulatto Charles, who probably w
from Saint-Domingue. Starting from the plantation of Manu
Andre, the insurgents gathered recruits from neighboring plant
tions until somewhere between 150 and 500 slaves, including m
roons, were in the field. Armed with cane knives, axes, hoes, and
few small arms and led by mounted chiefs with their "colors di
played and full of arrogance," they plundered plantation house
burning two of them, and killed two white men as they advanc
some fifteen miles to the southeast. The next day, however, two con
panies of voluntary militiamen and thirty regulars arrived and, u
der the command of General Wade Hampton, defeated the rebe
lious slaves in battle. The rebels were no match for these well-arme
and well-trained forces. Sixty-two blacks, apparently including tl
leaders, were killed in the encounter. Eighteen of those remainir
were convicted of rebellion, assassination, arson, and pillage an
were sentenced to be shot on their owners' plantations. Their heac
then were cut off and placed on poles as a warning to others.[23]

Nothing so extreme was soon to happen along the Atlantic coas
yet there, too, evidence of discontent remained plentiful enough
suggest that slaves eventually might combine in actual rebellio
Meanwhile reports of massive devastation by West Indian slav
continued to reach the United States and, probably, the ears (
slaves. Against that background a reputed conspiracy in Camde
South Carolina, in 1816 caused great alarm, and slaves everywhei
continued in unmistakable ways to manifest resistance and mak
clear their urge for freedom.[24]

Although many blacks apparently reconciled themselves to sla
ery, even forged bonds of loyalty and affection with their owner
and, so far as records show, displayed little overt resentment towar
whites in general, it is equally true that unmasked hatred for thei
oppressors smoldered in others. This emotion might be expressed i
isolated acts of violence or in the decision to run away, but it als

23. James H. Dorman, "The Persistent Specter: Slave Rebellion in Territorial Lou
isiana," *Louisiana History*, XVIII (1977), 393–404; New York *Evening Post*, Februar
19 and 20, 1811; Clarence E. Carter (ed.), *Territory of Orleans, 1803–1812* (Washing
ton, D.C., 1940), 915–19. Vol. IX of *The Territorial Papers of the United States*, 28 vols
"Summary of Trial Proceedings of Those Accused of Participating in the Slave Upris
ing of January, 1811," *Louisiana History*, XVIII (1977), 472–73; Harriet DeLonge t
John Peters, February 16 and May 14, 1811, in Peters Family Letters, New York Pub
lic Library; Isaac L. Baker to Stephen F. Austin, February 15, 1811, in Eugene C
Barker (ed.), *The Austin Papers*, Vol. II, Pt. 1 of American Historical Association, An
nual Report . . . for the Years 1919 and 1922 (Washington, D.C., 1924–28), 184.
24. Aptheker, *American Negro Slave Revolts*, 257.

ild take the form of quiet satisfaction at misfortunes suffered by
nites, the adversity seen as evidence that slavery violated divine
der. This is what happened in Virginia on the eve of the second
ir with England.
On December 26, 1811, fire consumed the Richmond Theater.
nong the seventy-two who died was an array of notables including
orge W. Smith, governor of the state, and Abraham B. Venable,
esident of the state bank. Blacks attending the performance were
ore fortunate. By lucky circumstance the location of exits leading
om their part of the theater allowed most of them to escape. Waves
sympathy for the unprecedented loss of life swept the nation,
aching as far north as Boston, where the city council passed a
solution of condolence. But among blacks in Virginia, the fiery
ene was lifted from the mundane to the providential. To them, it
ok on overtones of religious significance involving retribution and
dgment. Thus their response to the disaster was satisfaction and
pe rather than sorrow. Slaves in Henry County were heard to say
hey were glad that the people were burnt in Richmond, and
ished that all the white people had been burnt with them. That
od Almighty had sent them a little Hell for the white people, and
at in a little time they would get a greater."[25]
If such feelings became at all widespread among the black popu-
tion, southern whites would have much to dread from the war
ith England that by early 1812 seemed impossible to avert. Memo-
:s of British depredations and slave reaction during the American
:volution offered no ground for confidence in the forthcoming con-
ct. All evidence suggested that the new generation of slaves, still
:tter educated in the principles of freedom than their forebears,
ould be even more responsive to political appeals from opportu-
stic liberators than were their parents and grandparents in the
'70s and 1780s. Few could doubt that slaves in 1812 would wel-
me American involvement in war as a means of attaining their
:edom.
Slaveholders were correct in suspecting that slaves followed the
:veloping quarrel with England, understood war was near, and
anned to take advantage of hostilities when they began. War cre-
ed opportunities for slaves unknown in times of peace. Few of the

25. *Niles' Weekly Register* (Baltimore), I (January 4, 1812), 329–30; William Henry
ote, *Sketches of Virginia, Historical and Biographical, 2nd Series* (2nd ed.; Philadel-
iia, 1856), 321; Palmer, McRae, and Flournoy (eds.), *Calendar of Virginia State Pa-
rs*, X, 121.

recurring rumors of conspiracies in peacetime ever issued in op
rebellion, for slaves realistically assessed their chances in an arm
encounter with white Americans as poor and not worth the risk
But war would change everything. It was at times when white so
ety faced external challenge or was beset by internal dissension th
slaves were most likely to try to fulfill their desire for freedom.

Tom, a slave whom two justices of the peace in Montgome
County, Virginia, described—perhaps hopefully—as "young a
artless," disclosed his own expectations. As soon as war began,
intended to join the other slaves in his neighborhood in revolt.
point of added significance not likely to be lost on authorities w
that Tom learned about public affairs not from his master or oth
members of the slaveholding class, but "from the poor people in t
neighborhood" with whom he familiarly associated, and "by hea
ing the newspapers read."[27]

Tom lived in a predominantly rural county, but urban slaves, tc
looked at the nation's foreign problems as offering a way to becom
free. While "Poor Black Sam" proved his own loyalty to the whit
in 1812, he revealed the hostility of others when he informed t
governor and council of Virginia that "all the niggres" planned
rise up, seize the arms stored in the capitol, and destroy Richmon
English agents had been active in Richmond and Petersburg, Sa
continued, "[dis]rupting the niggres and tells them that as soon
this pact is made the Inglish will land and then they will be free."

The dread possibilities described by Tom and Black Sam made
impression on southern whites, who warned of the peculiar risks t
South incurred in fighting England. The likelihood of slave hostili
entered into congressional debate over war. John Randolph a
sumed his practiced anti–War Hawk stance to advise Congress
December, 1811, that "while talking of taking Canada, some of
were shuddering for our own safety at home." He had witness
"the alarms in the capitol of Virginia" and knew that "the nightbe
never tolled for fire in Richmond that the mother did not hug h
infant more closely to her bosom." An English invasion promise
disaster. "God forbid, sir, that the Southern States should ever s

26. Slave interview in Nottaway Jail, May 5, 1802, in Executive Papers, Virgin
State Library.
27. Palmer, McRae, and Flournoy (eds.), *Calendar of Virginia State Papers*,
121–22.
28. Robert S. Starobin (ed.), *Blacks in Bondage: Letters of American Slaves* (Ne
York, 1974), 139–40. For activities of a purported British spy in Richmond, s
Palmer, McRae, and Flournoy (eds.), *Calendar of Virginia State Papers*, X, 264–65.

enemy on their shores, with these infernal principles of French
ternity in the van."[29]
Although Congress overruled such forebodings and declared war
April, 1812, apprehensions of the sort Randolph voiced did not
aporate. While the country steeled itself for English attack, south-
ers continued their gloomy prophecies: "Unfortunately we have
o enemies," said the mayor of Richmond, "the one open and dered; the other nurtured in our very bosoms!" Slaves "want noth-
g but means and opportunity to break their shackles," warned
presentative Daniel Sheffey of Virginia in January, 1813. Assur-
ces of the slaves' incompetence to coordinate plans for freedom
uck him as unconvincing: "Man is strong, resolute, and ingenious
en liberty is concerned." Sheffey sharpened his familiar allusion
"the fate of Santo Domingo" by warning of the havoc that would
low if "ten thousand men landed on the Southern shores . . .
ith] fifty thousand stand of arms" for the slaves. "Every man
uld find in his own family an enemy ready to cut the throats of
s wife and children."[30]
Calhoun took note of such unbecoming predictions. He saw them
t only as signs of unmanly resolution in white leadership but also
confessions of weakness certain to embolden slaves. In South
rolina, he was proud to say, "no such fears in any part" were felt.
he great Camden conspiracy had not yet occurred.) Calhoun in-
sted that hostilities with England posed no threat to southern in-
itutions. On the contrary, war strengthened slavery, for in wartime
he public force and vigilance are of necessity the greatest."[31]
Calhoun was only partly correct. Thoroughly equipped, well-
ained white armies undoubtedly would experience great success
awing unarmed blacks. But their advantage would last only so
ng as enemy forces remained far from slaveholding areas, and this
ey could not be counted upon to do.
Southerners were more apprehensive about the war's possible ef-
ct on their property than Calhoun cared to admit. Even masters
nfident of the harmlessness of their slaves nonetheless expected
e appearance of a British army in their neighborhood to disrupt
e slave-master relationship, exactly as it had done a generation
rlier during the Revolution. They did not see how slave disci-

29. *Annals of Congress*, 12th Cong., 1st Sess., 451.
30. Quoted in Johnston, *Race Relations*, 118; *Annals of Congress*, 12th Cong., 2nd
ss., 401.
31. *Annals of Congress*, 12th Cong., 2nd Sess., 819, and 12th Cong., 1st Sess., 48.

pline—which was essential to coerced labor—could be maintain
in the face of invasion. At her estate near Washington, D. C., M
Margaret B. Smith was resigned to the loss of her slave proper
She awaited the arrival of the British armies, when "our enemy
home," as she described the slaves, would abandon their own
and flee to British lines. Local officials took every precaution to p
vent this from happening. When military necessity removed mili
from areas of large slave population, special patrols sometimes to
their place in order to keep the bondsmen at work. In Washingt
in the summer of 1813, Elbridge Gerry, Jr., expected to be call
upon to patrol more frequently now that the British approache
"and this is very necessary, for the blacks in some places refuse
work, and say they shall soon be free, and then the white peop
must look out."[32]

Such efforts at control proved only partly successful. It is true th
in 1812, as in 1776, many slaves and free blacks so closely identifi
with the views of their white countrymen as to serve loyally
American land and naval forces. It also is true that in both wa
many slaves (and white Americans, too), especially those dista
from the seacoast, evidenced little political awareness and thus co
tinued their regular routine almost as though war were not bei
waged. Yet the War of 1812, like the Revolution, found some slav
alert to the opportunity it offered to profit from their masters' mi
tary peril by gaining advantage within the slave system or by esca
ing from it altogether. Again, just as they did during the Revolutio
slaves took advantage of their masters' weakness by deserting t
plantations to take refuge on British ships and within British line
a course that in effect allied them with the enemy. The "Black pop
lation of these Countries," wrote a British admiral, "evince up
every occasion, the strongest predilection for the cause of Gre
Britain, and a most ardent desire to join any Troops or Seamen a
tive in the Country."[33] The mayor of Richmond told a similar stor
"The standard of revolt is unfurled," he reported. "Wherever pra
ticable these deluded creatures, regardless of consequences ha
flocked to it." In an effort to be completely evenhanded, some Britis
commanders allowed the slaves' owners to come within their lin

32. Margaret Bayard Smith, *The First Forty Years of Washington Society* (Ne
York, 1906), 90; Claude G. Bowers (ed.), *The Diary of Elbridge Gerry, Jr.* (New Yor
1927), 198–99.
33. Quoted in Sarah McCulloh Lemmon, *Frustrated Patriots: North Carolina an
the War of 1812* (Chapel Hill, N.C., 1973), 197.

d try to persuade the fugitives to return to their old allegiance.
w often these persuasions succeeded is not known.[34]
British Vice Admiral Sir Alexander Cochrane on April 2, 1814, is-
ed a proclamation inviting slaves to flee to British ships or mili-
y posts and designated a base for them on Tangier Island, near
e mouth of the Potomac River. Having placed themselves under
itish protection, the blacks enhanced British offensive capacity by
forming an active military role. Eventually two hundred escaped
ves joined with three hundred royal marines to form an inte-
ated battalion. A black marine corps took part in the major Ches-
eake campaigns of 1814, and black marines aided in assaults on
ginia. To the distress of white Americans, runaway slaves served
willing soldiers in military campaigns against their former mas-
s. "Our negroes are flocking to the enemy from all quarters,
ich they convert into troops, vindictive and rapacious," com-
ined Brigadier General John P. Hungerford as he observed this
m of slave rebellion taking place in Virginia. "They leave us as
ies upon our posts and our strength, and they return upon us as
ides and soldiers and incendiaries."[35]
In an effort to check such behavior, Virginia authorities kept some
litia units close to home rather than sending them to more dis-
at points to oppose the British advance. Partly this policy resulted
m fear of violence at the hands of unruly slaves; partly it was
signed to deprive the British of black manpower; partly it was
tated by reluctance to lose a valuable economic resource. "The
rthumberland [Virginia] slaves are every day effecting their es-
pe," ran one plea for military reinforcement, "and I am confident
at unless some vigorous measures are adopted and a sufficient
ce allowed us, this whole penninsula will be stripped of its most
luable personal property."[36]
In July, 1813, John Randolph, noting that the militia in his part
Virginia had been dispatched to fight the British, warned of "the
nger from *an internal foe* augmented by the removal of so large a
rtion of our force." The same danger in North Carolina brought

34. Palmer, McRae, and Flournoy (eds.), *Calendar of Virginia State Papers*, X, 368.
also *Annals of Congress*, 14th Cong., 2nd Sess., 1105, 1117.
35. Frank A. Cassell, "Slaves of the Chesapeake Bay Area and the War of 1812,"
rnal of Negro History, LVII (1972), 144–55; Palmer, McRae, and Flournoy (eds.),
endar of Virginia State Papers, X, 368. For an instance of spying by a slave, see
utenant Colonel R. E. Parker's report, Palmer, McRae, and Flournoy (eds.), *Cal-
ar of Virginia State Papers*, 338.
36. Palmer, McRae, and Flournoy (eds.), *Calendar of Virginia State Papers*, 338–39.

the militia company of Wilmington special treatment. "The pe
liar situation of the town as respects the enemy and the negroe
an official explained, "induced me to exclude them from a draft."
1814 the Wilkinson County Court in Mississippi Territory est;
lished a draft—not to bring men into the army, but to keep th
out. It was instituted, Jefferson Davis later explained, to make s
a sufficient number of men stayed at home to guard the slaves ratl
than enlisting for the defense of New Orleans.[37]

In some instances domestic unrest required American commar
ers to dispatch troops to troubled areas in order to awe slav
Charleston received a regiment of militia sent from the interior
the summer of 1812 for that purpose. On another occasion memb
of the White Oak militia of North Carolina were sent home wh
rumors of an imminent slave uprising reached their encampment
Beaufort. At another point in the war, forces were dispatched to t
Northern Neck in Virginia to guard slaves on the home front af
most of the local troops had been sent to the defense of Norfolk.
officer in the North Carolina militia stationed at Fort Johnson
pealed to the governor for "a few cavalry" to prevent a slave reb
lion "so probably and so much to be dreaded in this section of t
state."[38]

On at least one occasion, American forces operated direc
against slaves rather than against the British invaders. In the fall
1814, upon learning that British arms had fallen into the hands
blacks in Georgetown and Washington, General Tobias E. Sta
bury ordered troops to move against them for fear they would "
sult the females, and complete the work of destruction commenc
by the enemy."[39]

Slavery in the Chesapeake area and the Carolinas experienced
vere disruption as a consequence of war, but the southern front
presented American forces with equally challenging problems. H
tile Indians, blacks, and Spanish offered a major test of Unit

37. John Randolph to Josiah Quincy, July 4, 1803, in William Cabell Bruce, *Jc
Randolph of Roanoke, 1773–1833* (New York, 1922), I, 394; William Watts Jones
William Hawkins, July 13, 1812, in Governors' Papers, North Carolina Division
Archives and History; Haskell M. Monroe, Jr., and James T. McIntosh (eds.), *The
pers of Jefferson Davis* (Baton Rouge, 1971–), I, lxix.
38. Aptheker, *American Negro Slave Revolts*, 23; Thomas Brown to William Ha
kins, July 14, 1812, and Mathew Morris, "Report," July 18, 1813, both in Governc
Papers, North Carolina Division of Archives and History; Richard Brent to the G
ernor, February 10, 1814, in Palmer, McRae, and Flournoy (eds.), *Calendar of Virgi
State Papers*, X, 300.
39. Tobias E. Stansbury to Richard M. Johnson, November 14, 1814, in *Annals
Congress*, 13th Cong., 3rd Sess., 1633.

ates power on the long frontier extending westward from the At-
antic Ocean to the Mississippi River. Two years earlier, in October,
10, the United States had begun the process of annexing West
orida, but East Florida remained in Spanish hands, a haven for
gitive slaves and a site for the launching of guerrilla attacks
ainst Georgia as well as against the new American territory of
est Florida. So hateful to the planters' interests was the maroon
tlement in Florida that in the late summer of 1812 Georgia offi-
als, on their own initiative, sent the state militia across the border
ly to have it driven back by combined Indian and black forces.[40]
Soon after Congress declared war against England, the Spanish
owed British officers to assemble a force of black Cuban troops at
nsacola. The Tennessee *Herald* spelled out the fearsome implica-
ns of this development: "The same band which has initiated
ainst us the scalping knife and the tomahawk of the Indians will
t stop to renew upon the Mobile and Lower Mississippi the
gedy of St. Domingo." The area's nearest neighbors, Georgia and
uth Carolina, were not "in a situation to afford them assistance,"
 newspaper pointed out, for the danger of slave revolt distracted
nters in those states just as it did in the Southwest.[41]
Despite these early warnings, the Americans did not have to face
 to their vulnerability in that quarter until the summer of 1814,
en the British extended their operations to the Gulf of Mexico.
e Admiral Cochrane, British commander of the North American
ation, earlier pointed out the advantage of invading the United
ates from the south. The operation would require only a few Brit-
 troops, he supposed, for they would be joined by the Spanish
d by the Creeks and Choctaws. This massive force then would
ive up the Mississippi Valley to Canada, thereby overwhelming
 Americans and ending the war.
There was every reason to expect slaves to respond to the pro-
ted British campaign in ways destructive to American interests.
May, 1814, a report from the Gulf claimed that 2,800 Creeks, an
ual number of Choctaws, plus another thousand Indians near
nsacola stood ready to support a British invasion. They would be
ned, some predicted, by the slaves in Georgia.[42] Indians incited

40. *Niles' Weekly Register*, III (December 3, 1812), 235–37; Rembert Wallace Pat-
, *Florida Fiasco: Rampant Rebels on the Georgia-Florida Border, 1810–1815* (Ath-
, Ga., 1954), Chap. XIV.
41. Quoted in *Niles' Weekly Register*, III (October 17, 1812), 107.
42. Robert V. Remini, *Andrew Jackson and the Course of American Empire*,
3–1821 (New York, 1977), 235, 301.

against the whites could exert awful vengeance, as America
learned in the massacre at Fort Mimms in 1814, but the fury
blacks was to be dreaded still more, if for no other reason th
because, unlike Indians, the blacks were scattered throughout
white settlements.

"We must be prepared to act with promptness," General Andr
Jackson wrote in the summer of 1814, "or Mobile and New Orlea
by a sudden attack may be placed in the hands of our enemies, a
the negroes stimulated to insurrection and massacre, may dellu
[sic] our frontier in blood." By September, Governor William C.
Claiborne of Louisiana was warning Jackson of local fears of "I
mestic Insurrection; We have every reason to believe that
Enemy has been intriguing with our slaves." New black arriv
had been seen in New Orleans, he added, including Saint-Dom
guans "of the most desperate characters."[43]

As Jackson prepared his defense against the British advance,
eight-man committee of safety representing New Orleans and t
sugar-plantation district told him to expect no help from the
places: "The maintenance of domestic tranquility in this part of t
state obviously forbids a call on any of the White Inhabitants to t
defense of the frontier, and even requires a strong additional forc
While a British force prepared to drive inland, the sugar planters
Louisiana—no doubt remembering the great rebellion that ov
whelmed the region only four years earlier—appealed for a hundr
cavalrymen to be stationed along the Mississippi to suppress sla
insurrection.[44] The plea of the New Orleans citizens was support
by Secretary of War James Monroe, who advised Jackson in Septe
ber that "the militia of Louisiana will be less effective for gene
purposes from the dread of domestic insurrection, so that on t
militia of Tennessee your principal reliance must be."[45] Thus Jac
son's army at the Battle of New Orleans in January, 1815, was ma
up mostly of militia from Tennessee and Kentucky—states havi
relatively few slaves—together with smaller groups of regulars, fr
blacks, pirates, Indians, and Louisiana militia.

43. Andrew Jackson to David Holmes, July 21, 1814, in John Spencer Bassett (e
Correspondence of Andrew Jackson (Washington, D.C., 1926–35), II, 19; William C
Claiborne to Jackson, September 20, 1814, ibid., 55–56. See also E. Fromentin
Jacques Philippe Villeré, October 19, 1814, in Jacques Philippe Villeré Papers, H
toric New Orleans Collection, New Orleans.
44. Committee of Safety to Jackson, September 18, 1814, in Bassett (ed.), Co
spondence of Andrew Jackson, II, 51–53.
45. Quoted in Tommy R. Young II, "The United States Army and the Instituti
of Slavery in Louisiana, 1803–1815," Louisiana Studies, XIII (1974), 212.

With the approach of a British army, the large and competent
e-black population of New Orleans presented American military
inners with a problem faced nowhere else. "They will not re-
ain quiet spec[ta]tors of the interesting contest," Jackson de-
led. "They must be for, or against us." He proposed to assure
:ir allegiance and defuse a potentially explosive force by raising
·egiment from among them, which he then would deploy outside
: state. The plan aroused objections. Some "respectable citizens"
posed "putting arms into the hands of men of Colour," for doing
would "only add to the force of the Enemy." Members of the coun-
of defense—"men well-informed and well-disposed"—refused
endorse the enlistment of blacks unless "there could be a guar-
ty, against the return of the Regiment." If at the close of war,
y leaders explained, "the Individuals were to settle in Louisi-
a, with a Knowledge of the use of Arms, and that *pride of distinc-
n*, which soldiers pursuits so naturally inspires, they would prove
ngerous."[46]
This reasoning did not persuade Jackson to withdraw his plan.
: enjoyed total confidence in his ability to dominate common
ldiers, either black or white. But more important, he viewed en-
tment of free blacks as an essential safety measure, a device for
aintaining white control. "If they can be enrolled," he explained,
ney may when danger appears be moved in the rear to some point
nere they will be kept from doing us an injury. If their pride and
erit entitle them to confidence, they can be employed against the
nemy. If not they can be kept from uniting with him."[47]
Jackson soundly defeated the British at the Battle of New Orleans,
d the war ended with the slaveowners' worst fears unrealized.
)en rebellion had not occurred in Louisiana or anywhere else.
)netheless, numerous individuals had lost property, as an undermined number of slaves took advantage of the British military
esence to establish their freedom and followed the example set
· their forebears during the Revolution by seeking to accompany
e British as they withdrew from the United States. In the fall
1814, some three hundred former slaves from the Chesapeake
ea arrived at Halifax under British auspices; nine hundred more
ere expected to follow. In January, 1815, a British major general
New Orleans informed Jackson that a "considerable number" of

46. Andrew Jackson to William C. C. Claiborne, September 21, 1814, in Bassett
.), *Correspondence of Andrew Jackson*, II, 57; Claiborne to Jackson, October 17,
4, *ibid.*, 77.
47. Andrew Jackson to William C. C. Claiborne, October 31, 1814, *ibid.*, 88.

slaves had gathered at his headquarters with the intention of e
barking with the British army. Others already were aboard Briti
ships in Mobile Bay.[48]

Experience during the War of 1812, just as during the Revoluti
demonstrated the fragility of the slave-master relationship and
vulnerability to military challenge. Once more, southerners saw t
loyalty of slaves evaporate in the presence of an invading force. E
these painfully learned lessons had little immediate relevance
cause the end of the second war with England inaugurated a lo
period of peace for the United States. Secure on the continent
never before and facing no serious challenges from abroad, Ame
cans could confidently turn all their energies toward internal dev
opment. With the southeastern Indians defeated and their Engl
allies repulsed, a considerable part—but not all—of the southe
frontier had been made secure. The most conspicuous exception v
Spanish East Florida, which remained occupied by hostile India
and vengeful blacks organized as a maroon settlement. Along t
Apalachicola River only sixty miles from the United States bord
some 250 fugitive slave men and women held the "negro fort,"
abandoned British post, from which they issued invitations for o
ers to join them and launched guerrilla attacks against the proper
of their former owners in Georgia.

Secretary of War William Crawford, formerly a senator fr
Georgia, complained to Jackson that the Florida maroons joined t
Creeks in efforts "to inveigle" slaves from Georgia. Crawford's
port was hardly news to Jackson, who, partly in order to subdue t
maroons, had conducted earlier raids into Florida. Now Jackson
structed Brigadier General Edmund P. Gaines that "this fort mu
be destroyed" if it harbored fugitive slaves or held out "inducemer
to the Slaves of our citizens to desert."[49]

In August, 1816, under orders from Gaines, Lieutenant Color
Duncan A. Clinch "invested" the fort. When the blacks answered
demand for surrender by firing a cannon and hoisting a red flag w
the English Union Jack above it, Clinch proceeded to blow up t
fort's magazine. Among the few to survive the explosion were
black man and a Choctaw chief whom Clinch considered leaders

48. *Niles' Weekly Register*, VII (October 6, 1814), 54; Major General Lambert
Jackson, January 20, 1815, and Maunsel White to Jackson, February 20, 1815, b
in Bassett (ed.), *Correspondence of Andrew Jackson*, II, 151, 176–77.
49. William Crawford to Jackson, March 14, 1816, in Bassett (ed.), *Corresponde*
of Andrew Jackson, 236–37; Andrew Jackson to Gaines, April 8, 1816, *ibid.*, 238–

resistance. He ordered these men turned over to the Seminoles
torture and execution.[50]
)estruction of the Negro fort did not secure the southern frontier.
.ians in Florida continued for many years to conduct raids into
orgia, and Florida long remained a refuge for runaway slaves.
t the aggression went both ways. "It is quite common for the
ckers . . . to make incursions into Florida & steal or take off by
ce the negroes," wrote James Bankhead from his vantage point
t south of the Georgia border.[51]

n 1818, under orders from President James Monroe to clear
ited States soil of marauding Seminoles, Andrew Jackson led an
ny composed chiefly of Georgia militiamen into Florida with the
ention, his actions suggest, of making the Spanish province an
merican possession. When in the course of the campaign Jackson
otured and executed two British subjects, the entire incident be-
ne a matter of international dispute and, especially, of contro-
·sy within the United States government. There Jackson had more
enders than he had critics. Representative Henry Baldwin of
nsylvania put the matter bluntly and in a manner certain to win
nmendation in the South. The Georgia militia under Jackson, he
olained, "were, in fact suppressing an insurrection of slaves,
.ed by an Indian force, all assembled and armed for purposes hos-
: to the country."[52] Thus Jackson's aggression could be forgiven
:ause it had been conducted for the purpose of safeguarding slav-
· and in what was thought to be the national interest.

rhe next year Spain ceded East Florida to the United States, an
:nt Georgians, even in the colonial period, had regarded as essen-
l to the maintenance of slave discipline. Although for decades af-
1819 the Seminoles and blacks in the Florida swamps continued
resist American authority, requiring a long and costly military
npaign before they were subdued, the southern frontier at last
ild be considered secure.

3y 1819, with all European powers gone from territory east of the
ssissippi, slaves had lost a century-old source of external support.

0. John Bach McMaster, *A History of the People of the United States from the Revo-*
on *to the Civil War* (New York, 1915), IV, 432–33; John D. Milligan, "Slave Rebel-
usness and the Florida Maroon," *Prologue*, VI (1974), 4–18.
·1. James Bankhead to Christopher Van Deventer, January 15, 1818, in Christo-
r Van Deventer Papers, William L. Clements Library, University of Michigan, Ann
or.
2. *Annals of Congress*, 15th Cong., 2nd Sess., 1040. See also *ibid.*, 16th Cong., 1st
s., 1194.

No longer could black fugitives readily find a haven outside ʼ
United States, although some in Louisiana managed to flee to Tex
The eventual destruction of the maroon society in Florida depriv
slaves in Georgia and South Carolina of an external stimulus to fr
dom present since early in the eighteenth century. Slaves now sa
more completely into bondage. They became more thoroughly
part of American society because no alternative to it existed.

The diplomacy and military achievements of Jefferson's, Ma
son's, and Monroe's administrations went far toward providing
curity for the nation. A momentous part of those achievements v
the elimination of long-standing threats to slavery. By acquir
French and Spanish possessions lying on the path of American we
ward advance, the three Virginia presidents made possible ʼ
opening of a vast new region to a slave-based plantation system
is of at least equal importance to note that the same achieveme
also made slavery a more stable institution than it ever had be
before. Planters would have found it futile to try to develop ʼ
lands of Alabama and Mississippi with slave labor if an unfrien
government on the border encouraged slaves to escape or to rel

The removal of French and Spanish power also had the effect
strongly reinforcing the southern spirit of independence. Much
British defeat of French power in 1763, by removing a threat
American security, lessened the need for close colonial ties w
Britain and thereby made possible the colonial protests that led
revolution, so the confidence inspired by the accomplishments
the Virgina Dynasty allowed the South to resist national author

Southern leaders could risk defiance only because they felt lit
need for national protection against foreign threats. It was not ʼ
fault of southern statesmen that, despite their imperial achie
ments, slavery continued to be eroded by developments beyo
their control and menaced by interests they could not touch.

5

☖☖☖☖☖☖☖☖☖☖☖☖☖☖☖☖☖☖☖☖☖☖☖☖☖☖☖

Confronting Internal Dangers

ıvasion and revolt—the threats to slavery that so vexed eighteenth-
ıtury Americans—were joined after the Revolution by a chal-
ıge of a different order. Slavery, it now appeared, also could be
ıned by the quiet, eroding force of hostile public opinion even be-
·e many owners realized what was happening.

If the nearly absolute authority masters sought to exercise over
ıves ever was questioned by white members of the community
ıd its legitimacy destroyed, then owners—having lost their white
ies—might be compelled to make large concessions to their black
ıor force as the price of continued service. Should that happen,
: controls that kept blacks in a subservient caste would be loos-
ed, and slavery in its familiar, profitable form would disappear.
e plantation system then would change in unpredictable and dev-
ating ways, transforming all social relationships in the process.
is prospect proved nearly as disquieting as did the threat of in-
ırection itself. "We have among us in the very Bosom of our Coun-
· and Families, a property who although valuable as the means of
ır Cultivation can only continue so by being kept completely sub-
ıinate," explained the governor of South Carolina in November,
98.[1] If slaves grew insolent and proud and unwilling to submit to

. Governor's message to the Senate, November 29, 1798, in Governors' Messages,
1–1800, South Carolina Department of Archives and History.

their masters' will, and if that dissidence gained outside suppo
the economy and society of the South would break down becau
the core of the system, the slave-cultivated plantation, would
made inoperable. Such might be the outcome if critics of slave
grew in numbers and influence.

Slaveowners never constituted more than a minority in the to
southern white population. They could not by themselves, alone a
unaided, preserve the institution upon which the plantation syste
depended. The labor force could be kept subordinate only so long
masters enjoyed community support, not only for the institution
self, but also for the devices required to maintain discipline—str
rules enforced by the whip. The means necessary to control mu
never be allowed to come under outside scrutiny and supervisic
"If they take away the power of discriminatory punishment al
gether, they are no longer slaves," a South Carolinian wrote. "Th
will soon set the master's power at defiance, and be transform
into insurgents and out-laws."[2]

Servile behavior among blacks depended almost entirely on t
attitudes and conduct of whites, whose determination to exerc
coercive power defined slavery and maintained it. The instituti
had no other basis. Yet the apparent simplicity of this fact may
misleading. Whites never had everything their own way in relatic
with slaves. By its very nature, slavery involved a contest of wi
The will of the owners, who were intent on commanding respe
subservience, and labor from their slaves, was constantly pitt
against that of the bondsmen, who were struggling to retain co
trol of their own persons and to establish bearable conditions
survival.

The outcome of the battle—and *battle* is the word that best c
scribes master-slave relationships—almost always was inconc
sive. Neither contestant found it easy to impose unconditional s
render on the other. Accommodation and concession ordinar
were required of each. Advantage in the power struggle typica
fell to the owners, for they had much besides their own streng
and wit to rely on, while the slaves had little. All the instruments
the state, including the courts and militia, supported the owne
claims. Behind these lay the potent force of majority approval

2. Review of *The Tenth Annual Report of the American Society for Colonizing
Free People of Colour . . .* , in *Southern Review*, I (1828), 231.

e institution of slavery itself, as well as for the practices necessary
maintain it.³

But despite this mighty array of resources, well-informed masters
uld not approach these challenges with complete self-confidence,
· none of the auxiliaries to power enjoyed absolute immunity
subversion. Permanent majority support could not be taken for
anted. In February, 1794, Miles Parker of Gates County, North
rolina, made this point when he appealed his conviction on the
arge of assaulting a black man: "Some members of the jury were
endly to the emancipation of negroes and their equality with the
ites."⁴ If Parker was right, slavery in Gates County faced an un-
rtain future, for there, the verdict suggests, slaves had allies. Hard
explain away was the fact that a white man had been brought to
al for an offense against a black and that he had been found guilty.
future plantation contests in that neighborhood, slaves could be
pected to make full use of that strategic advantage.

Only a few years earlier, events of the revolutionary era had
oved that public opinion, the ultimate source of the master's au-
ority, was subject to manipulation by skilled propagandists. If
:ver men could organize support for a break with England, they
;o could mobilize an antislavery crusade. This is exactly what
gan to happen. Under that influence, majority endorsement for
.very became dubious. In the years immediately following the
volution, numerous antislavery critiques were published in both
rth and South, and slavery ended in the northern states—by 1804
: last holdout, New Jersey, had passed a gradual-emancipation
t. No one having an interest in preserving slavery could quite ig-
re these developments. An area of freedom on the border of the
.veholders' dominion would prove as unsettling in the nineteenth
ntury as it had been in earlier times.

By 1800 a number of subversive influences worked to undermine
.very. The South became a stronghold of republican thought, an
:ology that southern partisans employed in defense of their right

3. On paternalism and struggle and accommodation, see Eugene D. Genovese,
l, Jordan, Roll: The World the Slaves Made (New York, 1974), 5–7; Leslie Howard
ens, This Species of Property: Slave Life and Culture in the Old South (New York,
'6), 70–105; Bobby Frank Jones, "A Cultural Middle Passage: Slave Marriage and
nily in the Ante-Bellum South" (Ph.D. dissertation, University of North Carolina,
ipel Hill, 1965), 45–47.
4. Miles Parker's Affidavit, February court term, 1794, in Gates County Slave Rec-
ls, 1783–1867, North Carolina Division of Archives and History, Raleigh.

to be free from outside interference. Yet republicanism, with
hostility toward inequities in privilege, wealth, and status and
the exercise of arbitrary power, could be turned against planter i
terest. This was so because the single most important element pi
motive of aristocracy within the South was slavery, and slave
more starkly than any other institution, demonstrated the misuse
power. But republicanism was only one of several influences wi
potential for weakening the basis of the planters' life. A contemp
rary set forth the complexity of the threat: "Rewards and punis
ments, the sanctions of the best government, and the origin of lo
and fear, are rendered useless by the ideas excited by the Fren
Revolution; by the example of St. Domingo; by the lure of free i
groes mingled with slaves; and by the reproaches to masters a
sympathies for slaves, breathed forth from the Northern States."
    The writer was the republican idealogue John Taylor of Caroli
Although it is tempting to discount the lament as expressing oi
middle-aged regret for the passing of better days, Taylor's crotch
analysis was by no means uniquely his. By the first years of the ni
teenth century, common wisdom held that slaves had become l
humble, less easily disciplined than in earlier times. "Certain eve
which have taken place in the West Indies . . . with some interi
causes, have concurred to change considerably the habits of sub
dination among the Slaves," observed a resident of Northampt
County, North Carolina, in 1802. Northerners discerned a like tra
formation in the blacks who lived among them. By "wise regu
tions," Pennsylvania had been "kept undisturbed by negro conspi
cies, for more than half a century," wrote a Philadelphia edit
"carnal intercourse between whites and blacks, now scandalou
common, was extremely rare . . . and the blacks were more ind
trious, sober, contented, and useful . . . than they have ever been
any period, since their heads have been turned by the modern j
gon of liberty, and the rights of man."
    Whether observations in this vein reflected a truly new sp
among blacks or only changed perception by whites matters less
our purpose than the course of action the perception dictated.
cording to one North Carolinian, "Firm and steady policies are

    5. Taylor, *Arator*, 118. Taylor characterized slaves as "docile, useful and hap
unless interfered with. *Ibid.*, 119.
    6. Petition, September 1, 1802, in Petitions 1800–59, Legislative Papers, N
Carolina Division of Archives and History, Raleigh; "People of Colour," *Port Foli*
(May 23, 1801), 164.

spensably necessary to keep them in their present condition."[7] most no measure designed to stabilize slavery and to halt subver- on could be dismissed as too extreme for so vital an end.

Firm policies might not suffice, however, for among the internal :velopments thought to imperil slavery in the Early National Era as a major cultural change occurring in blacks themselves, a pro- :ss beyond the power of individuals to direct or to check. In the :ars following their arrival in America, Africans had been trans- rmed into African-Americans, thereby acquiring essential aspects ' the culture they were helping to create. Blacks everywhere, espe- ally those in the North, in the Chesapeake Bay area, and in urban :nters, soon shared the language and religion as well as many of e values characteristic of American society. Furthermore, in the 'ocess of turning New World wilderness into civilization, slaves in l regions demonstrated skills and accomplishments comparable ith those of their white countrymen. For example, Peter Deadfoot, venty-two years old, was described by his owner as "a tall, slim, ean limbed, active, genteel, handsome fellow, with broad shoul- :rs." He was "very sensible and smooth tongued." He was an indif- rent shoemaker, a good butler, ploughman, and carter, an excel- nt sawyer and waterman. He understood breaking oxen very well id was "one of the best scythemen, either with or without a cradle, America." In summary, said his master, "He is so ingenious a llow, that he can turn his hand to anything; he has a great show of ide, though he is very obliging." Peter Deadfoot's accomplish- ents may not have included reading and writing, but thirty-year- d Elleck, who called himself Alexander Brown and whose master :scribed him as "very artful," could read "pretty well." He was a icklayer, mason, and plasterer. "There is hardly any thing in a mmon way but what he understands, can behave very well," his aster reported.[8] Such men as these were obvious threats to slav- y, for they shattered one of the strongest justifications that could : advanced for maintaining it—the argument that Africans were vages suited only for routine, menial labor and were unqualified live in America as free persons.

The appearance of skilled, talented, acculturated blacks called r reassessment of slavery by the white population, a reassessment

7. Petition, September 1, 1802, in Petitions 1800–59, Legislative Papers, North rolina Division of Archives and History.
8. Windley (comp.), *Runaway Slave Advertisements*, I, 289–90; II, 357.

it generally did not get. Rethinking also was demanded by the ri
ing voices of antislavery protest that in the wake of the Revolutic
appeared in the South itself, sometimes even within plantatic
communities.

Antislavery agitation threatened to spread disruptive ide.
throughout society. Such concepts might even become an eleme
in localized plantation hostilities. Reformers' claims that slaves pc
sessed "inalienable rights," that punishments were excessive ai
unjust, or, most damaging of all, that slavery itself was wrong ai
ought to be ended might infiltrate the plantations to add furth
tension to already strained master-slave relations.[9]

But that was only part of the problem. Masters themselves mig
succumb to the antislavery argument and defect from slaveholdi
ranks. When in 1799 "Othello," ostensibly a free-black resident
Maryland, alluded to "that corrosive anguish of persevering in an
thing improper, which now embitters the enjoyment of life," I
identified a persistent problem. Some slaveowners believed ther
selves in the wrong and suffered in consequence. Some went so f
as to free their slaves.[10]

Troubled consciences offered the antislavery cause potential f
spectacular gains. On one of his early tours through Maryland, t
Methodist evangelist Francis Asbury found that the slaveown
John Willson "acknowledged the wrong done the blacks by takir
them from their country, but defended the right of holding them
Abolitionists managed to exploit this obvious weakness in the slav
holders' armor. Their success in encouraging manumissions pe
haps was related to the decline in agriculture that made slavehol
ing in parts of Virginia and Maryland temporarily less profitab
than it once had been. But however that may be, thousands
owners in the 1780s and afterward freed their slaves, offering mor
and religious justification for doing so. Even in regions where e
plicitly antislavery argument was never tolerated, masters neve
theless sometimes were inclined at least to relax discipline a
grant concessions to their bondsmen. "In many parts of this di

9. On this point, see an 1838 comment by Charles B. Shepard, quoted in Gui
Griffis Johnson, *Ante-Bellum North Carolina: A Social History* (Chapel Hill, N.
1937), 565.

10. James O'Kelley, *Essay on Negro Slavery* (Philadelphia, 1789), 42. On the d
puted issue of the southerners' sense of guilt, see Charles Grier Sellers, Jr., (ed.), *T
Southerner as American* (Chapel Hill, N.C., 1960), 40–71, and James Oakes, *The R
ing Race: A History of American Slaveholders* (New York, 1982), 117–22.

ict," ran a report from South Carolina, "negroes have every other
aturday, keep horses, raise hogs, cultivate for themselves every-
ing for home consumption, & for market, that their masters do."
this manner, generous and humane owners no doubt satisfied
eir sense of duty and salved their conscience; yet such laxity was
t without drawbacks for the rest of the community. Planters who
osened control made the lives of less indulgent masters more dif-
ult, while they also introduced a disruptive element into the lives
ordinary white folk who were trying to establish communities
sed on caste and patterns of "respectable" behavior. "Every mea-
re that may lessen the dependence of a Slave on his master ought
be opposed, as tending to dangerous consequences," advised a
oup of South Carolinians in 1816. "The more privileges a Slave
tains, the less depending he is on his master, & the greater nui-
nce he is likely to be to the public."[11]
When the master's philanthropy extended to manumitting his
aves, the menace became extreme. The growing numbers of freed
acks acted as a particularly unsettling influence on those who re-
ained slaves, a troublesome effect pondered even by antislavery
dvocates. "From this increase of free Negroes, their bondage will
come intolerable to the Slaves, & their Efforts to escape from it
ill probably produce a catastrophe not to be contemplated with-
t horror and dismay," predicted a committee of antislavery activ-
ts in 1796.[12] Such prophecy seemed well based, for despite the re-
rictions that hedged them, free blacks still enjoyed freedoms and
itiative beyond those accorded any slave. The emotions experi-
ced by slaves when they saw friends and relatives leaving as free
rsons may be imagined, although no writer seems ever to have
plored them.
One such incident that did enter the historical record suggests the
sruptive potential of the manumission vogue. In 1785 when the
ill of Joseph Mayo of Powhatan, Virginia, was opened, his heirs
arned that he had freed his large slaveholdings. The Mayo slaves
ubtless blessed their late master, but white neighbors found rea-
n to regret his generosity. News of the manumissions destroyed

---

11. Elmer T. Clark et al. (eds.), The Journal and Letters of Francis Asbury (London,
58), I, 442; petition, Orangeburgh, Amelia Township, December 4, 1816, Slavery
titions, 1800–30, Legislative Papers, South Carolina Department of Archives and
istory.
12. Report of the Committee for Improving the Condition of the Free Blacks
796], in Pennsylvania Abolition Society Papers.

discipline on nearby plantations and, according to one of Thoma
Jefferson's correspondents, "caused 2 or 3 combats between slave
and their owners, now struggling for the liberty to which they cor
ceive themselves entitled."[13]

Experiences of that sort taught lessons in caution and social r
sponsibility. However strong the antislavery appeal, property inte
est and concern for order kept all but the most pious or philar
thropic slaveowners firmly in line. But with nonslaveholders it wa
a different matter. When Hercules, a worker at the Nottingha
Forge near Baltimore, was returned to his owner in 1782, he e:
plained that he had "been back among the Dutch [Germans?], an
they use him kindly, and pay him good wages." In 1790 the slav
brothers Caesar and Jack escaped "into the frontier country" wher
their master supposed, they were harbored by free Negroes or "b
white persons who are enemies to slavery, and may think such
conduct warrantable." Perhaps most small farmers by the earl
nineteenth century identified their interests with those of the slave
holders and looked forward to owning slaves themselves. At ver
least, the majority of them apparently accepted the institution a
necessary for social control. Yet working against their support of th
masters' interests were counterclaims among which human sym
pathies ranked as the most compelling. The miseries and hardshi
to which slaves were subject caused even an aristocratic Sout
Carolinian to muse that "if the Quakers travelled this road, I shou
not wonder at their wishes to end slavery. The abuse is glaring an
wicked." In particular, the domestic slave trade, an essential featur
of the institution, came under attack by lower- and middle-clas
persons who saw its cruelty and did not profit from it. It was thi
aspect of slavery that first awakened the conscience of Benjami
Lundy, the Quaker abolitionist, when he observed the slave trade i
western Virginia. At about the same time, a traveler in that sta
noted that "the people on the road loaded the inhuman drivers wit
curses and execrations."[14] The loyalty of nonslaveholders to the sy:
tem was essential; yet their loyalty was suspect and never could b

13. James Currie to Thomas Jefferson, August 5, 1785, in Boyd (ed.), *Papers
Thomas Jefferson*, VIII, 342–43. For the legal problems encountered in carrying o
Mayo's will, see Hutchinson and Rachal (eds.), *Papers of James Madison*, IX, 150–5
14. Windley (comp.), *Runaway Slave Advertisements*, II, 258–59, 382; Alize Iza
to Ralph Izard, November 21, 1794, in Ralph Izard Papers, South Caroliniana I
brary, University of South Carolina, Columbia; [Thomas Earle], *Life, Travels, ar
Opinions of Benjamin Lundy* (Philadelphia, 1847), 15; Ulrich B. Phillips (ed.), *Plan
tion and Frontier, 1649–1863* (Cleveland, 1909), II, 55.

ken for granted. The support even of small slaveholders seemed to
ang in the balance. At the turn of the century it was common for
hem to free their slaves in their wills and to use that solemn occa-
on to record for the benefit of survivors fervent antislavery testimony. Would a younger generation succumb to similar influence
nd follow the emancipating example of their elders?

The fact that southern whites voiced antislavery opinion at all
roved that slaves possessed at least tentative allies in their inces-
ant struggle against bondage. For the present, these advocates remained few and eccentric, but if antislavery ideas someday ceased
eing the monopoly of prophets and passed to the multitude, slave-
wners would face a threat all but impossible to contain. One could
oresee a three-way contest in which slaveowners—always a mi-
ority—would find themselves pitted against the combined forces
f blacks and a white majority sympathetic to abolition. If that al-
iance materialized, the balance of power on the plantations almost
ertainly would shift, the master's authority would evaporate, and
avery would end. Much of the planters' effort from the Revolution
o the Civil War was designed to prevent the alliance from being
orged.

The endeavor achieved a large measure of success, yet the danger
ever entirely disappeared. Throughout the antebellum years, per-
ons of uneasy mind detected subversive influences everywhere. A
orth Carolinian in 1840 thought he could see campaigns at work
oth at home & abroad, which will render negro property very un-
afe & insecure. I really fear more for our own citizens than I do
om Northern influence."[15] The best defense was never to yield the
ightest ground to antislavery critics or their argument. Even well-
eaning owners, by excessive kindness toward their slaves, might
romote the very disorder they sought to avoid.

An impression prevailed that philanthropic influences in the late
ghteenth century and afterward had removed some of the most
xtreme impositions against slaves and had led to marked im-
rovement in their circumstance. Fewer barbarities than in colonial
ays and more consistent attention to physical well being, it was
ought, now characterized their lot. Thus, in 1794 on their travels
rough North Carolina, members of the great Izard family happily
ontrasted the plenty enjoyed by their own slaves back home in

15. Quoted in Johnson, *Antebellum North Carolina*, 506; David Brion Davis, *The
lave Power Conspiracy and the Paranoid Style* (Baton Rouge, 1970), 32–61; Steven A.
hanning, *Crisis of Fear: Secession in South Carolina* (New York, 1970), 255–56.

South Carolina with the misery and squalor of the unfortunates b
longing to their backward neighbors.[16] A degree of self-congratul.
tion showed through observations in that vein, obscuring the dai
ger of indulgence. Other persons no less concerned for the publ
good found the change alarming. They did not welcome relaxatio▮
as progress but, rather, they viewed them as signs of white weakne
in the relentless struggle that characterized race relations in tl
plantation South. While convention held that kindness and gene
osity brought greater benefits—that is, more productive labor—
than did severity, it also was believed that the kindness must ▮
freely granted and not extorted either by slaves or by white critic
Unthinking relaxation of the bonds of slavery, these persons argue
menaced the social order by inviting still further costly discord.[17]

Slaveowners everywhere would have found a complaint fro▮
Orangeburgh District, South Carolina, in 1812 illustrative of or
of the dread results to be expected from diminished rigor. In th.
plantation region, male slaves, "forgetting they were such"—th.
is, having been *allowed* to forget their status—attempted "to exe
cise among some of the lower classes of white people freedoms ar
familiarities which are dangerous to society." The petitioners con
plained especially about "the attempts which are made and some ▮
them with success at sexual intercourse with white females." Tl
lesson was easily drawn. Such boldness was "one of the cons
quences of softening their condition as slaves," a product of tl
"general disposition . . . to ameliorate" the treatment traditional.
accorded blacks. In the absence of state law prohibiting this sexu
license (the offense was not rape), citizens of the "incensed and i▮
dignant neighborhood" thought it necessary "to erect a tribunal ▮
their own and to measure out justice to the offender with their ow
hand."[18] The white community as a whole—slaveholder and no▮
slaveholder alike—had come to the support of slavery by compe▮
sating for certain masters' negligence or philanthropy. By no meai
incidentally, they also had helped maintain essential social distan◀
between slaves and "the lower classes of white people." By promp
extralegal action, the community had reinforced the subordinatic

16. Jordan, *White over Black*, 367–68; Alize Izard to Ralph Izard, November ▮
1794, and Ralph Izard to Alize Izard, December 7, 1794, both in Ralph Izard Pape▮
17. The debate continued. See the Minutes of the ABC Farmers' Club, 1846–▮
pp. 104–13, in Aiken County Records, South Caroliniana Library, University of Sou▮
Carolina, Columbia.
18. Petition, December 12, 1812, in Slavery Petitions, 1800–1830, Legislative F
pers, South Carolina Department of Archives and History.

sential to the maintenance of slavery and a caste system. They had
:monstrated further that in Orangeburgh slaves were to find no
lies.

Such persuasive display of community backing strengthened the
ands of masters in their day-to-day dealing with slaves. In the at-
osphere that evidently prevailed in Orangeburgh District, even
e most severe plantation discipline was unlikely to call forth re-
ike from the tenderhearted. The slaves now had no place to turn.
ney were overwhelmed by white unity. Plantation resistance had
st its political import. As long as the majority sanctioned slavery
id the means necessary to maintain it, the master held the upper
and on his own plantation and careless owners would be forced
to line. Any subversion by slaves would be temporary and its ef-
cts localized. But if the situation should be reversed, and non-
aveholding whites sided with blacks in the continuing struggle,
ie owners certainly would go down to defeat. As the Democratic
nator Stephen A. Douglas of Illinois liked to point out in the 1850s,
avery could not exist "for a day or an hour" in jurisdictions where
ie masters' claims failed to secure public sanction.[19] That condi-
on never prevailed in the South, but unlikely as it now may seem,
appeared for a moment to be on the verge of developing.

Religion supplied the principal subversive force. Beginning near
ie middle of the eighteenth century, a succession of evangelists—
iew light" Presbyterians, Baptists, Methodists—moved through
ie South gaining converts as they went, especially from lower- and
iddle-class whites and slaves. Whatever the literal content of the
.vivalists' message, its effect was to blur social distinctions. Those
ho came under its sway were likely to magnify their own conse-
uence while shedding some of their former deference by calling
ito question the values and behavior of their social betters, many
whom owned slaves.[20]

Slaves readily subscribed to the new gospel, finding in its teach-
ig and method more vivid promise of salvation than was offered
v the Anglicanism that previously had been virtually the sole
urce of their spiritual fare. For some of them, as for their white
eighbors, evangelicalism bespoke equality and even the prospect

19. Edwin Earle Sparks (ed.), *The Lincoln Douglas Debates of 1858* (Springfield,
., 1908), 160.
20. Donald G. Mathews, *Religion in the Old South* (Chicago, 1977), 28–38, 40–41,
–71; Rhys Isaac, "Evangelical Revolt: The Nature of the Baptists' Challenge to the
aditional Order in Virginia, 1765–1775," *William and Mary Quarterly*, 3rd ser.,
XXI (1974), 345–68.

of temporal freedom. It also set forth a persuasive scriptural cr
tique of slavery. Under the new dispensation, some slaves then
selves became preachers—unordained and unauthorized, bu
preachers nonetheless—who exerted great influence within th
black community.

Slaveowners were given much reason to look upon the new rel
gious developments with disapproval, even anxiety, for they wer
associated with discontent and rebelliousness and a general loo
ening of the bonds of slavery. At Essex County courthouse in Vi
ginia in 1767, Jupiter was tried and convicted "for stirring up th
Negroes to an insurrection, being a great Newlight preacher." Thre
years later, the Virginia planter Landon Carter mused on what h
regarded as the decline in trustworthiness of his slave Toney: "H
first religion that broke out upon him was new light and I believe
is from some inculcated notions of those rascals that the slaves i
this Colony are grown so much worse."[21]

Though blacks appear to have had special affinity for the gosp
as preached by Baptists, it was Methodists in particular who late i
the century occupied the vanguard of the small army of preacher
intent upon evangelizing the South. All but inseparable from Meth
odist gospel was an antislavery message paralleling the liberal vie
of human rights associated with the Revolution. Like other evang
lists, Methodists preached to free and slave alike. If overt condem
nations of slavery generally were absent from their services fc
blacks, a gospel of personal worth and spiritual liberation assured
was not. Further, it is unlikely that the antislavery views that man
evangelists held could be altogether hidden from black worshiper

Itinerant Methodist ministers did not hold back from attemptin
to proselytize whites to the antislavery cause. They were noted fc
their attempts to influence the behavior of new church members b
insisting upon emancipation as a corollary to salvation. The Rever
end Samuel Mitchell remembered the years when he rode circuit i
Virginia and "was in the constant habit of advising all such as a
tached themselves to the Methodist church to emancipate the
slaves."[22] Preachers urged nonslaveholding converts to become ac
vocates of emancipation. Not surprisingly, Methodist efforts pro
voked hostility from those who foresaw in their successes shifts i

21. Windley (comp.), *Runaway Slave Advertisements*, I, 56; Jack P. Greene (ed
Diary of Landon Carter, I, 378.
22. Catterall (ed.), *Judicial Cases*, I, 183–84.

inion that, if allowed to grow unchecked, promised social discord
d the consequent doom of slavery.[23]
At their Baltimore conference in 1784, Methodist bishops chal-
ged the existing social order by adopting emancipation as an of-
ial goal. Few could doubt the sincerity of their pronouncements,
; preachers and their converts displayed no hesitancy in moving
yond antislavery rhetoric to direct action. Not only did they spread
antislavery gospel; they sometimes defended slaves from the im-
sitions of patrols, helped fugitives elude their pursuers, and acted
other less overt ways to undermine slaveholding society.
From the sheriff of King William County, Virginia, in 1789 came
report certain to give pause to those fearful of the rising white
mpathy for slaves. At a rural schoolhouse east of Richmond,
ethodists and Baptists "two or three times a week" held night-
ne religious meetings for whites, slaves, and free blacks. These
terracial gatherings disrupted plantation discipline, complained
e sheriff: "Our Negroes are not to be found when we are in want
them, but are at such meetings." Under evangelical influence,
acks apparently considered themselves almost emancipated. They
oved freely about the countryside and stole "everything they can
y there hands on." Fully as outrageous was the disdain pious
ites displayed for the authority of patrols charged with maintain-
g order among slaves and confining them to plantations. When on
e occasion the patrol tried to break up the Methodists' meeting,
Ir. Charles Neale through one of them out of the doore & said that
ey should not take up any negro that was there." If Methodist in-
ence were not checked, warned the sheriff, "Our negroes wood
xt under the same pretence disobey the orders of there Masters
der the pretence of Religion." Only one conclusion was possible:
f there is nothing done with those people we shall not have a negro
command."[24]
Doubtless the situation the sheriff described was extraordinary;
t sympathy for blacks and antagonism toward the instruments of
cial control, if manifested at all, signified danger. The burgeoning
ligious enthusiasm fostered by Baptist and Methodist preachers

23. For two such instances, see Wesley M. Gewehr, *The Great Awakening in Vir-
ia, 1740–1790* (Durham, N.C., 1930), 247, and Clark *et al.* (eds.), *Journal and Letters
rancis Asbury*, I, 355, 442, 488.
24. Johnston, *Race Relations*, 97–98. For a former slave's understanding of the
sters' dread of Methodist egalitarianism, see [John Thompson], *Life of John
ompson, a Fugitive Slave . . .* (Worcester, Mass., 1856), 19.

brought blacks and whites together in situations that ignored, ev
defied, the social and political order. At the end of such a path l
the fall of slavery. Religiously inspired opposition to slavery in t
Early National Era constituted a grave internal threat to the pla
tation order.

It was not that slaveowners opposed the spread of religion amo
lesser whites or even among slaves. Indeed, beginning in the mi
1830s, a "mission to the slaves" became central to southern Prot
tant activity. But masters expected their slaves to be inculcat
with a faith that reinforced slavery rather than undermined it.
Presbyterian missionary assigned to North Carolina found th
slaveowners welcomed "intelligent" ministers, but were "oppos
to those ignorant preachers who endeavor to work more upon t
Passions & Sympathies of the negro by loud unmeaning bawlin
instead of truth."[25] They expected the result of preaching to be pa
fication and spiritual ease, not enthusiasm and unrest.

Although some believed religion contributed to slave docility, ot
ers found the newly converted to be less humble, less slavelike th
before. The Louisiana planter Bennet Barrow thought he knew w
sixteen of his neighbor's slaves ran away: "All this grows out of h
having them preached to for 4 or 5 years past—greatest piece
foolishness any one every [sic] guilty of." As born-again Christiar
some slaves preferred to devote themselves to religious exercis
rather than to the owner's tasks. If daytime routine left them
room for their new concerns, they would pursue them at night, t
time custom conceded to be their own. Night meetings ruin "t
servants," a North Carolina owner complained. Not even the mo
pious master was likely to count the spiritual welfare of bondsm
as worth the sacrifice of discipline and labor. Religious activi
among slaves could be tolerated only within limits: "We all seem
live in peace & quietness," wrote a South Carolina planter, "&
putting a stop to all this pretended Religion the Negros gits the
Rest of nights."[26]

25. Donald G. Mathews, "The Methodist Mission to the Slaves, 1829–1844," Jo
nal of American History, LI (1965), 615–31; D. A. Campbell to Absalom Peters, S
tember 15, 1834, in American Home Missionary Society Papers, Amistad Resea
Center, Tulane University, New Orleans.

26. Edwin A. Davis (ed.), Plantation Life in the Florida Parishes of Louisia
1836–1846, as Reflected in the Diary of Bennet H. Barrow (New York, 1943), 323–
N. H. Harding to Absalom Peters, August 16, 1829, in American Home Missiona
Society Papers; Hugh McCauley to Isaac Ball, June 2, 1814, in Ball Family Pape
South Caroliniana Library, University of South Carolina, Columbia.

Most objectionable to the slaveowners was the evangelists' min-
ing of religious zeal with secular policy. The practice was opposed
·cause it so nearly proved successful. For a few years during the
'80s there was reason to expect liberal ideas eventually to domi-
ite the white population of Virginia and Maryland and thus bring
ıout the collapse of slavery in the upper South. No such prospect
emed at all likely in either South Carolina or Georgia, where reli-
on and philosophy offered only feeble and easily handled chal-
nges. Only a few antislavery voices were heard in Georgia—at the
ademy at Augusta, for example, and on one brief but notable oc-
sion from the judicial bench. The protest in South Carolina was
st as ineffective.[27]
There, a combination of great planters, the near equivalent of an
igarchy, controlled affairs. Among South Carolina gentry there ex-
ted no group parallel to Virginia's aristocratic critics of slavery.
ıng before abolitionism had caused much stir elsewhere, political
ndidates whose background suggested weakness in support of
avery found they had little chance of winning elections in South
ırolina. With the conspicuous exceptions of Henry Laurens and his
n John (whose great wealth derived in part from the slave trade),
rtually all leading South Carolinians in the revolutionary and
ırly National eras stood foursquare behind slavery. Efforts to
rculate contrary views, even within the confines of the upper
ass, were scarcely tolerated, as Henry Laurens himself discovered.
1785 he ventured to give a copy of Richard Price's much-read
ımphlet in defense of the American Revolution to John F. Grimké,
ıe of the state's wealthiest planters. Grimké shared the pam-
ılet's amazing antislavery message with his still richer friend
alph Izard. The two magnates were predictably indignant. Grimké
hought himself almost affronted by having the pamphlet pre-
nted," because it advocated "measures for preventing too great an
equality of property and for gradually abolishing the Negro trade
ıd Slavery." They "reprobate" your work, Laurens informed the
ıthor.[28]

27. Adam Boyd to Committee of Correspondence, November 25, 1797, and Isaac
iggs to President of the Society, September 10, 1790, both in Pennsylvania Aboli-
n Society Papers; Charlton, "Judge and a Grand Jury," 206–15.
28. Robert L. Brunhouse (ed.), "David Ramsay, 1749–1815: Selections from His
ritings," Transactions of the American Philosophical Society, n.s., LV, Pt. 4, (1965),
3; Richard Price to Thomas Jefferson, July 2, 1785, in Boyd (ed.), Papers of Thomas
ferson, VIII, 258.

Before the westward spread of cotton culture, up-country farm
ers, having few obvious economic ties to slavery and not much sym
pathy for it, might have acted as a countervailing influence to lo·
country planters, but that potential could not be realized becau·
earlier generations had apportioned representation in the Gener
Assembly so as to deprive the up-country of effective political voic
Such opposition to slavery as did appear secured no permanent to
hold in any part of South Carolina society. Even the resistance to i
spread, which early in the century surfaced in up-country countie
withered by 1820 in the face of the westward-moving cotton cultu·
and rising land prices.[29]

The clergy were not immune to such influence. The fate of an
slavery religious protest in South Carolina, as eventually throug
most of the South, was foreshadowed by a clerical gathering
Charleston. There, in January, 1795, twenty-three Methodist min
ters from the South Carolina low-country drew up a statement a
firming the "impropriety" and "baneful consequences" of slaver
They then took note of the trend that soon was to overwhelm the
southern efforts. Falling under their censure were those Method
ministers who had "become the patrons of Slavery as well as t
holders of Slaves themselves; to the Scandal of the ministry, and t
strengthening of the hands of Oppression."[30] Not even antislave
clergymen could easily resist conforming to social norms.

In Virginia, antislavery ideas spread more widely than in mc
other parts of the South. By 1782 humanitarians in the state leg
lature had acquired enough influence to enact a law permitting i
dividuals to manumit their slaves without first securing speci
permission from state authorities. The new measure led to rap
increase of the state's free-black population. Their numbers gre
from three thousand in 1780 to thirty thousand in 1810.[31] Those w
distrusted blacks found this a deplorable development. In Accom

29. Examples of up-country antislavery thought—all expressed in the afterma
of a slave-conspiracy scare in Camden, South Carolina—appear in Grand Jury P
sentments from Chester, November, 1816, Fairfield, November 19, 1816, Kersha
November 19, 1816, Lexington, October, 1816, Richland, October, 1816, and Yo
October 29, 1816, all in Grand Jury Presentments, South Carolina Department
Archives and History.
30. Quoted in George C. Rogers, Jr., *Charleston in the Age of the Pinckneys* (N
man, Okla., 1969), 143.
31. William Waller Hening (comp.), *The Statutes at Large, Being a Compilation*
All the Laws of Virginia . . . (Richmond, 1810–23), XI, 39–40. For statistics on grow
see Jordan, *White over Black*, 406–407, and Ira Berlin, *Slaves Without Masters: T*
Free Negro in the Antebellum South (New York, 1974), 46–47.

ounty in the 1780s, free blacks were popularly thought to be unre-
onstructed Tories, covertly maintaining British sympathies and
heltering runaway slaves. But even when they did nothing illegal
r overtly subversive, their mere presence—"a race or nation of
eople between the masters and slaves"—made slaves discontented
nd hard to control.[32] Slavery, one could believe, would be more
ifficult to maintain now that humanitarians had persuaded the leg-
lature to ease the avenue of escape from it.

Under religious tutelage in the mid-1780s, antislavery sentiment
rew confident enough for its advocates to seek enactment of a
radual-emancipation law. The Virginia law of 1782 had *allowed*
anumissions; under terms of the new proposal the state would
quire them. But antislavery advocates were not to have their way.
y 1785, when petitions supporting their measure reached the Gen-
ral Assembly, defenders of slavery had mobilized to resist their
ritics. While antislavery partisans had been circulating petitions
mong small farmers and church members, their opponents were
raveling through the state gathering signatures urging defeat of a
easure that would multiply the free-black population and revolu-
onize the state's social structure.

The pro-slavery petitions, signed by 1,244 Virginians, reveal the
ttitude and interests of those early defenders of slavery. They cited
cripture to counter the evangelists' claim that slavery conflicted
vith religious principles. Further, they argued, victory in the Revo-
ution confirmed the right to private property. Abolition would vio-
ate that natural right and thus surrender a patriotic accomplishment. They dwelt at length on the dangers posed by free blacks,
vhom they termed "banditti." These objections no doubt carried
much weight, but so, too, did another point. Slavery, the petition-
rs implied, was a distinctively American institution essential to
ontinued growth. Persons who tried to destroy it were, at best,
entimental and impractical reformers. At worst, they were disor-
anizers, opponents of progress, enemies seeking to tear down the
ountry.[33]

Confronted by such a formidable argument, the gradual-emanci-
ation plan failed to win a hearing in the state legislature. The lawmakers' decision was made easier by the abolitionists' inability to

32. Johnston, *Race Relations*, 42; McColley, *Slavery and Jeffersonian Virginia*, 151;
Hutchinson and Rachal (eds.), *Papers of James Madison*, VIII, 403–404, 442, 477.
33. Fredrika Teute Schmidt and Barbara Ripel Wilhelm, "Early Proslavery Peti-
ions in Virginia," *William and Mary Quarterly*, 3rd ser., XXX (1973), 133–46.

gain overt support from the older, traditional source of antislavery thought in Virginia, the great liberal spokesmen who during the recent struggle for independence had identified themselves with the cause of human rights. While antislavery groups were preparing their petition campaign, Methodist leaders traveled to Mount Vernon in hope of enlisting the aid of George Washington. The general disappointed them. He gave the visitors "his opinion against slavery" but declined to sign their petition, although he promised that if the legislature took up the measure, he would write a letter of support.[34]

Thomas Jefferson did not go even that far. At the height of the revolutionary era, Jefferson showed signs of becoming an active proponent of antislavery measures, but his enthusiasm soon was checked and then as rapidly declined. Eventually he assessed the problems involved in antislavery programs as beyond the wisdom of his generation. In neither large ways nor small ones would he follow a course designed to weaken slavery. He even declined appointment as executor of Thaddeus Kosciuszko's will, which authorized use of the revolutionary hero's estate to acquire slaves for the purpose of freeing and educating them.[35]

It had become clear that despite the resounding words of the revolutionary era, the self-interest of slaveowners would not permit general emancipation. Though finely honed consciences found evils and inconsistencies in slavery, it nonetheless had been an accepted part of life in Virginia during nearly all the commonwealth's existence. Its removal would require major readjustments from everyone in the state, black and white alike. If slavery ended, the old familiar problems and anxieties associated with it would be replaced by new ones fully as difficult and painful as the old.

Perhaps the strongest objection raised to any emancipation plan was the obvious fact that it would remove from the black population the controls that now kept most of them profitably employed at their masters' work and in a well-defined servile position. The behavior of those already freed did not seem reassuring. Although many newly manumitted blacks lived the kind of sober, industrious lives that commended them to substantial white citizens, a number of them conspicuously did not. Even abolitionists sometimes de-

34. Clark et al. (eds.), Journal and Letters of Francis Asbury, I, 489. With respect to slavery, George Washington wrote to Alexander Spotswood on November 23, 1794, that "I shall frankly declare to you that I do not like even to think, much less talk of it." Phillips (ed.), Plantation and Frontier, I, 56.
35. Catterall (ed.), Judicial Cases, IV, 178–79.

ored the idleness and intemperance in which some free blacks in-
dlged, and found their wayward conduct a strong obstacle against
opular commitment to emancipation. The presence of a landless,
villy irresponsible class was an object of dread nearly everywhere
n early America, perhaps in no place more strongly than in Vir-
nia, where in the seventeenth century unruly poor whites had
:en a source of political and social unrest and a menace to law and
roperty.[36] If landless whites, bound to the ruling class by ties of
ice and culture, once had flirted with rebellion, how much greater
ne danger to be expected now from landless and alien blacks!

Abolitionists in the upper South also encountered strong opposi-
on in efforts to aid blacks already free. They had concentrated
neir activities in the city of Alexandria. There, as in the South's
ther urban centers, the black population rapidly increased in the
780s. The discrimination and poverty that commonly afflicted the
ewly freed aroused compassion in some whites but suspicion in
thers. As oppressed and relatively unassimilated people—outsid-
s—the blacks' loyalty to existing social and political arrange-
nents could not be taken for granted. Would they become sober,
roductive workers? Would they be reconciled to the permanent
ondage of their fellow blacks? Free blacks in the North already had
iken an active antislavery stance. Would they themselves be con-
:nt to remain a caste at the bottom of society? What terrible social
onvulsions might they precipitate?

Virginia and Maryland abolitionists attempted to remove the
nxiety such questions generated by providing free blacks with
:hools. This was a less oblique assault on poverty and unrest than
may at first appear. As a device for instilling conventional values,
ducation might serve as a tranquilizing influence. Looked at more
enerously, education also could help outsiders become participat-
ig members of society. The schools taught skills that might be ex-
ected to promote economic and social mobility. The educational
xperiments in Alexandria and elsewhere thus demonstrated aboli-
onist assumptions that blacks formed part of the social order and
hould be encouraged to rise within it. But these assumptions
lashed with the intentions of persons pledged to the opposite:
:lacks must forever remain outsiders—subordinate to whites, pref-

36. Alexander Addison to the Society, December 6, 1790, Report of the Virginia
bolition Society, May 5, 1797, George Drinker to Joseph Bringhurst, December 10,
804, Report of the Choptank, Maryland, Abolition Society, April 26, 1797, all in
:nnsylvania Abolition Society Papers; Edmund S. Morgan, *American Slavery*,
15–270.

erably as slaves—and the existing social order must be perpetuate Not easily eliminated was the suspicion that free blacks retaine sympathy with slaves and, in conjunction with them, would act a fatal counterbalance to white power.

Not surprisingly, the educational activities of the antislayery s cieties came under attack even before revelations of major slav plots magnified racial antipathies. Their most effective critic wa the distinguished young physician and planter Elisha Cullen Dic (he served as consulting physician during George Washington's las illness). His early objection could be dismissed as prophecy, but Ga briel's conspiracy four years later made his views appear realisti and unanswerable.

Abolition societies, he warned, tended to produce "the most ser ous calamities" in the South. Abolitionist schoolteachers "cor stantly" inculcated "natural equality among the blacks of every d scription. They are teaching them with great assiduity the onl means by which they can at any time be enabled to concert an execute a general insurrection." Literate free blacks would teac their skills to slaves and thus make coordinated resistance eas Prudent citizens, it followed, must unite to suppress antislaver activity.[37]

By the time Dick penned his warning, the wave of fear that fo lowed Gabriel's conspiracy had swept across the state. Blacks di not wait for whites to tell them how to respond. Education an emancipation became less important to them than survival. The now made themselves as inconspicuous as possible, avoiding abol tionists and no longer attending the societies' schools. White abol tionists, too, gave in to the constraints of popular disapproval. S low did the fortunes and prospects of Virginia abolitionists fall tha a year later the reporter for the society at Alexandria declared, "W are in fact dead, and I may say, I have no hope of reanimation." The conclusion was inescapable: No effective measures promotin the demise of slavery and the elevation of free blacks were at a likely to be put forth in Virginia or anywhere else in the South.

Thoroughly foreshadowed though it was, such pessimisr emerged suddenly. Even as late as the spring of 1800, Methodist

37. Berlin, *Slaves Without Masters*, 82–83; Archer McLean to William Rogers, Feb ruary 15, 1796, and Report of the Alexandria Society, May 28, 1801, both in Pennsy vania Abolition Society Papers; Elisha Dick to James Monroe, September 26, 180(in Palmer, McRae, and Flournoy (eds.), *Calendar of Virginia Papers*, IX, 178.
38. James Wood, Address of the Virginia Abolition Society, May 22, 1801, in Penr sylvania Abolition Society Papers.

parently hardly felt it at all. On May 2, only three months before
velation of Gabriel's conspiracy, the Methodist bishops set forth a
nvigorated campaign to promote emancipation. Their recent fail-
e to move Virginia legislators to enact a gradual-emancipation
v had not proved disspiriting, for the momentum of continued
urch growth appeared to belie the permanence of such reversals.
a printed address, the bishops directed each annual conference
instruct special committees of elders, deacons, and traveling
eachers to gather signatures from all their "acquaintances and all
e friends of liberty" calling upon the southern state legislatures to
ovide for gradual emancipation.

The bishops did not intend to confine their campaign to the South
r to make it solely a denominational effort. They urged persons
the North to join the crusade by exerting their influence on
quaintances in the slave states, "whether those friends be Meth-
ists or not." This activity was not designed as an experiment
a one-time enterprise. The bishops directed that pressure on
e southern state legislatures "be continued from year to year, 'till
e desired end be fully accomplished.' " In effect, the rapidly grow-
g Methodist church announced its transformation into an aggres-
ve antislavery society. Its goal, declared the bishops, was "equal
erty."[39]

News of the Methodists' plan and reports of Gabriel's conspiracy
ached South Carolina at nearly the same time, a coincidence no
ubt adding to the alarm expressed by state officials over both.
nator Jacob Read sent a copy of the bishops' printed address to
e governor with a warning. If South Carolinians allowed Meth-
ists to proceed with their petition drive, they would "bring down
e firebrands to our houses and daggers to our throats. . . . Quakers
d Methodists have long been sapping the existence of the South-
n States," Read charged. "The former are however harmless when
mpared to the latter." The governor placed a copy of the Method-
document before the state legislature along with his own obser-
tion of "its improper tendency, as highly incompatible, with the
hts of all the Southern States; and extremely interesting to this
ate in particular."[40]

39. [Methodist Episcopal Church], *The Address of the General Conference of the*
thodist Episcopal Church, to All Their Brethren and Friends in the United States,
ltimore, May 23, 1800 (N.p., n.d.).
40. Jacob Read to John Drayton, July 18, 1800, in Governor's Message to the Sen-
e, November 25, 1800, in Governors' Messages, 1791–1800, South Carolina Depart-
ent of Archives and History.

Citizens in Charleston did not wait for the legislature to act. mob confronted the city's leading Methodist preachers, burned the petitions, and escorted the Reverend George Daugherty to the tov pump. There they held his head under the spout until he near drowned. Not only did public opinion in South Carolina thus che the petition campaign at its beginning, but the Methodist clergy work among slaves was made more difficult as owners all over t state became leery of allowing them to preach on their plantatior At the same time, the legislature controlled religious services f blacks by forbidding them to be held at night or behind clos doors.[41]

Popular opposition and legislative action halted antislavery a tivity in South Carolina, as it had elsewhere in the South, before had a chance to become politically effective. Yet one of its troub some side effects, the free-black population, remained. The proble of the free blacks, a group likely to oppose slavery and by its me existence to weaken it, grew more urgent as their numbers conti ued to rise. Southern determination to perpetuate slavery strengt ened the motive to eliminate free blacks.

No doubt many white persons were sufficiently informed of t course of the Saint-Domingue revolt to know that it originated an uprising by the colony's free mulatto population. If that cla could initiate insurrection in one slave society, presumably it cou do so in another. Accordingly, a group of slaveholders in the upp South joined with northern philanthropists to develop a plan to r move the troublesome element from the country. A number of ear antislavery writers, recognizing "the race problem" as being an o stacle to any plan to end slavery, earlier had ventured proposals make emancipation more palatable by exporting freed blacks. Son blacks appeared to welcome the idea. In Boston in 1788, a grou requested the city council to help them emigrate to Africa.[42] But was prejudice and fear of insurrection rather than hopes for abol tion that infused the scheme with whatever appeal it had in tl South. In 1800, as a response to Gabriel's conspiracy, the subje first gained official consideration in Virginia.

First discussed in secret by the House of Burgesses, the propos

41. Albert Deems Betts, *History of South Carolina Methodism* (Charleston, S. 1952), 92, 169, 170.
42. St. George Tucker to John Page, March 29, 1790, and John Pemberton to Co mittee of the London Society, November, 1788, in Pennsylvania Abolition Socie Papers.

ɔn received endorsement from an array of persons regarded as
ʌders in the upper South. John Marshall, chief justice of the
ʌited States; Bushrod Washington, the first president's nephew;
d Henry Clay, a rising young political star—all soon ranked in the
ʌdership of the colonization movement. At the same time, philan-
ɾopists and clergymen in the northern and southern states favored
ɂ project as both a humanitarian measure benefiting oppressed
ople and a missionary enterprise likely to promote the conversion
Africa. Diplomatic conflict leading to war with England in 1812
ɂvented implementation in the first years of the century. But with
ace restored, the plan emerged as an enterprise to be conducted
a nationwide scale.

ʌn 1816 the American Colonization Society was formed in Wash-
ʒton, D.C., in part for humanitarian motives, in part to lessen the
ɂelihood of slave unrest by removing the slaves' most obvious al-
s. The society's efforts came to little. The number of persons to be
ʌnsported was too great and the society's resources were too small
make the project feasible, even had slaveowners generally re-
ʌved to support it. Approval for the society's program—never very
tensive—rapidly declined, especially in the lower South. The ac-
ɾity of its agents and the spread of its publications, some warned,
ɔuld incite slaves just as other antislavery propaganda did. A
ɾiter in the *Southern Review* set forth the society's probable effect
slaves: "Conceiving that there is some power at work for their
ʌief, the nature of which they do not accurately understand—
ɔnstantly reminded that there are those in the world who think
ɂm the victim of injustice, and who have the power to protect
ʌd relieve them—they contract of course, the anxious restlessness
ʌich is the natural effect of anticipated good deferred."[43] In short,
ʌonizationists would encourage slaves in waging their plantation
ɾuggles for autonomy.

White southerners soon concluded, although with much hesi-
ʌncy, that free blacks could be tolerated, that they were a lesser
ʌnger to plantation order than was colonizationist propaganda.
ɂee blacks continued to be seen as a social problem and a source of
ʌd and encouragement to disruptive slaves, but their concentration
cities and towns reduced their irritating effect. Few free blacks
ʌed in rural, agricultural regions where they might contaminate

43. Review of *The Tenth Annual Report of the American Society for Colonizing the
ɂe People of Colour...*, 228–29.

the large numbers of plantation slaves. Further, in the 1820s a
1830s the continued westward spread of plantation slavery reduc
the proportion of slaves likely to be in contact with them. At t
same time, state legislatures restricted the possibility of furtl
manumissions and placed the free-black population under incre;
ingly rigid controls designed to minimize its subversive potenti

Meanwhile, internal sources of dissent lessened. The church
that had so boldly challenged southern society before 1800 modifi
their critical stance. For the most part they abandoned their eff(
to undermine the worldly order in which they functioned. No mc
harsh condemnations emerged from church councils. Abolition
clergymen left the South voluntarily or were expelled. Silence,
course, never was total. Here and there, mostly in the upper Sou
Quakers, Baptist Friends of Humanity, and resolute evangelic;
continued to expound the ideals of an earlier day and throughc
the 1820s supported tiny antislavery societies. But however mu
these homegrown dissidents annoyed slaveowners, they function
so far from the centers of power and so clearly diverged from t
mainstream of sectional development as to seem merely embarra;
ing rather than dangerous.

Nonslaveholders, too, ceased being the imminent threat they h.
seemed at the start of the century, when antislavery preachers a
peared to be mobilizing them in the slaves' favor. Many of the sm;
farmers who aspired to become planters themselves or who liv
among them in close economic and social association wholly ;
cepted the planters' views and leadership, while others, unwilli
to join the consensus, chose to leave the South rather than stay ·
to fight dubious battles.[44]

However, remaining and scattered throughout the region was ·
unabsorbed nonslaveholding element—upland farmers not bou·
economically to the planters, and, especially in the cities, artisar
teachers, tradesmen, and laborers of every sort—whose ties wi
slavery were loose or nonexistent. Their allegiance to the plante·
values and leadership could not be assumed. Chiefly on their ;
count, the specter of crumbling support for slavery and thus of
changed balance of power within the South never could be co·
pletely dispelled.

44. *Annals of Congress*, 16th Cong., lst Sess., 292, 1354; William T. Allan in *Libe
tor*, August 25, 1843; John Rankin, *Letters on American Slavery Addressed to Mr. Thon
Rankin . . .* (Newburyport, Mass., 1837), 72; Avery O. Craven, *The Coming of the C
War* (New York, 1942), 95; John D. Barnhart, "Sources of Southern Migration i·
the Old Northwest," *Mississippi Valley Historical Review*, XXII (1935), 49–62.

The challenge to planter dominance offered by liberal theorists
d evangelicals had been met successfully. The spread of cotton
ture had secured for slavery a tight hold on the South, making it
ssible for the many who would defend it to overcome the few in-
e the section who would end it. No organized group remained to
estion slavery or to contest the planters' control. Nonetheless, the
ential for challenge by nonslaveholders remained. And always
itributing to insecurity was knowledge that disruptive aboli-
nist influences still might come from outside the South, influ-
es that slaves—and nonslaveholders—might find seductive and
it slaveholders would have no tested means to forestall.

6

Growing Antislavery Pressures

In the first years of the new century antislavery sentiment studd
northern public discourse and newspapers, particularly those
Federalist persuasion. Although these criticisms of southern ins
tutions could be read as reflections of pure philanthropy, they c
ried obvious political implications as well. Federalist authors cou
not hide their delight in exposing the hypocrisy of Jeffersoni
Democrats who celebrated liberty and republicanism while livi
from the labor of slaves.

Even if partisan politics sometimes appeared to furnish both
casion and motive for northern strictures against slavery, that
planation by no means detracted from their subversive impact
the South. Neither did it lessen their influence on northern opini
Antislavery and antisouthern ideas appeared so often in northe
print, sermons, and conversation as to become commonplace.
that way they acquired the authority of any other conventional
lief. In 1821 Representative Henry Meigs of New York could spe
with little likelihood of contradiction, of northerners' and southe
ers' twenty-year-long "series of sarcasms upon each others custor
modes of living, and manners."[1] In the North antislavery early
came a cultural given.

New Englanders in particular came to see themselves as mora

1. *Annals of Congress*, 16th Cong., lst Sess., 943.

perior to residents of the slave states, a conviction some of them
de little effort to conceal. Thus, as early as 1806 a South Carolin-
, evidently feeling no need for elaboration, referred to "the in-
bitants of New England, some of whom look upon their Southern
ethren as an inferior race of men." Such northern self-pride could
use even persons who moved from New England intending to
ke the South their home to experience a sense of loss rather than
pe and anticipation. "I can assure you I am not very well pleased
th South Carolina," wrote Susan Blanding in 1808, shortly after
e arrived in Camden. "I think a person to quit the Northern states
spend their life in the South, must make a great sacrifice, yes,
crificing a land of Liberty for a land of slavery . . . a land of luxury,
quired by the hearts blood of the poor ignorant Africans—such
deed is the difference."[2]
Moral self-satisfaction came to seem inseparable from northern
rth, and its development did not need to await the arrival of ag-
essive abolitionism in the 1830s. In 1816 James K. Paulding wrote
northern men who floundered "into Virginia . . . loaded with a
ck of prejudices as large as a pedlar's [sic]." And in 1820 residents
Laurens District in South Carolina complained of the supercil-
us air assumed by northern-based "Hawkers and Peddlers" who
ave generally a great aversion to the southern and western or
aveholding States." Little happened afterward to lessen Yankee
ejudice. "Texas and Arkansas are to me more truly foreign than
nada or the West Indies or even Van Diemensland," wrote a Con-
cticut clergyman in 1848.[3]
Such private aversion was easily transmitted to public and offi-
al bodies. Although Congress long remained immune to antislav-
y pressures, state legislatures more readily succumbed. Thus in
bruary, 1805, Pennsylvania dispatched an intemperate resolution
its southern counterparts: "The House of Representatives un-
sitatingly, declare, that Slavery in any shape, within the United
ates, is a blot on the American character; and that they will, with

2. William James Ball to Isaac Ball, November 24, 1806, in Ball Family Papers;
san Blanding to the Blanding Family, December 2, 1808, in William Blanding Pa-
rs, South Caroliniana Library, University of South Carolina, Columbia.
3. [James K. Paulding], *Letters from the South, Written During an Excursion in the
mmer of 1816* (New York, 1817), I, 31; Grand Jury Presentment from Laurens Dis-
ct, November, 1820, in Grand Jury Presentments, South Carolina Department of
chives and History; James T. Dickinson to George Whipple, March 6, 1848, in
erican Missionary Association Archives, Amistad Research Center, Tulane Univer-
y, New Orleans.

ardour, seize any occasion, to lend their aid, to wipe off and prev[e] the extension of the foul stain."[4]

Slaveowners deplored the mounting northern criticism of sou[th] ern institutions as menacing, insulting, unconstitutional interf[er] ence with local affairs. Its effect, complained the astute south[e]rn partisan John Taylor of Caroline, was exactly as intended—it und[er] mined slavery by encouraging slave resistance.[5] Northern antisla[v] ery critics, as expected, yielded nothing to the objection, but ea[ch] developed a response derived in part from their impression t[hat] widespread discontent already prevailed among slaves. They c[on] strued the well-publicized slave plots of 1800–1803 as events jus[ti] fying opposition to slavery rather than as reason to abandon it. O[nly] by freeing the slaves, they argued, could catastrophe be avoided. [In] this way northern antislavery activity early became associated w[ith] fears for the physical safety of American society. By rebelling a[nd] plotting to rebel, slaves contributed to the growth of a northern [an] tislavery movement.

The threat of insurrection gave calls for emancipation an urgen[cy] they might otherwise have lacked and provided antislavery p[ro] grams an attraction that religious and moral argument alone co[uld] never have supplied. White southerners warned that antislav[e] agitation would promote slave rebellion, but early abolitioni[sts] were just as insistent that their program offered a means of averti[ng] disaster rather than of encouraging it. As long as slavery existed, t[he] American Convention for Promoting the Abolition of Slavery warn[ed] in 1801, the danger of race war would persist.[6]

Northerners had to explain to themselves and to others why th[ey] were so troubled about an institution that already had been end[ed] in their own section. Slavery, abolitionists insisted, was a natio[nal] problem; the Constitution, with its package of sectional comp[ro] mises, had made it so. Each part of the Constitution pertaining [to] slavery had its northern critic, but the most objectionable clau[se] (second only to the three-fifths compromise) concerned military [af] fairs. The Constitution's provision for federal military aid to su[p] press insurrection made the South's volatile labor system a natio[nal] concern. If rebellion broke out, abolitionists explained, northe[rn]

4. Commonwealth of Pennsylvania, Resolution Addressed to the Legislature [of] North Carolina, February 20, 1805, in James Turner Papers, Vol. III, in Govern[or] Papers, North Carolina Division of Archives and History.
5. Taylor, Arator, 115, 118–19.
6. American Convention for Promoting the Abolition of Slavery, Minutes of [the] Proceedings of the Convention of Delegates . . . 1801 (Philadelphia, 1801), 38–39.

diers would be called upon to march against the South's blacks,
d northern taxpayers would share the burden of financing the
mpaign. Even if by some miracle slaves remained quiet in peace-
ne, involvement in foreign war—and that seemed likely as long
the Napoleonic Wars continued—would make them an immedi-
e danger, or so events of the preceding century taught. In any
ture conflict northern soldiers would be saddled with a dispro-
rtionate share of the military burden because white southerners
uld have to stay at home to control dissident slaves. "Take away
ose [southern] whites who must remain to watch over the Slaves,
d how many will there be, to act against the enemy? . . . Who
ught the Battles of Independence?" These embarrassing ques-
ns—some of them soon to be given added pertinence by the War
1812—appeared in the Boston *Repertory* on April 24, 1804.[7]
Discussions of slavery in this way assumed the pragmatic qual-
y that characterized them for some years after 1800. Still it was
l but impossible to bar abstract questions of right and wrong
m discussion of an institution that so glaringly clashed with the
equently celebrated national ideals of liberty and equality. The
aves of religious revivals that periodically swept America, reach-
g a height in the 1740s and continuing into the new century, en-
uraged a moralistic approach to all public issues. At the same
ne, the revivals brought about a reordering of values in those who
me under their sway. Emerging from the experience with sharp-
ed awareness of their own individuality and worth, new converts
ere likely to seek equal social station and recognition for them-
lves. Some extended to others, even to slaves, the concern they felt
r their own personal dignity. Moved by heightened religious sen-
bility, some of them called for the end of slavery, less because they
d calculated its damage to society and the economy than because
ey now counted it a great wrong perpetrated against fellow hu-
an beings.
Contributing to the strength of the religious argument, as evan-
licals shaped it, was their overpowering sense of doom. Although
r some persons, as the historian Linda Kerber once observed, ev-
y age is an Age of Anxiety, the early years of the Republic were
ceptionally so.[8] Optimists might find in those troubled times re-

7. Quoted in Kerber, *Federalists in Dissent*, 40. See also *Annals of Congress*, 9th
ng., lst Sess., 370–71.
8. Kerber, *Federalists in Dissent*, 158. See also Page Smith, "Anxiety and Despair
American History," *William and Mary Quarterly*, 3rd ser., XXVI (1969), 416–24.

juvenation and hope, but others detected in the same events or
decline. Evangelicals in particular viewed sin and self-indulgen
and growing secularism (which they believed characterized the ag
as an invitation to God's wrath.

Some of the evangelicals considered slavery the most flagrant
the many sins in which Americans, individually and collective
indulged. Retribution must be expected. Persons who suppos
themselves wise enough to fathom God's ways speculated that t
divine punishment would precisely fit the crime. Already the rigl
eous discerned signs supporting prophecy that a slaveholding n
tion would be destroyed in a holocaust of slave rebellion and ra
war. They could not easily ignore the portent of Saint-Doming
and the warnings supplied by Gabriel and the unnumbered, most
anonymous black conspirators who succeeded him.

Through such ominous associations the antislavery argume
early acquired the evangelical quality that in the 1830s became
hallmark and helped supply its proponents with their abundar
remorseless energy. Abolition, argued its religious advocates, w
not primarily a matter of secular policy and rational choice;
was, above all else, a religious duty. American Home Missiona
Society agents who worked in the southern states in the late 182
and 1830s sent back to society headquarters complaints that sla
ery was a threat to virtue and pure religion and was an obstacle
evangelizing the South. They decided that slavery impeded the ca
rying out of God's will and at the same time menaced the natior
security.[9]

These solemn convictions help explain why abolitionists in tl
1830s, unlike their more secularly oriented predecessors of a gener
tion earlier, seldom heeded even the most urgent warnings of tl
perils of antislavery agitation. Religiously motivated abolitionis
were unlikely to be deterred by difficulties met in carrying out the
program or by warnings of the risks involved in emancipation, f
they were demanding what they believed ought and must be dor
not what was popular or comfortable to do. Judgment would com
whether the nation was ready to accept it or not. History could l
cited as proof: "The strong arm of omnipotence bro't deliverance
the oppressed, without paying the least respect to the courtly po

9. Daniel Gould to Absalom Peters, July 31, 1826, and November 10, 1828, Hu
Carlisle to Peters, July 28, 1830, James H. Fowler to Peters, June 19, 1834, all
American Home Missionary Society Papers.

ians of Egypt," wrote the secretary of an obscure southern anti-
very society as early as 1820.[10]
Until well into the 1820s, the tie between evangelicalism and an-
lavery was closer in the South than in most parts of the North.
avery long remained a legal institution in Pennsylvania, New
rk, and New Jersey; yet untraveled farmers and villagers in those
ates, when they thought of slavery at all, must have viewed it
a totally exotic practice of no concern to them, in spite of the cen-
s returns that showed New York City having as many blacks as
arleston. In postrevolutionary years northern preachers infre-
ently dwelt on their parishioners' responsibility for slavery and
cial injustice within their own states, an omission that struck the
glish-born Methodist missionary Francis Asbury, who in 1795 re-
arked the inequity of New York masters having for the most part
aped the verbal lashings to which Methodist preachers regularly
bjected slaveholding Virginians.[11]
Northern states were not quite so barren of religiously inspired
tislavery activity as Asbury evidently thought; nevertheless, he
is correct in believing that some of the most prominent northern
ancipationists, organized as the American Convention for Pro-
oting the Abolition of Slavery, asked for less drastic action against
very than evangelical faith required. Unlike later antislavery ad-
cates, they seldom demanded immediate emancipation. Even so,
ey could not avoid arousing opposition. They found at an early
te that even their moderate approach provoked misgivings. Anti-
very activity, their opponents warned, eventually would lead to
il war.[12]
The rather moderate members of the American Convention, how-
er, were not the only early critics of slavery. There were other abo-
ionists near the beginning of the century, particularly those re-
aining in the South, who, unlike the more distinguished members
the American Convention, had no close ties with dominant ele-
ents in society. They saw themselves, instead, as outsiders hurling
allenges at powers and principalities. They seldom adjusted their
etoric or program in order to secure favor and influence or to

10. *The Emancipator (Complete), Published by Elihu Embree, Jonesborough, Tennes-
, 1820 (Rpr.; Nashville, 1932), May 31, 1820, p. 22. All further citations to the
mancipator are to this reprint of the original.
11. Clark *et al.* (eds.), *Journal and Letters of Francis Asbury*, II, 62.
12. George Benson to William Rogers, February 19, 1791, in Pennsylvania Aboli-
n Society Papers.

avoid recrimination. In their situation the effort would have fail
in any event, for they could do little to hide the fact that they we
bent on elevating the humble and bringing the mighty low.

After official bodies of the leading evangelical churches that c
erated in the South relaxed their early antislavery zeal, southe
antislavery groups would be confined mostly to the hill country
western North Carolina and Virginia and to east Tennessee. In th
relative isolation, Quakers and members of evangelical churches i
mained unreconciled to slave-plantation society. Their small, tigh
knit antislavery societies issued condemnations and supplied je
miads to abolitionist editors, who in turn circulated their writin
throughout the country. In that way these otherwise obscure a
isolated persons spread their antislavery message far and wide. B
they were powerless in their own region to slow the economic a
social developments that throughout antebellum years tied slave
to progress. The further these obscure people traveled from the se
of power, the more alienated they became, the less restrained gr
their program, and the more remorseless was their message. N
surprisingly, some of the most impassioned antislavery protest e\
written came from those little-known southerners.[13]

In essays published in the 1820s, these backwoods abolitioni
reiterated their belief in the likelihood of retributive judgment co
ing upon the nation through slave insurrection and their convicti
of Christian duty to work to avert it. But in those years one did n
have to fret about "judgment" and "duty" and "retribution" in c
der to be concerned about the prospect of slave revolt. Even unl
lievers and rationalists, who scoffed at such abstractions as "n
tional sins" and "imputed guilt" and who were unperturbed by t
prospect of divine punishment, admitted to worry about slave i
volts, for these events, unlike God's prospective judgment, actua
had taken place both in the United States and the West Indies. Fa
ing such dangers, one need not decide whether they were punis
ments dealt by the hand of God or by the will of the incensed a
outraged blacks acting by and for themselves.

It was possible to dread the prospect of slave insurrection a
to seek ways of averting it while at the same time accepting it

13. James Brewer Stewart, "Evangelicalism and the Radical Strain in Southe
Antislavery Thought During the 1820s," *Journal of Southern History*, XXXIX (197
379–96; Merton L. Dillon, *Benjamin Lundy and the Struggle for Negro Freedom* (l
bana, Ill., 1966), 52–54; Merton L. Dillon, "Three Southern Antislavery Editors: T
Myth of the Southern Antislavery Movement," *East Tennessee Historical Socie*
Publications, XLII (1970), 47–56.

ing just. A Quaker abolitionist newspaper on one page could warn
uthern readers of the "unwise and impolitic" practice of main-
ning "inveterate and desperate" black enemies "in our homes,
d about our farms, and in our towns and cities," and print on the
xt page a poem calling down God's vengeance against white op-
essors. To help "avert the impending storm" forecast by such
ssages, Elihu Embree, a Quaker ironmaker, in 1820 founded the
mancipator in Jonesborough, Tennessee. "The Slavery of the Afri-
ns in the United States," he wrote, "if continued a few generations
iger, will produce such scenes of misery and destruction for our
sterity . . . as have not been exceeded in the history of man." [14]
Comprehending—as few others in those days did—the conflict
tween master and bondsman that was inherent in slavery, Em-
:e directed against the institution the distaste for war and vio-
ice that was inseparable from his Quaker faith. Embree's first-
nd observations in Tennessee led him to emphasize the harshest
pects of slavery and to interpret the institution much as did Sena-
: James Burrill of Rhode Island, who viewed slavery only from
ur. Burrill, too, found no place for sentimentality and illusion
ien describing slavery. If it could be called a patriarchal system
Virginia and the Carolinas, it was not so in the West: "The greater
imber of slaves, in new countries," he told the Senate, "will be
nnected with their master by no other tie than that heartless one
bargain and sale." [15]
Embree likewise found few elements of paternalism in the mas-
:-slave relationship as he saw it function in the new West. Instead,
olence lay at its core. Embree characterized the slave population
America as a nation held in unwilling bondage by exploitative
pressors. "I view the slaves as prisoners of war," he wrote, who
ccording to the laws of nations have the right to seize any oppor-
nity to free themselves—nor have we doubt that they will em-
ace every opportunity that promises success." [16]
Viewing master and slave as locked in an adversary relationship,
nbree portrayed abolitionists as "mediators, between the oppres-
r and the oppressed," arbitrators attempting to end a protracted
ur. Their purpose, wrote Embree, was not to encourage insurrec-
on, as slaveholders charged, but to avert violence by promoting
iancipation. Their efforts, Embree thought, would be regarded by

14. *Emancipator*, April 30, 1820, pp. 12, 13; October 31, 1820, p. 112.
15. *Annals of Congress*, 16th Cong., 1st Sess., 218.
16. *Emancipator*, September 30, 1820, p. 85.

slaves as conciliatory and thus would "appease" their "restless a dissatisfied disposition."[17]

Although predictions of slave violence of the sort that filled E bree's newspaper were almost as old as American slavery itself, th conspicuously surfaced in public prints for the first time only 1819 and 1820 during congressional debates over the admission Missouri. The Missouri issue brought slavery to public attenti and injected it into national politics as never before. Not even t long agitation preceding abolition of the slave trade in 1808 creat anything like the widespread public concern that accompanied t Missouri issue. All across the North, while Congress debated the fa of slavery in the new state, local meetings and antislavery so eties—and in some instances state legislatures—passed anti-M souri resolutions designed to register grass-roots disapproval of t further spread of slavery into the Louisiana Purchase.[18]

The political ambitions of out-of-favor New Englanders no dou helped precipitate the opposition and perhaps shaped congression debates on the issue, as southern critics then insisted. But whatev their own views on slavery may have been and whatever their m tives, congressmen representing certain districts in the Northea would have found it imprudent to ignore the diffused antisouthe and antislavery opinions that even then formed part of the thoug of many northern voters.

A slow, steady flow of antislavery tracts had appeared in rece years, most of them written by Quakers or evangelicals who h lived in or at least had visited slave states. These writings, fill with supposedly accurate information about slavery, had reach sympathetic clergymen and politicians as well as laymen and that way achieved a pyramidal effect on public opinion. Althou their influence cannot be measured, it seems likely that to them large part must be credited the generalized sense that slavery w wrong, that it was an outworn remnant of the barbaric past, a sy tem contrary to the genius of the new nation. However that may b it is evident that abolitionists had faith in the power of their wr ings to influence political decisions. Before antislavery petitio reached the Senate in March, 1818, someone placed a copy of Jo Kenrick's *Horrors of Slavery* on every senator's desk.[19] But explici

17. *Ibid.*, 87; October 31, 1820, p. 100.
18. The entire episode is treated in Glover Moore, *The Missouri Controver 1819–1821* (Lexington, Ky., 1953).
19. *Annals of Congress*, 15th Cong., 1st Sess., 237.

olitionist arguments such as Kenrick's—which unsympathetic
iders found easy to dismiss as fanatical—were not the only per-
isive force moving congressmen to question the wisdom of allow-
g slavery to spread into the West.

Statistics, themselves value-free and untouched by either poli-
s or moralism, further supported the view that in the national
erest slavery ought to be ended. By constitutional mandate, the
iited States government every ten years conducted a census and
due time made the results available as official public documents.
us in 1791, 1801, 1811, and again in 1821, the government pub-
hed the facts of population change. Federalists in particular, with
ir interest in the tangible—in banks and currency, in taxation, in
iff policy, in growth itself—found the information disclosed by
 census both fascinating and frightening, for the columns of num-
rs that filled its pages confirmed the racial imbalance to which
irmists had called attention, even in colonial days. Blacks in-
ased in the South at a rate considered highly dangerous to na-
nal safety. Slave population grew by 33 percent from 1800 to
10, the census showed, and by a further 29 percent in the next
cade.[20]

As early as 1806 Samuel Blodgett prepared a manual in which he
w from comparative statistics an antislavery lesson. Free states
reased in population and wealth more rapidly than slave states;
e labor was more productive than slave labor. The author pro-
led explicit antislavery instruction for persons interested in na-
nal well-being. The United States should encourage commerce
d "useful emigration," wrote Blodgett. "This we ought to do, to
ice our country immediately in a state unvulnerable to foreign
vaders."[21] But such a policy, his northern readers must have
own, the slave states were in no position to implement. Blodgett's
blication confirmed northern self-satisfaction and self-pride. To
rthern eyes, the South, doggedly tied to slavery, held back na-
nal progress, even endangered national security.

A few years later, after the 1810 census rendered Blodgett's work
t-of-date, Adam Seybert prepared yet another statistical abstract.
is also presented, but in still more striking form, the enumerable
licators of national growth. Seybert showed that in all indices of

20. U.S. Bureau of the Census, *Negro Population, 1790–1915* (Washington, D.C.,
 8), 26, 28, 29.
21. Samuel Blodgett, *Economica: A Statistical Manual for the United States of
erica* (Washington, D.C., 1806), 80–82.

progress but one, slave states lagged behind every other section
the country. Only in the increase of slave population did the Sou
outstrip the North.[22]

The alarming fact, made evident by publications such as the
was the large part of the total population made up of slaves and t
speed with which that part grew. When critics placed this inforn
tion alongside the then commonly held notions about blacks—the
propensity to violence, the danger they posed in wartime, their u
assimilability—the reader could hardly fail to conclude that in t
South's slave population the nation faced a severe and intensifyi
problem.

Not surprisingly, statistics delineating the expansion of slave
were turned to the support of antislavery arguments and progran
As early as 1804, Congress heard alarms over census revelatio
One-fifth of the nation's total population—one-half the populati
of some states—was enslaved, said Representative David Bai
"Their circumstances, their barbarism, their reflections, their hop
and fears, render them an enemy of the worst description." Ba
expanded upon his dread of the enslaved blacks. "If they are igr
rant, they are, however, susceptible of instruction, and capable
becoming proficient in the art of war." Not racial prejudice, as it
commonly understood, but fear was reflected in Bard's antislave
position.[23]

By the time the Missouri issue reached Congress in 1819, the s
tistics of population growth had become a staple in antislave
argument. Abolitionists recognized the census data as a resour
of peculiar power. Such facts were unanswerable. Numbers po
sessed an objectivity that could not be dismissed as easily as cou
the more familiar but disputed charges of the cruelty and sinfu
ness of slavery. However, antislavery reliance on the census ca
ried with it a troublesome corollary. The force of these statisti
depended for the most part on the assumption that blacks we
unassimilable, that they constituted, as Embree wrote in the Ema
cipator, an enemy nation within America, whose presence mea
constant struggle and peril.

Much in the recent experience of white Americans encourag
such conclusions. Memories of Saint-Domingue, Gabriel's consp

22. Adam Seybert, *Statistical Annals: Embracing Views of the Population, Co
merce, Navigation, Fisheries . . . of the United States of America . . .* (Philadelpl
1818), 24, 38, 53.
23. *Annals of Congress*, 8th Cong., 1st Sess., 995–96.

·y, and subsequent plots were not easily erased. Thus statistical ·guments, based as they often were on a particular analysis of ave temperament and inclination, served better to support the ·ogram of the American Colonization Society, which aimed to ansport blacks to Africa, than that of persons who advocated eir incorporation into American society. But despite the varied ;es to which they might be put, statistics long continued to bolster e antislavery argument. The Presbyterian O. P. Hoyt predicted 1827 that by 1880 the nation would contain four million more acks than whites. Throughout the 1820s Benjamin Lundy made e of similar population projections in his *Genius of Universal* ·nancipation, as did abolitionists in the 1830s and afterward, to pport the call to eliminate a problem that seemed to threaten the tional future.[24]

Related to the disquiet produced by population data was a fact of omentous political import, especially in the eyes of northern Fed- alists. Constitutional mandate linked both congressional repre- ntation and membership in the Electoral College to the size of the ave population, thereby adding to southern influence in setting tional policy. The three-fifths compromise, which made this pos- ble, was a festering grievance, particularly to New England poli- ians, who found in slavery the key to southern political power.[25]

All this could only strengthen the determination of restrictionists block the extension of slavery into Missouri. When Representa- e James Tallmadge of New York introduced his proposal to make issouri a free state and to ban slavery from the rest of the Louisi- a Purchase, southerners understandably fought back—to save eir political lives, if for no other reason. They detected in efforts close the West to slavery a grave challenge to their position in e Union. Restrictionists, it appeared, aimed to erect a western all beyond which southern institutions could not go. Southern aders found the probable effects of such containment intolerable— rpetual minority political status for the South and eventual ra- al conflict arising from confinement within narrow geographical unds of a rapidly growing black population. Less often mentioned

24. *Freedom's Journal*, May 11, 1827; *Genius of Universal Emancipation*, IV (No- mber, 1824), 17; Amos A. Phelps, *Lectures on Slavery and Its Remedy* (Boston, 1834), 9; John Greenleaf Whittier, *The Works of John Greenleaf Whittier* (New York, 1892), I, 71.

25. Kerber, *Federalists in Dissent*, 36–39; James M. Banner, Jr., *To the Hartford nvention: The Federalists and the Origins of Party Politics in Massachusetts, '98–1818* (New York, 1970), 101–104.

was the further likelihood that a ban on the South's territorial e
pansion would lead to decline in the price of slaves with conseque
financial loss to all who held such property.[26]

Southern spokesmen also found in the Missouri controversy a
immediate danger. The much-publicized congressional debate ov
slavery, they charged, would encourage slave resistance and pr
mote insurrection, for slaves could not be prevented from learni
that powerful men outside the South—their friends and potenti
allies—had called their servile status into question. The prospect
unmanageable slave restiveness led southerners to reassert their o
position to public discussion of slavery. Southern political pow
and manipulative skill, of the sort John C. Calhoun eventually ma
tered, might be sufficient to block national antislavery legislatio
but pacification of slaves made hopeful by congressional debat
would prove a more formidable task.

In addressing the Missouri issue, southern congressmen confin
their attention almost exclusively to the effect restriction wou
have on them, their slaves, their section. In the most precise sen
of the term, they reacted to the issue as provincials. Charles Pinc
ney of South Carolina stood alone among southern statesmen
placing the matter in spacious context. The senator looked beyor
the bounds of his own state and section to count the worth of slave
to the entire nation. America's prosperity and world position, Pinc
ney asserted, derived from the forced labor of blacks. Destroy sla
ery, and the financial and commercial structure of the United Stat
together with its international eminence, such as it was, also wou
be destroyed.[27]

Such a remarkable but wholly eccentric analysis of the America
economic system could not be accepted by northern congressme
who, in their own fashion, doubtless were as culture-bound as we
their southern colleagues. They ignored Pinckney's insights as we
as his conclusion. They refused to acknowledge the constructive ro
of slavery in American foreign and domestic trade and in northe
capital accumulation and their own section's involvement with
Instead they charged slavery with being a source of national wea

26. The discussion of slavery, which raised doubts about its future, was thoug
to lower slave prices. See Johnson, *Ante-Bellum North Carolina*, 564–65. In paral
concern, John Quincy Adams believed that criticism of the United States Ba
caused decline in the price of bank stock. John Quincy Adams and Lewis Cond
*Report of the Minority of the Committee on Manufactures, Submitted to the House
Representatives of the United States, February 28, 1833* (Boston, 1833), 6.

27. *Annals of Congress*, 16th Cong., 1st sess., 1313–15.

ess, an obstacle to continued progress, even a threat to the nation's existence.

In this way northern opponents of the admission of Missouri suceeded in identifying the restrictionist position with the national terest, while nearly all advocates of slavery continued to focus on urely sectional concerns. In the Missouri debates, nationalism and ntislavery became one. From that time forward, persons ambious for the continued growth of American power and having a rge vision of the nation's future indicted slavery as an obstacle ustrating national achievement. For the idealistic, slavery was a oral blot canceling out the virtues upon which greatness supposlly depends; for others, who imagined themselves realistic and ractical, it was a source of political and military weakness that ventually would prevent the United States from playing its desned large role in world affairs.

During the Missouri debates, Representative Tallmadge pictured r his colleagues the alternatives offered for their choice: a strong, osperous, influential nation without slavery or a weak, distracted ation if slavery continued its growth. According to his premise, avery divided and weakened society; social unity brought strength. aniel P. Cook, the youthful antislavery congressman from Illinois, ovided a still more graphic critique. Slavery, said Cook, "is callated to invite invasion, and no one will deny that it exposes the ate to domestic violence." His reminder of the Indian wars that companied the recent conflict with England carried an approprie warning: England "arrayed the savages against us" during the ar of 1812, and some future enemy also might arm the slaves.[28]

Cook's reference to the military menace inherent to a servile popuition embodied a theme restrictionists succeeded in tying explicy to the Missouri issue. They dwelt upon the opportunities for trigue slaves offered to external enemies. At first glance, the arment, though appropriate to an earlier time, now seemed out-ofate. Recent diplomatic triumphs brought slaveholders a greater egree of security than they ever had enjoyed before. As we have en, the purchase of Louisiana in 1803 pushed American boundaes well to the west of slave population. Shortly afterward, a series military adventures and diplomatic negotiations culminating in e Adams-Onis Treaty of 1819 dislodged the Spanish from all their ncient positions east of the Mississippi. By these means Americans

28. *Ibid.*, 15th Cong., 2nd Sess., 1206; 16th Cong., 1st Sess., 1111.

acquired undisputed control of the southern frontier, except for th
nagging presence of a number of Indian tribes, and these soc
would be removed west of the Mississippi. Thus a prime incitemer
to slave violence and an encouragement to would-be runaways ;
last was eliminated. By 1820, for the first time since slavery w;
introduced in the English colonies two centuries earlier, slavehol.
ers need feel no concern that foreign powers were in a position 1
endanger master-slave relations. But almost before southern whit
adjusted to their new freedom and prepared to exploit it, restri
tionists came forward to shake the complacency the new situatic
invited. Expansion of slavery into the trans-Mississippi West, an
slavery congressmen warned, would renew the danger that soutl
erners supposed diplomacy had eliminated forever.

Harrison Gray Otis, representative from Massachusetts, explaine
why this was so. He looked farther west than Missouri and to a di
tant future, when the vast Louisiana Purchase would be people
with slaves, its population at last reaching the western frontie
There in the far Southwest and on the Pacific coast, American settl
ment would collide with Spanish, English, and Russian interest
All the old rivalries that plagued Americans in the past would t
renewed, and with them, Otis warned, would come fresh dangers •
"intrigue and revolution." Although the entire nation might suff
from the resulting collisions, slaveholders would bear the chief bu
den, for once again, slaves would serve as willing instruments •
European hostility to the United States.[29]

But it was not European rivals alone who would threaten slave
as it followed its westward course. So volatile were slaves thougl
to be under every circumstance that the likelihood of a free-blac
population within the United States inciting slaves gave pause eve
to persons of antislavery reputation. It led Tallmadge, who was r
advocate of servile rebellion, to express strange inconsistencies i
policy. Although he was the author of slavery restriction, Tallmadg
announced his opposition to proposals to exclude slavery from Al
bama Territory, because "surrounded as it was by slaveholdir
states, and with only imaginary lines of division, the intercours
between slaves and free blacks would not be prevented and a *servi*
war might be the result."[30]

Slave rebellion was a specter neither friend nor foe of extendir
slavery to Missouri easily dismissed. Its stubborn presence becan

29. *Ibid.*, 16th Cong., 1st Sess., 254.
30. *Ibid.*, 15th Cong., 2nd Sess., 1203.

ident when congressmen of both persuasions addressed them-
lves to the "diffusion" argument, a defense of the right to extend
avery that owed its sole claim for consideration to fears of insur-
ction. In order to justify their expansionist program on other
ounds than self-interest, southerners urged its necessity as a
fety measure. Confinement of a growing slave population would
oduce pressures that at last would explode into violence. South-
n spokesmen thus accepted the restrictionists' prophecy of ulti-
ate slave revolt, but by advocating "diffusion," they turned the
ospect to their own advantage. Slaves might indeed rebel, they
greed, but only if restrictionists succeeded in their campaign to
onfine the black population behind artificial, politically designed
arriers.[31]
Let slavery be spread through new regions, and all predicted
angers would disappear. Slavery then would remain the institu-
on its defenders claimed it now was—gentle and humane and
aracterized by paternalistic relationships. Enjoying these advan-
ges, slaves would have no reason to become dissatisfied. Such dis-
untled slaves as there were would find collusion difficult, for they
ould be scattered so thinly that revolt would be hard to arrange
nd, if attempted, would easily be put down. Only if Congress con-
ned slavery to its present range and the black population grew in-
easingly dense, as census statistics indicated was its tendency,
ould severity and rigor out of necessity come to characterize it.
  Restriction would have other, equally disastrous results. Failure
spread slavery would make life for nonslaveholding southern
hites difficult and unpleasant. Many would decide to leave in or-
er to escape the region's ever-growing black population. Thus
ould the older South be further depleted of white population and
e section's already ominous racial imbalance be made still more
enacing. The Tallmadge Amendment, some warned, would result
the "negro-izing" of the South.[32]
  Although neither party to the contest had everything its own way,
e South achieved a significant victory in the Missouri Compro-
ise. Congress in 1820 agreed to admit Missouri as a slave state and
open the southern portion of the Louisiana Purchase to slavery.
hile the Missouri settlement plunged abolitionists into despair,
uthern leaders could take satisfaction from the result.[33] Yet their

31. *Ibid.*, 1276; 16th Cong., lst Sess., 1012, 1085.
32. *Ibid.*, 16th Cong., lst Sess., 315, 1532.
33. "Hell is about to enlarge her borders; and tyranny her domain," wrote Elihu
mbree in *Emancipator*, September 30, 1820, p. 89.

optimism was tempered by recognition of the dangers that the d
bates revealed, not only to the South's continued political influen
in the Union, but to the survival of the Union itself. The apprehe
sion felt in the wake of the compromise brought forth Jefferson
famous, oft-quoted admission that the controversy "like a fire b
in the night, awakened me and filled me with terror. I considered
at once the knell of the Union," a sentiment that we may suppo
was shared by others less given to eloquent statement.[34]

The issues raised in the debates did not soon disappear. In pa
ticular, the specter of black violence, made vivid by the congres
men's bold depictions, left sharp imprints on the consciousness ev
of persons who lived far from the probable scenes of terror. Perha
the controversy was responsible for staging apocalyptic visions ev
in a mind customarily so controlled as that of John Adams, wl
wrote in 1821: "Slavery in the Country I have seen hanging over
like a black cloud for half a century. If I were as drunk with enth
siasm as Swedenborg or Wesley, I might probably say I had se
Armies of Negroes marching and countermarching in the air, shi
ing in Armor. I have been so terrified with this phenomenon that
constantly said in former times to the Southern Gentlemen, I cann
comprehend this object: I must leave it to you."[35]

If thoughts of slavery could thus agitate an aged resident
Quincy, Massachusetts, who surely knew he was not likely ever
be confronted by angry black hordes, how much more severely mu
the composure of slave-state residents have been shaken by the co
centrated attention abolitionists and the United States Congre
had turned to the subject!

Insurrection was the abolitionists' aim, declared Senator Willia
Smith of South Carolina, even while he joined his colleague Philli
Barbour of Virginia in expressing confidence in the loyalty and d
cility of slaves. Not "one among twenty" slaves in South Carolir
could at that moment be incited to rebellion, said Smith, a calcul
tion perhaps not wholly reassuring to persons aware of the sma
and often obscure beginnings of revolution. But even loyal slave
the senator believed, could be contaminated by antislavery sent
ments of the sort so freely expressed in Congress during the Missou

34. Thomas Jefferson to John Holmes, April 22, 1820, in Paul Leicester Ford (ed
Writings of Thomas Jefferson, X, 157–58.
35. John Adams to Thomas Jefferson, February 3, 1821, in Lester J. Cappon (ed
*The Adams-Jefferson Letters: The Complete Correspondence Between Thomas Jeffersc
and Abigail and John Adams* (Chapel Hill, 1959), II, 571.

bates. Those ideas could not be depended upon to remain con-
ed within the halls of the capitol. Representative Edward Colston
 Virginia was much upset when he spied a black face among lis-
ners in the gallery. How far might the subversive ideas expressed
 congressional debate be spread by such agents? No doubt it was
is consideration that led Colston to accuse a New England con-
essman of endeavoring through antislavery speeches to "excite a
rvile war" and of being "no better than Arbuthnot or Arbruster
he British citizens executed in Spanish Florida in 1818 by General
ndrew Jackson], and deserves no better fate."³⁶

The fears expressed by southern congressmen were to be realized
rhaps earlier than they had imagined. Slaves commonly were
ought to grow more restive in the 1820s under influences emanat-
g from the North and, especially, from Washington. This percep-
on, recorded by white observers, depended upon connections that
ay in truth not have existed. The balkiness of slaves, if it did in
ct increase, perhaps arose from some source other than external
imulus. Yet southern alarm appeared not altogether unfounded,
r in South Carolina evidence soon appeared to suggest a tie be-
ween resistant blacks and northern antislavery activity. The great
ave conspiracy that rocked Charleston in the summer of 1822 ap-
rently owed part of its inspiration to the well-publicized congres-
onal debates over slavery in Missouri.

36. *Annals of Congress*, 16th Cong., 1st Sess., 267; 15th Cong., 2nd Sess., 1205.

7

❀❀❀❀❀❀❀❀❀❀❀❀❀❀❀❀❀❀❀❀❀❀❀❀❀❀

From Denmark Vesey to
Nat Turner

Up and down the southern coast in 1820, slaves struck the whi
population as being exceptionally hard to control. Reports from Vi
ginia, South Carolina, and Georgia told of mounting discontent. S
menacing did blacks appear that officials of all three states warne
Secretary of War John C. Calhoun to prepare for desperate sla\
attacks on federal military installations. In Virginia discontente
and belligerent slaves might be deluded enough, thought Governc
Thomas M. Randolph, to try to seize the federal arsenal near Ricl
mond. A moment's relaxation would encourage "that necessary co
sequence of a system of slavery, occasional Rebellion." The governc
doubted that full-scale revolt was near, yet he was unwilling "b
any omission . . . to provoke audacity, or even to excite hopes, whic
at the least must produce insubordination."[1]

Randolph agreed with conventional wisdom   hopes for freedo
made slaves harder to control and exaggerated the perpetual prol
lem of keeping them at work on the masters' terms. Recently, son
whites believed, the slaves' expectations had received encourag
ment from events beyond southern control. The Missouri debat
and abolitionist activity had led them to speculate, as at no tin

1. John C. Calhoun to James Bankhead, July 27, 1818, in Robert L. Meriwether
al. (eds.), *The Papers of John C. Calhoun* (Columbia, S.C., 1959–), II, 427; Decius Wa
worth to John C. Calhoun, January 15, 1820, *ibid.*, IV, 580; Thomas M. Randolph
John C. Calhoun, April 18, 1821, *ibid.*, VI, 57.

ce the Revolution, about the possibility of changing their condi-
n. Now these outside influences must be counteracted in order to
bilize slavery and forestall insurrection. Blacks must be taught
ain that their hopes were illusory and their would-be allies inef-
tual. Slave resistance must lose its political import.
To promote security, Randolph suggested removing locks and
yonets from the weapons stored near Richmond, thereby making
m useless to mutinous slaves who might manage to storm the
senal. Calhoun complained that on account of a recent congres-
nal cut in military appropriations the War Department could ill
ord the expense. Nevertheless he promised to find the money
mewhere, for "in a point so important nothing ought, if possible,
be left to hazard."[2]
f slaves appeared menacing in Virginia, their discontent in South
rolina seemed still more dangerous. As early as the summer of
18, reports reached Calhoun of "indications lately of turbulence"
Charleston. When, a few months later, anxieties among whites
creased, Calhoun ordered the federal arms and ammunition that
re stored in the city removed to the harbor and the greater pro-
tion of Fort Moultrie.[3]
The tightening of security in Charleston and elsewhere in the
board South helped relieve at least one source of apprehen-
n. With skill and a bit of luck, rebellious blacks might have cap-
red some lightly defended federal arsenal. Thus armed, they could
ve converted a local uprising into a formidable regional threat.
was this possibility that prompted Calhoun, after taking emer-
ncy measures, to establish policy designed to make sure nothing
the sort ever happened. Following reorganization of the army on
ne 1, 1821, he ordered one company of artillery deployed to each
senal in the slave states as surety that any attack by blacks would
repulsed.[4] This became standard practice, thus rendering suc-
ssful slave revolt all but impossible, however widespread unrest
ght be. With the arsenals virtually impregnable, no source of
ms in significant quantity was anywhere available to rebels. Fire-
ms would remain a monopoly in the hands of whites.
Southern governments always had tried to make sure that only
 white population had access to weapons. There had been sur-

2. John C. Calhoun to Thomas M. Randolph, April 30, 1821, ibid., VI, 84.
3. John C. Calhoun to James Bankhead, July 27, 1818, ibid., II, 427; Calhoun to
n Geddes, December 31, 1819, ibid., 529.
4. John C. Calhoun to Thomas M. Randolph, April 24, 1821, ibid., VI, 72.

prising exceptions, as in the days of free-and-easy relations in ear
South Carolina, when blacks served as armed militiamen.[5] B
this was a temporary aberration not to be repeated in later yea
Colonial and state governments required white militia members
supply themselves with arms, and every household was expected
be so equipped. In practice, however, purchase of weapons son
times exceeded the means of ordinary persons. Far more disconce
ing was the thought that in regions where white population w
sparse, even possession of a gun promised to be of little help
standing off an embodied mass of angry blacks.

A report from North Carolina in 1813 claimed that "the se
board in general has a scattered population of Whites—they poor
generally without arms & ammunition," and as late as 1831, Be
jamin Cabell wrote from Danville, Virginia, to express his doub
"whether upon an emergency we could turn out 20 efficient pieces.
Such deficiencies may have been exceptional, yet it remains tr
that the disparity in strength between whites and blacks during t
first two or three decades after 1800 was less than it came to be
later years. In parts of the South early in the century, initial adva
tage in a test of power conceivably would lie with blacks on accou
of their superior numbers, a possibility both critics and defende
of slavery went to great lengths to point out. Yet in any such raci
clash the blacks' numerical advantage would disappear as soon
the white militia could be mobilized. Accordingly, in the first yea
of the new century, every slave state made special exertions
supply itself with efficient, well-equipped militia units, and inc
viduals able to afford the cost armed themselves and cultivat
marksmanship.[7]

After American independence the states and national governme
established armories, where weapons and ammunition were stor

5. Clarence L. Ver Steeg, *Origins of a Southern Mosaic: Studies of Early Carol
and Georgia* (Athens, Ga., 1975), 105–106.

6. Christopher Dooley *et al.* to Governor William Hawkins, January 23, 1813,
Governors' Papers, North Carolina Division of Archives and History; Benjamin Ca
ell to John Floyd, September 20, 1831, in Executive Papers, Virginia State Libra
See also Benjamin Oliver to James Monroe, September 23, 1800, and Thomas Ne
ton to James Monroe, December 29, 1800, both in Executive Papers, Virginia St
Library.

7. [Joseph Blunt], *An Examination of the Expediency and Constitutionality of P
hibiting Slavery in the State of Missouri* (New York, 1819), 11–12; Jacob Read
Charles Pinckney, June 10, 1807, in Charles Pinckney Papers; [Paulding], *Letters fr
the South*, II, 247; James Semple to Lieutenant Alexander McRae, May 6, 1808,
Executive Papers, Virginia State Library.

ady for use against foes, either foreign or domestic. The arsenal at
ayetteville, North Carolina, appears to have been established spe-
fically as a resource against insurrection. By this means, the con-
st between slaves and masters became a most unequal one. How-
er, this fact did not altogether reassure the white population,
ho sometimes became unnerved by the prospect that these vital
vernment stores, meant for their own defense, might fall into
e hands of slaves, as indeed Gabriel in 1800 was said to have
tended.[8]
In Charleston in 1822, the free black Denmark Vesey, plotting re-
ellion, showed himself fully aware of the whites' superior fire-
ower as he developed plans for arming his coconspirators. The par-
cipants in Vesey's scheme were enterprising and industrious, but
ere as unsuccessful as Gabriel in overcoming their lack of weap-
s. Vesey's men, witnesses reported, made or secured 300 daggers
d some 250 picks and bayonets (authorities never located any of
ese, a striking fact that has encouraged some historians to doubt
eir existence and, consequently, to doubt the reality of the plot
elf). They also systematically noted the location of firearms in
res and houses. These they planned to seize at the start of the
volt. But the advantage thus gained was certain to be only tem-
rary. Vesey's preparations, resourceful though they were, could
ve counted for little against the white militia and the large store
firearms cached by the United States government—as Calhoun
cently had directed—at Fort Moultrie.[9]
There were still other reasons, if more were needed, for doubt-
g the possibility of successful rebellion in antebellum years. The
evalence of strong slave families created attachments that must
ve led to second thoughts on the part of many would-be rebels.
reign enemies, once a source of encouragement and potential
d for slave revolt, had practically disappeared. Although Saint-
mingue still provided inspiration to slaves—major inspiration

8. Lemmon, *Frustrated Patriots*, 196; Gerald W. Mullin, *Flight and Rebellion*,
2–203.
9. Richard C. Wade, "The Vesey Plot: A Reconsideration," *Journal of Southern His-*
y, XXX (1964), 154–55. Some slaves understood their disadvantage: Report of In-
view with Slaves in Nottoway Jail, May 15, 1802, Lewis' statement, 1802, Bob's
position in trial of Frank and Sancho in Halifax County, April 23, 1802, all in
lave Insurrection Folder," Executive Papers, Virginia State Library; slave testi-
ny in "Criminal Action Concerning the 1831 Insurrection of Slaves," in Onslow
unty Miscellaneous Records, North Carolina Division of Archives and History, Ra-
gh. For similar views in a much earlier time, see Horsmanden, *New York Con-*
racy, 244–45.

for Vesey and his followers—its distance from the American coa
and its own distracted condition made intervention unlikely. Aft
1815, the year that saw the generation-long European wars en
the United States seemed unlikely to be drawn into foreign confli
or to face invasion. Slaves could no longer hope for aid from th
quarter. By 1819, except for the sparsely settled Spanish state
Texas, all foreign territories touching upon the slave states ha
come under the United States flag. The United States Army had i
flicted costly defeats on the Indians during the War of 1812, ar
most of the remaining southern tribes, which once might have c
fered support to slave resistance, were moved west of the Missi
sippi River in the 1830s. Beginning shortly afterward, the Sen
noles in Florida, whose troublesome habit it was to harbor fugitive
were subjected by the United States Army to a long and bloody w
of attrition.

The only remaining sources of encouragement and aid to sla
resistance were whites and free blacks living within the Unite
States itself. This was a danger nineteenth-century slaveowne
could not dismiss or take lightly. Abolitionists and antisouthe
congressmen already exerted a disruptive effect on master-slave r
lations, and their activities were unlikely to diminish. Evidence a
peared to suggest in the Vesey plot, as it had on earlier occasion
that blacks knew their status was at issue in northern-based p
litical maneuvers and reform movements and that they might l
tempted to act in response to them. To white southerners the pc
sibility of their doing so, instead of subsiding, appeared to grow ev
more menacing, as abolitionists intensified their merciless conder
nations of the slaveholding South.

Southern whites dwelt upon the dangers that confronted the
rather than on their own armed strength and the blacks' relati
weakness and isolation. Their failure to view events in perspecti
helps account for the thunderbolt effects of the exposure in M;
1822, of Denmark Vesey's plot to seize Charleston. Although such ;
event would have brought distress at any time, its impact doul
less was magnified because it so nearly coincided with the marsh;
ing of antislavery, antisouthern political forces during the Missou
controversy.

Vesey's scheme did not take Charleston residents altogether I
surprise. For many months before the day the slave Devany Priole;
revealed the first inkling of a planned uprising, abundant sig
pointed to the blacks' discontent. Much of the unrest resulted fro

cent official suppression of the African Methodist church, a mea-
ure adopted after city authorities decided that religious meetings
ad become seedbeds of sedition. In June, 1818, legal action was
ken against the black ministers. Four were given the choice of
aving the state or being imprisoned. These measures left blacks
the city, including Vesey, much aggrieved, for the church had
rved as a treasured center of spiritual and social life and provided
rare source of esteem for the class leaders, the men responsible for
hurch activities.[10] The ensuing resentment grew so ominous that,
s we have seen, authorities advised the War Department to take
mergency precautions.

These measures did not prevent Charleston blacks—slave and
ee—from continuing to discuss among themselves means for reme-
ying their grievances. For a number of reasons, they thought their
hances of doing so were good. Like other persons in South Caro-
na, Vesey was familiar with the tumultuous history of Saint-
omingue, a colony he had visited as a youth, and imagined its
overnment would support black revolt on the mainland. Further,
ublic discussions of slavery were common enough by the 1820s for
heir general import to reach those from whom such information
deally would be kept hidden. Even rural areas far more isolated
han Charleston did not remain untouched by subversive notions.
n Edgecombe County, North Carolina, for example, black preachers
ere reported to have convinced their congregations that "the na-
ional government had set them free . . . and that they were being
njustly held in servitude."[11] Wherever that kind of misinformation
irculated, whether in rural North Carolina or in Charleston, the
esult was likely to be unrest and reluctance to fulfill the role of
lave. Knowledge that the masters' authority had been called into
uestion and that the white population was divided in its support
f slavery encouraged the impression that bondage was temporary
nd early deliverance a possibility.

Vesey had read some of the Missouri debates, especially the anti-

---

10. Marina Wikramanayake, *A World in Shadow: The Free Black in Antebellum
South Carolina* (Columbia, S.C., 1973), 125–28. For general accounts of the Vesey
onspiracy, see *ibid.*, 133–53; John Lofton, *Insurrection in South Carolina: The Tur-
ulent World of Denmark Vesey* (Yellow Springs, Ohio, 1964); and William W. Freeh-
ing, "Denmark Vesey's Peculiar Reality," in Robert H. Abzug and Stephen E. Maizlish
eds.), *New Perspectives on Race and Slavery in America: Essays in Honor of Kenneth
M. Stampp* (Lexington, Ky., 1986), 25–47.

11. Johnson, *Ante-Bellum North Carolina*, 525; Aptheker, *American Negro Slave
Revolts*, 81.

slavery speech delivered by Rufus King, and was said also to ha
owned, even earlier, an antislavery pamphlet—exactly which or
never was ascertained. Joel R. Poinsett may not have been alt
gether mistaken when he wrote from Charleston in the wake
Vesey's conspiracy that the "discussion of the Missouri questic
at Washington, among other evils, produced this plot. It was co
sidered by this unfortunate and half instructed people as one
emancipation."[12]

Unfolding events in Charleston in the summer of 1822 appeare
to confirm some of the white South's deepest suspicions—Sain
Domingue continued to inspire American blacks, and discussion
slavery, either by Congress or by abolitionists, encouraged expect:
tions of freedom. Evangelical religion, it appeared, also operated
a powerful influence among Charleston blacks. Vesey himself wa
an avid reader of the Bible. For years he had served as an inform:
religious teacher, pointing out to others scriptural passages that h
interpreted as condemning slavery and promising deliverance. H
thus harnessed to his cause the religious spirit that missionaries
the evangelical churches had fostered among blacks. Vesey's plar
also gained the support of Gullah Jack, a sorcerer in whose gr
tesque and misshapen person lingered remnants of African religiou
belief that appealed to those plantation slaves who had assimilate
fewer elements of Christianity than had blacks in Charleston.[13]

Among the myriad influences that were suspected of embolder
ing slaves were the many outsiders—northerners, foreigners, trar
sients—whose business or whim happened to bring them to th
city. During the trials of the Vesey conspirators, a witness testifie
that though a Scottish sailor "had a white face he was a negro i
heart." A German peddler reputedly sympathized with blacks, an
a stranger named Andrew S. Rhodes had been heard to defend th
right of slaves "to fight for their liberty." The court suspected tha
this short list did not come close to identifying all the pro-black
who had infiltrated Charleston.[14] The voicing of such suspicions re
vealed once again the slaveholders' awareness that they lived in
world full of elements uncommitted, even hostile, to their systen
and that these might someday coalesce and overwhelm them.

12. Joel R. Poinsett to James Monroe, August 13, 1822, in James Monroe Paper:
13. Gerald W. Mullin, "Religion, Acculturation, and American Negro Slave Rebel
lions: Gabriel's Insurrection," in John H. Bracey, Jr., August Meier, and Elliott Ruc
wick (eds.), *American Slavery: The Question of Resistance* (Belmont, Calif., 1971), 16C
John Oliver Killens (ed.), *The Trial Record of Denmark Vesey* (Boston, 1970), 61, 64.
14. Killens (ed.), *Trial Record*, 148–49, 152–53.

But that day had not yet come. The conspirators' zeal and moti-
ation did not exceed the whites' determination to crush them. After
esey's plan was exposed by a slave informer, much as Gabriel's had
een a generation earlier, Charleston authorities set about to prove
 blacks as well as to anxious whites that the white population re-
ained solidly in control of the city and were united in resolve. A
ourt investigated the conspiracy in all its ramifications and traced
to its furthest origins. Authorities arrested 131 blacks and finally
onvicted 49. Thirty-seven of these, including Vesey and Gullah
ack, were hanged. The court spared the remaining 12 on condition
eir owners send them out of the state. The state legislature freed
evany Prioleau for having exposed the conspiracy and granted him
lifetime pension.

By such means, blacks learned again, as white Charlestonians in-
ended, that every participant in a plan for revolt, every person re-
otely implicated with discussion of the right to freedom signed his
wn death warrant. Misguided masters might be indulgent and for-
iving, but the state would be ruthless in dealing with black rebels.
his was powerful deterrent indeed, but not even this lesson could
bsolutely assure that slaves elsewhere would refrain from develop-
g similar plans, nor could it guarantee their quiet acceptance of
avery. Resistance was certain to continue, and its tie to political
evelopments and to social change always remained a possibility.

Slave society, like every other, contained its portion of desperate
ersons willing to act in disregard of personal risk. Further, and
erhaps in the long run equally troublesome to slaveowners, noth-
g could altogether stamp out the slaves' inclination to resist au-
hority in ways short of coordinated rebellion. External influences
ontinued to reinforce slave recalcitrance. One of the strongest
orces operating against slave docility was the persistent agitation
f white critics. In the 1820s, as politicians and abolitionists contin-
ed to debate the legitimacy of slavery, resistance might be ex-
ected to become still more difficult to contain.

While slaveowners could do little to eliminate this irritant at its
orthern source, they could undertake to lessen its impact on slaves.
ne means of achieving at least the outward appearance of servility
and realistically this was the most that could be hoped for) was to
eep slaves under constant surveillance and to punish deviance
henever it appeared. Following Vesey's conspiracy, patrols, an
ld device designed to control and intimidate blacks, were made
ore efficient. Harsh laws strictly enforced were intended to pre-
ent unauthorized slave assembly and slave movement off the plan-

tations, the instruction of slaves to read, their unsupervised instruction in religion, slave contacts with northern subversives, and the
circulation of seditious literature. Some twenty years earlier, a
northerner had provided the rationale for such restrictive measures:
"Every thing which tends to increase their knowledge of natural
rights, of men and things, or that affords them an opportunity of
associating, acquiring, and communicating sentiments, and of establishing a chain or line of intelligence, must increase your hazard
because it increases their means of effecting their object."[15] Constant vigilance, supplemented by ruthless suppression of the slight-
est sign of black unrest, discouraged even minor forms of resistance
though it could not prevent them.

Although the goal of perfect tranquillity was impossible to attain,
repression became thorough enough to bring perceptible change in
slave life. Unrestricted movement through the countryside became
more difficult than it once had been. Increasingly rare were the easy
social gatherings that had been a relieving feature of slavery in the
eighteenth century and that had so clearly facilitated Gabriel in developing his conspiracy. The slaves' religious meetings—a source of
racial cohesiveness and inspiration—came under the scrutiny of
whites and, as we have seen, for a time virtually were abolished in
Charleston. Thereby an important element of independence was lost
to the city's slaves, and the continued development of autonomous
black culture was impeded.

Relations between blacks and whites were altered in the 1820s as
well. Nonslaveholding whites in earlier days sometimes formed
easy, friendly relationships with blacks. These never entirely ceased,
but as slavery faced new domestic threats, such associations increasingly became furtive and exceptional, for those who formed
them risked being viewed with suspicion and being treated con-
temptuously.[16]

But despite these valiant efforts in the 1820s to protect slavery, its
subtle undermining continued, and white southerners found themselves nearly powerless to halt the process. Subversive influences
continued to work upon the black population in spite of all countervailing efforts. Ordinarily slaves learned of antislavery political developments at Washington or in the North only through chance re-

15. *American State Papers, Class VII: Post Office Department*, 27.
16. Catterall (ed.), *Judicial Cases*, I, 319; II, 319–30, 362, 419; *State v. Jacob Boyce*,
Superior Court of Law, Spring Term, 1847, in Perquimans County Slave Papers,
1759–1864, North Carolina Division of Archives and History, Raleigh.

arks by whites. But on rare occasions, especially in the upper
uth, they were exposed directly to antislavery teachings. In Aust, 1818, the Reverend Jacob Gruber, presiding Methodist elder
om Carlisle, Pennsylvania, preached at a camp meeting in Mary-
nd. Some three thousand whites and four hundred blacks, many
them slaves, attended the service. For most preachers the pres-
ce of blacks would have signaled discretion, but not for Gruber,
no only a short time earlier had been pastor of a black church in
altimore. To the outrage of whites, Gruber presented the camp
eeting with an antislavery sermon. Slavery, he told the biracial
ngregation, contradicted the Declaration of Independence and
less modified would lead to insurrection and racial war. The way
aves interpreted Gruber's remarks is nowhere recorded, but his
essage and the text from which he preached, "Righteousness ex-
eth a nation; but sin is a reproach to any people" (Prov. 14.34),
uld hardly have been lost even on untutored listeners.[17]

Gruber's camp meeting sermon was a highly exceptional event.
obably few southern blacks ever experienced such frank antislav-
y indoctrination. But its repercussion surely did not end with the
ur hundred who attended his service. It was not fanciful to sup-
se that Gruber's preaching had geometrical effect extending well
yond the locality where it took place, for the blacks who heard
m could not be counted on to keep the experience to themselves.
ne sentiments Gruber expressed that day could be expected to
read among the slave population in ever-widening circles.

Whites generally succeeded in shielding slaves from direct ex-
osure to antislavery sentiments of the sort voiced by indiscreet
ethodist preachers, but they failed to do the same for free blacks.
pecially in Maryland and Virginia, such persons enjoyed ready
cess to abolitionist thought. Throughout the 1820s, Benjamin
undy's journal, the *Genius of Universal Emancipation*, with its
arsh condemnation of slavery and slaveholding society, was pa-
onized by free blacks in the upper South as well as those in the
orth. While they lived in Baltimore in the late 1820s, both Lundy
nd his coeditor William Lloyd Garrison associated with members
 the free-black community, whom they counted among the most

17. William P. Strickland, *The Life of Jacob Gruber* (New York, 1860), 105–109,
0–41; Donald G. Mathews, *The Methodists and Slavery: A Chapter in American Mo-
lity, 1780–1845* (Princeton, N.J., 1965), 35–36; John B. Boles, "Tension in a Slave
ociety: The Trial of the Reverend Jacob Gruber," *Southern Studies*, XVIII (1979),
9–97.

loyal of their supporters. *Freedom's Journal*, the short-lived new paper edited in New York in the late 1820s by Samuel Cornish an John Russworm, also circulated among blacks in Virginia an Maryland, thereby carrying into slave country its message urgi black uplift and resistance to slavery.[18] It is impossible to suppo that the information contained in these journals and the hopes an expectations they inspired among blacks who were free remaine unshared with blacks still enslaved.

An event of particular interest to the southern free-black com munity in the 1820s occurred in New York, when the state legisl ture completed the emancipation process it had started at the en of the preceding century. On July 4, 1827, all remaining slaves the state were set free. The occasion assumed significance exten ing well beyond New York, for it came at a time of sectional tensi and growing awareness of racial issues by whites and of heightene anticipations by slaves. Southern free blacks welcomed the Ne York emancipation as a prophetic event. On the auspicious day, t Friendship Society of Baltimore, a black fraternity, held a dinner celebrate the occasion. The members drank toasts to John Jay, t New York advocate of emancipation; to Elisha Tyson, a renowne Quaker abolitionist in Maryland; and to *Freedom's Journal* and t *Genius of Universal Emancipation*. On the same day, blacks in Fre ericksburg, Virginia, assembled to toast *Freedom's Journal* and the own state: "May Virginia, and her sister slave states, show to t people of Colour on the 4th of July 1828, that they have approved the example set them by the legislature of New York." In July, 182 blacks in Richmond commemorated the New York accomplishmen once more.[19]

These occasions allowed blacks in the upper South, responding abolitionist influence from the North, to take antislavery stand The influence was not likely to end with them, for free blacks cou not be prevented altogether from associating with slaves. On th account, southern whites dreaded free blacks as a threat to slaver a subversive force that must be closely watched. Nevertheless, was slaves, not free blacks, who had the opportunity to carry an slavery impressions throughout the South. Maryland and Virgini the southern states where antislavery influences were stronges

18. Dillon, *Benjamin Lundy*, 89, 99, 145; *Freedom's Journal*, July 13 and 20, 182
19. *Freedom's Journal*, July 13 and 20, 1827; "At a Public Dinner Held by the Fr Colored People of Richmond, July 4, 1829," in American Colonization Society Pape Manuscripts Division, Library of Congress.

;o were the states that in the 1820s supplied many of the slaves
10 cultivated the new cotton plantations of the Gulf states. Thus
:re widely sowed among the South's black population the aboli-
nist and evangelical convictions that whites exercised usurped
wer, that slavery was wrong, and that someday the wrong would
 made right. These same slaves had the greatest opportunity to
1rn that the white population was far from united in support of
1very.
Antislavery influences conveyed a message of hope rather than of
spair. They counseled slaves to be patient for a while longer until
e combination of circumstances that already had brought deliv-
ance to blacks in the North worked the same release for them. A
ntinued pacific reading of the abolitionist message would depend
1ally, however, on evidence of liberal trends within the South that
1uld indicate movement toward freedom. Such evidence, always
ant, became increasingly hard to detect.
Persons of authority in the South in the 1820s seldom expressed
1ubts about the legitimacy of slavery. By that time, slaveholders
1d progressed far toward establishing dominance over the region.
though acquiescence in their control never was total and did not
tend to equal degree through all geographic areas, the slavehold-
s' position was enhanced early in the new century when a portion
 the disaffected and potentially disaffected whites migrated to new
ntiers, often to those north of the Ohio River. Most of the dissi-
nts who chose to remain either harbored their opinions in silence
 expressed them where few in the South could hear.[20] Seldom in
tebellum years did any come forward publicly to disclose resent-
ents. But in Virginia, especially, there were notable exceptions.
Part of the basis for discord became apparent in the late 1820s. At
at time nonslaveholders in Virginia's western counties opened a
w chapter in their long political struggle for enlarged represen-
tion in the General Assembly. Insofar as slavery entered the dis-
1te, it was from considerations of politics rather than philan-
ropy. Disaffected westerners saw slaves more as symbols of the
1equal power wielded by eastern planters than as objects of hu-
anitarianism. In July, 1829, a petition from residents of Augusta

20. *Annals of Congress*, 16th Cong., lst Sess., 1354; John Spencer Bassett, *Slavery
 the State of North Carolina* (Baltimore, 1899), 98; *Niles' Weekly Register*, XXXVI
1ly 25, 1829), 345, 357; Dillon, *Benjamin Lundy*, 108–109; William T. Allan in *Lib-
ator*, August 25, 1843; Avery O. Craven, *Coming of the Civil War*, 95; Barnhart,
ources of Southern Migration," 49–62.

County called for emancipation, less because slavery was unju
than because they found it harmful to white society. But ev
though few western Virginians manifested much sympathy for t
rights and aspirations of blacks, the bitterness that characteriz
the intersectional contest within the state gave slaveowners pau:
for by skilled manipulation sectional antagonisms might turn we
ern farmers toward support of emancipation projects.[21]

Discord within Virginia took forms other than sectional rival
While Virginians west of the Blue Ridge Mountains were calling f
legislative reapportionment, small farmers and mechanics in ea
ern counties demanded extension of the suffrage. Neither these a
tagonisms nor their antislavery implications were new. Some fifte
years earlier, "Mr. Richardson" had promised "something warml
that if English armies invaded Virginia, as then seemed likely, "
would volunteer his services . . . at the hazard of all he possesse
but if the Negroes were to rise in an insurrection and destroy the
masters, he would not turn out and risk his life for any set of m
that would deprive him of his just right." Likewise, the presence
blacks—the property of well-to-do men—and the crimes they som
times committed awakened in poorer whites a sense of alienatie
and powerlessness that might nourish resentment toward slav
owners as well as toward slaves. A petition opposing leniency for
slave accused of molesting a poor white woman in Loudon Coun
illustrates the process. The document called attention to the da
gers to be expected from slaves—a familiar point—but it also r
vealed a further threat to slaveholders' dominance: the disaffectie
of the lowly. If the court let the accused slave off easily, said t
petitioners, "there is no telling where crime is to end among th
class. . . . The community will not be safe from their outrages; ar
especially females in the humble walks of life, who have not throv
around them the protection of wealth and of influential friends—\
claim to be as human as the mass of folks."[22]

The petitioners' unintended revelation of festering social ranc
in eastern Virginia may well have given state authorities pause, f
they could not fail to know that wherever slaves lived, white so
darity was essential to maintain their subjugation. Slaveowners i
curred risks when they neglected to give adequate attention to t
concerns of lesser members of society. Despite its brutality, slave
was a fragile institution depending for its continuance on comm

21. *Niles' Weekly Register*, XXXVI (July 25, 1829), 356–57.
22. Johnston, *Race Relations*, 99–100; J. N. Rose *et al.* to the Governor, July 1
1831, in Executive Papers, Virginia State Library.

y support. Inducements to unity among whites undoubtedly were
ong. Perhaps racial interests could bridge all schisms, but no one
t had measured the cohesive power of race or found the point at
ich white solidarity would break.

Eastern planters were foolhardy when they delayed granting all
ite males equal participation in political affairs. The new south-
stern states, in contrast, moved quickly to establish full white
inhood suffrage and equal representation. These measures har-
onized with democratic trends in the country at large, but they
so served the peculiar interests of slaveholders. Fully incorporat-
ᵤ all white males into the body politic reduced the potential for
ngerous social cleavage. Planters of eastern Virginia begrudged
ᵉ necessity to make political concessions to disfranchised and un-
rrepresented whites in their state, but they, too, found it neces-
ry to set aside their objections in the interest of welding the white
pulation into a solid whole.

A delegate to the Virginia constitutional convention in 1829 ex-
ained why this was so: "The time is not far distant when not only
rginia, but all the southern states, must be essentially military,
d will have military governments. . . . We are going to such a state
fast as time can move. The youth will be taught not only in the
ts and sciences, but they will be trained in arms." That policy
uld be required, he explained, in order to meet forthcoming chal-
ges, either internally from slaves or externally from the North.
the looming emergency, the state would need to call forth "every
e white human being and to unite them in the same common
erest and government."²³ When all are needed for military serv-
, all must be admitted to political privilege. The ancient Athen-
s had known as much.

Aside from such prophecy, some read into the convention's delib-
ation grand designs that, if present at all, were not to be achieved.
e mildly antislavery editor Hezekiah Niles of Baltimore believed
e convention's effects would reverberate throughout the South
d lead to the eventual end of slavery in the entire section. "The
eatest question before the Virginia convention," he wrote, "is the
rpetual duration of slavery or the increase of a generous and free
ite population."²⁴ As Virginia went, so would go the South. At
ke was the future of slavery itself.

Niles exaggerated. The momentous implications he saw in the

23. Charles Henry Ambler, *Sectionalism in Virginia from 1776 to 1861* (Chicago,
0), 161.
24. *Niles' Weekly Register*, XXXVII (October 31, 1829), 145.

debates were not there, for slavery itself was not openly at iss
Instead, deliberation centered on the basis of representation a
suffrage in Virginia. Should property remain the significant det
minant for both? But since "property" included slaves, slavery
came a legitimate topic for discussion both in the convention a
outside it, provoking alarm similar to that aroused a decade earl
during the Missouri debates. To voice any doubt at all about sou
ern institutions, some believed, was to take the first step towa
destroying them. The editor of the Charleston *Mercury* pointed c
the danger of Virginia's public examination of slavery. Such sc
tiny gave false encouragement to slaves; it also prompted northe
meddlers to enlarge their efforts. "Already do the advocates of at
lition rejoice even at the agitation of the subject and confiden
predict the day of triumph," wrote the editor.[25]

Slaves became more restive, whites believed, as the date for t
convention drew near. "We have lately been seriously alarmee
reported Oliver Cross. But then he added, as though resigned
the fact, "We are always more or less alarmed." As owners fear
slaves themselves followed the developing controversy, gatheri
from it hope where little hope was warranted. In Mathews Coun
slaves supposed that the election for the convention had liberat
them, though their masters tried to conceal this fact, and that
would receive "free papers" on August 1. Some, it was said, h
made up their minds to revolt if the papers were withheld.[26] E
dence of growing antiplanter sentiment among portions of the wh
population gave to slave unrest—a persistent feature of plantati
life—greater than usual purposiveness. Resistance now signifi
more than merely individualized opposition to the slave's o
condition; it had found an apparently attainable goal that in t
immediate past neither master nor slave could have formulat
Cleavage within white society had strengthened the slaves' positic
Convening of the constitutional convention suggested for the fi
time since the 1780s that emancipation in Virginia was a distir
possibility rather than a utopian goal.

Much evidence in the summer and fall of 1829 pointed to bc
increasing slave unrest and corresponding concern among whi
that the unrest could not be contained. At the end of the year, t

25. Ambler, *Sectionalism*, 146.
26. Oliver Cross to Garrett M. Quarles, September 3, 1829, in Executive Pape
Virginia State Library; Aptheker, *American Negro Slave Revolts*, 82; Colonel Tompk
to William Giles, July 18, 1829, in Executive Papers, Virginia State Library.

vernor of Virginia noted in his annual message that a "spirit of
satisfaction and insubordination was manifested by the slaves
different parts of the country from . . . [Richmond] to the sea-
ard."[27] From Accomac County came a particularly startling re-
rt. Slaves there had undertaken a mass exodus to New York and
nnsylvania. Some went "off in gangs and armed, bidding defiance
the citizens," while others—maroons—took refuge on islands in
esapeake Bay and fought off would-be captors.[28]
New incitement from the North deepened anxiety. On September
, 1828, in Boston, David Walker finished composing a pamphlet
dressed to his fellow blacks and sent it to the printer. *Walker's
peal, in Four Articles Together with a Preamble to the Coloured Citi-
1s of the World, but in Particular, and Very Expressly to Those of the
1ited States of America* was no ordinary antislavery tract nor was
author a typical abolitionist. Walker, a North Carolina–born free
1ck, had lived in Charleston at the time the city's black population
thed with the discontent that Denmark Vesey would mobilize for
volt. Sometime in the mid-1820s, sharing the anger of other black
utherners and acquainted with the arguments and aspirations of
ch revolutionaries as Vesey, he arrived in Boston.[29] There, while
1king his living by dealing in used clothes, he devoted himself to
iting for *Freedom's Journal* and furthering organization of the
y's blacks. But as the title of his pamphlet suggests, his concerns
tended well beyond the limits of Boston. *Walker's Appeal* spoke to
race rather than to a class or community. It called on colored
ople everywhere to unite in action to end their subjugation.
acks should rely on themselves to restore their rights and not wait
whites to extend rights to them. Instead of cringing in humility,
1cks should radiate pride; instead of submission, they should defy
who would oppress and exploit them.
Walker understood that in strict sense no people could be kept

27. Theodore M. Whitfield, *Slavery Agitation in Virginia, 1829–1832* (Baltimore,
0), 54; Benjamin Brand to R. R. Gurley, August 18, 1829, in American Coloniza-
n Society Papers. For insurrectionary alarms in North and South Carolina and
orgia, see Thomas P. Hunt to R. R. Gurley, September 3, 1829, Francis Kinlock to
R. Gurley, January 19, 1830, and Samuel K. Talmadge to R. R. Gurley, May 29,
9, all *ibid.*
28. Colonel Joyner *et al.* to the Governor, August 13, 1829, in Executive Papers,
ginia State Library.
29. Donald M. Jacobs, "David Walker, Boston Race Leader, 1825–1830," *Essex
titute Historical Collections*, CVII (January, 1971), 94–107. Peter Hinks generously
owed me to read chapters of his manuscript study of David Walker, in which he
s forth important new evidence for the Walker-Vesey connection.

enslaved without their own consent. That consent, he insisted, mu
be withdrawn. Walker did not overtly counsel race war, though t
militant posture he advised blacks to assume seemed calculated
invite retaliatory violence. Blacks, he implied, would be justified
destroying their tormentors, and they were quite competent to t
task. "I do declare," he wrote, "that one good black can put to dea
six white men."[30]

The boast had a long tradition in Walker's home state. During
insurrectionary alarm in Bertie County, North Carolina, in 18(
Mrs. Dwyer's Plato was heard to declare that "the negroes were
much stronger than the white people that one black would be
match for two or three whites." Plato's notion persisted. In 183 |
planter in Hertford County, just to the north of Bertie, complain
that he had lost control of his labor force. Nothing he did cou
persuade them of their weakness. They had repudiated the idea th
was essential to servility: "By reason or calculation, their min
cannot be convinced of the great disparity between them and t
whites."[31] David Walker's sentiments were those of Plato and t
Hertford County slaves. His pamphlet was designed to persua
blacks to believe in an idea essential to successful resistance—th
in no respect, martial capacity not excepted, need they feel in a
way inferior to their white oppressors. But on account of the gro
ing armed strength of the whites, Walker's advice would have be
more realistic had it been given in 1800 rather than in 1828.

Before the year ended, *Walker's Appeal* came into the hands of fr
blacks in Savannah. Shortly afterward, authorities discovered cc
ies in other cities up and down the coast and even as far from Bost
as New Orleans. To distribute his pamphlet, Walker had employ
his intimate knowledge of the communication network command
by black southerners and northern seamen, black and white, w
penetrated southern harbors. The pamphlet soon went into a seco
edition and then a third, as it circulated among northern blacks a
in slave country.[32]

Such widespread distribution could not have been unorganize
Evidently Walker, or someone acting for him, had set into operati

30. Herbert Aptheker, *"One Continual Cry": David Walker's "Appeal to the Colo
Citizens of the World," 1829–1830, Its Setting, and Its Meaning* (New York, 1965),
31. Bertie County Slave Papers, 1800–1805, North Carolina Division of Archi
and History, Raleigh; Solon Borland to Roscius C. Borland, August 31, 1831, in G
ernors' Papers, North Carolina Division of Archives and History.
32. Clement Eaton, "A Dangerous Pamphlet in the Old South," *Journal of South*
History, II (1936), 1–12.

ɔlan to put his *Appeal* into the hands of southern blacks. The pam-
ılet soon turned up in Wilmington, North Carolina, Walker's for-
ɜr home, and there the slave Jacob Cowan confessed. He had been
alker's designated agent through whom some two hundred copies
ipped from New York were to be funneled to blacks in other towns
roughout the state. Cowan's master soon sold him to an unsus-
cting purchaser in Mobile, Alabama.[33]
The unsettling effect on whites of *Walker's Appeal* is understand-
ɪle. The writings of white abolitionists were regarded as an out-
ge, yet they possessed the comparative virtue of being directed
tensibly only toward members of their author's own race. Now
ɪveholders confronted a black revolutionary bent upon inciting
her blacks to throw off bondage. No wonder southern whites
und the pamphlet a cause for alarm. They saw it as a threat to
ɛir physical safety as well as a challenge to their labor system and
white supremacy.
Wilmington's police chief read the pamphlet and took time to
mmarize its message for the governor of North Carolina. The *Ap-
al* contained passages, wrote James F. McRae, "treating in most
 flammatory terms of the condition of the slaves . . . exaggerating
ɛir sufferings, magnifying their physical strength and underrating
ɛ power of the whites; containing also an open appeal to their
tural love of liberty; and throughout expressing sentiments to-
lly subversive of all subordination in our slaves; and inculcating
inciples wholly at variance with existing relations between the
ʋo colours of our southern population."
McRae appended to his perceptive summary a worrisome ob-
rvation designed to put the governor on guard. Already the *Ap-
al*—or the whites' reaction to it—had accomplished part of its
ission. "A very general and extensive impression," he believed,
ɪas been made on the minds of the negroes in this vicinity that
easures have been taken toward their emancipation on a certain
not distant day."[34]
With such authoritative evidence of sedition before him, the
ɔrth Carolina governor dispatched urgent messages to police offi-

<hr/>

33. Marshall Rachleff, "David Walker's Southern Agent," *Journal of Negro History*,
ːII (1977), 100–103; William H. Pease and Jane H. Pease (eds.), "Walker's *Appeal*
ɪmes to Charleston: A Note and Documents," *Journal of Negro History*, LIX (1974),
9–92.
34. James F. McRae to John Owen, August 7, 1830, in Governor John Owen's Let-
 Books, 1828–30, Governors' Papers, North Carolina Division of Archives and
story.

cers throughout the state and to the state senators. They must al
their neighborhoods to intercept subversive writings and to dete
signs of insurrection. But along with these instructions went t
governor's strange confession. He himself considered all efforts
suppression futile. Little could be done to correct the state's perilo
situation. Not even doubled vigilance would guarantee security. '
is mortifying to know," he concluded, "that we are suffering an e
without the possibility of a remedy."[35]

Others, even if sharing Governor John Owen's sense of doom, we
inspired to adopt defensive measures. Throughout much of t
South, the alarm led to passage of new legislation designed furth
to suppress and humble blacks and thereby to safeguard slavery.
the emergency, lawmakers gave renewed attention to the proble
of the free blacks. The *Appeal* had reminded whites of a fact th
would have preferred to forget: Bonds of unity between free blac
and slaves remained strong. *Walker's Appeal* contributed to antag
nism toward free blacks and encouraged proposals to restrict th
activity, even to expel them from the South. At the same time,
agents of the American Colonization Society discovered, the pa
phlet steeled the blacks' determination to remain where they were

Despite the flurry of lawmaking and the widespread air of eme
gency generated by Walker's pamphlet, only persons with sho
memory found either the occasion or the reaction altogether ne
Walker told southern whites only what they always had know
Slaves wanted freedom; they remained in bondage only because s
perior force and white unity compelled them to do so; and wh
opportunity appeared, they would rebel in an attempt to chan,
their condition. Walker had tried to impress upon blacks his id
that they themselves were responsible for their continued enslav
ment. Slavery was not only something done to them; it was som
thing they did to themselves. What restrained slaves from rising
and destroying the whites at this very moment? asked one whi
Virginian. "Nothing but an universal horror of so diabolical
act."[37] Only the blacks' compassion saved the whites from destru
tion. The writer had grasped the insight Walker sought to convey
blacks. They *allowed* whites to oppress them, and it was in the

    35. John Owen, Circular Letter, August 19, 1830, *ibid.*
    36. Josiah F. Polk to R. R. Gurley, August 13 and September 20, 1830, in Americ
Colonization Society Papers.
    37. Oliver Cross to Garrett M. Quarles, September 3, 1829, in Executive Pape
Virginia State Library.

wer *now* to end their degradation. Southern whites lived at the
fferance of their slaves. The *Appeal* was designed to remove the
ves' reticence and hesitation, much as Thomas Paine in *Common
nse* aimed in 1776 at destroying vestiges of American loyalty to
e king.

Despite the obvious grounds for deepening southern concern after
29, some whites failed to support the repressive measures that
ost whites evidently believed essential. In some places, philan-
ropy warred with prudence and a noticeable lag occurred be-
een the stimulus Walker provided and the appropriate response.
North Carolina, free blacks were allowed to vote as late as 1835,
hen a constitutional amendment finally excluded them from the
lls, and some white persons, especially in Virginia and North
rolina, persisted in urging humanitarian programs to benefit
ves. Tyron McFarland, for one, could not understand such folly.

1831 the North Carolina legislator, famed for his advocacy of
te-financed schools for the poor, requested the governor to send
m a copy of *Walker's Appeal.* He had heard frightening things
out the pamphlet and often referred to it in his political speeches,
t for all its notoriety, he had never had a chance to read it, had
ver even seen a copy. Neither had his constituents. Now he must
ve the pamphlet in order "to prove to some individuals that their
eas as to slaves are founded on 'faulse philanthropy.' " Some in-
uated voters in Richmond County, he regretted to say, criticized
s stand against allowing the instruction of slaves. He needed
mething as persuasive as Walker's pamphlet to convince doubt-
s, and perhaps himself, too, that he was right to advocate keeping
ves in ignorance and, as he explained, that "I have no selfish or
human wish to gratify, all I wish is the good of my Country and
sterity."[38] Repression of blacks, insisted McFarland, was not mo-
ated by prejudice or cruelty, but only by the stern necessity of
f-preservation.

At the time McFarland sent his request to Governor Montfort
okes, the legislator apparently did not yet know that only a few
ys earlier in Southampton County, Virginia, an episode of overt
cial war had occurred. No pamphlet would be needed now to con-
ce southern whites of their peril. For the first time in twenty
ars, a considerable body of North American slaves had rebelled,

38. Johnson, *Ante-Bellum North Carolina,* 601; Tyron McFarland to Montfort
kes, September 3, 1831, in Governors' Papers, North Carolina Division of Archives
d History.

and for the first and only time in United States history, slaves h
indiscriminately slaughtered scores of white citizens. Nat Turne
slave revolt provided sufficient evidence to convince remaini
skeptics that slaves did indeed pose a grave threat to the lives a
security of white southerners.

On Sunday evening, August 21, 1831—the fortieth anniversary
the start of slave participation in the revolt in Saint-Domingue
Nat Turner and five other slaves launched a violent crusade agair
whites in their neighborhood, beginning with the family of Turne
master. Other slaves, perhaps as many as seventy in all joined t
attack, which finally left at least fifty-seven whites—men, wome
and children—dead.[39]

There is no proof whatever that Turner or any of his recruits h
read *Walker's Appeal* or even knew it existed. There is no proof eith
that they ever saw copies of William Lloyd Garrison's *Liberator*
another Boston production—or any other abolitionist writing,
though many took for granted that Turner, at least, surely mu
have done so. In fact, no one at the trials and investigations th
followed the revolt produced evidence to associate Turner or mer
bers of his band with any of the alien influences to which southe
whites customarily attributed slave disaffection. This negative e
dence, far from providing reassurance, was in itself unnerving, f
it demonstrated that slaves required no prodding from outside a;
tators to cause them to rise up in fury against whites.

The only influence ever shown to have operated on Turner, besic
the all-important condition of slavery itself, was the religious teac
ing offered by the Bible and spread by evangelical preachers. Bo
the Bible and preachers were everywhere. They could neither
hidden from slaves nor restricted to those who could be trusted
interpret their message "correctly" and use it "wisely." Nothi
could be done to alter the fact that the black population long a
had acquired the essentials of Christianity. By now Biblical lesso
of justice and retribution had blended with the grievances of slave
to generate violence in Southampton County.

Surviving sources of information about the Turner revolt le
unmistakably to that conclusion, and it was the lesson some dr

---

39. The most thorough account, with accompanying documents, is Henry Irv
Tragle, *The Southampton Slave Revolt of 1831* (Amherst, Mass., 1971). This volu
contains Nat Turner's invaluable confession as recorded by Thomas Gray (pp. 3(
21). For the perspective of a white participant, see F. N. Boney, *Southerners All* (N
con, Ga., 1984), 108–12.

the time. But for most white southerners, that was not its most
ɔealing lesson or, in the end, the most influential one. Few relin-
ished belief that outside influences in some way inspired the
ɩbreak. Hostile ideas filtering in from the North, conventional
sdom charged, set Turner on his murderous course.

Benjamin Cabell, member of the aristocratic Virginia family,
ɔught he understood the force that drove Turner and his follow-
ɔ. "The damnable spirit of fanaticism," Cabell declared, "engen-
red by northern publications and perhaps disseminated by mis-
ɔnaries as well as through the P. office, seems to pervade the
ɩntry at distant and remote points." Mrs. Lawrence Lewis of Al-
ɩndria could be still more specific: "To the Editor of the 'Libera-
ɔ'. . . . we owe in greatest measure the calamity," she told her Bos-
ɩ cousin Harrison Gray Otis. N. D. Sutton of Bowling Green in
roline County offered his own explanation. He was perfectly
ɩisfied that "these traveling preachers and peddlers have been in-
umental to a great degree in producing the present state of
ɩngs." From this premise Sutton drew an obvious, popular moral.
ɩves "should not be permitted to have preaching at anytime nor
ɔuld they be permitted to go about contracting for themselves."
North Carolina, too, where evidence of slave discontent appeared
nost as flagrantly as in Virginia, observers agreed that religion
d northern fanaticism must be charged with creating the slave-
ɔners' problems.[40]

When Governor John Floyd of Virginia finally offered the gover-
r of South Carolina his own reasoned theory of its cause, he had
d nearly three months to ponder the meaning of the South-
ɩpton revolt. But for all its ripening, his analysis hardly improved
on those offered earlier. Much thought had left him "fully per-
aded" that the "spirit of insubordination" that inflamed Turner
d threatened to ignite similar revolts "had its origin among . . .
ɔ Yankee population, upon their first arrival amongst us."[41] It was

40. Benjamin Cabell to John Floyd, September 20, 1831, and N. D. Sutton to John
ɔyd, September 21, 1831, both in Executive Papers, Virginia State Library; Mrs.
ɩwrence Lewis to Otis, October 17, 1831, in Samuel Eliot Morison, Life and Letters
Harrison Gray Otis, Federalist 1765–1848 (Boston, 1913), II, 260; Calvin Jones to
ɔntfort Stokes, December 28, 1830, in Governors' Papers, North Carolina Division
Archives and History. Inconclusive evidence suggesting a wider conspiracy involv-
ɔ northern free blacks and abolitionists and poor white southerners appears in
theker, American Negro Slave Revolts, 303–304, and Ira Berlin (ed.), "After Nat
ɔrner: A Letter from the North," Journal of Negro History, LV (1970), 144–51.
41. Tragle, Southampton Slave Revolt, 275–76.

an explanation the South Carolina governor—whose state then ¿
proached the Nullification Crisis—was prepared to accept.

"They began first, by making them religious," Floyd wrote, "
telling the blacks God was no respecter of persons—the black m
was as good as the white—that all men were born free and equal
that the white people rebelled against England to obtain freedo
so have the blacks a right to do." Finally, continued Floyd, "c
females and of the most respectable were persuaded that it w
piety to teach negroes to read and write . . . that they might re
the Scriptures." Government shared blame with misguided, pic
women. Officials had grown lax. Under a permissive regime, la
designed to restrict slaves "became more inactive." While autho
ties looked the other way, black preachers found in northern-p
duced religious tracts and "incendiary publications" the subversi
ideas that they communicated to slaves in unsupervised church se
ices. Through the agency of black preachers, Floyd believed,
widespread conspiracy had taken shape to destroy white control
Virginia. "In sum," he wrote, "the Northern incendiaries, trac
Sunday Schools, religion and reading and writing" produced T
ner's revolt.[42]

Floyd omitted only one important element from his wide-rangi
indictment. He did not take into account the crucial part played
grievances inseparable from slavery in explaining the Southampt
fury. It was a pardonable oversight, for conventional wisdom h
that the lot of slaves in the Old Dominion was enviable. Only t
ungrateful, the infatuated, or the misled would reject so fortunat
condition. But that benign view neglected aspects of slave life t
had little to do with its incidents of work, food, clothing, and shelt
No more clearly than most of his white contemporaries did the V
ginia governor see the fierce wounds produced even in well-treat
slaves by the reality of bondage and forced submission. No spok
man for the state could be expected to acknowledge as legitim
the aggrieved slaves' sense of injustice.

The deep-seated grievances and the motives of earlier slave reb
had long been on record, revealed by witnesses in the numerc
trials resulting from the Gabriel and Vesey conspiracies and fr
others less well-known. Curiously, only a few statements made
the Southampton rebels survive; yet even this sparse evidence
tablishes the circumstance that led slaves to support Turner's d
perate venture. Just as Turner himself—as recorded in the sta

42. *Ibid.*, 430–32.

:nts he made to Thomas Grey—was moved not by uncommonly
rsh treatment but by the demands of retributive justice, so his
lowers struck out against unmerited bondage and the impositions
despotic masters. When the first reports of violence reached
arby neighborhoods on the morning of August 22, 1831, some ill-
ormed persons assumed that the traditional enemy, the British,
ist have invaded Virginia once again. Among slaves the assump-
n did not produce alarm, however, for blacks—slave and free
ke—generally looked upon the British with much favor. The slave
irdy felt no regret at being told that British armies marched
-ough Virginia. "He said that 'If they really were in the County
ling white people . . . it was nothing and ought to have been done
ig ago—that the negroes had been punished long enough.' "[43]

On the morning of the revolt, before many outside the immediate
:a grasped exactly what was happening, Nancy Parsons, a young
nite woman, came upon a slave lying along the road "kicking up
; heels" in his own unique posture of ecstasy. The prospect of the
itish presence accounted for his immoderate joy. Wasn't he afraid
the British? Isaac answered no and "that if they came by he
iuld join them & assist in killing all the white people—that if they
:cceeded he would have as much money as his master." Ever since
29, when his hopes for emancipation aroused by the constitu-
nal convention of that year were dashed, Isaac had felt the im-
sitions of his bondage more keenly. "If he had been set free two
urts ago," he explained, "this would not have happened."[44]

In Onslow County, North Carolina, many miles from Southamp-
1, slaves responded much as did slaves in Virginia to the excite-
:nt Turner's revolt produced and to the prospect of freedom. Jacob
ked about his own plans. "He said that 'If they rose he had a
etty good sword, that he would be amongst them . . . and since
it time at Mr. Hawkins he . . . wished that the camp meeting was
arcr than it was, so that he might aid in destroying the whites.' "
metimes, it appeared, slaves moved toward revolt from a gener-
zed sense of injustice, as did Turner, but they might also be
ompted by specific, personal grievance, as was Jacob, who still
iarted from the unspecified incident "at Mr. Hawkins."[45]
Similarly, in Virginia near the site of the revolt, the master's im-
)derate exercise of power led Frank to support the rebels: "His

43. Aptheker, "One Continual Cry," 106; Tragle, Southampton Slave Revolt, 202.
44. Tragle, Southampton Slave Revolt, 189.
45. Criminal Action Concerning the 1831 Insurrection of Slaves, September 20,
i1, in Onslow County Miscellaneous Records.

master had crop[p]ed him [cut off his ears]," he explained, "and
would be crop[p]ed before the end of the year."[46] Turner's most
timate coconspirators were confident that their initiative wou
arouse the other slaves' deep-seated hatred and would rally them
revolution. When Jack first learned of the plan "to rise and kill
the white people," he objected, reasoning that Turner's band was
too small to accomplish so large a scheme. But Hark, one of Turne
few confidants, discounted the objection. He predicted that "as th
went on and killed the whites the blacks would join them." M
slaves, Hark believed, shared his own hatred and would join t
revolt.[47]

There was little time at the end of August and start of Septemb
1831, for white citizens to undertake extensive efforts to locate t
wellsprings of revolt. Mobilization to subdue the rebels seemed
be the sole necessity. Alarm was widespread. Officials across t
state border ordered out the North Carolina militia, some units
guard the immediate border area, others to rush to the aid of th
embattled neighbors. Word of the revolt reached both Mayor J.
Holt at Norfolk and Governor John Floyd at Richmond at alm
the same early hour on August 23. Lacking means to coordina
military plans, each official acted independently of the other to me
the emergency. Both men interpreted the news from Southampt
as evidence that a state of war existed. Accordingly, both mobiliz
massive military force. Within a few hours, Floyd dispatched troc
and cavalry, drawing forces especially from Richmond, Norfolk, a
Brunswick. The mayor likewise ordered the volunteer and mili
units under his command to move to Southampton. But the Norfe
authorities went still further. At their own initiative and withc
consulting Governor Floyd, the mayor and his advisers request
help from federal forces. Colonel James House, commandant of Fe
tress Monroe, responded at once by dispatching three compan
from the First Artillery Regiment and marines and sailors from t
USS *Natchez* and the USS *Warren*, two warships then stationed
Hampton Roads. At the same time, the commander of the Unit
States naval yard depot agreed to furnish equipment for the volu
teer company hastily formed at Norfolk and Portsmouth.[48]

46. Tragle, *Southampton Slave Revolt*, 214–15. Emphasis added.
47. *Ibid.*, 196.
48. *Ibid.*, 16–19, 42, 264–65, 269–70, 424–25; George C. Dromgoole to Natha
Mason, August 23, 1831, in Nathaniel Mason Papers, Southern Historical Collecti
University of North Carolina, Chapel Hill.

Concern that use of federal troops without the governor's request
sregarded constitutional nicety was allayed by a letter from the
nited States adjutant general to Colonel House expressing "the en-
re satisfaction of the President and Secretary of War, at the promp-
tude with which you dispatched three companies of Artillery . . .
the request of the civil authority, on this lamentable and unfore-
en occasion." Federal military authorities cooperated still further.
fore the summer ended, five companies of troops had been moved
om the northern seaboard to Fortress Monroe to meet the addi-
nal outbreaks that hourly were expected. As an additional pre-
ution, the navy announced plans to discharge the black mechan-
s who had been employed at naval installations at Portsmouth,
vhich will increase the number of white men in that town about
ur hundred."⁴⁹

Although Governor Floyd did not at all minimize the gravity of
e emergency, he could not conceal his displeasure that Norfolk
ficials had appealed for federal troops. No doubt it was comfort-
g to know that the United States had made good on its constitu-
nal obligation to help put down rebellion—a fact perhaps not
st on those slave states that soon afterward refrained from sup-
rting South Carolina in its nullification adventure. Nevertheless
e mayor had erred, the governor believed, in requesting federal
d. Sending troops to the interior left the seacoast, with its large
ack population, dangerously depleted of military force. But more
the point, resort to federal troops may have suggested to blacks
at the people of Virginia were too weak to cope with their own
cial problems, that the maintenance of slavery depended on fed-
al force. Such an impression could only make slaves contemptu-
s of their white masters. Widespread insubordination—refusal to
 disciplined, reluctance to work—must be the result. And what
ould happen, asked Floyd, if someday foreign war required with-
awal of federal troops, leaving Virginia to defend herself? How
uld slaves respond then? It was something to think about.⁵⁰

Important though such considerations were, it is doubtful that
ey entered the minds of many persons in the last days of August,
31. At that moment, they could think of little else than how to
ve themselves from the ferocious blacks. Women and children es-
cially were afflicted with terror as word of Turner's onslaught

49. Tragle, *Southampton Slave Revolt*, 58, 19–20; William Murdaugh to John
oyd, September 24, 1831, in Executive Papers, Virginia State Library.
50. Tragle, *Southampton Slave Revolt*, 271–72.

spread. Many fled to woods and swamps and remained there for a extended period. If it were possible, even greater panic appears have been experienced in North Carolina than in Virginia. Rumo swept the state that Wilmington had been burned and its white ci zens massacred. A black army two thousand strong was said to l advancing on Raleigh. Nearly a thousand women were reported have gathered for protection at Halifax, a similar number at Mu freesboro, and still others at defensible points in Gates and Nort ampton counties.[51]

Alarm was slow to subside. On September 29, more than a mon after Turner's band was destroyed, twelve hundred men, wome and children fled their homes in the northern part of Pittsylvan County, Virginia, and collected at "Col. Estes's" on report that s hundred slaves had attacked a camp meeting. When similar r mors continued to spread with like effect and no factual base, sor citizens began to calculate their impact on blacks. James Peir thought that "the rumours afloat, and the alarms with which t people have been so unfortunately harassed . . . and the fact whi cannot and does not escape the notice of the Slaves, that many pe sons are under great apprehensions, must of necessity, bring t Slaves to think on the subject, and are unfortunately too much ca culated to encourage them to make such attempts."[52]

At last some concluded, no doubt correctly, that the continuir rumors of impending violence lacked any foundation whatever, ar that immoderate response to them made whites appear ridiculot "I believe indeed," wrote Benjamin Cabell, "that the blacks ther selves have in some instances, had the address to put reports in circulation in order to enjoy the spectacle resulting from the una countable panic of the whites."[53] If so, this was indeed grim hum and reckless in the extreme, for when whites mobilized to suppre

51. *Ibid.*, 85; [Samuel Warner], *Authentic and Impartial Narrative of the Tragi Scene Which Was Witnessed in Southampton County (Virginia) on Monday the 22nd August Last* . . . [New York, 1831], 19–25; Pattie Mordecai to Ellen Mordecai, Se tember 16, 1831, and R. Lazarus to George W. Mordecai, October 6, 1831, both Pattie Mordecai Collection, North Carolina Division of Archives and History, Raleig
52. Benjamin Cabell to John Floyd, [October 6, 1831], and James Peirce to Jo Floyd, October 10, 1831, both in Executive Papers, Virginia State Library; Debor Shea (ed.), "Spreading Terror and Devastation Wherever They Have Been: A Norfo Woman's Account of the Southampton Slave Insurrection," *Virginia Magazine of H tory and Biography*, XCV (1987), 65–74.
53. Benjamin Cabell to John Floyd, October 19, 1831, in Executive Papers, V ginia State Library.

volt, real or imaginary, they did not scruple from inflicting repris-
s. The massacre of whites in Southampton County was followed
imediately by a massacre of blacks. Although no one kept tally
eets, almost surely far more blacks than whites were murdered.
"Last Tuesday and Wednesday [August 23 and 24] there was
mething like 40 negroes kill'd by the Murfreesboro Company, the
overnor Guards, and the *ballance* of the enemy was kill'd and
ken by the Virginians on Thursday. . . . Negroes are taken in . . .
id executed every day," reported Robert S. Parker, who had been
the seat of war. On August 25, he continued, "there was a negro
om Ahosky Ridge bending his course toward Southampton, and
idertook to pass through the Boro' and when he had got as far
rough town as Mr. Manny's office, there were about 8 or 10 guns
ed at him by the Guard, they then cut off his head, stuck it on a
ole, and planted the pole at the cross streets."[54]
Indiscriminate murder and torture characterized efforts to sup-
ess revolt and uncover conspiracy. At Enfield, North Carolina, a
eptic about the reality of the purported conspiracies reported
at "the good people about town have taken a free negro to the Vice
screwed him up to extort confessions & failing in their object
reaten to shoot him forthwith."[55]
It was hard for whites anticipating destruction to separate the
iilty from the innocent. "We have testimony that will implicate
ost of the negroes in the county," wrote a resident of Sampson
ounty, North Carolina. The frightened whites in neighboring Du-
in County responded to an alleged conspiracy by putting "10 or
5" to death. At the height of the panic at Murfreesboro, a black man
as shot and beheaded for having predicted "there would be a war
etween the black and white people."[56]
Although no one recorded the effects of the insurrection on the
acks who survived the reprisals, Charity Bowery, who was a slave
North Carolina near the Virginia border, remembered some six-
en years afterward that "the brightest and best men were killed in

54. Robert S. Parker to Rebecca Manney, August 29, 1831, in John Kimberly Pa-
rs, Southern Historical Collection, University of North Carolina, Chapel Hill.
55. S. Whitaker to the Governor, August 26, 1831, in Governors' Papers, North
rolina Division of Archives and History. See also William Kauffman Scarborough
1.), *The Diary of Edmund Ruffin* (Baton Rouge, 1972–89), II, 207–209.
56. William Blanks to the Governor, September 13, 1831, and T. Borland to the
overnor, September 18, 1831, both in Governors' Papers, North Carolina Division
Archives and History.

Nat's time. Such ones are always suspected. All the colored foll
were afraid to pray in the time of the old prophet Nat. There was r
law about it; but the whites reported it round among themselve
that if a note was heard, we should have some dreadful punishmen
and after that, the low whites would fall upon any slaves they hear
praying or singing a hymn, and often killed them before their ma
ters or mistress could get to them."[57]

In Southampton County a reign of terror against free blacks i
well as slaves followed the revolt. "Many white people of low cha
acter take advantage of the prejudice excited against them to ma
treat and abuse them so that they are obliged to flee from the
homes to save their lives." Their only recourse, the report conti
ued, was to take refuge "in the houses of those benevolent white me
that will afford them protection. Mr. [Joseph] Lewis and [Car
Bowers have a number of them at their plantations."[58]

Whites in North Carolina subjected free blacks to similar repri
als. At Elizabeth City in September, 1831, two white men broke in
the home of a free black and killed him. One of the murderers wz
apprehended, but, wrote an agent of the American Colonization S
ciety, "I feel satisfied should our Grand Jury find a true bill again
the murderer he will be acquitted. . . . The mere imprisonment
this man has already caused considerable excitement among ou
nonslaveholding population." In such an atmosphere, a number
blacks who previously had been unresponsive to proposals to ser
them to Africa now welcomed the chance to leave. Others fled to tl
North.[59]

Whites caught up in the hysteria suffered in their way as well. "I
almost every section of our county," wrote a resident of Southam
ton, "conversation instead of being as it was a month since, ligl
and cheerful, is now clothed in dismal forebodings.—Some of ou
citizens will leave us—and all agree, that they never again can fe
safe, never again be happy." A well-to-do resident of Wilmingto
regretted "holding so much property here, and if not actually tie
down to this place, would gladly remove to the north." Suppressio
of revolt, the writer believed, had left the fundamental problem co

57. John W. Blassingame (ed.), *Slave Testimony: Two Centuries of Letters, Speeche
Interviews, and Autobiographies* (Baton Rouge, 1977), 267.
58. Jonathan McPhail to R. R. Gurley, September 22, 1831, in American Colon
zation Society Papers.
59. Miles White to R. R. Gurley, October 1, 1831, and John C. Ehringhaus to R.
Gurley, September 29, 1831, both *ibid.*

onting southern whites unresolved: "In the bosom of almost every
mily the enemy still exists."[60]
The perception of continuing, unavoidable danger fed the milita-
sm that for years had characterized southern culture. State and
cal governments endeavored to bring militia units to a high state
f preparedness. Volunteer groups were formed to help defend the
cial order. Eighty-eight students at the University of Virginia
rmed an association to study military tactics under an instructor
ppointed by the faculty and asked the governor to supply them
ith arms. At the University of North Carolina, students organized
volunteer company and requested sixty stand of arms.[61]

Not surprisingly, the emergency led citizens to call upon govern-
ient to solve a problem that seemed beyond the capacity of individ-
als. Some demanded expulsion of the free blacks. Some thought
avery should be ended gradually and the freed slaves removed.
ome called for more severe laws regulating all blacks. Others of-
red no specific remedy, but merely pointed out the state's perilous
ndition and pled for legislative action—any action—that might
ring security.

Such evidence of widespread concern led to an unprecedented de-
ate in the Virginia General Assembly. For the first and last time, a
uthern legislature subjected slavery to public examination. Yet
ie scrutiny produced no evident gains, for as discussion proceeded,
became clear that no action could be taken. Compensated eman-
ipation at state expense appeared too costly, even if a plan could
e agreed upon. Emancipation without compensation would de-
troy property rights and in any event was politically impossible.
here simply was no politically feasible solution.

No legislator placed a bill calling for emancipation before the
eneral Assembly. Instead, the entire matter of slavery and free
lacks was referred to a select committee, which failed to agree on
recommendation. When the committee chairman moved to dis-
harge the body on the ground that legislation on slavery was "in-
xpedient," Thomas J. Randolph offered a substitute resolution fa-
oring gradual emancipation of slaves born after July 4, 1840, to be

60. *Liberator*, January 28, 1832; Rachel Lazarus to G. W. Mordecai, October 6,
831, in Pattie Mordecai Collection.
61. Joseph Caldwell to the Governor, September 17, 1831, and Joseph B. Southell
nd 67 others to the Governor, September 17, 1831, in Governors' Papers, North
arolina Division of Archives and History; Robert M. Patterson to John Floyd, Octo-
er 24, 1831, in Executive Papers, Virginia State Library.

followed by their colonization. His motion to submit the propos
to popular referendum encountered strenuous objection on th
ground that public discussion would have dangerous consequence
Controversy would sharpen the long-evident divisions between ric
and poor and between slaveowners and nonslaveowners. It woul
aggravate the slaves' discontent, making them still harder to cor
trol. Willoughby Newton painted the scene: "The hustings—th
muster ground—nay, sir, every crossroad and grog-shop, will l
made the scene of angry debate, and noisy declamation, upon th
agitating subject. What must be the inevitable consequence? . . . R
volt and insurrection among our slaves."[62]

Newton's misgivings already had been foreshadowed during th
debate, when several legislators voiced resentment not only towar
free blacks and slaves but toward slaveowners as well. "At all tim
the non-slave-holders of Virginia are subjected to the most outr;
geous imposition by the presence of this population," sai
George W. Summers of Kanawha County. Small farmers performe
patrol duty "to protect the slave-holder in the enjoyment of th;
which it is the interest of non-slave-holders, should not exist." Thes
were ominous sentiments indeed, for they revealed social divisior
that imperiled the consensus upon which slavery depended. A
though he was a man of substance and the owner of land and slave
Thomas J. Randolph put himself forward on this occasion as chan
pion of the small farmers. He accepted the validity of their grie
ance: "It has been the practice, if not the policy of the large slav
holder," he said, "to make the poor man the instrument of the
police and their punishments to their slaves; which has begotte
hostility between the slave and the less wealthy."[63] But to acknow
edge the grievance, as Randolph did, was not to relieve it.

The General Assembly succeeded in solving no part of the raci;
problem. When it adjourned, the petitions that had called for emar
cipation and for expulsion of free blacks remained unanswered
Rather than finding solutions, the legislators had opened forbidde
subjects to examination and had revealed seldom-exposed tension
It was partly to counteract the divisive result such action was e:
pected to have that Thomas R. Dew, professor at the College of Wi

---

62. Joseph C. Robert, *The Road from Monticello: A Study of the Virginia Slave
Debate of 1832* (Durham, N.C., 1941), 19, 98.
63. *Ibid.*, 86; Alison Goodyear Freehling, *Drift Toward Dissolution: The Virgin
Slavery Debate of 1831–1832* (Baton Rouge, 1982), 122–69; Robert, *Road from Mo
ticello*, 96.

am and Mary, prepared a major defense of slavery in the form of a
review of the General Assembly's debates. Slavery could not—and
would not—be ended, Dew argued; and the free blacks could not be
removed. Freedom or moves toward freedom would produce dis-
ord and violence. Only forthright defense of slavery could guaran-
e tranquillity.[64]
Dew came forward with his ingeniously structured proslavery ar-
ument at an opportune moment. Recent events in Virginia sug-
ested the need to bolster the slaveholders' position in the face of
iternal dissension among whites and discontent among slaves. At
ie same time, vigorous abolitionist agitation was under way in the
orth. Southern institutions, it appeared, were about to be sub-
cted to a pincerslike attack against which defense and justification
ould be needed as never before.

64. Dew's argument appeared as Thomas R. Dew, *Review of the Debate in the Vir-
nia Legislature of 1831 and 1832* (Richmond, 1832).

8

A Pacific Crusade

By the time Nat Turner's rebels tore through Southampto County, William Lloyd Garrison had published the *Liberator* fc nearly eight months in Boston, and copies of the newspaper ha carried his shrill abolitionist message to the slave states. The cor junction of events made certain that some Virginians would blam Turner's violence on Garrison's rhetoric. Soon officials throughot the South were demanding suppression of the *Liberator* in the nam of public safety, and state legislators were calling for Garrison's ex tradition from Massachusetts to be tried for the crime of incitin slaves to revolt.[1]

There was some irony in all of this, for already in 1831 Garriso had progressed far toward the nonresistant position that late would make him notorious. Although early opponents of slaver commonly believed slaves would be justified in rising against thei oppressors, neither Garrison nor the many abolitionists who pre ceded him urged slaves to revolt. Garrison often advised the oppo site. His views decrying slave violence had been on record for man months—ever since the alarm produced throughout the South b *Walker's Appeal*.

Garrison lived in Baltimore in 1829 and was just beginning hi

---

1. Wendell Phillips Garrison and Francis Jackson Garrison, *William Lloyd Garr son, 1805–1879* (Boston, 1885–89), I, 239–42, 247–48.

ectacular career when copies of the *Appeal* came to light in several
uthern cities. With characteristic flouting of the expedient, he had
ded to his published statement deploring the pamphlet an admir-
g comment on "the bravery and intelligence of its author." But
er, in answer to charges that he endorsed Walker's militancy, Gar-
on declared the contrary to be true: "We do not preach rebel-
n—no, but submission and peace."² Slaveholders might doubt
e sincerity of Garrison's disclaimer, yet he had voiced what re-
ained standard abolitionist policy throughout the 1830s. While
ely asserting the slaves' theoretical right to rebel, abolitionists
stomarily shrank from the prospect of their doing so. It was partly
avert such a disaster, Garrison insisted, that he founded the *Lib-
tor* at Boston in January, 1831. He would try to persuade whites
end slavery before they became the victims of their vengeful
ndsmen.

He insisted that he had no connection with Turner's revolt, but
pended to the disclaimer was an assertion that must have infuri-
ed southern readers. Slaves, he wrote, "would be justified in using
taliatory measures more than any people on the face of the earth."
eir use of violence in the cause of liberty was as fitting as that of
e American revolutionary patriots.³ Garrison's distinction be-
een the right to revolt and the wisdom of doing so was not par-
cularly subtle, yet it is easy to understand why in the emotional
mosphere of 1831 southerners ignored Garrison's clear distinction
d read his words as a message urging blood and destruction. To
aveowners, assertion of the injustice of slavery seemed equivalent
inviting insurrection. Even if the worst did not happen—even if
 good fortune antislavery propaganda did not lead to overt rebel-
n—at very least such criticism would undermine plantation dis-
line, with consequent decline in labor productivity and in the
lue of slaves.

Garrison found in the blacks' status as slaves sufficient cause for
volt, but he also agreed with his southern critics who held that
tside influences might stimulate disorder. The Southampton reb-
, he wrote, had found inspiration in a worldwide movement to-
rd freedom, of which the antislavery campaign and his own ca-
er formed only a part. According to Garrison, ideological currents

2. *Genius of Universal Emancipation*, X (January 15, 1830), 147; *Liberator*, January
1831.
3. *Liberator*, September 3, 1831.

impinging upon the South from many directions prompted slav
to rebel—"voices in the air, sounds from across the ocean, invit
tions to resistance above, below, around them!"[4] Southerners wou
have found this an especially alarming observation, for Garris
implied that the impulse to throw off bondage was irresistible a
that it might not be within anyone's power to prevent slaves on th
own initiative from striking for freedom.

Slaveowners unhesitatingly rejected advocates of emancipati
as "fanatics," but they could not be so sure that the northern m
jority would similarly repudiate them and their program. To t
contrary, evidence suggested growing northern affinity for antisla
ery thought. Even though in 1831 abolitionists comprised only
tiny, obscure element in the northern population, the disquieti
fact could not be evaded that a generalized antislavery, antisout
ern sentiment had long pervaded much of the North and apparent
intensified. The course followed by a number of northern congre
men and publicists during the Misssouri controversy, together wi
a myriad of lesser events, amply supported that conclusion.

Abolitionism's seditious effect in undermining slavery, souther
ers believed, could be detected among softhearted white men a
women even within the South. How else could be explained the
insistence on teaching slaves to read and their winking at violatic
of regulatory laws? Further, a large body of potentional abolition
recruits existed among the South's many nonslaveholders. What, f
example, would a slaveholder make of this lament written by
farmer in Iredell County, North Carolina, in 1825: "The great m
of our county seem determined to engross all the best land of t
country—and then how are the poor to live amongst their slav
and overseers?"[5] Slaveowners must seize every available means
limit the abolitionists' opportunity to subvert members of their ov
race as well as the black population. But suppose the effort faile
Suppose that, under the promptings of northern-based fanatics a
the encouragement of corrupted southern whites, slaves made a d
perate bid for freedom through a revolt too widespread and inten
for southern resources to subdue. In that extremity, it was true, t
Constitution offered recourse. Yet its provision for federal milita

4. *Ibid.*, October 15, 1831.
5. John Floyd to James Hamilton, Jr., November, 1831, in Tragle, *Southampi
Slave Revolt*, 175; Christopher Houston to Placebo Houston, April 23, 1825, in G
trude Dixon Enfield (ed.), "Life and Letters of Christopher Houston" (Typescript
Perkins Library, Duke University, Durham, N.C.).

d would count for little if an abolitionized northern public sym-
thized with the insurgents instead of with their masters.
If present trends continued, southern spokesmen believed, slave-
lders eventually would find themselves isolated and friendless
hen calamity struck. The day might even come when a hostile
orth openly promoted insurrection. A northern black editor early
rmulated the possibility. "The nation cannot bear everything,"
rote John Russworm in 1827, "and if the indignation of the people
ould compel our government to withdraw her protection, and
ve notice that the slave states shall be left to themselves, I tremble
r the consequence." In the same year, one of Benjamin Lundy's
uthern correspondents, anticipating imminent revolt, expressed
milar dread. North-South political disputes and cultural differ-
ces, he suggested, already had grown so intense as to destroy
mity between the sections. Thus, predicted the Kentuckian, when
e slaves unleashed their fury, besieged southern whites would
and alone, and the hostile North would "laugh at their calamity
d mock when their fear cometh."[6]
Here and there in the 1820s, northerners voiced sentiments sug-
sting that such predictions already had acquired a factual base,
at a common front uniting whites in support of slavery no longer
uld be taken for granted. In 1826, Judge Benjamin Tappan, a
tive of Massachusetts then living in Ohio, startled an agent of
e American Colonization Society with his remark that he hoped the
aves would rise up and cut the throats of their masters. In the
me year, a writer in the Genius of Universal Emancipation, pon-
ring his responsibility toward slavery, arrived at a conclusion like-
ise hostile to southern white interest: "I would inquire whether
e slave has not a resort to the most violent measures, if necessary,
 order to maintain his liberty? And if he has the least chance of
ccess, are we not, as rational and consistent men, bound to justify
m?" The writer stopped short of advocating encouragement and
d to black rebels, but not very far short. Conversation with Quak-
s in Pennsylvania and Ohio in 1829 led Josiah F. Polk, an agent of
e American Colonization Society, to conclude that "some of them
ould grieve to see the Southern States freed from this curse with-
t the severest chastisement." Polk shared the opinion already held

6. Freedom's Journal, April 13, 1827; Genius of Universal Emancipation and Balti-
re Courier, II (May 19, 1827), 218. See also Thomas Law to John C. Calhoun, August
, 1821, in Meriwether et al. (eds.), Papers of John C. Calhoun, VI, 328, and Annals of
ngress, 9th Cong., 2nd Sess., 626–27.

by some slaveholders, "that in the event of a formidable insurre
tion in the South scarcely a man would cross the line to aid in i
suppression, even *at the hazard of the dissolution of the Union.*"[7]

It was in the uneasy atmosphere generated by such sentimen
that both southerners and abolitionists assessed the slave violen
of 1831. Abolitionists could not escape their reputation as access
ries to the Southampton revolt, though the accusation fell harde
on Garrison, whose newspaper more outspokenly than any oth
condemned slavery and slaveholders. Southern white leaders mig
take comfort, however, in knowing that even in the North, whe
slavery fell under general disapproval, persons concerned for soci
order and intersectional harmony denounced the abolitionis
policy and the rhetoric in which their arguments often were pr
sented. Following Turner's revolt, Francis Wayland, president
Brown University, requested Garrison to stop sending him the *Li
erator.* Its attitude toward slaveowners, he complained, was "me
acing and vindictive," prejudicing them against "cool discussion"
slavery. Still worse, the newspaper's presentation of "the miseri
of the slaves" was "calculated to arouse their most destructive pa
sions [and to urge] them on to resistance at all hazards."[8]

Garrison and his associates continued to insist that such criti
misunderstood the abolitionists' purpose. Their program, who
pacific in intent, was designed to prevent repetition of the catastr
phe that had struck Virginia. In thus responding to his opponen
Garrison utilized one of the oldest themes in antislavery argumer
A powerful objection advanced against slavery since at least t
early eighteenth century was the near certainty that an enrag
slave population someday would rise up and destroy its oppresso
This familiar expectation as motive for urging emancipation ha
been joined more recently by the potent but still relatively nov
force of moral and religious duty. Thus the antislavery crusade
the late eighteenth and early nineteenth centuries represented ;
amalgam of old prudential and newer idealistic elements. The tv
strands of antislavery thought were never again separated and pe
sisted until slavery finally was destroyed, though sometimes or
sometimes the other was emphasized.

7. Benjamin C. Peers to R. R. Gurley, October 13, 1826, in American Colonizati
Society Papers; *Genius of Universal Emancipation and Baltimore Courier,* I (Augu
26, 1826), 403; Josiah F. Polk to R. R. Gurley, December 17, 1829, in American Co
nization Society Papers.
8. Francis Wayland to Garrison, November 1, 1831, in Antislavery Collection, B
ton Public Library.

While religious revivals in the 1820s supplied new dynamism to ntislavery argument, sharpening political rivalries between North nd South joined events in Europe and South America to augment ears of revolt. The result by 1830 was the marked urgency with which abolitionists faced the slavery issue.

Freedom was in the air. In 1827 Nathaniel Paul, black pastor of he First African Baptist Society in Albany, New York, identified ome of the diverse forces that he thought would impel slaves to try o cast off their bonds: "the catastrophe and exchange of power in he Isle of Hayti, the restless disposition of both master and slave in he southern states, the constitution of our government, the effects f literacy and moral instruction, the influence and spread of the oly religion of the cross of Christ, and the irrevocable decree of lmighty God."[9] Paul's catalog barely hinted at an additional timulus to antislavery thought. Principles of liberty inseparable om the Age of Revolution still generated expectations that supported liberal political movements throughout Europe as well as in merica. While oppressed peoples on the Continent battled for liberty in the 1820s, white Americans applauded their efforts and rayed for their success.

In particular, the struggle of the Greeks to win independence from urkey aroused admiration. "Greece & the Greek cause are the eigning topic," reported a South Carolinian from Boston in 1824. By the end of the decade, the Polish revolt against Russian despotism supplemented the Greek struggle as an object of American esteem, and in 1830 the triumph of liberal forces in France was cheered in Washington. Humanitarian urges could shift focus as eed required, and when the shift occurred, black people, slave or ree, might well be beneficiaries. "Three little girls a few weeks since xpressed the wish to form a society for the benefit of the Greek children," reported E. M. Balch from Maryland in 1830, "but since hey have learned that they are no longer in need of their mite they ave interested their youthful zeal and tender feelings in behalf of he unfortunate people of colour." Such flexibility was not likely to be confined to children. Although rebellions by white Europeans ad no immediate relation to slavery, the example of a people rising n behalf of freedom—an example that so many Americans clearly dmired—bore transferable implications for a country pledged to etaining a large part of its population in bondage. Some slavehold-

9. Nathaniel Paul, *An Address, Delivered on the Celebration of the Abolition of Slavery in the State of New York, July 5, 1827* (Albany, N.Y., 1827), 16.

ers frankly acknowledged the prospect. Upon hearing a Virginia ma
tron express extravagant sympathy for the rebellious Greeks, Joh
Randolph, with reference to nearby blacks, retorted, "The Greek
madam, are at your door."[10]

Revolutionary movements acquired an unmistakable antislaver
cast when in the wake of the Napoleonic Wars Spain's possessior
in the Western Hemisphere threw off colonial ties and also provide
for emancipation. The significance for the American South coul
not be missed. The slave states faced new isolation as the free terr
tory surrounding them grew. No sooner had the Missouri Compro
mise opened a door through which slaves and plantation agricu
ture could enter the West than the South American revolution
diminished the boon by creating a free neighbor on the souther
and western border. Who in the 1820s could doubt that an antislav
ery Mexico sooner or later would encourage slave unrest in th
United States and offer refuge to black fugitives from the South, a
all earlier neighbors had done? Indeed, the entire Latin America
revolutionary example could be expected to unsettle North Amer
can slavery. "A secret influence is imperceptibly conveyed from th
land of Bolivar to the miserable slaves," said a northern Presbyte
rian preacher. "It invites them to freedom. You cannot intercep
that influence."[11]

Of mounting concern, too, was the aggressive antislavery move
ment under way in England, with its proclaimed goal of abolitio
throughout the British Empire. In the late 1820s, an array of notabl
English reformers gained parliamentary support for emancipatio
in the British West Indies. Antislavery Americans followed the prog
ress of British abolitionism admiringly but also with apprehen
sion, for the measure promised to revolutionize race relations i
areas well outside British territory. Success of the parliamentar
reformers, it appeared, would force Americans to act against slaver
sooner than they might find convenient. Slavery in the Unite
States, some believed, could not long survive emancipation in th
West Indies. Such prophets counted partly on the prestige and er
couragement the British example would supply to American anti
slavery reformers. But more than that, they measured the effec

10. M. C. Darby to Mrs. Manigault, June 22, 1824, in Manigault Family Papers
E. M. Balch to R. R. Gurley, July 4, 1830, in American Colonization Society Papers
Robert Dawidoff, *The Education of John Randolph* (New York, 1979), 63–64.
11. O. P. Hoyt at Potsdam, N.Y., in *Freedom's Journal*, May 11, 1827.

ritish abolition would have on American slaves. Abolition in the ritish Empire, wrote John Quincy Adams, "may prove an earthuake upon this continent."[12] A northern periodical accounted for the unsettling effect comuonly expected to flow from success of the British antislavery uovement: "Their slave population is in the immediate neighborood of our own. They speak the same language. The intercourse is usy, constant, and unavoidable."[13] Despite all efforts to keep them uolated and ignorant, slaves still would manage to learn about uents that affected their status, even when those events occurred ur from regions where they lived. It was in South Carolina and ueorgia, states long having close economic and social relations with ue Caribbean islands, that the impact of British emancipation was upected to be the most severe. "Let those resolutions be carried uto effect in the West Indies," remarked a Georgia planter, "and in ux months I shall see the effect on my slaves."[14] The *Christian Spectator* addressed to American celebrators of foreign revolution a mencing question about the ultimate consequence of British antislavery. When the British West Indian slaves become free, "who will say uat a war of extermination [in the American South] will not ensue, u which the African cause may excite as much sympathy and as beral contributions in England and in the West Indies, as the ureek cause has done in this country?"[15]

Such speculation, with its mingling of painful memories of Saintuomingue and prospects of renewed foreign intrigue, could only udd to the planters' concern. It was tempting for anglophobes to uspect the traditional enemy of evil intent and impossible to doubt ue evil intent of northern abolitionists. The northern-based antiuavery movement was a front, some concluded, for hostile English uterest bent on spoiling the American experiment in republicanism und economic freedom. Conspiracy was in the air. "It is somewhat ungular that the passion of humanity should, at the same instant of ume, have seized so strongly upon New England and Old England,"

12. Charles Francis Adams (ed.), *Memoirs of John Quincy Adams Comprising Porons of His Diary from 1795 to 1848* (Philadelphia, 1874–77), VIII, 269. See also [Elott Cresson] to R. R. Gurley, November 10, 1831, in American Colonization Society uapers.

13. *Christian Spectator* as quoted in *Freedom's Journal*, March 23, 1827.

14. Quoted in American Anti-Slavery Society, *First Annual Report . . . 1834* (New ork, 1834), 22.

15. Quoted in *Freedom's Journal*, March 23, 1827.

observed a Virginia congressman, "that this passion would hav
been so strongly and so singularly enlisted in favor of the blac
slaves."[16]

Aspersions such as these may have confirmed some persons in a
ready established resistance to antislavery argument, but they di
little to lessen reformers' admiration for the steady British advanc
toward emancipation and nothing to allay apprehension that enc
ing slavery in the British West Indies would increase disconten
among slaves in the United States. Abolitionists remained cor
vinced that antislavery measures in America must parallel Englis
accomplishment. The alternative, they insisted, would be race wa
As the British moved toward emancipation in the 1820s and earl
1830s, hardly any element in antislavery argument loomed large
than warnings of eventual slave uprisings. These would come soor
abolitionists repeatedly warned, unless Americans agreed to mak
drastic changes in race relations. To those who reply "that the dan
ger *may be distant*," said Yale College professor Benjamin Sillimar
"I answer, it *may* also be near."[17]

The many new influences awakening northern reformers to th
menace of slavery led some of them by 1831 to seek to coordinat
their efforts through national organization. Free blacks were at th
forefront of the project. After they and a few white reformers dis
cussed the subject at the First Annual Convention of People of Colo
held at Philadelphia in June, 1831, hopes rose for early agreemen
on "an enlarged and extensive plan" of antislavery action. But th
project had not proceeded far when the Southampton revolt inter
vened, bringing with it general reassessment of reform policy. Som
were led to caution, others to greater initiative by Nat Turner'
exploits.

It was a troublesome and confusing time. Reformers, watchin
the turbulent national scene, tried to assess not so much their ow
chances for success as the probable effect their actions would have
either to lessen or increase turmoil. Some abolitionists found in th
tensions of sectional politics a compelling reason to delay organizec
activity. In the early 1830s, the bonds of national union were bein
tested as never before by South Carolina's threatened nullificatio

16. *Annals of Congress*, 15th Cong., 2nd Sess., 1370.
17. *Abolition Intelligencer*, I (May 7, 1822), 7, 9, 10; *Genius of Universal Emancipa*
tion, VI (November, 1824), 17; Phelps, *Lectures on Slavery*, 109, 210; Whittier, *Work*
of John Greenleaf Whittier, VII, 33–34; American Anti-Slavery Society, *First Annua*
Report, 19–20; Benjamin Silliman, "Some of the Causes of National Anxiety," *Africa*
Repository, VIII (August, 1832), 170.

the Tariff of 1832. National authority faced unprecedented chal-
nge at the hands of slaveowners. Understanding of this fact rein-
rced antislavery and antisouthern impressions among nationalis-
: New Englanders; it also produced caution. Even northern
embers of the American Colonization Society feared their rela-
vely conservative program would contribute to southern political
saffection. Accordingly, they proceeded with still greater wariness
an usual.[18] In that tense atmosphere, a number of antislavery ad-
cates concluded, any action promising still further intersectional
scord ought to be shunned.

Among some antislavery reformers in New York and New En-
and, however, considerations of duty managed to overrule caution
en in that troubled time, and voices calling for expanded antislav-
y action continued to be raised. In particular, free blacks, whose
terest in emancipation bore an immediacy no white reformer
uld match, viewed Turner's revolt as opportunity for antislavery
complishment rather than as cause for retreat: "This insurrection
the south," wrote the Philadelphia black reformer James Forten,
vill be the means of bringing the evils of slavery, more promi-
ntly before the public, and the urgent sense of danger . . . will lead
something more than mere hopes and wishes." But early opti-
ism of the sort Forten displayed was tempered when reformers
uged the deep anxiety resulting from Nat Turner's revolt. "The
outhampton affair has paralyzed our Philadelphia friends," ex-
ained Arthur Tappan of New York, "and nothing has been done or
n be done there now, towards organizing a National Society."[19]
Nearly two years were to pass before the three antislavery
oups—New Yorkers, New Englanders, and Pennsylvanians—
uld bring themselves to assume the risks involved in forming
e American Anti-Slavery Society. During that extended interval,
arrison and others who were bent upon intensifying antislavery
ort clarified their attitude toward violence. They also scrupu-
usly defined their relationship to the slaves. In these undertakings,
uakers exercised influence beyond their numbers.

18. Charles Tappan to R. R. Gurley, March 13, 1830, in American Colonization
ciety Papers. Of Garrison, Tappan later would write, "I sometimes wish Arthur
ppan had let him lay in Baltimore jail—." Charles Tappan to R. R. Gurley, August
1831, ibid.
19. James Forten to William Lloyd Garrison, October 12, 1831, in Antislavery Col-
tion, Boston Public Library; Lewis Tappan to Garrison, January 21, 1832, ibid.;
rtram Wyatt-Brown, Lewis Tappan and the Evangelical War Against Slavery (Cleve-
d, 1969), 107.

The hesitancy Quakers displayed toward national organizati
did not obscure the fact that no religious group could claim a long
more firmly established antislavery commitment. So closely ide
tified were they with the cause that others regarded their support
essential. Any new abolitionist campaign must build on the ba
Quakers had created. Their commitment to nonviolence was sin
larly venerable. No antislavery program that seemed at all likely
result in bloodshed could win their endorsement.

Apprehension about the possibly violent effect of abolitionis
was felt in other quarters of the reform community as well. Indee
the entire "benevolent empire," the informal coalition of New Yor
and Boston-based reform societies, would follow Quakers and t
American Peace Society in shying from programs that seemed pr
ductive of violence and confusion rather than of peace and order.

It was against this background that the founders of the Americ:
Anti-Slavery Society drafted their platform and decided upon
mode of operation. They found in Quaker belief and practice mea
to allay the fears produced by the specter of slave revolt. The me
and women who convened at Philadelphia in December, 1833,
form the new society specifically renounced violence in the antisla
ery cause. And they also pointedly rejected cooperative effort wi
slaves. The society's Declaration of Sentiments, drafted by Garriso
set forth the new organization's principles and intended plan of o
eration.[20] These were altogether pacific and on the Quaker mod
There is every reason to suppose, however, that this feature of t
document accurately reflected views then held not just by Quake
but by the great majority of northern opponents of slavery, with t
possible exception of the free blacks.

Garrison's Declaration of Sentiments forthrightly condemn
slavery. Slavery was a sin that ought not to be tolerated for anoth
instant, but despite its enormities, wrote Garrison, slavery shou
be combated solely by means of moral suasion. Abolitionists r
nounced all use of "carnal weapons." They would argue the wror
done the slaves, the danger of keeping them longer in bondage, ar
the duty of immediately setting them free. While they would pla
no limit on verbal assaults, they would not take up arms again
slaveholders. More important, in view of prevalent insurrectiona:
fears, they would instruct slaves to follow their peaceful exampl

20. Garrison's "Declaration of Sentiments of the American Anti-Slavery Societ
is most conveniently found in Louis Ruchames (ed.), *The Abolitionists: A Collection
Their Writings* (New York, 1963), 78–83.

at the words abolitionists employed to alter opinion among
ites might also reach slaves was an incidental and unsought
obability. Such an outcome was neither calculated nor desired.
olitionists would direct their condemnations to free persons
ne—to the white electorate, whose opinions on slavery presum-
ly could be changed and mobilized. They would not address their
guments to slaves, who in any event could be assumed already to
ve made up their minds on the subject. Slaves needed no "moral
asion" concerning slavery—except for what was regarded as the
l-important counsel to remain at peace.

Garrison took care, nonetheless, to note that white Americans in
e revolutionary era finally grew impatient with petitions and pro-
st, the unavailing tactics of moral suasion. When the colonists no
nger could endure oppression, they took up arms against English
spots. Garrison did not face up to all the implications of that his-
ric fact, nor did he expand upon the analogy. Instead, he advised
ves, whose grievances he acknowledged to be greater than those
the colonists, to be more noble and self-restrained than white
nericans had been. Slaves should continue uncomplainedly to suf-
r oppression until deliverance came—at the hands of others.

Despite its simplistic quality and detachment from reality, Garri-
n's counsel was politic, the only advice possible at a time when
olitionism was suspect in the North and feared in the South, and
hen slaves nearly everywhere were thought to stand at the brink
rebellion. Any other program than the one adopted at Philadel-
ia probably would have aroused such widespread revulsion
ainst antislavery activity as to bring the movement to an abrupt
d.[21]

But these policies were not adopted solely out of expediency; they
flected the abolitionists' own convictions. Few of them in the
30s were bloody-minded enough to wish to provoke slave revolt
d race war. Further, they did not yet envision themselves acting
concert with blacks to end slavery. The widespread support for
e position taken at Philadelphia is indicated by the fact that anti-
avery groups throughout the North incorporated it in the plat-
rms and constitutions of all other antislavery societies founded in
e 1830s. The only important dissenters were free blacks. Although
veral black people took part in forming the American Anti-Slavery
ciety and endorsed its program, probably members of that group

21. See Bertram Wyatt-Brown, "William Lloyd Garrison and Antislavery Unity: A
appraisal," *Civil War History*, XIII (1967), 5–24.

felt less drawn toward pacifism than did white reformers. Some
an early date apparently even thought of direct military support
slave rebellion. Thus in 1832, George Carey of Cincinnati, an ea
black follower of Garrison, opposed an abolitionist project to fou
a college for blacks at New Haven. He favored instead a site outsi
the United States. If it were located in Canada, he explained, "
could have a military department attached to the college."[22]

The decision not to enlist slaves in the antislavery campaign
corded with abolitionists' principles and their perception of poli
cal necessity and was adopted chiefly for those reasons. But it a
harmonized with the paternalistic attitude humanitarians co
monly held toward the objects of their philanthropy and probat
seemed even more acceptable to them on those grounds. Abolitio
ists seldom articulated paternalism. They never stated that th
thought themselves superior to slaves. They did not hint that th
regarded blacks as moral or intellectual defectives who requir
their aid. Indeed, the important role played in the movement
such persons as Frederick Douglass and Charles and Sarah Remo
suggests the opposite assumption. Yet, in the long run, their paci
advice to slaves and their unilateral conduct of the abolitionist ca
paign encouraged a sentimental attitude toward slaves, an attitu
that had remained for the most part recessive before the 1830s.

Although racial prejudice had not been absent even among
formers in earlier years, it acquired new bases as the antislave
movement proceeded. This outcome certainly was not intende
and it ran counter to the abolitionists' persistent and sincere effor
to combat prejudice as a chief bulwark of slavery. White abolitio
ists eloquently defended black equality and black capacity. Yet e
ments of their campaign worked against the outcome they desire
Slaves, who once had been romantically pictured as fierce, wrong
warriors about to break their bonds and devastate the South, grad
ally were transformed in abolitionist writings into pathetic, helple
victims, trembling to accept the benevolence of wise and compete
white reformers. This view of slaves harmonized with reformist
titudes toward other "defectives"—the poor, the blind, the insar
the deaf and dumb—who also required aid from their more fort
nate betters.[23] Such attitudes, first reflected in action, soon we

22. Carey to Garrison, May 15, 1832, in Antislavery Collection, Boston Pub
Library.
23. See David Rothman, *The Discovery of the Asylum: Social Order and Disorder
the New Republic* (Boston, 1971).

ꞁstallized in language and print, and finally were perpetuated as
ıth. The image of blacks as incompetents accompanied, perhaps
ʼengthened, notions of its opposite—the moral, even genetic, su-
ꞃiority of whites.

Despite its nobility of purpose, philanthropic activity fostered
ꞇh beliefs, for however unselfishly aid might be extended, the
ꞁer unavoidably assumed a position of superiority before the re-
ꞇient. Such posture had been inseparable from the philanthropic
ꞃrk of the constituent societies of the antislavery American Con-
ꞃtion and of the various "humane societies" whose object in the
20s and earlier was to aid blacks and protect them from kidnap-
ꞃs and other would-be exploiters. Although totally unintended,
ꞇh paternalism and prejudice received heavy reinforcement from
ꞇ program abolitionists adopted in response to the political situ-
ꞇon they found themselves in during the early 1830s. Their deci-
ꞃn to make the antislavery movement a pacific enterprise confined
ꞇely to free persons cast slaves in a subordinate, inferior role,
ꞃile also denying them the right to participate in their own
ꞇeration.

Despite these unfortunate ultimate effects, the pacific tactics and
ꞁilateral action decided upon by the founders of the American
ꞇti-Slavery Society reflected shrewd appraisal of prevailing fears
ꞇd power relationships. Although the abolitionists' Quaker-like
ꞃgram may to a later age seem inevitable, persons at the time did
ꞇ find it so.[24] Instead of the self-denying policies adopted at Phil-
ꞇlphia in 1833, abolitionists might have decided to employ
ꞇves' evident desire to be free as a major weapon in their crusade.
ꞇey could have advised slaves to abandon their masters and flee to
ꞇ North. They could have mobilized northern free blacks and mili-
ꞇt whites into invading guerrilla bands. They could have an-
ꞃunced an alliance with slaves and proclaimed a war for libera-
ꞃn. These tactics seem unthinkable (though white southerners at
ꞇ time would not have been surprised to find them implemented),
ꞇt only because they are so at variance with the peaceable tactics
ꞇually adopted and so unlike the mode of operation almost uni-
ꞃsally adopted by other nineteenth-century protest groups. In
ꞃrt, they seem "un-American."

Yet as abolitionists surely knew, the means they rejected had

24. Bertram Wyatt-Brown makes this point and explores the possible range of
ꞇtics in his "William Lloyd Garrison and Antislavery Unity," 5–24.

found ample precedent in the American past. They were mod
of hostility eighteenth-century enemies freely employed agaii
American colonists. The Spanish, French, and English at vario
times had undertaken tacit alliances with slaves and had urg
them to escape and to rebel, though always for political and natic
alistic purposes, not primarily for philanthropic ones.

In contrast, the goals as well as the methods of the nineteen
century American antislavery movement reflected its origin in re
gious and humanitarian principles and in prudential concern. B
as slaveholders generally understood, abolitionism also possess
unmistakable political overtones. It was related to, and was in so
sense a product of, fundamental social and economic changes th
by the 1820s were moving the northern states toward open rival
with the South for the right to control the nation and to set its futt
course. If the time should arrive when its political aspects becar
dominant and took command, then abolitionists might cast asi
moral suasion and at last resort to modes of rivalry made famili
to earlier Americans by Spanish, French, and English enemies.
the eighteenth century, hostile powers had not shrunk from explc
ing slave discontent, inviting slaves to flee their masters and c
couraging them to violent resistance—all in order to achieve poli
cal and imperialistic ends. The same things might be done again.

9

☙☙☙☙☙☙☙☙☙☙☙☙☙☙☙☙☙☙☙☙☙☙☙☙

A Disruptive Influence

ot for a moment did white southerners believe the abolitionists'
peated denials of insurrectionary intent. From the slaveholders'
int of view, nothing in their record inspired trust. If abolitionists
cerely wanted to avoid provoking rebellion—so southerners
ought—they would not persist in issuing the kind of propaganda
at might persuade nonslaveholders to withdraw support from the
anter class, thereby making revolt more likely. Neither would they
nduct their campaign in such a way as to encourage slaves to be-
ve they had partisans in the North. But antislavery activity, under
y circumstance and in any shape, was not something toward
hich slaveholders could afford forbearance. It struck at the source
their livelihood and the foundation of their status, power, and
lf-esteem. "It is my property they seek to take," complained James
arbour of Virginia; "it is my person, my safety, my happiness, that
e put to hazard."[1]
By the 1830s, slaveholders' growing awareness of the abolitionist
reat eclipsed every impulse toward tolerance. The most aggres-
ve vehicles of antislavery propaganda, the Boston *Liberator* and
e New York *Emancipator*, lay so far to the north as to be physi-
lly unassailable. But offending editors close to the border lived
peril. The violence that border-state mobs directed against anti-

1. *Annals of Congress*, 16th Cong., 1st Sess., 330.

slavery editors in the mid-1830s—James G. Birney in Cincinna
Elijah P. Lovejoy first in St. Louis and then in Alton, Illinois
represented release of long-standing tension.[2] Slaveholders a
their partisans had been incited almost beyond endurance by
recent, well-organized and well-financed abolitionist propagan
campaign. In May, 1835, the American Anti-Slavery Society 1
solved to flood the nation with antislavery publications. Newsp
pers, pamphlets, and tracts would be sent everywhere, especia
into the slave states, where antislavery agents themselves dared n
go. While the mails carried abolitionist ideas to the South, a sm
army of lecturers would march across the North voicing the abc
tionist gospel.

All went as planned. The lecturers kept their appointments, a
abolitionist presses in New York turned out thousands of pages
print, many bearing well-executed woodcuts illustrating the suffe
ings of slaves. Slaveholders regarded the literature as insulting
themselves, but worse, it might fall into the hands of slaves, wl
even if not literate, could understand the vivid pictures. And near
as troublesome, it might persuade impressionable southern whit
to question the peculiar institution.

Although abolitionists already had learned that the way of t
antislavery advocate was hard, few could have foreseen the wave
hostility aroused by their propaganda campaign of 1835. Mo
greeted abolitionist lecturers almost everywhere they went in t
North, and in the South, arrival of the antislavery publicatio
provoked hysterical responses. Reports of increased slave unrest a
companied the furor. In the summer and fall of 1835 at widely sep
rated points, alleged servile conspiracies were uncovered. Abolitio
ists, southern whites charged, instigated these new plots just as th
bore responsibility for the Nat Turner atrocity.[3]

In the ensuing panic, southern whites directed violence agair
slaves and free blacks, against whites suspected of being abolitic

2. Betty L. Fladeland, *James G. Birney: Slaveholder to Abolitionist* (Ithaca, N
1955), 130–43; Merton L. Dillon, *Elijah P. Lovejoy, Abolitionist Editor* (Urbana, I
1961), Chaps. VII-XIII.
3. Russell B. Nye, *Fettered Freedom: Civil Liberties and the Slavery Controver
1830–1860* (East Lansing, Mich., 1949), 41–85. A conspiracy allegedly involvi
white men is described in Edwin A. Miles, "The Mississippi Slave Insurrection Sc
of 1835," *Journal of Negro History*, XLII (1957), 48–60, and Laurence Shore, "Maki
Mississippi Safe for Slavery: The Insurrectionary Panic of 1835," in Orville Vern
Burton and Robert C. McMath, Jr. (eds.), *Class, Conflict, and Consensus: Antebell
Southern Community Studies* (Westport, Conn., 1981), 96–127.

A Disruptive Influence   179

ts, and against antislavery publications. A mob at Charleston
urned the mail as it arrived by ship from New York. Southern state
gislatures demanded from their northern counterparts laws sup-
ressing antislavery societies and throttling the abolitionist press.
itizens' meetings posted rewards for delivery into their hands of
e best-known antislavery advocates—"dead or alive." Similar re-
ction was not unknown in the North. At about the same time that
harlestonians burned abolitionist pamphlets, a mob in Philadel-
nia destroyed boxes of such literature while the city's mayor
oked on.[4]

President Andrew Jackson grew apprehensive as he saw mobs in
oth North and South take law into their own hands. "The spirit of
ob-law is becoming too common and must be checked, or ere long
will become as great an evil as servile war," he told the postmaster
eneral. Yet as a slaveholder and Tennessean, Jackson, too, was re-
elled by the abolitionists' "attempt to stir up amongst the South
e horrors of a servile war." Although the stern disciplinarian knew
e remedy, he also knew the federal system prevented its being im-
osed. "Could they be reached," wrote the president, "they ought to
e made to atone for this wicked attempt, with their lives." But if
olitionists could not legally be hanged, they might at least be
ade ineffective. Thus in his annual message of 1835, Jackson asked
e northern states to enact laws suppressing abolitionist activity
d called upon Congress to close the mails to "incendiary publica-
ons intended to instigate . . . insurrection."[5]

Congress passed no such law, in part because southern members,
creasingly conscious of "state rights," refused to concede the na-
onal government's authority in such matters. Neither did any
orthern state legislature grant either Jackson's request or the
outhern demand to outlaw abolitionist agitation.

Although some northern state governors—especially Edward Ev-
ett of Massachusetts and William Marcy of New York—expressed
mpathy for the South's plight, no legislature went further than
nsuring abolitionists for their "incendiary" actions. The legisla-

4. Wyatt-Brown, *Lewis Tappan*, 149–63; Frank Otto Gatell, "Postmaster Huger
d the Incendiary Publications," *South Carolina Historical Magazine*, LXIV (1963),
3–201; Gary B. Nash, *Forging Freedom: The Formation of Philadelphia's Black Com-
unity, 1720–1840* (Cambridge, Mass., 1988), 277.
5. Andrew Jackson to Amos Kendall, August 9, 1835, in Bassett (ed.), *Correspond-
ce of Andrew Jackson*, V, 360; James D. Richardson (ed.), *A Compilation of the
essages and Papers of the Presidents* (Washington, D.C., 1896), IV, 1394.

tures of only three states—Maine, New York, and Ohio—bother
to reply at all to southern requests for repressive legislation, ar
none of these responses came near to satisfying slaveholders' d
mands. From the viewpoint of southerners, this was an ominous r
fusal, for it led to an inescapable conclusion: The South must star
on its own resources in defense of slavery. John C. Calhoun read tl
situation gloomily: "Not a step has been taken [by northern state:
not a law has been passed, or even proposed; and I venture to asse
that none will be."[6]

Disheartening though these failures were, the South for the pre
ent was not quite so friendless as Calhoun's statement implied. E
ery northern state contained its share of influential persons eager
demonstrate to their slaveholding countrymen that abolitionis
were as objectionable north of the Ohio River as south of it. Inste:
of truly representing spontaneous rank-and-file sentiment, the mo
that plagued abolitionist lecturers often resulted from encourag
ment and support—sometimes instigation—by such promine
citizens. Throughout the 1830s, dozens of violent antiabolitioni
episodes across the North testified to the influence of persons be
upon maintaining cordial relations with the South and leaving sla
ery undisturbed. Some northerners found nearly as unwelcome .
did southerners the prospect that antislavery activity would add
already threatening intersectional discord and perhaps even inci
race war.[7]

Antislavery partisans themselves, it appeared, were no long
united in attitude toward slave revolt. John Farmer drew a histor
cal analogy from the disagreement. The flinty New Hampshire ab
litionist marveled at the stand taken by those who shrank from tl
thought of slave insurrection: "How near they are approximating
the old tory doctrines of the Revolution." But more typical was W:
liam Oakes, an eminent botanist with unimpeachable abolitioni
credentials, who expressed relief to find so many of his associat
again going on record against violence. "Let it be fully understood
he wrote, "that 3/4 of the abolitionists do not believe even in defe:
sive war, much less in the 'sacred right' of insurrection." Oak

6. Garrison and Garrison, *William Lloyd Garrison*, II, 73–76; William L. Marcy
John Gayle, [1835], in Miscellaneous Manuscripts, New-York Historical Socie
Richard K. Cralle (ed.), *Speeches of John C. Calhoun* . . . (New York, 1853), II, 531.
7. Leonard L. Richards, *"Gentlemen of Property and Standing:" Anti-Abolition*
Mobs in Jacksonian America (New York, 1970); Lorman Ratner, *Powder Keg: Northe*
Opposition to the Antislavery Movement, 1831–1840 (New York, 1968).

ted, too, the reassuring fact that "they all rejoice to use any op-
rtunity to speak to slaves & entreat to them to wait in patience
er so long rather than recourse to insurrection." To those who
ewed repetition of such points as more ritualistic than convincing,
akes offered evidence designed to calm: After a half-dozen years of
tensified antislavery effort, slave insurrections were no more com-
on than before the campaign began.[8]
Oakes's observation could not be disputed. Despite repeated
arms, Nat Turner as yet had no imitator. Suspicion nonetheless
n deep, and the South's having been spared further overt rebellion
d little to remove objections to antislavery agitation, for as plant-
s understood, the undermining of slave discipline in forms short
outright revolt could ruin the plantation South.
Slaveowners never underestimated the threat to their welfare
osed by the rising antislavery movement. Few and scorned as were
e declared adherents of abolitionism, southerners suspected that
e values they represented were not so generally despised as mob
tion against them might suggest. They could not forget that, de-
ite plentiful evidence of northern antiabolitionist sentiment, no
orthern state government had acted to halt abolitionist activity.
is omission constituted a troublesome paradox that southerners
und hard to ignore and northerners could not explain away. On
e hand, governmental nonaction could be excused as reflecting
thing more than traditional commitment to freedom of expres-
on; on the other hand, it could be understood as proceeding from
ofound and as yet unacknowledged changes in the North that
entually would challenge planter influence in national affairs. The
tter explanation seemed the more credible, for despite the con-
icuous presence throughout the free states of southern sympathiz-
s, the section as a whole appeared to be changing from a region
mply adhering to values and institutions somewhat different from
ose of the South into a rival, perhaps even an overt enemy, with
olitionists helping supply motive power for the transformation.
ose individuals in the North who were committed to a free-labor
stem and who advocated governmental policies designed to foster
mmercial and industrial growth found in the antislavery move-
ent an auxiliary to their purpose. The abolitionists' morally de-
ved hostility to the plantation South complemented their own am-

8. William Oakes to Samuel E. Sewall, August 20, 1835, in Antislavery Collection,
ston Public Library.

bition and helped elevate their drive to power from expediency high ethical ground.[9]

The ambition of some opponents of slavery evidently extend into the South itself to embrace more aims than only persuadi owners to substitute free labor for the labor of slaves. Abolitionis some suspected, schemed both to subvert the nonslaveholdir whites' allegiance to the planters and to forge an alliance wi blacks. The ultimate success of their efforts seemed possible, for t natural affinity of the three groups might someday effect such union, with dire consequence to plantation society. Blacks th would be transformed from being merely a neutral element arou which moral controversy raged into a positive force in an interse tional struggle for power.

The understanding that slaves played a political role in the nati reached far into the past. It was a role recognized and made opei tive by the three-fifths compromise of the Constitution. To that e tent, slaves were made adjuncts of southern power within the n tion and became inseparable from it. But slaveholders long h regarded slaves also as potential enemies, recruits for hostile u against the white South. When a generation earlier Jefferson ai Monroe conferred about a site for settling blacks found "guilty insurgency," Jefferson set forth an all-important condition: "\ should prefer placing them with whatsoever power is least likely become an enemy, and to use the knolege [sic] of these exiles predatory expeditions against us."[10]

Misgivings that an enemy might turn to its own advantage t blacks' desire for freedom became still more pressing with the ri of aggressive, organized antislavery activity after 1830. In the g ometry of external relationships, the North then assumed the hc tile position earlier occupied by Spain, France, and England. Fr blacks at that point entered into the racial configuration almost ominously as did slaves, for whether located in North or South a whether free or slave, black people were counted as being natur allies of northern antislavery forces. Southern free blacks, existi only at the sufferance of whites, rarely made common cause wi slaves in any overt way and practically never challenged whi

9. Julian P. Bretz, "The Economic Background of the Liberty Party," Americ Historical Review, XXXIV (1929), 250–64; Margaret Shortreed, "The Antislave Radicals: From Crusade to Revolution, 1840–1868," Past and Present, XVI (Nove ber, 1959), 65–87.
10. Jefferson to Monroe, June 3, 1802, in Executive Papers, Virginia State Libra

minance. The relative autonomy enjoyed by their northern coun-
parts allowed them to act far differently. Uncertainty as to how
rthern free blacks would respond to their independence troubled
eir white neighbors. Shortly after the Southampton revolt, a resi-
nt of Parkersburg, Virginia, worried that just across the river in
io lay a free-black settlement whose residents enjoyed "the same
ivileges nearly as free men." On that account, he added, "we have
great deal to fear." Even northern whites sometimes doubted the
alty of free blacks. "There is much uneasiness," reported a Stark
unty, Ohio, resident in 1830, "in consequence of a colony that is
w forming in upper Canada, which no doubt will be a source of
uble some day to these western states."[11]
Worrisome though these people were, especially to white south-
ers, no plan for removing them could be agreed upon. The chief
ficulty in finding an alternative to their immigration to Africa—
project that early proved chimerical—was their supposed affinity
th antislavery northerners. In 1836 the Maryland legislature con-
dered a plan to expel them from the state on the familiar ground
at they constituted both a nuisance and a danger. But the pro-
sal never came out of committee, not because the lawmakers
ted them less objectionable than was alleged, but because the
ggested remedy promised still greater danger. Expulsion of free
acks, said the committee, "would be to send them to the free
ates, to make easier the path for runaway slaves, and to league
th fanatic abolitionists." It was better to keep these troublesome
ople in the South, where they could be watched and controlled,
an to send them to the North, where they would swell enemy
nks. "Especially do I object to the colonization of our Negroes
on our northern frontier," said a Georgian in 1858. "They facili-
te the escape of our fugitive slaves. In case of civil war, they would
come an element of strength to the enemy."[12]
Although southern whites spent much time discussing the free-
ack problem, their greater concern naturally lay with abolitionist
fluence on slaves. Suspicion of abolitionist-induced disaffection

11. J. B. Creele to John Floyd, November 26, 1831, *ibid.*; William D. Barrett to
R. Gurley, March 3, 1830, in American Colonization Society Papers. The specter
rsisted: In 1846 an abolitionist predicted that 20,000 blacks from Canada would
d Mexico by attacking the United States, and in 1857 an antislavery preacher in
ntucky advised that "40,000 Negroes in Canada are training and plan to come
wn and slit the throats of the slaveholders." *Liberator*, May 22, 1846; John Fee to
ecutive Committee, July 15, 1857, in American Missionary Association Archives.
12. Brackett, *Negro in Maryland*, 24; Catterall (ed.), *Judicial Cases*, III, 61.

focused on the upper South, where, white southerners suspecte
slaves had been contaminated by antislavery doctrine filteri
across the border as well as by their close knowledge of the prec
dent set by Nat Turner. Outside influences, some observed, ma
border-state slaves ambitious for freedom and hard to discipline. I
longer were they tractable workers. Their unsavory reputati
spread well beyond the region. Thus citizens of South Carolina
the 1830s protested importation of slaves from Virginia and Mar
land on grounds that those "Villains of the North" would demora
ize their own more isolated and therefore uncorrupted slaves.[13]

Abolitionists relished as evidence of progress the attitudes amo
slaves that their owners viewed with alarm. They, too, took f
granted that slaves transported from the upper South to the dev
oping plantations of the Gulf states carried liberating ideas wi
them, ideas for which abolitionists gladly took credit. Throu;
transfer of slaves from the upper to lower South, predicted the R(
erend Amos A. Phelps, the "whole mass will be leavened; and t
spirit of insurrection—the creature of oppression . . . will not th
be dead. . . . On the contrary, it will be instinct with life."[14] Phelp
a founder of the American Anti-Slavery Society, did not recoil fro
the prospect of rebellion, even though it was totally at variance wi
the professed pacifism of the society he had helped establish.

In contrast, the abolitionist Beriah Green, president of the co
vention that organized the American Anti-Slavery Society, conti
ued to hold the more conventional belief that antislavery activi
protected southern whites against vengeful blacks. Only the fa
that slaves were pacified by northern reformers' efforts in their b
half, Green claimed, prevented rebellion. In Kentucky, where an
slavery ideas circulated rather freely in the early 1830s, Robert
Finley, an agent of the American Colonization Society, likewise cre
ited his own activity with giving slaves hope of eventual freedo
and thereby tempering their hostility. A North Carolina planter
1835 believed he detected among slaves in his neighborhood sor
of the influences antislavery reformers spoke of: "It seems that t
abolition question so much talked of latterly has gotten to the
[ears] and they have taken up the idea that the northerners will fr

13. Catterall (ed.), *Judicial Cases*, III, 61; Grand Jury Presentment from Beaufo
April 17, 1832, in Grand Jury Presentments, South Carolina Department of Archiv
and History.
14. Phelps, *Lectures on Slavery*, 211.

em which has [led] some of them to exult in anticipation of
:edom."[15]
Although the extent of slaves' accurate knowledge of antislavery
tivity remains unmeasured, their frequent escapes from border
:as testify to their understanding that in one part of the country
acks were free, and there refuge could be found. No other response
the deepening sectional conflict should have been expected. Pre-
dent could be found in the past, when members of their grandpar-
ts' generation had acted in much the same way upon learning
at foreign powers across the border offered sanctuary from colo-
al masters.
The understanding led to unsettling consequences after 1830 as
e tempo of attempted escapes increased. By 1834, as a device for
tercepting runaways, authorities regularly assigned guards to
cket boats sailing between Baltimore and Philadelphia. Although
ost escapes to the North appear to have been acts of individual
speration, sometimes they approached the magnitude of mass
ovement, as in 1829 in Virginia, when slaves "in gangs" left Ac-
mac County, and again in September, 1832, when a band of some
ghteen slave men in Northampton County sailed in a stolen boat
om Chesapeake Bay to a wharf in New York City. Shortly after-
ard, thirty more Northampton slaves unsuccessfully tried to du-
icate the feat. These events, wrote Abel P. Upshur, "proving the
ter insecurity of this property among us, have rendered it of very
tle value. . . . The impoverishment and ruin of the people will be
e necessary consequence."[16]
Even as far south as the lower coast of North Carolina, slaves
eamed of similar exploits. In Onslow County in 1831, the slave

15. American Anti-Slavery Society, *First Annual Report*, 12; Robert S. Finley to
R. Gurley, April 12, 1831, in American Colonization Society Papers; John Blount
Charles W. Jacocks, October 3, 1835, in Charles W. Jacocks Papers, North Carolina
vision of Archives and History, Raleigh. Slave testimony about the extent of knowl-
ge of abolition activity is hard to come by, but see remarks by Frederick Douglass
Liberator, May 19, 1843, and by Booker T. Washington in Louis R. Harlan (ed.),
e *Booker T. Washington Papers* (Urbana, Ill., 1972–84), I, 218. See also Stanley Feld-
in, *Once a Slave: The Slaves' View of Slavery* (New York, 1971), 185–87, 273–75.
16. Catterall (ed.), *Judicial Cases*, IV, 81; Colonel Joynes to William Giles, August
, 1829, in Executive Papers, Virginia State Library; Upshur to the Governor, Oc-
er 4, 1832, in Palmer, McRae, and Flournoy (eds.), *Calendar of Virginia State Pa-
s*, X, 278; American Anti-Slavery Society, *First Annual Report*, 54. For other, simi-
incidents, see John W. Blassingame, *The Slave Community: Plantation Life in the
tebellum South* (Rev. ed., New York, 1979), 206–208.

Peter revealed that "there is about thirty head about here that
for going to the free states, that they were going in the vessel b
longing to Col. Dudley."[17] From such bold undertakings, souther
ers learned that antislavery activity threatened economic disasl
even if it did not lead to violence. Mass escapes demonstrated th
through its recently expanded antislavery reputation, the North c
erted a seriously disruptive influence on the South's society a
economy. Slave response to the lure of the North could be taken
evidence that an abolitionist-slave political alliance might be in t
making. Further, it revealed to slaveowners unpleasant truths th
eventually would prove to be their nemesis: Total control of the
labor force was impossible, and preventing slave contact with forc
hostile to the planters was impossible.

In the lower South and in interior regions, the slaves' knowled
of the antislavery North probably was less detailed than in stat
along the border, but even in isolated areas it may not have be
wholly lacking. Slaves bought from the upper South—and su
trade was constant—were likely to bring with them contaminati
information that they could pass to others, a result owners und
stood but found no way to avoid.

Border-state slaves were not the only source of subversive infc
mation available to slaves of the lower South. Occasional travele
and the ubiquitous Yankee peddler offered them as well as the
owners glimpses of a different world. Rafts and steamboats on t
Mississippi arrived from the free states, with sometimes seducti
effect on slaves along the river. Situations unique to a particul
locality might be responsible for disruption, as in southern Georgi
where lumbermen from Maine spent winters working in the regior
great live oak forests. There they labored alongside slaves to prepa
timbers for New England shipyards and, according to a suspicio
neighbor, tried to incite them to rebel.[18] Neither these northe
woodsmen nor many members of the small army of travelers wl
regularly made their way through the South were likely to be avow
abolitionists. Slaves nonetheless could learn from them that wor

17. Criminal Action Concerning the 1831 Insurrection of Slaves, in Onslow Cou
Miscellaneous Records.
18. Willie Lee Rose (ed.), *A Documentary History of Slavery in North America* (N
York, 1976), 416. On the whites' suspicion of peddlers and the slaves' response
them, see *Annals of Congress*, 16th Cong., 1st Sess., 1024. An account of a slave w
ran away with a peddler is in George P. Rawick (ed.), *The American Slave: A Comp
ite Autobiography* (Westport, Conn., 1972), XIX, 121.

s elsewhere—including blacks—led lives very unlike their own,
ıd some would find the difference inviting.

Such enlightening contacts, necessarily infrequent and limited to
latively few persons, did not go far toward counteracting the iso-
ting effect that movement into the undeveloped Southwest had on
aves as well as on their owners. But isolation, which might have
elped stabilize slavery, was made less stultifying by advances in
chnology, especially in the 1840s and afterward, and by the grow-
ıg popular enthusiasm for politics. With multiplication of news-
ıpers and ever-improved means of travel, white southerners—and
aves too—enjoyed expanded opportunity to learn about faraway
ents and to be influenced by them. The inland South then lost
ıme of its isolation, with unsettling consequences. Absorption in
ıe heated electoral campaigns of the 1830s and 1840s brought
ackcountry whites into periodic contact with national affairs. Poli-
cs opened curtains for slaves as well. Not even black people were
together deprived of the diversion and enlightenment offered by
olitical activity. Slaves, along with their masters, heard political
iscussions, watched parades and rallies, listened to rumors. As
ırly as 1830, a complaint about this reached the governor of North
arolina. Slaves, said the writer, were permitted to assemble "at
ıusters, elections and other places where they acquire insolence
ıd audacity." In North Carolina in 1836, a slave remembered, "there
ıme a report from a neighboring plantation that, if Van Buren was
ected, he was going to give all the slaves their freedom. It spread
ıpidly among all the slaves in the neighborhood, and great, very
eat was the rejoicing." The "negroes in Georgia are already saying
ɔ each other that great men are trying to set them free and will
ıcceed, and many other expressions of similar import," the Geor-
ıa politician Howell Cobb was told in 1844. In South Carolina on
ıe eve of the Civil War, when special precautions respecting slaves
ɔmmonly were thought essential, ten percent of the audience at
ɔlitical rallies, James H. Hammond estimated, were black.[19]

The topics commonly discussed in electoral campaigns—tariffs,
ınks, land policy—must have been incomprehensible and of ab-

19. Calvin Jones to Montfort Stokes, December 28, 1830, in Governors' Papers,
ɔrth Carolina Division of Archives and History; Blassingame (ed.), *Slave Testimony*,
ı6; John W. H. Underwood to Howell Cobb, February 2, 1844, in Ulrich B. Phillips
d.), *Correspondence of Robert Toombs, Alexander H. Stephens, and Howell Cobb,*
ɔl. II of American Historical Association, *Annual Report . . . for the Year 1911* (Wash-
gton, D.C., 1913), 55; Steven A. Channing, *Crisis of Fear*, 39.

solutely no interest to most blacks. But occasionally it was othe wise. Slavery itself became an issue in some elections. Thus in 184 when Democrats accused the Whig presidential candidate of abo. tionist leanings, slaves in Georgia, Emily P. Burke remembere "were all bold enough to assert publically that 'when Willia Henry Harrison became President of the United States, they shou have their freedom.'" Doubtless, not "all" Georgia slaves said ar such thing, but the fact that a similar independent report came fro Alabama at about the same time suggests at least some substan for both accounts.[20]

Political use of the slavery issue continued through the 185C with predictable effect on slaves. In 1856 when John C. Fremont ra as candidate of the new, antislavery Republican party, and again 1860 when opponents branded Abraham Lincoln the abolitioni choice of an abolitionist party, southern white voters' frankly e pressed concern could not be confined to themselves. At such time slaves learned from local politicians that their status was a point contention, that somewhere white men and women advocated fre dom for blacks. In his fourth annual message, delivered Decemb 2, 1856, President Franklin Pierce referred to abolition as "a forei object" that could be accomplished only "through burning citie and ravaged fields, and slaughtered populations, and all there most terrible in foreign complicated with civil and servile war." Pierce's sentiments achieved printed form, circulated through th South, and, like other written material, may have been compr hended by slaves.

Much rarer opportunities for abolitionist indoctrination a peared, one from so distinguished a source as William Tecumse Sherman, the later scourge of the South. Despite his well-earne Civil War reputation, Sherman was never an abolitionist symp. thizer, and his supplying slaves with antislavery literature in 184 while stationed at Fort Moultrie signifies neither subversive nor i surrectionary intent. Rather it suggests his contempt for abolitio ists and his confidence in the docility of slaves. It also supplies th incidental information that apparently some of the slaves he asse ciated with could read. Sherman found ridiculous an abolitioni pamphlet written "by that crazy fool Bob Levering," but the slave

20. Rose (ed.), *Documentary History*, 412; *Liberator*, January 22, 1841.
21. Richardson (ed.), *Messages and Papers*, VII, 2931–32.

 whom he gave Levering's essay "for their amusement," as he said,
 ay well have regarded it differently and perhaps put it to unin-
 nded use.[22]

So far as is known, publications of the sort Sherman treated
 ith such abandon seldom reached slaves in the Deep South, but
 uch as in the 1820s, antislavery literature continued to circulate
 nong free blacks in Baltimore and Washington and to a lesser ex-
 nt in towns in Virginia.[23] The news and ideas such material con-
 yed to free-black readers could not easily be concealed from
 aves there and, eventually, from slaves in more remote southern
 gions as well.

It is, of course, unnecessary to demonstrate external influence in
 rder to account for the high value blacks placed on freedom. The
 aves on President James K. Polk's Mississippi plantations, for ex-
 mple, who made life miserable for the overseers by persistently
 emanding better treatment and running away, may not even have
 nown there was a North, to say nothing of being informed about
 ne antislavery movement. When they fled beyond the immediate
 eighborhood, their goal apparently was not to reach a free state
 ut to go to Tennessee. So far as the records show, Polk's slaves did
 ot even enjoy access to religious teachings, which, for many, pow-
 fully reinforced aspirations for freedom. Yet for all their apparent
 norance, his slaves—like countless others—repeatedly proved, to
 ne pain of overseers, that they wanted to be free.[24]

In the case of the slaves on Polk's plantation, "evil" poor-white
 eighbors were blamed for encouraging and aiding resistance. The
 harge well may have been true, for although slavery and the racial
 ttitudes that supported it now received massive endorsement at all
 cial levels, some southern whites still remained outside the con-
 nsus, and much as in colonial days, behaved toward slaves in a
 anner subversive of the institution. Especially in those rural areas
 here small farmers and still-poorer whites were numerous, and in
 ties, where social barriers of every sort were frail, slaves came into

22. Sherman to Ellen B. Ewing, February 8, 1844, in William Tecumseh Sherman
 pers, Ohio Historical Society, Columbus. The pamphlet was Robert E. H. Levering,
 ne Kingdom of Slavery . . . (Circleville, Ohio, 1844).
    23. Ethan Allen Andrews, Slavery and the Domestic Slave Trade in the United States
 oston, 1836), 36–37, 57.
    24. John Spencer Bassett (ed.), The Southern Plantation Overseer as Revealed in His
 tters (Northampton, Mass., 1925), 54, 63, 146–47, 263.

contact with lower-class whites in ways that violated some notion of racial etiquette.[25] The loyalty of urban dwellers to slavery, some assumed, could not be depended on. H. W. Connor in 1849 believe that though most of Georgia still solidly supported slavery, Savannah and Augusta could not be counted on: "The cities all of the are becoming more and more unsound and uncertain and all for th same reason"—their northern and foreign-born population. Bu there were native apostates as well. Nearly anywhere, though especially in cities, one could find persons willing to engage in unauthorized trade with slaves, exchanging whiskey, finery, even nece sities for farm products, possibly stolen from masters or whi neighbors. By thus establishing an independent economic connec tion with slaves, these merchants challenged the exclusiveness the slave-master relationship. Further, by such commerce they ider tified their interests with those of the slave rather than with th slave's master, thereby creating the possibility of an additional po litical threat to the institution. In 1831 in Virginia, N. E. Sutto complained of the scene at "every village" of blacks and white "vending and trad[ing] in various ways. . . . The exhibition of whi and black mingling together beggars description. . . . What I ask to be expected but disorder and consequences of the most dangerou and alarming results[?]"[26]

If even in those propriety-assailing situations certain barriers be tween the races seldom were breached, such interracial familiarit nevertheless nurtured attitudes incompatible with the submissio that plantation discipline required. Partly on account of that inflt ence, urban slaves, it was thought, significantly differed from slave in rural areas. In towns, blacks developed a sense of independenc copied the manners and attitudes of their white associates, and be came resentful of close supervision. Not surprisingly, planters con monly tried to prevent their field slaves from associating with tow slaves, who enjoyed varied sources of information and range of so cial contact. Blacks displaying unslavelike traits and urban white

25. For examples, see Bassett (ed.), *Southern Plantation Overseer*, 66; State v. Jace Boyce, Superior Court, Spring Term, 1846, in Perquimans County Slave Paper 1759–1864, Case of Amos Ellis, in Criminal Actions Concerning Slaves, 1817–19, Wayne County Records, North Carolina Division of Archives and History, Raleig Catterall (ed.), *Judicial Cases*, II, 329, 355; Phillips (ed.), *Plantation and Frontier*, II, 8
26. H. W. Connor to John C. Calhoun, June 12, 1849, in J. Franklin Jameson (ed *Correspondence of John C. Calhoun*, Vol. II, Pt. 2 of American Historical Associatio *Annual Report . . . for the Year 1899* (Washington, D.C., 1900), 1188–89; N. E. Sutto to John Floyd, September 21, 1831, in Executive Papers, Virginia State Library.

areless of racial barriers should be given no chance to sow in rural
aves the seeds of discontent that unfitted them for steady labor.
onetheless, despite taboo and precaution, slaves and white people
ontinued to mingle in social situations, drinking and playing cards
gether, on terms that approached equality. An occasional white
erson still flouted every expectation by helping slaves escape, as
e fugitive John Brown discovered when he found a poor man will-
g to provide him with a forged pass in exchange for an old hen.
nd sexual barriers still were broken, sometimes in forms threat-
ning to the social order. "Do not many of our pretty white girls
ven now, permit illicit negro embraces at the South?" was the un-
ttling question addressed to the rice magnate Robert F. W. Allston
1 1858.[27] Transgressions such as these, originating within the
outh, had no discernible ties to northern antislavery, yet their ef-
cts on the social order were similar, and the eventual coalescence
f the two was not unlikely.

The slaveholders' distrust of white dissidents in their midst had a
ng history, as we have seen. Early in the century, slaves in Virginia
pparently took for granted the sympathy and good will of neigh-
oring lower-class white people, even for violent schemes. Thus Ga-
riel, plotting his rebellion in 1800, intended to spare Quakers,
Iethodists, Frenchmen, and poor women who owned no slaves.
wo years later, Virginia slaves, questioned about newly revealed
lots, testified that "the poorer kind of white people in and about
tichmond" offered to aid their projected insurrection.[28] Whether
he slaves' expectation was well-founded or not, such testimony
robably would not have been offered had not both slaves and
laveholders judged it entirely credible. When in 1815 a white Vir-
inian named George Boxley developed an elaborate plan to free the
laves by means of insurrection, these suspicions gained substance.
ut by at least the 1820s, relations between the races clearly were
eteriorating, while white solidarity strengthened. Although the
conomic opportunity that slavery and cotton offered the ambitious
vhite southerner doubtless contributed to the change, solidarity
lso was furthered by the steady flow of small farmers and antislav-

27. James Harold Easterby (ed.), *The South Carolina Rice Plantation, as Revealed*
 the Papers of Robert F. M. Allston (Chicago, 1945), 146; [Brown], *Slave Life in Geor-
ia*, 72.
28. Peter Randolph's Interview with Slaves Accused of Insurrection, May 5, 1802,
 Executive Papers, Virginia State Library. See also Enoch Sawyer to "Dear Sir,"
1ay 10, 1802, in Perquimans County Slave Papers.

ery dissidents out of the South, thereby removing rather than co: verting a source of opposition. Thus, by the time of Turner's revol slaves contemplating violent plans no longer realistically coul hope to receive significant aid from white southerners, though the: were rare exceptions, as in North Carolina, where in 1831 a sla⌐ preacher accused of organizing a conspiracy was "proved" to ha⌐ gone to "Mr. Gibbs and asked him if he would join them for th⌐ were about to rise," and in Mississippi, where in 1835 white men- not all of them "respectable"—were implicated in an alleged sla⌐ conspiracy.[29]

Evidence of stress within southern white society reappeared ⌐ the 1850s, however, generating new doubts about the permanenc of racial solidarity. Only this unease makes comprehensible the u⌐ tempered hostility southern whites directed against Hinton Row⌐ Helper's *Impending Crisis* (1857), with its antislavery arguments a⌐ dressed to southern nonslaveholders. "All attempts . . . to widen t⌐ breach between classes of citizens are just as dangerous as efforts ⌐ excite slaves to insurrection," observed Calvin Willey in the 18⌐ report on public education in North Carolina.[30] Occasionally whi⌐ disloyalty surfaced as apparent fact rather than mere suspicion ⌐ potential. Thus, on the eve of the Civil War, a woman wrote fro⌐ South Carolina that in the Abbeville District "five negroes are to ⌐ hung, twenty white men implicated all southern born, the po⌐ white *trash* who have associated with negroes and are jealous of t⌐ higher classes and think insurection [sic] will place all on a footin⌐ and they get some plunder in the bargain."[31]

Although white leaders sometimes doubted the constancy of no⌐ slaveholders and fretted over signs of class division, such disconte⌐ as poorer whites felt in antebellum years by no means necessari⌐ manifested itself in sympathy for blacks. One can hardly claim, f⌐

29. *Annals of Congress*, 16th Cong., 1st Sess., 292, 1354; William T. Allan in *Liber tor*, August 25, 1843; John Rankin, *Letters on American Slavery*, 72; Avery O. Crave⌐ *Coming of the Civil War*, 95; Barnhart, "Sources of Southern Migration," 49–6 Isaiah H. Spencer to the Governor, September 20, 1831, in Governors' Papers, Nor⌐ Carolina Division of Archives and History.

30. Johnson, *Ante-Bellum North Carolina*, 79.

31. Quoted in Steven A. Channing, *Crisis of Fear*, 272–73. For other comments ⌐ the nonslaveholders' disaffection, see John H. McHenry to R. M. T. Hunter, Februa⌐ 21, 1850, in Charles Henry Ambler (ed.), *Correspondence of Robert M. T. Hunt⌐ 1826–1876*, Vol. II of American Historical Association, *Annual Report . . . for the Ye⌐ 1916*, (Washington, D.C., 1918), 105–106; Conway P. Wing to Milton Badger, Augu⌐ 3, 1848, John McMillan to Milton Badger, March 25, 1853, and Joseph McKee ⌐ Milton Badger, July 28, 1845, all in American Home Missionary Society Papers.

xample, that the small farmers in Virginia who in the late 1820s
nd early 1830s agitated for constitutional change at the slavehold-
rs' expense were motivated by racial philanthropy, or that the
ovement in North Carolina in the 1850s to change the basis of
xation, again at slaveholders' expense, intended benefits to slaves.
onslaveholders in plantation areas commonly were integrated
to the planter-dominated society and economy and seldom mani-
sted disapproval of slavery. Economic and social grievances might
ad yeoman farmers outside such areas to resent, even oppose,
anters and the institution that sustained them, but even so, they
ere not often disposed to take up the slaves' cause.[32] Nevertheless,
e effect of class division, even if not so calculated, was to destabi-
ze slavery.

Relations between whites of low degree and blacks became less
iendly in the immediate antebellum decades than they once had
een, thus diminishing the likelihood that slaves could find depend-
ble nearby allies in their freedom struggles. Two different forces
ntributed to the estrangement. Mounting fears of abolitionism
nd sedition, carefully fostered by the molders of southern opinion,
ade intimate relationships of the kind that sometimes prevailed
 the seventeenth and eighteenth centuries suspect and dangerous.
Vhites who in an earlier day might have followed their inclinations
ward friendship with blacks now were likely to be deterred by the
mbarrassment and risk that accompanied charges of "abolition-
m." At the same time, an antagonism born of distrust and fear of
acks became increasingly evident among nonslaveholders.

The prolonged series of alarms, marked especially by Gabriel's
nd Vesey's conspiracies and culminating in Turner's revolt, took its
ll on interracial sympathies. Among the consequences of these
vents was confirmation of the distrust whites long ago had begun
 feel toward blacks. Some nonslaveholders, now regarding them
s enemies beyond reconciliation, vowed to wage a war of annihi-
ation should another Turner-like episode occur. In such event,
acks must be shown no mercy; all should be held responsible for
e deeds of a few. "They must be convinced that they must and will
e soon destroyed if their conduct makes it the least necessary,"
rote a North Carolinian. Yet not even such ruthlessness quite guar-
nteed slaveholders blind support for their interests. That lower-

---

32. Eugene D. Genovese, "Yeoman Farmers in a Slaveholding Democracy," *Agri-*
ultural History, XLIX (1975), 331–42.

class antipathy toward blacks carried with it resentment towar
slaveholders is suggested by the North Carolinian who vowed i
1832 that "we will not be harassed to protect ourselves from injur
by other peoples negroes but if one blow is struck we will murde
them indiscriminately."[33]

And of course that is exactly what they did. Whenever black
manifested a disposition toward violence, a spirit of untempere
vengeance was raised against them. The ferocious reprisals that fo
lowed Turner's rebellion were not unprecedented. In 1811, at th
time of the great insurrection in Louisiana, a visitor to New Orlean
reported that "about 150 negroes have been killed in various ways–
Only two white men killed and three good dwelling houses burnt
In the aftermath of Gabriel's conspiracy, Governor James Monro
received draconian advice: "Where there is any reason to believ
that any person is concerned, they ought immediately to be hanged
quartered and hung up on trees on every road as a terror to th
rest. . . . It will not do to be too scrupulous now," Joseph Jones ha
gone on to warn, "but to slay them all where there is any reason t
believe they are concerned."[34]

In Monroe's day, officials could check application of such sent
ments, but in an era characterized by democracy, they would hav
difficulty doing so, even if so inclined. Ruthless though Monroe
correspondent was in 1800, he nonetheless confined his advocacy c
slaughter to persons suspected of conspiracy. In the 1830s, a moo
of far greater severity captured the population. White southerner
then warned slaves and abolitionists of the merciless retributio
that awaited all blacks in the event of revolt by a few. Even exter
mination was considered.[35] Warm relationships between slaves an
nonslaveholders could not be expected to flourish in that kind o
atmosphere.

If white southerners had come to distrust blacks, blacks with a
much cause feared whites, slaveholders and nonslaveholders alike

33. Solon Borland to Roscius C. Borland, August 31, 1831, in Governors' Paper:
North Carolina Division of Archives and History; Johnson, Ante-Bellum North Care
lina, 519. See also Eric Foner, Nat Turner (Englewood Cliffs, N.J., 1971), 24, 67, 69–7C

34. Isaac L. Baker to Stephen F. Austin, February 25, 1811, in Barker (ed.), Austi
Papers, Vol. II, Pt. 1, p. 184; Joseph Jones to Monroe, September 9, 1800, in Executiv
Papers, Virginia State Library.

35. Joseph Speed to Gerrit Smith, December 17, 1835, in Gerrit Smith Paper:
Syracuse University Library, Syracuse, N.Y.; Tragle, Southampton Slave Revolt, 69
William M. Atkinson to R. R. Gurley, September 10, 1831, in American Colonizatio
Society Papers.

aves could never long put aside knowledge of the wrath that
vaited them on account of the missteps of their fellows as well as
themselves. Joseph Riddick of North Carolina no doubt was cor-
ct in concluding, upon disclosure of a slave plot in 1802, that
aves seemed more alarmed at the news than did the whites, for in
nes of rumored conspiracy, slaves were rounded up with little dis-
imination and condemned on the flimsiest of grounds, and fear
ve license to unprovoked violence.[36]
The hysteria and violence surrounding conspiracy alarms gener-
ly came only at long intervals. In ordinary times, the principal
urce of friction with white persons other than the slaves' owners
y in the imposition of the patrols, the community police force that
ually was manned by the neighborhood's small farmers. Folklore
well as slave narratives fully illustrate the slaves' irritation with
ese men who had authority to intrude into their homes and inter-
re with their leisure-time activities. Slaves would have resented
em in any event, but their resentment was greater because pa-
ollers sometimes could not resist the opportunity to tyrannize
er blacks and with little or no excuse to inflict cruelties both large
d small. By doing so, however, they risked reprisals. In 1802 at
whatan, Virginia, defiant slaves declared the patrols "had already
en permitted to go on too long but that it should not be long be-
re a Stop should be put to them," and in 1798 in Bertie County,
orth Carolina, a band of slaves "did attack, pursue, knock down
d lay prostrate the patrollers of said county."[37]
But such bold defiance was highly unusual, for most slaves must
ve known they had little chance to get the better of this official
m of the state. The most they could expect to do was to trick,
miliate, and sometimes inflict pain. Still, these incidents did not
present moves in a parlor game of wits. The frequent, petty, inter-
cial clashes that occurred in the course of the patrols' carrying
t their assignments may be regarded as incidents in the smolder-
g warfare waged between blacks and nonslaveholders, racial war-
re that characterized the antebellum South. "Many negro slaves
e allow'd by their owners to Raise and keep dogs . . . that do great
jury to our stocks and if we kill these dogs they will kill our dog,

36. Riddick to Benjamin Williams, June 18, 1802, in Governors' Papers, North
rolina Division of Archives and History.
37. Horatio Turpin to James Monroe, January 22, 1802, in Executive Papers, Vir-
ia State Library; Called Court, May 31, 1798, in Bertie County Slave Papers,
00–1805.

our horse, or our Cow," complained a group of nonslaveholdir
farmers in 1830.[38] The slaves' interference with the patrol struck
blow, however slight, against slavery itself, for the patrollers we
the slaveholders' surrogates, carrying out measures thought esse
tial to maintain the social and economic order. The functions a
signed the patrol and the pay they received helped bind them to tl
slaveholder and assure their continued support.

Slaves were not resourceless in the conflict, as the aggriev(
small farmers learned. Yet since law and society intended tl
blacks' subservience, whites were in a position to inflict severe r
taliatory injury with only moderate risk to themselves. How cor
mon such offenses were is difficult to say, but evidence from Sou
Carolina extending over four decades suggests their prevalenc
From Charleston in 1792 came a complaint of indiscriminate m(
violence directed against blacks in the wake of insurrectiona
alarm: "Whilst we wish to punish the disorderly we cannot but re
robate the inhuman practice of murdering the peacable and inoffe
sive." Existing laws are "entirely inadequate to prevent the preva
ing crime of murdering negroes, whereby our land is becomir
stained with blood, and the pages of our records crowded wi
instances of unexpiated murder," reported a Kershaw grand ju
in 1808.[39]

Ten years later, residents of the same district again complained
the "inadequacy of the punishment attached to the crime, in pr
venting persons of malignant dispositions from murdering slaves
At the same time, a grand jury in Fairfield called attention to "tl
great and growing evil" of "many instances of murder and cru
treatment of Slaves in this District and other parts of the State
And again, in 1819 petitioners from Kershaw warned of a "fast i
creasing" evil—"slaves wantonly abused and crippled by loose ai
licentious men."[40]

Perhaps as a response to these and similar complaints, the sta
legislature in 1821 imposed punishment for murder of slaves, but
grand jury in Richland nine years later found that the offense st
was considered "nearly nominal, no instance having yet occurred

---

38. Quoted in Johnson, *Ante-bellum North Carolina*, 556.
39. Grand Jury Presentments from Charleston District, September 21, 1792, a
from Kershaw District, November 14, 1808, both in Grand Jury Presentments, Sou
Carolina Department of Archives and History.
40. Grand Jury Presentments from Kershaw District, April 14, 1818, and N
vember 19, 1819, *ibid*; Grand Jury Presentment from Fairfield District, Novemb
1818, *ibid*.

hich the penalty has been enforced, although many and increasing
ıstances have occurred characterized with the deepest guilt." In
ght of the data from South Carolina, Frederick Law Olmsted's re-
ort of 1860 becomes more believable. Olmsted wrote of meeting a
aveholder in Mississippi who boasted as evidence of his unusual
rtue that he had never shot one of his slaves.[41]

It is not clear whether the offenses against blacks of the sort that
appear to have been so flagrant in parts of South Carolina were at
ıe hands of their owners or of other persons. But the retributions
ıat commonly followed slave violence almost certainly can be
ıarged for the most part to nonslaveholders in whom festered a
ıalignant dread of blacks and, perhaps, envy and resentment to-
ard their masters.

If the lowest class of white persons disliked both master and slave,
ıe feeling was mutual. Narratives of fugitive slaves, often written
ıder abolitionist tutelage, and recollections of elderly former
aves frequently allude to the contempt blacks felt for "poor
hites." These degraded persons, it appears, fell under the scorn of
aves and southern gentry alike. In expressing derogatory opinion
· an entire social class whose culture and deprivations in some re-
ects resembled their own, slaves only mirrored attitudes of their
ıasters—and these were attitudes calculated to strengthen slavery
y discouraging the creation of interracial bonds.[42]

Planters had good reason to look down upon poor whites and to
ıcourage blacks to do the same. They were scorned by planters less
ır shiftlessness and lack of social grace than because their lowly
atus suggested they might someday become allies of slaves, as
ıey narrowly had missed doing in colonial days. Indeed, in spite of
ıcial pressure, a few of them still manifested such meager racial
ride as to associate on terms of near equality with free blacks and
aves to whom they sometimes offered aid and comfort. The aid
as reciprocated. A number of elderly blacks in the 1930s remem-
ered slavery days when poverty-stricken white persons had ap-
ealed to their parents for food and other kinds of assistance.[43]
anters felt compelled to check these inclinations, for they signified

41. Grand Jury Presentment from Richland District, October, 1830, ibid.; Freder-
k Law Olmsted, A Journey in the Back Country (New York, 1860), 62–63.
42. See Eugene D. Genovese, "'Rather Be a Nigger than a Poor White Man': Slave
rceptions of Southern Yeomen and Poor Whites," in Hans L. Trefousse (ed.), Toward
New View of America: Essays in Honor of Arthur C. Cole (New York, 1977), 79–96.
43. Rawick (ed.), American Slave, II, 87; George P. Rawick et al. (eds.), American
ave: Supplement, Series I, Vol. II, pp. 135–36, and Vol. V, p. 320.

a break, however slight, in white solidarity and to that extent u̇
dermined slavery. The fostering of prejudice in both poor whit(
and slaves helped reduce the possibility of the two groups ev(
coalescing.

Slaves only feebly resisted their owners' effort to drive a wed̦
between them and the group whose sympathy could have provid(
strength to both. Most slaves fell into the trap their owners d
signed; they commonly joined the masters in holding poor whites ḭ
contempt. Probably most never questioned why they did so, but
few pondered the matter and found an explanation. Many years ä
ter emancipation, Tom Woods still remembered the "white fol̦
[who] wasn't much better off dan we was. Dey had to work hard aṙ
dey had to worry 'bout food, clothes and shelter, and we didn't. Lo
of slave owners wouldn't allow dem on deir farms among deir slav(
without orders from de overseer. I don't know why unless he wä
afraid dey would stir up discontent."[44]

While slaveowners were defining poor whites as members of
subordinate caste scarcely on a level even with slaves, they al̦
tried to persuade blacks that they themselves were inferior beiṇ
suited for no other role than that of slave.[45] The effort was uti̧
tarian. Obviously slavery would be made more stable if blacks cou̧
be convinced of their limitations and come to view their servi
status as being appropriate to persons of their small capacity. Wh(
slaves adopted as their own the masters' view of the poor white
they thereby also conceded the masters' view of their own infeṙ
ority. Anyone willing to associate with blacks on terms of familiari̧
and equality is thereby rendered contemptible—so ran the thoug̦
process. "Anyone as poor as I am and as lacking in all that the woŗ
honors is not worth my regard," the slaves were supposed to fe(
Their contempt for poor whites was a manifestation of self-coṙ
tempt nurtured by planters for their own purposes.

But just as slaves never altogether relinquished ties with po(
whites, neither did they fully accept as valid the allegation of the
own hopeless inferiority. Their religion, with its gospel of worth aṙ
redemption, and the positive roles and relationships that the sla҅
community afforded, tended to promote a feeling of self-worth sṵ

44. Rawick (ed.), *American Slave*, VII, 354.
45. Rawick *et al.* (eds.), *American Slave: Supplement, Series I*, Vol. II, pp. 167, 1̧
Blassingame, *Slave Community*, 177, 202–203. On the ideas masters sought to incṵ
cate in slaves, see Thomas L. Webber, *Deep Like the Rivers: Education in the Sla̧
Quarter Community, 1831–1865* (New York, 1978), 27–58.

cient to counteract efforts to denigrate them. In any event, slaves
aw that despite the pretensions to superiority by masters and
verseers, the whites were, after all, human beings much like them-
elves, whose judgment in practical matters did not always exceed
heir own and whose individual strength was no greater.[46] Their
masters, too, made mistakes, suffered misfortune, became ill, and
ied. The mystique in which whites tried to cloak themselves, if not
ransparent, was easily rent. Thus the authority and position of
whites depended chiefly upon force, and this was an element that
slaves, too, could muster. Resistance to impositions made by one's
equal—or inferior—was tempting; although risky, it also was easy
and sometimes successful. From Bradley and Drew counties in Arkansas came word in 1858 that "the slaves are refusing to be flogged,
and much trouble is apprehended." Similar accounts of slaves who
refused to be disciplined and got away with it are plentiful.[47]

Recalcitrance of this sort apparently increased in the 1850s and
thus coincided with menacing northern political developments.
Less extreme instances of slave resistance and jousting for position
probably occurred on practically every plantation. Planters lived in
fear that such commonly witnessed evidences of initiative would
grow, be coordinated, and spread beyond control. In reality, however, the means by which slaves could organize resistance were
severely limited. Plantations were scattered, slaves were closely
watched, and, perhaps most important of all, the majority of white
southerners of every social degree—despite troublesome defections—combined to support the planters' authority. So severe were
the sanctions against extending aid and sympathy to slaves that few
white southerners chose to champion their cause. Nevertheless, the
possibility remained alive. And here and there, especially in the upper South, antislavery voices continued to be heard.

For a long time, abolitionists shied away from even the prospect
of attempting to intervene in the southern racial conflict. Indeed, as
we have seen, they advised slaves to moderate their resistance and
wait for moral suasion to work its emancipating effect. Throughout
the 1830s they refrained from any attempt to reach into the South,
to make contact with slaves, or to encourage their resistance. They

46. [Brown], *Slave Life in Georgia*, 204–205; Webber, *Deep Like the Rivers*, 91–101.
For an example of slaves ignoring work instructions they judged faulty, see Jack P.
Greene (ed.), *Diary of Colonel Landon Carter*, I, 568.
47. Blassingame, *Slave Community*, 317–20; Corydon Fuller Journal, June 4, 1858,
in William L. Clements Library, University of Michigan, Ann Arbor.

remained uncommitted in the ongoing struggle that took place o
most plantations and in most southern communities. Whatever di
content abolitionist activities aroused in blacks was unintended an
was seldom exploited. "The weapons of our warfare are not carnal
insisted the abolitionist Simeon S. Jocelyn in 1834. "Palsied be th
arm that would unsheathe the sword of violence."[48]

Surprisingly, in view of the vigor and frequency of statements i
that vein, abolitionist attitudes toward slaves rapidly underwei
transformation beginning in the late 1830s, until by the 1850s
number of prominent abolitionists had renounced pacifism as a tac
tic and unabashedly begun to urge slaves to act in concert wit
them to promote emancipation.

The easy abandonment of pacifism and nonengagement by a dy
namic abolitionist element is readily accounted for. Slaves ampl
proved to northerners their desire to be free, both by running awa
and by resisting their owners' impositions. Although the Southamp
ton revolt of 1831 was never repeated, evidence of slave restivenes
accumulated on a scale sufficiently large to demonstrate its destruc
tive potential to the slave system. At the same time, growing num
bers of abolitionists judged their program of moral suasion a fail
ure. They had not broken the South's will to maintain and exten
slavery. Neither had they converted a northern majority to thei
program. But their own determination to end slavery remained un
diminished, even grew. The conjunction of these phenomena soo
led abolitionists to reconsider their policy of disengagement fron
slaves and, with scarcely a pang, to abandon it. If the white popu
lation would not end slavery peacefully, then blacks, always eage
for freedom, might be encouraged to end it themselves by force.

48. American Anti-Slavery Society, *First Annual Report*, 21.

10

Toward an Abolitionist-
Slave Alliance

After the Southampton revolt in 1831, no large-scale slave uprising
devastated any part of the American South. But that good fortune
brought less relief than one might expect, for on individual plantations unrest and slave escapes appeared on a scale large enough
to warn of their destructive potential and possible acceleration.
Revolt might be brewing anywhere. Planters liked to profess complete confidence in the loyalty and docility of the slave population.
They boasted of sleeping with doors unlocked and of old ladies left
alone in remote plantation houses.[1] Yet the insurrectionary panics
that periodically swept parts of the South belied the vaunted self-
assurance.

There was good reason not to be truly confident, for even if most
of the rumored conspiracies turned out to have no basis, a haunting
reality still could not be shrugged off: Acts of violence continued to
be directed at owners and overseers, and slaves persisted in exploiting every opportunity to gain advantage within the slave system.
They ran away as they always had done, some for a limited time to
nearby woods and swamps, some to southern cities, some to northern free states or to Mexico or Canada. Such experiences confronted
planters with almost daily demonstration of their vulnerability,

---

1. Charleston *Courier* cited in *Liberator*, March 24, 1845; Scarborough (ed.), *Diary
of Edmund Ruffin*, I, 556–57.

lending to antislavery agitation a menacing aspect quite unrelate
to its moral censoriousness. The abundant evidence of disconten
influenced abolitionists as well, leading some of them to reexamin
their policy of disengagement from slaves.

A particularly dramatic event on the high seas hastened the re
consideration. In June, 1839, a slave ship flying the Portuguese fla
landed in Cuba with a cargo of newly captured Africans. There som
of them were transferred to the Spanish vessel *Amistad* and the
launched toward an unspecified destination. During the passage
the slaves mutinied, killed several white crewmen, and took contro
of the vessel. They tried to sail the ship home to Africa, but survivin
white crew members managed to thwart the plan and instead ma
neuvered the boat into Long Island Sound.[2]

There the blacks were seized and imprisoned. At once began
lengthy court battle over disposition of the captives, with a commit
tee of abolitionists directing efforts to prevent their being delivere
to Spanish authorities. Massive publicity surrounded the affair a
the case eventually made its way to the Supreme Court, which or
dered the captives freed and returned to Africa. Not only did thes
complex legal maneuvers bring much favorable attention in th
North to the antislavery cause, but the court battles also gave man
abolitionists for the first time an opportunity to defend the rights o
black people in a practical rather than a theoretical way. The spe
cial circumstance that allowed them to aid these slaves could no
be brushed away—it was mutiny and murder that brought th
Amistad's human cargo into northern waters. Blacks themselves
with no prompting from white allies, thus projected the issue of vio
lence into the foreground of abolitionist concern. Mutiny aboard th
Amistad confronted abolitionists with the fact of black rebellion. I
that manner, they were given opportunity to condone violence i
the movement against slavery, to accept its creative possibilities
and—perhaps still more important—to make common cause with
blacks. But for the moment, despite their acquiescence in the slaves
forceful escape from bondage, most abolitionists still distinguished
between the slaves' resort to violence through their own choice and
abolitionists' use or advocacy of it. Most also seem not yet to have
recognized the utility to their cause of an abolitionist-slave alliance

Abolitionist response to the *Amistad* affair nevertheless suggest

2. For an account of the entire episode, see Howard Jones, *Mutiny on the "Amis
tad": The Saga of a Slave Revolt and Its Impact on American Abolition, Law, and Diplo
macy* (New York, 1986).

w lightly held and easily relinquished was the ideal of nonresist-
ce. Few condemned the blacks for what they had done. On the
ntrary, abolitionists accepted and justified the mutiny as they
arshaled all their resources to prevent the rebels' return to slav-
y. Among the leaders in the campaign that eventually sent the
utineers as free men to Africa was Lewis Tappan, the well-known
angelical abolitionist, who happened also to be one of the most
nfirmed of nonresistants. Tappan easily bent his principles to ac-
mmodate rebellion in the cause of freedom. If he recognized the
consistency, it did not appear to trouble him. His example was by
means an isolated one.[3]
Two and a half years later, in November, 1841, mutiny on the
reole, a brig transporting slaves from Virginia to Louisiana, pro-
ded abolitionists with a similar though less celebrated opportu-
ty to defend the cause of black rebels. After seizing command of
e vessel, the mutineers sailed to Nassau, where authorities reased most of them. Furious at British disregard of American prop-
ty rights, southerners talked of war. Abolitionists ridiculed the
ospect. Gamaliel Bailey's *Philanthropist* drew a ludicrous picture
the threatened conflict. If the nation decided to fight over the in-
dent, the editor wrote, slaveholders would be forced to stay "at
me to protect their families against the slaves," while antislavery
orthern freemen" would be called upon to fight "for the coast-
se slave trade."[4] Again abolitionists reproached the South for its
ilitary weakness in the face of an enslaved "internal enemy," and
ain they defended rebellious slaves.
As abolitionist response to the *Amistad* and *Creole* mutinies made
ear, the consensus for nonresistance, fragile from the start, dis-
ayed unmistakable signs of fracture by the 1840s. For many, paci-
m, even in its most earnestly proclaimed phase, had been only a
osen strategy designed to fit the times rather than a matter of deep
nviction. When circumstances changed, strategy could be changed,
o, with no resultant pangs of conscience. Especially among those
olitionists eager to translate antislavery fervor into direct politi-
l action, nonresistance was lightly held and easily relinquished.
s passing would have grave consequence for slaveholders.
Some of the same abolitionists who in the late 1830s led the move-

3. Wyatt-Brown, *Lewis Tappan*, 205–20.
4. The incident aroused far less interest than did the *Amistad* mutiny, but see Wil-
am Ellery Channing, *The Duty of the Free States; or, Remarks Suggested by the Case
the Creole* (Boston, 1842), and *Philanthropist*, January 5, 1842.

ment to transfer antislavery from the sphere of moral reform in
the arena of party politics were among the first to alter their stan
toward slaves and slave resistance. Those politically disposed r
formers, who were more likely to be lawyers, editors, or busines
men than clergymen, held commonplace attitudes with respect
power and its uses. They viewed slaveholders and "the slave powe
as political enemies to be confronted by ordinary worldly mea
and defeated. If southerners would not relinquish slavery in r
sponse to moral influence exerted through persuasion and pray
then they would be deprived of their slaves by earthly instrumen
of coercion. If slavery could not be ended peacefully, with consent
the owners, it would be ended in some other way. Political pow
offered itself as the coercive means most readily at hand and t
most attractive way to effect this goal. Individuals hostile to t
South on account of the policies of its congressional political leade
likewise found in antislavery activity a weapon congenial to the
needs. For some of them, the encouragement of slave violence w
not out of the question.[5]

The abolitionists' entrance into party politics did not lead ine
tably to encouragement of slave resistance or to efforts to forge
alliance with slaves. But as nonresistants readily understood, t
decision to resort to politics and thus to coercion meant that su
strategies no longer were theoretically precluded. "We dread t
tendency to ballots," wrote Garrison in 1843. "They are but one r
move from bloodshed."[6] As Garrison realized, behind majority ru
lay force, the power to coerce minorities and to destroy dissente

The trend toward direct action notably strengthened in the la
1830s, when abolitionists came to view southerners less as errir
fellow citizens than as overt enemies. In their eyes, the sharp resis
ance manifested toward abolitionist efforts in that turbulent de
ade rapidly transformed slaveholders from being misguided fello
countrymen into stubborn foes. The violence encountered by no
resistant abolitionists invited violence in return. Northern mo
aroused intense hatred in some. It was hard to remain a forbearir
and forgiving Christian in the face of disrupted lectures, wreck

5. Larry Gara, "Slavery and the Slave Power: A Crucial Distinction," *Civil W*
History, XV (1969), 4–18; Bretz, "Economic Background of the Liberty Party," 25
64; Richard H. Sewell, *Ballots for Freedom: Antislavery Politics in the United Stat*
1837–1860 (New York, 1976), 3–23.
6. *Liberator*, September 22, 1843.

wspaper presses, a murdered editor, a burned Pennsylvania Hall,
ttered slaves.[7]
White abolitionists seldom thought of fighting slaveholders them-
lves, but some began to consider the possibility of encouraging
ves, the planters' natural enemies, to do so. Abolitionists who fre-
iently had justified their program as offering the only means to
oid interracial warfare began in the late 1830s to view insurrec-
n in a different light. Rather than recoiling from the prospect,
ey were attracted by it. Insurrection came to be welcomed as the
timate means, perhaps the only means, of ending slavery and de-
roying the power of slaveholders.
Jabez Delano Hammond of Cherry Valley, New York, was one of
e earliest white advocates of deliberately fomenting rebellion as
 antislavery device. Such extremism came unexpectedly from
at source. Hammond fit no pattern for the malcontented of that
 any age. He was not an obscure, downtrodden figure; there was
thing in the biographical record to show alienation or dogged
nse of failure; neither can his easy marriage with violence be cred-
d to the impetuosity of youth or to romantic desperation. Ham-
ond was a respected Otsego County judge and past the age of sixty
en he revealed his militant program. Earlier he had served un-
markably as a member of the Fourteenth Congress of the United
ates and as a New York state senator. A serious student of politics
 well as an experienced politician, he soon would write an ac-
aimed and still-consulted political history of New York. Oddly
ough, despite his unbounded hatred for the South, Hammond was
t usually identified at the time as an abolitionist, though his wife
ore the badge of that fellowship.[8]
The prospect of voluntary emancipation by slaveholders had dis-
peared, Hammond decided as early as 1839, and he saw little
ore reason to anticipate the "spread of correct views" in the
orth. "The only way in which slavery at the South can be abol-
hed is by force," he concluded. Hammond proposed that abolition-

7. See the impassioned statements in Alvan Stewart to Samuel Webb, May 28,
38, and June 25, 1840, in Alvan Stewart Papers, New-York Historical Society, New
rk, N.Y. A strand in Quaker thought, and perhaps in other Protestant thought as
ll, insisted on the need for retributive justice for slaveholders. See Josiah F. Polk
R. R. Gurley, December 17, 1829, in American Colonization Society Papers.
8. Allan Johnson and Dumas Malone (eds.), *Dictionary of American Biography*
ew York, 1928–36), VII, 205–206; Wesley Bailey to Gerrit Smith, March 6, 1845,
Gerrit Smith Papers.

ists establish two military academies patterned after West Poin
one in Upper Canada and another at Matamoras in Mexico, bo
centers of southern black refugees and both beyond easy interfe
ence by slaveholders or the United States government. From the
academies, black youths trained in the art of war would be d
patched to infiltrate the South. There they would blend into t
slave population, encourage sabotage, and foment slave uprisin;
Such military agents, said Hammond, in a phrase disposing of t
conventional agents of moral suasion, would prove "the most su
cessful Southern missionaries."[9]

At first Hammond revealed his unorthodox views only in priva
correspondence, perhaps to no one except his radical New Yo
neighbor Gerrit Smith. But Hammond's violent proposals repi
sented no passing mood, and before another decade passed, he h;
published a version of them in the form of a fictionalized sla
autobiography, *Julius Melbourne*. Its pages repeated his advice
1839: Philanthropists should begin to recruit black armies instea
of "raising funds to pay abolition lecturers." With undisguised re
ish, he pictured the day "when the rich rice and cotton fields of t
south will be drenched with human gore . . . and when the gorgeo
palaces which now adorn the southern plantations will be enve
oped in flames."[10]

Few abolitionists were so forward or so bloodthirsty as Hai
mond. Most conscientiously shied from such livid scenes and co
tinued to insist that their activity was designed to prevent violen
rather than promote it. Yet prospects for a peaceful end to slave
through the agency of repentant white Americans continued to r
cede. Blacks, both North and South, taught white abolitionists
surer way.

Beginning in the late 1830s, the arrival in the North of growir
numbers of fugitive slaves acquainted abolitionists with the eage
ness of slaves to free themselves independent of outside advice
agency. The behavior of northern free blacks likewise was instru
tive. Few of them, as it turned out, adhered to nonresistance. Whi
abolitionists found that free blacks, from whose consciousness t
fact of slavery could never long be absent, were ready on their ov
initiative to take up arms to defend fugitives—and themselves

9. Jabez Delano Hammond to Gerrit Smith, May 18, 1839, in Gerrit Smith Pape
10. [Jabez Delano Hammond], *Life and Opinions of Julius Melbourne . . .* (Syr
cuse, N.Y., 1847), 237.

)m slave catchers and from authorities who would enforce the fu-
tive slave laws. In several northern cities they formed vigilance
mmittees, sometimes in cooperation with whites, to safeguard
naways and prevent kidnappings. In the course of their risky pur-
its, members on occasion used force, broke the law, and otherwise
sisted authority.[11] No one absorbed in such desperate activity was
:ely to stop for very long in order to ponder its implication for the
ture of nonresistance theory. Thus the enterprise of aiding run-
vays ineluctably moved its advocates forward to new positions,
th free blacks conspicuously in the vanguard. It was but a short
:p from helping fugitives elude the clutches of the law in the North
urging them to escape from the South.
White abolitionists thus awoke to both the propensity of slaves to
:e themselves and the eagerness of free blacks to help them in do-
g so. Abolitionists, white and black alike, soon learned to exploit
ese developments, not alone for their humanitarian purpose, but
so for their utility in arousing northern antislavery sympathies.
:cordingly, they made the fugitive an important adjunct to their
use on the lecture platform and in their publications.
But abolitionists also learned from fugitives a threefold practical
sson that extended well beyond propaganda value. First, each suc-
ssful escape freed at least one slave and, by demonstrating to both
vner and bondsman the vulnerability of slavery, weakened the en-
'e system; second, these were the accomplishments of direct ac-
on, not of moral suasion; third, they undeniably were the work of
aves themselves. Only in an indirect way, if at all, could they be
edited to the abolitionists' influence.
Even white abolitionists who continued to be nonresistants would
ad themselves uncomfortable if they asked the victimized slaves
free blacks to follow their own pacific example. The trend instead
as toward justifying and even encouraging black resistance rather
an continuing to voice old pleas for patience. By adding their sup-
rt, abolitionists now assumed a major role in the campaign slaves
d free blacks already had initiated to destroy slavery.
The flight of slaves in the 1840s and 1850s was viewed as a serious
oblem, especially by owners in the upper South, who found that
e ease of escape significantly weakened their control. For the pres-
t, the erosion in absolute numbers could be borne, but the facility

11. Jane H. Pease and William H. Pease, *They Who Would Be Free: Blacks' Search*
Freedom, 1830–1861 (New York, 1974), 206–12.

with which escapes took place forecast a time when the loss wou become ruinous. Abolitionists appeared to be ready to hasten th day. A few—whites and free blacks alike—already had carried the hatred of slavery and their willingness to defy the law to the poi of entering slave states themselves and helping slaves escape. The well-publicized incidents, with the prison literature some of the engendered, made an important contribution to the romanticizi of abolitionism.[12] Of greater significance to the evolution of nort ern relationships to slaves, however, were less dramatic events ta ing place in state legislatures. At the same time that individu northern citizens on their own initiative were aiding slaves to c cape and to elude would-be captors, some northern states enact personal liberty laws denying the use of state facilities and the a of state officials for the enforcement of the federal fugitive sla law.[13] The implication of such legislation for the plantation Sou could not be missed. Northern states had unmistakably put the selves in the position of being accessories to the South's racial co flict, even when waged on remote plantations, and had become co mitted partisans of the slave.

It may have been his understanding of these implications of t fugitive slave issue that persuaded the New York philanthrop Gerrit Smith, with whom the radical Judge Hammond was in f quent correspondence, to prepare his "Address to the Slaves of t United States" for presentation to a Liberty party convention he at Peterboro, New York, in January, 1842. The address generally h been ignored by historians of the antebellum United States; yet b cause of its shift away from the policies of pacifism and disengag ment that had been written into the platform of the American An Slavery Society, Smith's work stands as a milestone in the proce that would lead to the destruction of slavery. It was in some respec a declaration of war against the South in the vein made familiar Lord Dunmore's proclamation of November, 1775, to the slaves Virginia, inviting them to escape. Unlike most earlier abolitionis Smith recognized slaves as active participants in the struggle f emancipation. His address proclaimed a hitherto unacknowledg

12. Notable examples of this genre are Joseph C. Lovejoy, *Memoir of Rev. Char T. Torrey, Who Died in the Penitentiary of Maryland, Where He Was Confined for Shc ing Mercy to the Poor* (New York, 1847); Daniel Drayton, *Personal Memoir of Dar Drayton, for Four Years and Four Months a Prisoner (for Charity's Sake) in Washing Jail* (Boston, 1855); George Thompson, *Prison Life and Reflections . . .* (Hartford, 185
13. Thomas D. Morris, *Free Men All: The Personal Liberty Laws of the North, 178 1861* (Baltimore, 1974), 107–29.

iance between abolitionists and slaves and set forth radically new
es for both groups.
Smith announced his abandonment of the "almost universally
ld" conviction "that the friends of the slave have no right to com-
unicate with him." Instead, it was the abolitionists' duty to be the
ves' "advisors, comforters, and helpers." Their obligation ex-
nded well beyond sympathy and rhetoric. Duty also required
em to take direct, aggressive action against the slave system. Ac-
rding to Smith, "the abolitionist has a perfect moral right to go
to the South, and use his intelligence to promote the escape of
norant and imbruted slaves from their prison-house." Slaves had
parallel responsibility: They were duty-bound to run away. The
y of prayer and persuasion had passed; now both parties—slaves
d abolitionists—should *act* in the cause of freedom.[14]
The address counseled against violence. Smith did not suggest, as
s friend Hammond had done, that slaves murder and burn in a
ike for freedom. Nevertheless he insisted on their right to take
om their masters or other white persons food, clothing, horses,
ats—whatever they needed to make good their escape. Few abo-
ionists could object to Smith's urging slaves to run away, though
e antislavery Virginian Samuel M. Janney thought the advice un-
cessary. But they found it hard to approve his counsel to steal,
pecially to steal even from persons in the free states. Despite objec-
on, Smith's address was endorsed by the Liberty party convention
New York and by antislavery groups in Illinois and elsewhere.[15]
Yet acceptance of the revolutionary principles of direct action
ainst slavery and alliance with slaves did not come easily for
. Gamaliel Bailey, for one, entered his protest: "Our business is
nply with the master." In this respect, the Cincinnati editor wrote,
would continue to stand firmly on the principles of the American
ti-Slavery Society as Garrison formulated them in 1833. Reform-
s, thought Bailey, ought to avoid taking positions too far in ad-
nce of public opinion. Bailey interpreted Smith's address as a
ll for slave rebellion. To appear to sanction violence, he warned,
uld further close the minds of southerners while it also im-
ded the growth of antislavery sentiment in the free states. A still

14. *National Anti-Slavery Standard*, February 24, 1842.
15. Samuel M. Janney to J. Miller McKim, December 1, 1843, in Antislavery
llection, Cornell University, Ithaca, N.Y.; Alice Eliza Hamilton to Gerrit Smith,
ptember 22, 1842, in Gerrit Smith Papers; Minutes of the Illinois State Anti-
very Society, May 26, 1842, Chicago Historical Society, Chicago; Sewell, *Ballots
Freedom*, 90.

more serious matter: If abolitionist advice encouraged slaves to r
volt, the result might be extermination of the race rather than i
liberation.[16] Opposition in this vein did not bury Smith's proposal. On the co
trary, his advice soon was repeated. In 1843 the New England An
Slavery Convention endorsed a similar address to the slaves writt
and presented by no less a confirmed nonresistant than Willia
Lloyd Garrison. The event proved that some New England abo
tionists, too, now were prepared to accept the logic of their relatio
ship with slaves. They would abandon their earlier policy of dise
gagement and attempt to forge an open slave-abolitionist coalitio

Garrison's address, like Smith's, warned slaves to attempt
insurrections, not because revolt was wrong or unjustified, b
because it would fail. Instead of fighting hopeless battles on the
masters' plantations, Garrison advised, slaves should make eve
effort to escape to the North. In reaching that conclusion, howeve
Garrison moved closer than had Smith to justifying, even encou
aging, the use of violence. "By precept and example," wrote Gar
son, slaveholders "declare that it is both your right and duty
wage war against them, and to wade through their blood, if nece
sary, to secure your own freedom."[17] Despite such language, Gar
son remained a pacifist himself, but he neither expected nor advise
slaves to follow his example.

Both Smith's and Garrison's addresses represent a major compr
mise of the principle of moral suasion. And both closely resemb
the policy followed in the eighteenth century by foreign enemi
of English America, who planned to use slaves as instruments
struggle for empire. Through their ostensibly peaceful nineteent
century prose echo the Spanish king's proclamation directed
Anglo-American slaves in 1733 and Lord Dunmore's proclamati
of 1775 as well as Admiral Cochrane's less famous proclamati
during the War of 1812.

The white abolitionists' change in policy paralleled that of nort
ern free blacks as they, too, consciously moved toward open allian
with slaves. After escape to the North, some fugitives managed

16. *Philanthropist*, February 9, April 6, and August 27, 1842. See also *ibid.*, S
tember 22, 1841.
17. *Address of the New England Anti-Slavery Convention to the Slaves of the Uni
States with an Address to President Tyler, Faneuil Hall, May 31, 1843* (Boston, 184
3–13. The address is also in *Liberator*, June 2, 1843. On Garrison's authorship,
Henry Wilson, *History of the Rise and Fall of the Slave Power in America* (Bost
1872–77), I, 563.

aintain ties with family and friends in the slave states. For many,
ese perhaps represented no more than ordinary bonds of human
mpathy, but others made the crucial ideological leap of extending
ersonal relationships to embrace an entire people. From such ex-
anded consciousness came resolve to destroy the institution that
ept most blacks in bondage and degraded all of them. Northern
ee blacks, even though resident in ostensibly free states, early rec-
gnized that to the existence of slavery must be charged the preju-
ce and discrimination that burdened every aspect of their lives.
In the growing northern cities, particularly in Boston, New York,
ad Philadelphia, but also in smaller places such as Detroit, Pitts-
urgh, and Columbus, a community of free blacks had developed
arallel to the slave community in the South. The functions of the
vo were similar. In each instance, an oppressed and exploited
eople, barred by law and custom from equal participation in soci-
y and the economy, had come together for mutual aid and sup-
ort. In each instance, too, the formation of the community and its
aport were largely ignored by white people.
Members of the slave community helped each other in their psy-
ological resistance to slavery. The community fostered in its mem-
ers a sense of self-worth in the face of calculated efforts at degra-
ation. It offered support against the cruelties and burdens that
ere inseparable from slavery. The slave community thus was a
lf-help organization that made it possible for blacks to survive the
deal of slavery and through whose collective action members
metimes extorted from masters and overseers concessions that in-
vidual effort would not likely have achieved.[18]
Free-black communities in the North offered their members much
e same kind of aid and support, necessarily tailored, however, to
e North's market economy, which had only the most primitive
presentation in the rural South. Their free-state location allowed
em to act more openly in their own behalf than was possible for
aves. It also provided the added opportunity to speak freely against
avery with little fear of retribution and with the possibility of in-
uence. Further, the northern setting allowed them more openly to
sturb slavery by providing refuge for fugitives and defending
em from slave catchers, though blacks in the South did these
ings, too.
At least as early as 1796, Boston blacks founded the African Soci-

18. The most thorough treatment is Blassingame, *Slave Community*.

ety, principally for mutual aid and charity, but almost inevitab
one of its chief concerns came to be abolition. In 1808 it published
formal antislavery statement. Members of Boston's African Mason
Lodge, a fraternal order whose purpose was racial solidarity ar
mutual aid, likewise periodically listened to condemnations of sla
ery: The noted black leader Prince Hall, for example, delivered ;
antislavery oration before the lodge in 1797. Free blacks in t
North, as in the South, stood in the vanguard of opposition to pr
posals by the American Colonization Society to send them to Afric
and in doing so, they proclaimed ties with slaves that white sout
erners could only view as ominous. In 1817 black Philadelphia:
responded to colonization plans by resolving that "we never w
separate ourselves voluntarily from the slave population of th
country; they are our brethren by the ties of consanguinity, of su
fering, and of wrong." Free-black intransigence on this subjec
when borrowed by Garrison, became basic to the abolitionist pr
gram of the 1830s. As the fugitive slave issue grew in politic
prominence after the 1830s, urban blacks throughout the Nor
formed vigilance committees to help runaways and, especially,
protect them from recapture. Thus by the time organized antisla
ery activity among white northerners achieved prominence, nort
ern free blacks already had created an antislavery tradition th
closely tied them to the southern slave community, thereby lendi
to their activity strength and authenticity difficult for white abo
tionists to equal. Northern blacks and white abolitionists join
forces in the moral suasionist antislavery campaign of the 183(
but under stress of urgencies that white reformers were not likely
experience, black abolitionists more readily than their co-worke
soon moved from pacifism, with its faith in moral power, reaso
and good will, toward advocacy of direct antislavery action.[19]

In the late 1820s, a group of black youths, students in the Ne
York African Free Schools, talked of schemes "for the freeing ar
upbuilding of our race." They made a solemn pact, one of them r
membered, "that when we had educated ourselves we would ;
South, start an insurrection and free our brethren in bondage." A
though none of the band ever quite fulfilled that youthful pledg
one of them, Henry Highland Garnet, came near to doing so wh

19. Horton and Horton, *Black Bostonians*, 28–29, 30, 54, 58; Aptheker (ed.), *Doc
mentary History*, I, 71; Pease and Pease, *They Who Would Be Free*, 8–12, 171.

the 1840s he ventured to commit northern black leadership to
iance with slaves and advocacy of black revolt.[20]

Northern blacks on several occasions had answered mob violence
th counterviolence, as in riots at Cincinnati in 1829 and Philadel-
ia in 1832, and again in fugitive-slave rescues in the 1840s and
50s. Especially noteworthy among these incidents was a martial
counter at Christiana, Pennsylvania, in 1851, when free blacks
d their white sympathizers repulsed a posse called out to capture
gitives and in the process killed the fugitives' owner.[21] Such re-
onse did more than confirm familiar observation that human be-
gs under physical attack commonly try to defend themselves and
y strike back. Those demonstrations of black prowess in defense
rights flew in the face of the vulgar contention that blacks were
ecially qualified for slavery and meekly accepted it. They should
placed near the extreme of the continuum of well-thought-out
ack response to oppression that extends from the self-help organ-
tions of the 1790s to military service in the Civil War. These
amatic illustrations of determination to defend freedom against
ther encroachment formed the background for the bold policy
tements enunciated by black spokesmen in the 1840s. At a con-
ation of blacks held at Buffalo in 1843, the issue of slave violence
ealed its political face as black spokesmen proclaimed impa-
nce with moral suasion and drafted incendiary messages ad-
essed to their still-enslaved brethren in the South.

Much of the Reverend Samuel Davis' address opening the pro-
edings at Buffalo took the form of a sustained paraphrase of Pat-
k Henry's famous prerevolutionary speech in the Virginia House
Burgesses in which Henry proclaimed the futility of verbal pro-
t against British policy and the expediency of resort to arms. Da-
compared black military action in the cause of freedom with
ent, much-admired revolts in Greece and Poland. In support of
ropean rebels, Davis observed: "Money, as well as arms and am-
inition, were sent out from our own land. And not only these,
ny of freedom's noblest sons largely volunteered their own serv-
s, risking their lives and fortunes to the dangerous chances of

20. Alexander Crummell, *The Eulogy of Henry Highland Garnet, D.D., Presbyte-
1 Minister . . .* (Washington, D.C., 1882), 25–26; Pease and Pease, *They Who Would
Free*, 238.
21. Jonathan Katz, *Resistance at Christiana: The Fugitive Slave Rebellion, Chris-
1a, Pennsylvania, September 11, 1851* (New York, 1974), 81–103.

war with the infidel, tyrant Turks." The lesson was obvious: Nort
ern blacks should encourage and welcome revolt in the South, a
when revolt began, they should join forces with embattled slav
"No other hope is left us," said Davis, "but in our own exertions a
an 'appeal to the God of armies!' "[22]

The militant tone of the convention having been set, it was Ga
net's turn to speak. For an hour and a half, he exhorted delegates
support a slave uprising. "Brethren, arise, arise!" he cried. "Stri
for your lives and liberties. Now is the day and hour." Despite h
choice of language, the tactics Garnet advocated were not those
Nat Turner, whose men had massacred indiscriminately, but i
stead resembled those of a general strike. No one, said Garnet
echoing advice given earlier by David Walker—should consent to l
a slave. Slaves should resolve to be slaves no longer. They shou
confront their owners with the pronouncement that they want
"their liberty and had come to ask for it, and if the masters refus
it, to tell them, then we shall take it, let the consequence be what
may."[23] Violence certainly would be the result, but Garnet mai
tained a shred of nonresistance principles when he pointed out tha
under his plan, the violence would be initiated by masters, not l
slaves. In any event, the end sought now required new modes
action. Freedom would not come in that generation, thought Ga
net, without the shedding of blood.

Frederick Douglass, who recently had fled from slavery in Mar
land and still was identified with the nonresistant Garrisonian
spoke eloquently against Garnet's counsel. He favored "trying t
moral means a little longer." He "wished in no way to have a
agency in bringing about" insurrection. Convention delegates fro
Cincinnati joined Douglass in deploring a course certain to lead
violence. Garnet's plan, said one of them, "would be fatal to t
safety of the free people of color of the slave States, but especia
so to those who lived on the borders of the free States." Such
opinion must have had powerful impact on persons who knew of t
terrible retribution often visited on blacks in time of suspected co
spiracy. Not surprisingly, a majority of delegates refused to auth
ize the printing of Garnet's address as representing the sentimen
of the convention, though a motion to do so failed by only one vote

22. *Minutes of the National Convention of Colored Citizens Held at Buffalo on*
15th, 16th, 17th, 18th and 19th of August, 1843 . . . (New York, 1843), 6.

23. *Ibid.*, 12–13; Aptheker, *Documentary History*, I, 226–33.

24. *Minutes of the National Convention*, 13–19.

As the narrowness of defeat suggests, Garnet's address would not
set aside and forgotten. It too accurately reflected the mood and
shes of growing numbers of abolitionists, white as well as black,
be ignored for long. Four years later a national convention of
acks held at Troy, New York, ordered it printed in a slightly modi-
d version, and in 1849 a convention in Ohio agreed to publish an
ition of five hundred copies, together with *Walker's Appeal*, its
eological ancestor.[25]
Further evidence of the weakened hold of pacifism and moral sua-
on on free-black leaders appeared in 1847, when Charles Remond,
ho had strongly opposed Garnet's sentiments at the Buffalo con-
ntion, reversed himself and in an address at Abington, Massachu-
tts, advised slaves to rise in insurrection. Although the abolitionist
ess chose to minimize Remond's about-face, the influential Boston
ily *Whig* gave his views much hostile attention. The newspaper
s ready to accept slave revolt if slaves themselves determined
that course, but it could not tolerate a northern abolitionist—
rticularly not a black abolitionist—urging them to the act. Re-
ond was "a traitor to the country, to the Constitution, to Hu-
anity." Some white abolitionists, too, had difficulty accepting such
ld attempts to interfere in the South's domestic affairs. The Bos-
n politician Ellis Gray Loring complained to Garrison and de-
anded that the American Anti-Slavery Society disavow Remond's
ntiments, but even as he did so, he admitted to suspecting that
cifism's sun was setting. In the confrontational atmosphere of the
40s, views like Remond's could not be repressed. Loring had "no
ubt that (like the doctrines of Young Ireland) they are destined to
in a certain currency."[26]
Their currency among black abolitionists was not to be denied.
1849 Douglass, who more than anyone else could take credit for
e early rejection of Garnet's address, now openly advocated slave
volts. Sentiment favorable to insurrection continued to grow. In
e late summer of 1850, a convention of some fifty fugitive slaves
d a number of well-known radical abolitionists, both black and
ite, met at Cazenovia, New York. The gathering was occasioned
passage of the hateful new Fugitive Slave Law as well as by the
prisonment at Washington, D.C., of the abolitionist William L.
aplin for the crime of aiding slaves to escape and supplying them

25. Pease and Pease, *They Who Would Be Free*, 239.
26. Boston *Daily Whig*, July 3,1847. See also *ibid.*, July 9, 1847, for a defense of
ve violence by "J. C."; Loring to Garrison, June 28, 1847, *Liberator*, July 9, 1847.

with weapons. Talk of violence and insurrection and consolidatir an abolitionist-slave alliance dominated the sessions.[27]

The delegates pledged to help fugitives and advised them to u arms against would-be captors rather than be returned to slaver But the Cazenovia convention did not limit its concern to blac] who had fled to the North, and by focusing on slaves, its membe clearly intended to inaugurate an intensified stage in the interraci struggle. The delegates went far beyond merely encouraging slav. to flee to the North, the course Smith and Garrison had recor mended a few years earlier. Slaves were held as prisoners of war " an enemy's country," said the delegates, and thus had "the fulle liberty to plunder, burn and kill" to make good their escape. Alor with its advocacy of open revolt, the convention proclaimed a p litical and military alliance between northern and southern black "When the insurrection of the Southern Slaves shall take place, ; take place it will," so ran their message to slaves, "the great mass the colored men of the North . . . will be found by your sid with deep-stored and long-accumulated revenge in their hearts, ar death-dealing weapons in their hands." The new militant spir spread well beyond the abolitionists of central New York to swee away pacifism in unexpected places. Soon after the Cazenovia co vention adjourned, the nonresistant Parker Pillsbury, addressing, ; he supposed, a nonresistant Garrisonian gathering at Salem, Ohi found himself instead speaking to an assembly of whites and blac] now determined to arm themselves to fight slavery. Not even Pil] bury's eloquence could persuade them to resume their more mo erate former course.[28]

Few prominent white abolitionists before the late 1850s cou' bring themselves to endorse slave insurrection, still less to adv cate white participation. Nonetheless they, too, were irresistibly a tracted to the prospect of violent overthrow of slavery, few more than Garrison himself, once the very figurehead of nonresistan theory. Garrison depicted for slaves earlier and perhaps more easi accomplished emancipation than most hitherto had thought po sible. "Your blood is the cement which binds the American Unic together," he wrote in 1843; "your bodies are crushed beneath t] massy weight of this Union; and its repeal or dissolution would e sure the downfall of slavery." The South was able to maintain i

27. *National Anti-Slavery Standard*, August 29, September 5 and 12, 1850.
28. *Ibid.*, October 10, 1850.

stitutions, Garrison continued, only because "the whole military
ower of the nation is pledged to suppress all insurrections."[29]
Startling as Garrison's idea may have seemed in the 1840s, it was
r from being new. As early as 1820, John Quincy Adams, starting
om the same assumption, had predicted that secession would be
llowed by civil war, slave rebellion, and the consequent end of
avery. When Benjamin Lundy presented a similar forecast to New
ngland audiences during his lecture tour in 1828, Garrison heard
e idea, probably for the first time. In an early demonstration of his
arvelous receptivity to radical thought, Garrison adopted Lundy's
ew as his own. "What protects the South from instant destruc-
on?" asked Garrison in 1832. "OUR PHYSICAL FORCE. Break the chain
hich binds her to the Union, and the scenes of St. Domingo would
e witnessed throughout her borders."[30] It was an attractive pros-
ect for the radical abolitionist, beautiful in its simplicity and ease
accomplishment, satisfying for its embodiment of merited retri-
ution. In 1832 the prediction that slave violence would follow in
e wake of disunion also could be read as a political warning ad-
essed to southern leaders not to make good their threats of nulli-
ation and secession. The writings of Samuel Cornish soon after-
ard must have held even greater pertinence for southerners fearful
ot only of slave revolt but also of the disruptive effect of class di-
sions in white society. Dissolution of the Union, the black editor
edicted in 1837, would allow slaves to join oppressed "honest
hite laborers" in an uprising marked by "anarchy, bloodshed and
pine."[31]
Implicit in Garrison's notorious disunionist proposals of the 1840s
d 1850s was the expectation that slave revolt would follow seces-
on. Garrisonian disunionism, often dismissed as a visionary, non-
sistant device whereby scrupulous persons sought to separate
emselves from evil, thus presented a practical, militant aspect.
idden behind its pacific countenance lay the means for promoting
ave rebellion and assuring its success. Slavery, Garrison continued
 believe, could not long survive withdrawal of federal support.
hen antislavery politicians in the mid-1840s called upon the na-

29. *Liberator*, June 2, 1843.
30. Adams (ed.), *Memoirs of John Quincy Adams*, V, 210; Garrison to Editor of the
ston *Courier*, August 11, 1828, in Walter M. Merrill and Louis Ruchames (eds.), *The
tters of William Lloyd Garrison* (Cambridge, Mass., 1971–81), I, 65; *Liberator*, June 7,
32. See also *Liberator*, November 10, 1831, and March 10, 1832.
31. *Colored American*, September 2, 1837.

tional government to sever all its ties with slavery, they perhaps ha
uppermost in mind this political outcome rather than merely tl
austere goal of promoting national moral purity.

The movement in the 1840s for national disassociation from sla
ery gained momentum from proposals to annex Texas. That issu
more than any other, rendered the Union intolerable to many an
slavery northerners. Texas constituted a long-standing problem f
both abolitionists and slaveholders. Its attractions had been ob
ous for many years, and failure of the Adams-Onis Treaty of 1819
include the region within United States boundaries was an omissic
later diplomats and politicians would much regret and seek
remedy.

The fact that Texas was not a United States possession did n
prevent American citizens from wishing to settle there. America
moving into the Mexican state in the 1820s found an undevelope
nearly uninhabited region admirably suited to plantation agricu
ture and slave labor. But to their dismay, they also discovered th
they had placed themselves under a regime in which, unlike tl
United States, the revolutionary impulse toward emancipation ha
not been checked. In 1829 the Mexican government proclaimed tl
end of slavery, no matter the interests of settlers in Texas who can
from slave states and fully expected to surround themselves wi
familiar institutions. Mexican policy proved hardly less dismayi
to Americans left at home. White southerners could not face wi
equanimity the prospect of a free-labor state growing up on the
western border. It would constitute a barrier to the further wes
ward advance of slavery with consequent build-up in the East of a
explosive servile population. Its mere existence would encoura
unrest in the neighboring black belt and offer another refuge
fugitives.[32]

Texans' pleas and fervid representations to the Mexican gover
ment brought them special exemption to the ban against slaver
but they understood its provisional character. They never felt secu
about the permanency of the exemption they had been grante
When in the early 1830s Mexican officials began a process of poli
cal centralization, American settlers faced loss of most of the a
tonomy they until then enjoyed. Americans in Texas proved as d
voted to "states' rights" as did southern planters, and for much t

32. Phillips (ed.), *Plantation and Frontier*, II, 250; Stephen F. Austin to Mary Aus
Holley, August 2, 1835, in Eugene C. Barker (ed.), *The Austin Papers, October 183
January 1837* (Austin, Texas, 1927), III, 102.

ne reason. They protested the consolidating tendencies under
.y in Mexico and the consequent lessening of local control, for
:y dreaded being governed by an antislavery Mexican majority.
e resultant friction between state and central government—be-
:een Texan minority and Mexican majority—led first to protests
d then to revolution and the establishment of the Republic of
xas. It would be hard to exaggerate the role of slavery in bringing
out these events.[33]

As the revolutionary movement in Texas proceeded, encouraged
d aided by persons in the United States, many of them in the
uth, abolitionists launched a full-scale campaign against annex-
on. Their efforts received a favorable response, for whatever per-
asive arguments might be advanced in support of acquiring Texas,
possible to hide from northern voters was the fact that addition
so vast a region would considerably increase southern political
luence while also assuring continued growth of slavery. And to a
ople whose economic interests diverged so sharply from those of
: South these seemed consequences worth resisting.

Anti-Texas northerners also summoned to their support the same
irit of nationalism that a generation earlier had proved so fertile
ource of opposition to the spread of slavery into the Louisiana
rchase. Slavery, they again argued, produced internal dissension
d military weakness; it embittered intersectional relations; it ined invasion and insurrection. Acquisition of new slaveholding
:as would enfeeble the nation. Annexation, wrote the sanguinary
dge Hammond, "should be resisted unto blood."[34]

All these were prospective, intangible, perhaps imaginary dan-
rs. In contrast, southerners found in an independent Texas real
d immediate threats. Under the rule of an antislavery, Mexican
ijority, Texas would have proved an intolerable neighbor for the
:at planters of Mississippi and Louisiana, but still more widely
jectionable in the South was the prospect of a feeble, independent
xas falling within the orbit of a hostile European power. The Ten-

33. Paul D. Lack, "Slavery and the Texas Revolution," *Southwestern Historical*
arterly, LXXXIX (1985), 181–202. For a quite different interpretation of the back-
und of the Texas Revolution and the war with Mexico, see Eugene C. Barker, "The
luence of Slavery in the Colonization of Texas," *Mississippi Valley Historical Re-*
v, XI (1924), 3–36, and Seymour V. Connor and Odie B. Faulk, *North America*
ided: The Mexican War, 1846–1848 (New York, 1971), 3–32.
34. Hammond to Gerrit Smith, March 15, 1836, in Gerrit Smith Papers. "Every
lition of a slave state increases the danger of foreign invasion, and domestic insur-
tion, and thereby weakens the nation." *Signal of Liberty*, April 6, 1842.

nessee jurist John Catron alluded to a pressing consideration: t
unpleasant fact that Texas touched "our great 'Slave and Indi
border' " and thus in unsympathetic hands offered potential for
citing unbearable disorder throughout the South. Catron's hc
that "our relations with Texas . . . may be so settled as to leave
further cause of apprehension from the poor Mexicans, or the (mu
to be dreaded) *English*" was shared by other southern statesm
in the 1830s, who anxiously watched the fortunes of the infa
republic.[35]

The government of Texas proved stable enough to meet m
southern expectations as it followed the United States model in
development as a slaveholding republic. But diplomatic trends so
presented new worries to western-border watchers. England a
peared to be gaining influence within Texas; even British acqu
tion of the republic seemed not out of the question. Southern
found this prospect far more menacing than Mexican control e
had been. Long dreaded by slaveowners—but admired by black
as home of destructive antislavery influences, England now was
mored to have projected schemes for emancipation on a her
spheric scale. England planned to free the slaves in Cuba and Bra
by force, wrote a Washington editor, "and when she has acco
plished her purpose . . . she will be prepared to enforce the sa
principle as to us."[36]

All this was an old story for southerners, made no less disturbi
by familiarity. Once again, the South apparently faced the situati
that so often in times past had menaced its interests—the preser
of a strong, hostile power on its border. If Texas were abolitioniz
through English influence, slaveholders would find themselves in
absolutely untenable position. Bordered on north and west by a
gressive enemies offering haven for runaways, slavery would be
unstabilized as to be doomed. If by some miracle planters escap
that fate, another—equally dreaded—eventually would overta
them: Barred from further expansion to the west, the ever-growi
slave population would decline in value and eventually become
explosive force to the ruin of the South.

35. John Catron to Andrew Jackson, June 8, 1836, in Bassett (ed.), *Corresponde*
of Andrew Jackson, V, 401.
36. David M. Pletcher, *The Diplomacy of Annexation: Texas, Oregon, and the M*
can War (Columbia, Mo., 1973), 79–84, 120–25; Washington *Semi-Weekly Un*
September 4, 1845.

outhern annexationists in the 1840s did not try to cloak their
cern or hide their motives as they confronted the prospect of
as slipping out of their control forever. Texas must be secured
the United States in order to safeguard slavery where it already
sted and to clear the path for its continued diffusion into the
st.[37] Northern politicans made political capital out of the obvi-
. The "Real object" of Texas annexation, said Henry Waldron, a
nmission merchant from Hillsdale, Michigan, and later Radical
publican congressman, was "perpetuation of Slavery and the po-
cal power of the Slave States."[38]

3y annexing Texas, the United States annexed a war, for the gov-
ment of Mexico never had acknowledged the independence of
rebellious state and had always vowed to reconquer it. But
ansionist-minded Americans did not allow this fact to check
ir ambition. The desire to acquire other Mexican territory in the
st—California and New Mexico—also was strong, as was the
e to punish the unstable Mexican government for its various
nsgressions against United States citizens. Hardly less compel-
g was the widespread popular desire to confront England and
strate her schemes to interfere in hemispheric concerns. War
h Mexico in 1846 thus became surrogate for war with England,
more welcome for its prospect of rich territorial reward on the
ific coast as well as increased security for slavery.

ome persons at the time more than half-expected England to en-
the war in support of Mexico and in so doing to utilize a time-
rn tactic against the United States. "The English in case of war,
uld doubtless do all they could to make the slaves rise and would
ply them with the necessary arms and ammunition to make
m really formidable," predicted William Tecumseh Sherman. If
thought made the soldier uneasy, abolitionists welcomed the
spect. Samuel May, facing the war he had opposed, decided
idst all the gloom that "one ray of hope shines through. If En-
nd engages with Mexico in a war against the U.S., *Slavery must*
." The abolitionist Abby Kelley indulged in wilder fantasy as she
visioned a million slaves "ready to rise at the first tap of the

7. Washington *Semi-Weekly Union*, October 23, 1845. See also John C. Calhoun's
t Hill Letter, May 15, 1845, in *Niles' Weekly Register*, LXVIII (June 4, 1845), 232.
8. Hillsdale (Mich.) *Whig Standard*, September 15, 1846. See also Joshua R. Gid-
gs to Joseph A. Giddings, April 28, 1844, in Joshua Giddings Papers, Ohio Histori-
Society, Columbus.

drum." They, together with the twenty thousand blacks in Canac
would join with Mexicans and hostile Indians to overwhelm t
United States Army.[39]

Although when war began, slaves in Texas tried to take adva
tage of the conflict by fleeing to Mexico—a course Texans believ
Mexican authorities encouraged—the potential for revolt across t
South could not be realized. The campaigns were staged far frc
the centers of slave population, and the early success of Unit
States forces prevented invasion by Mexican armies whose col
manders might have exploited slave discontent much as the Briti
had done with such effect during both the Revolution and the W
of 1812. Yet the conflict entailed risks, as planters understoc
Southerners warned of the consequence of sending too many wh
men to combat. Residents of Pensacola, Florida, believed slav
there intended to rebel "as soon as a sufficient number of the wh
men went off to war," and South Carolinians experienced simil
apprehensions. Although the war brought slaves little opportun
to change their condition, those living close to Mexico followed t
fortunes of the armies and dreamed of the benefits defeat of t
Unted States might bring. In Louisiana, the former slave Solom
Northup remembered, slaves cheered news of Mexican victories a
mourned Mexican defeats.[40] But nowhere, except in Texas itself, c
the war occasion an unusual degree of slave restiveness, still les:
strike for freedom.

The war's destructive effect on slavery came indirectly. Conque
of Mexico provoked intense political struggle between North a:
South for control of the newly acquired area. The Wilmot Proviso
1847 set the premise for years of bitter debate. Slavery, Represe
tative David Wilmot had resolved, should forever be barred frc
any territory acquired from Mexico. Although political comprom:
in 1850 put the issue in abeyance for a time, the Kansas-Nebras
Act of 1854 renewed the controversy in still more virulent form.
its repeal of a portion of the Missouri Compromise, all the Louisia
Purchase lay open to the advance of slavery and the plantation s:
tem. Free-soil political groups bent upon containing—and thus

---

39. Sherman to John Sherman, January 4, 1846, in Rachel Sherman Thornc
(ed.), *The Sherman Letters* (New York, 1894), 29; May to J. B. Estlin, May 30, 1846
Antislavery Collection, Boston Public Library; *Liberator*, May 22, 1846.

40. *Liberator*, June 5, 1846; Steven A. Channing, *Crisis of Fear*, 54; Solon
Northup, *Narrative of Solomon Northup: Twelve Years a Slave* ... (Auburn, N
1853), 248.

nately destroying—the slaveholding South mobilized to resist
is development, with warfare in the new Kansas Territory the
ost celebrated result.

By the late 1850s, the South faced in the new Republican party a
litical force determined to check southern power and southern
pansion and to dominate the Union for its own purposes. It could
counted on to exclude plantation interests from effective partici-
tion in national affairs and to enact legislation designed to carry
t its leaders' declared intention to put slavery on a course toward
ltimate extinction."

An external enemy now menaced the South as none had done
ice 1815. By appeal to principles of human rights, northerners
uld justify to themselves and to others their intention to destroy
uthern power. To protest that Republicans, their abolitionist part-
rs, and slaveowners all were fellow Americans did not hide the
ith. Republicans were avowed enemies of planter interest; through
actment in the 1840s and 1850s of the personal liberty laws de-
;ned to protect fugitive slaves, northern states had made them-
lves partisans of the South's "internal enemy." Abolitionists had
clared themselves not merely advocates of the freedom of blacks
t their allies in an ongoing struggle for liberation. In that manner,
ave-master discord in southern households, workplaces, and plan-
tions became linked still more closely to sectional rivalries, and
idence of even apparently minor class antagonisms among white
utherners assumed major import as they acquired association
th the larger conflict.

11

$\cdot$⊕⊕⊕⊕⊕⊕⊕⊕⊕⊕⊕⊕⊕⊕⊕⊕⊕⊕⊕⊕⊕⊕⊕⊕⊕⊕⊕$\cdot$

Intimations of Violence

Organization of the Liberty party in 1839 and of its successors, t
Free Soil party in 1848 and the Republican party in 1854, signal
the emergence of a northern political force antagonistic to slave
and to planter influence. For the first time since elimination
French, Spanish, and English power in North America, the sla
states faced grave external danger. Moral-based opposition to t
South and to slavery, once associated almost solely with zealous
ligious reformers, now unmistakably was bound to power in t
form of northern political parties.

For the moment, the role slaves might play in the new situati
remained unsettled. Although by the 1850s abolitionists showed l
tle reluctance to welcome and even encourage slave resistance as
adjunct to their efforts, political party spokesmen—whether L
erty, Free Soil, or Republican—never acknowledged ties to t
slaves and never spoke of joining with them to overthrow the sou
ern planters. Republican leaders, seeking the widest possible su
port, customarily denied having abolitionist goals and shunned a
sociation with proclaimed abolitionists as well as with blacks. B
the logic of the politicians' antisouthern position made their stan
unconvincing and, as it proved, short-lived. Southerners, in a
event, thought they protested too much. The planters never d
guised their suspicion of a party that harbored and rewarded su
consistent opponents of the South as the outspoken politicia

:nry Wilson, Charles Sumner, Joshua Giddings, and Benjamin
ade. Politicians of that brand, thought a South Carolinian, were
t "the representatives of the Northern abolitionists—they are
nply the tools of the latter."[1] Antislavery, one might argue, had
come the motive force in northern politics.

A political force hostile to southern legislative policies and terri-
rial ambitions, as the Republicans were, could not be expected to
main forever unsympathetic to abolitionist intent. As southerners
derstood, the politicians' disavowal of abolitionism could not
de either their antislavery or antisouthern purpose. Neither, when
e time was right, would it prevent them from combining with
tves in efforts to hasten the South's downfall. Slaves then would
sume both a political and military role in a power struggle among
lite Americans.

At an early date, some abolitionists acknowledged that a majority
white voters were unlikely to accept essential features of their
ogram. Slaveholding southerners surely could not be expected
do so. Even though by sentiment northerners inclined toward
th antislavery and antisouthern positions, racial bias and desire
r national tranquillity prevented majority endorsement of aboli-
nism. Thus some abolitionists despaired of ever creating a con-
nsus favorable to the ending of slavery. Slavery, they decided,
as not likely to be ended by rational, peaceful means. Violence
one, it appeared, could "cut the Gordian knot," and that kind
initiative would come most effectively and appropriately from
tves themselves.[2]

At the middle of the nineteenth century, the peace movement and
onresistance had lost authority nearly everywhere. Honored in
eory though such principles still were, few accomplishments
uld be credited to their influence. On the contrary, as daily news
vealed, it was force and violence that moved the peoples of Europe
ward the valued goals of national unification and parliamentary

1. Thomas H. Seymour to Milledge Luke Bonham, December 30, 1859, in Milledge
ke Bonham Collection, South Caroliniana Library, University of South Carolina,
lumbia.
2. Jabez Delano Hammond to Gerrit Smith, May 18, 1839, and Artemas V. Bentley
Gerrit Smith, November 8, 1852, both in Gerrit Smith Papers; Alvan Stewart to
muel Webb, June 25, 1840, in Alvan Stewart Papers; Gerrit Smith to Frederick
uglass, August 28, 1854, in Gerrit Smith, Speeches of Gerrit Smith in Congress (New
rk, 1856), 401; Abraham Lincoln to George Robertson, August 15, 1855, in Roy P.
sler et al. (eds.), Collected Works of Abraham Lincoln (New Brunswick, N.J.,
53–55), II, 318.

democracy. Recent revolutions in the Germanies, Italy, and Frar had made a mockery of pacifism. For that generation, the conc sion seemed inevitable: Persons who sought to change the politi or social order must resort to worldly weapons in order to transl ideals into reality. Moral suasion remained useful for creating public opinion favorable to reform, but after minds had be changed, an entrenched old order still must be overthrown befc the new order could take its place. "Garrisonians . . . would & will plant the wilderness of this world with the rose of Sharo wrote a New England abolitionist in the late 1850s, "but there nee a rough breaking up team to prepare the way. The ugly drage heads must be cut off & their necks singed & their dens destroyed Such bloody procedure would not be the work of moral suasionis

When in the 1830s abolitionists were subjected to mob violer made possible by the unwillingness or inability of local gove ments to protect them, they took strong stands in support of "l and order" and self-righteously condemned those who violat them. Yet in more tranquil moments, they admitted to an ambi lence toward the value of both and toward the legitimacy of t devices used to maintain them. They were likely to reject man-ma law when it conflicted with their principles and to appeal for sa tion instead to the Higher Law. After all, slavery was fully support by statute, and order as it existed in the United States embraced t bondage and subordination of black people. The state obviously w competent to enforce wicked laws as well as good ones and cou maintain evil as well as beneficent institutions. Benjamin Drew Boston journalist and abolitionist, recognized the paradox. Gove ment, he concluded, is the instrument by which privilege maintai its dominion. Therefore violence against the state may be the or means for shifting power relationships. "A strong police must wat the motions of the oppressed," he wrote. "This system of police u ally answers its atrocious purpose very well. It wields the la against offenders, and instills into the oppressed the fear requis to suppress any overt act toward their rights as human beings.

3. Daniel Mann to Lysander Spooner, January 16, 1859, in Antislavery Col tion, Boston Public Library; Edmund Quincy believed moral reform would succ when its converts resorted to "ballot-boxes . . . Senates . . . battlefields." Massac setts Anti-Slavery Society, *Nineteenth Annual Report* (Boston, 1851), 83. See a Charles Burleigh's statement in Cincinnati *Gazette*, April 29, 1852, and the curi program in John M. Spear, *Twelve Discourses on Government; Purported to Have B Delivered in Boston, Massachusetts, December, 1852, by Thomas Jefferson of the Sp World* (Hopedale, Mass., 1853), 36, 40–41.

lentally, it hinders the commission of crimes, prevents mobs . . .
d keeps the streets quiet, and is so far beneficent in its actions.
t it cannot be denied that the cause of liberty in the world has
en much indebted to mobs." As a means of advancing a righteous
use, Drew concluded, abolitionists might properly defy the laws
d institutions through which the dominant maintain oppression.[4]
Even though some abolitionists tried, no counterinfluence man-
ed to halt or even slow the trend toward acceptance of force in
e slavery controversy. As sectional political disputes drove North
d South further apart in the 1850s, old zealots persisted in their
ll for violent overthrow of slavery, and new ones came forth to
n them. At the same time, some northern black abolitionists, to-
ther with a few discouraged whites, concluded that the United
ates offered black people no hope of justice and that emigration
Africa or perhaps Haiti was their only recourse. Others, however,
solved not to advise blacks to abandon the sharpening struggle by
eing the country. Instead, they boldly advocated physical defense
personal rights and early overthrow of the South's institutions.
acks in several northern cities supplemented their venerable vigi-
nce committees with military companies, ostensibly for their own
otection against kidnappers, and in 1857 delegates to a black con-
ntion in Ohio resolved to study military tactics and "to become
ore proficient in the use of arms." "The time is not far distant
nen the slave must be free," said Mary A. Darnes as she presented
e Attucks Blues of Cincinnati with a company flag, and she added
i not by moral and intellectual means it must be done by the
vord." In 1859 Martin R. Delany, sometimes called the Father of
ack Nationalism, began serial publication of his militant novel
ake; or, The Huts of America, whose main theme was the organi-
tion by a slave of a slave rebellion throughout the South. "I am
r war," Delany wrote, "—war upon the whites."[5]
Jabez Delano Hammond, the bellicose New York county judge,
ntinued to beat the drum for military invasion of the South as the
ost effective means to end slavery. Ten thousand men bearing
ms and ammunition sufficient to equip five times as many slave

4. Drew, A North-Side View of Slavery, 7.
5. Pease and Pease, They Who Would Be Free, 217–19; Howard H. Bell, "Expres-
ns of Negro Militancy in the North, 1840–1860," Journal of Negro History, XLV
60), 11–20; George W. Williams, History of the Negro Race in America from 1619 to
80 (New York, 1883), II, 145–46; Martin R. Delany, Blake; or, The Huts of America
ston, 1970), xxiii.

recruits could sweep through the South and liberate every slave,
wrote. Hammond's greatest regret, as he explained in the sixtee
page letter outlining his scheme, was that he himself was then t
old to lead such an invasion and slave revolt.[6]

Perhaps few other white northerners dreamed of martial plans
the sort Hammond designed. Yet the growing inclination to prepa
for military encounter was undisguised. A coterie of abolitioni:
supported warfare in Kansas in the mid-1850s, and in 1855 citize
in Grand Rapids, Michigan, founded a military company "for t
protection of Northern rights and Northern men." Its leaders a
nounced their intent to organize similar companies "in every ci
town, and village north of Mason and Dixon's line."[7] The most stri
ing evidence of the altered view toward force was the change th
took place in the 1850s among ostensibly nonresistant Garrisoni;
abolitionists. At the formation of the American Anti-Slavery Socie
in 1833, no member demurred from the society's official policies
barring violence as a tactic, counseling against slave resistance, a
focusing persuasive efforts solely on whites. Less than a quarter ce
tury later, abolitionist conventions renounced each of these po:
tions and endorsed its opposite.

A group of abolitionists in the late 1850s proclaimed an allian
with slaves, justified and encouraged slave insurrections, and a
nounced their readiness to aid rebels. They thus confessed their b
lief in the bankruptcy of moral reform as well as in the strength
racial bias. The barriers that white Americans had erected again
abolitionism and racial justice, they believed, could be breach
only by blacks themselves and only by violent means.

In October, 1857, a biracial National Disunion Convention mee
ing at Cleveland endorsed slave rebellion. The membership i
cluded, among others, the blacks Charles Remond and his sist
Sarah and William Wells Brown, and white radicals Susan
Anthony, Abby Kelley, Charles C. Burleigh, Parker Pillsbury, ar
Aaron Powell—all of them identified with the Garrisonian wing
the antislavery movement. But the language of their resolutio
made that relationship hardly credible. "It is the duty of the slav
to strike down their tyrant masters by force and arms," agreed t
delegates, "whenever the blow, however bloody, can be made eff

---

6. Jabez Delano Hammond to Gerrit Smith, February 28, 1852, in Gerrit Sm
Papers.
7. *Liberator*, July 20, 1855.

e to that end." And, they continued, "whenever we behold them
the battle-field of Freedom, we will give them every aid and com-
rt in our power."[8]
So alluring, especially to certain New Englanders, was the pros-
ct of insurrection that the Massachusetts Anti-Slavery Society's
nvention in January, 1857, devoted most of its sessions to discuss-
g the possibility.[9] On that occasion, one speaker after another pro-
aimed the right of slaves to rebel and the duty of northerners to
d them. Garrison entered the discussion, not in doctrinaire sup-
rt of nonresistance, but in oblique endorsement of rebellion, a
sition for which association with militant blacks perhaps had pre-
red him. "A man has no right to consent to be a slave," said Gar-
son, echoing both David Walker's Appeal written nearly thirty
ars earlier and Henry Highland Garnet's Buffalo address of 1843.
le is bound in duty to seek freedom," Garrison continued, "and he
ust seek it in a manner accordant with his own ideas of right, de-
ling that point for himself." Parker Pillsbury, who seven years ear-
r had been shocked by the northern blacks' propensity to vio-
nce, concurred with Garrison, but asserted the duty of rebellion
en more starkly: "It is as well a sin to be a slave as to hold a slave."
Garrison's close friend Henry C. Wright, a name once inseparable
m nonresistance, now stepped forward to join Garrison in urging
e opposite principle. "It is the right and duty of the people of the
orth, themselves being witnesses, to incite the slave to insurrec-
n," said Wright, "and to furnish them with arms and ammunition
carry out their purpose." The Boston orator Wendell Phillips en-
rsed Wright's counsel: "If a negro kills his master to-night, write
s name by the side of Warren: say that he is a William Tell in
sguise. . . . I want to accustom Massachusetts to the idea of insur-
ction, to the idea that every slave has a right to seize his liberty
the spot."
The view of slavery as warfare rather than as a paternalistic re-
tionship had been expressed considerably earlier by some aboli-
nists, especially by those who had firsthand experience with the
stitution. "Some men go for the abolition of Slavery by peaceful
eans," said the former slave Frederick Douglass in 1848. "So do I;
m a peace man but I recognize in the Southern States at the mo-

8. Ibid., November 6, 1857. See also American Anti-Slavery Society, Annual Re-
rts for 1857 and 1858 (New York, 1858), 183.
9. Most of the proceedings are in Liberator, February 13, 1857.

ment . . . a *state* of war." But it was Richard Hildreth, novelist ar
historian, who most fully set forth the concept. Africans had bee
captured in war, he wrote, "sold upon the coast of Guinea to a ce
tain Yankee slave-trader," transported to America, and resold to tl
planters. "Slavery then is a continuation of the state of war. It
true that one of the combatants is subdued and bound; but the w;
is not terminated."[10] Abolitionists who abandoned nonresistan
only reluctantly may have found advocacy of violence easier if th
could believe, with Hildreth, that they did not initiate conflict, b
only recognized a battle already under way. Perhaps it was h
awareness of this struggle of conscience that led Abby Kelley,
birthright member of the Society of Friends, to assure fellow abo
tionists that the "question is not whether we shall counsel the slav
to forsake peace, and commence war; *the war exists already, ar
has been waged unremittingly ever since the slave has been*
bondage."[11]

All this talk of violence, however bold, was solely a matter
theory. The convention that heard abolitionists voice their milita
sentiments proposed no plans for implementing them. Instead, aft
expressing encouragement, they waited for slaves to take the initi
tive and rise in open revolt.

At this point, abolitionists confronted a problem. Such slave ir
tiative, without assurance of outside material aid, was not likely
be taken, for slaves knew as accurately as did their masters th
revolt had no more chance of success in the 1850s—perhar
less—than it had under Nat Turner's leadership in 1831. Slaves ge
erally lacked arms and ammunition, but even with them, so the fo
mer slave Solomon Northup believed, revolt would mean "certa
defeat, disaster and death."[12] But this rational appraisal could ha
done little to reassure southern whites as they read abolitionist
inciting remarks, saw slaves escape into the North, and watched tl
growth of antisouthern political forces. The numerous souther
newspaper reports of servile plots and violence in the 1850s serv

10. Philip S. Foner (ed.), *The Life and Writings of Frederick Douglass* (New Yor
1950–55), II, 115; Richard Hildreth, *Despotism in America: An Inquiry into the N
ture, Results, and Legal Basis of the Slave-Holding System in the United States* (Bosto
1854), 35–36. See also Frederick Law Olmsted, *A Journey through Texas; or, A Sadd
Trip on the Southwestern Frontier* (New York, 1857), 123: "In Texas, the state of w
in which slavery arises, seems to continue in undertone to the present."
11. *Liberator*, February 13, 1857.
12. Northup, *Narrative*, 248–49; Olmsted, *Journey in the Back Country*, 474–7
See Chancellor Harper's explanation for the slaves' failure to revolt in E. N. Ellio
Cotton Is King, and Pro-Slavery Arguments . . . (Augusta, Ga., 1860), 607–609.

reminders of the insecurities inherent in a slaveholding society.
ese accounts chart the rising temper of slaves, but they also trace
e deepening concern of southern whites, who now faced opposi-
on not only from relatively powerless—and familiar—abolitionist
formers but also from potent antislavery, antisouthern politicians.
When the newly organized Republican party entered national
litics in 1856 by running John C. Fremont, a dashing figure of
tislavery reputation, as its first presidential candidate, southern
liticians freely charged Republicans with planning abolition,
en insurrection. In that way, those slaves who had access to news-
pers or political discussion gained the impression that their free-
m was at stake in the election. Fremont's defeat dashed their
pes for early deliverance. The result was a wave of loose talk
nong slaves, especially in the upper South, of how they might se-
re the liberty the polls had denied them. That the rash of alleged
nspiracies in Tennessee in the fall of 1856 had firmer grounding
reality seems unlikely, for all evidence suggests that, except in
e rarest, most desperate circumstance, slaves made rational cal-
lation of the probable results of their acts.[13] They could not help
t know by the 1850s that resort to open warfare was all but cer-
in to fail. Northern aid for runaways was readily at hand, but ma-
rial support for revolt remained highly unlikely.

Most slaves in the 1850s who found bondage intolerable fled from
instead of fighting to alter or abolish it. "Flight not fight is the
aves' ultima ratio," wrote the abolitionist J. Miller McKim in
57. "An antislavery movement has crossed the line." Flight, in it-
lf, somewhat changed the institution. On plantations from which
aves made good their escape, the remaining slaves gained satisfac-
n and hope. A traveler in Chicot County, Arkansas, found in 1857
at "all the slaves looked sorrowful, and displeased" when they
w a captured runaway led back to his master. It was commonly
ought, too, that slaves in the upper South were treated with
eater consideration on account of the ease of escape and that
aves in southern Texas near the Mexican border enjoyed similar
dulgence.[14]

13. Charles B. Dew, "Black Ironworkers and the Slave Insurrection Panic of 1856,"
urnal of Southern History, LXI (1975), 321–38.
14. McKim to Maria Weston Chapman, November 19, [1857], in Antislavery Col-
tion, Boston Public Library; Corydon Fuller Journal, May 6, 1857; Olmsted, Jour-
y through Texas, 266; Harrison A. Trexler, Slavery in Missouri, 1804–1865 (Balti-
re, 1914), 97; Rawick et al. (eds.), American Slave: Supplement, Series I, Vol. II,
121; Berlin, Slaves Without Masters, 351–52.

Fugitives absolutely must be captured, an overseer advised, or a plantation discipline would be lost, an impression that suggests th destructive potential of northern encouragement to runaways. Su cessful escapes encouraged further escapes. In 1845 John Thom Berryhill Plantation near Stevensburg, Virginia, advertised for Joh Roberts, his twenty-five-year-old blacksmith and shoemaker, wh "no doubt will attempt to go to the North, and has, likely, free p pers." Thom gave his version of why his slave had fled: "Sever have left the county; and he will no doubt attempt to follow." I some plantation areas bordering free states, flight became ep demic. From Martinsburg, Virginia, in 1847 came word that "slav are absconding from Maryland and this portion of Virginia in gang of tens and twenties and the moment they reach the Pennsylvan line, all hopes of their redemption are abandoned." And three yea later, slaves in Montgomery and Prince George counties in Mar land were said to be running away "in droves."[15]

The increasing tempo of the "nullifying flights" meant that ow ers in some areas now held their property in uneasy tenure. Pro imity to the free states made escapes from the upper South mo likely to succeed, but even in the lower South success was by r means unknown. Slaves in Louisiana, Arkansas, and Texas had a cess to the Indian nations and to Mexico. In Texas in the 1850 slaveowners on their own account several times organized arme bands to invade the Mexican state of Coahuila in pursuit of run ways. In 1855 three companies of Texas militia, acting under th governor's order, raided Mexico for the same purpose. Texans su pected persons of Mexican extraction of sympathizing with slav and aiding their flight across the border, a situation that perhap contributed to the Anglo-Texans' long-lasting scorn for the Mex cans who lived among them.[16]

The apparently increased restlessness of slaves in the 1850s an their demonstrated eagerness to escape to the North encourage two radical northerners to project schemes designed to effect in

15. Bassett, *Southern Plantation Overseer*, 54, 65; Washington *Semi-Weekly Unic* October 2, 1845; Charles J. Faulkner to John C. Calhoun, July 15, 1847, in Chauncey Boucher and Robert P. Brooks (eds.), *Correspondence Addressed to John C. Calhou 1837–1849*, Vol. II of American Historical Association, *Annual Report . . . for the Ye 1929* (Washington, D.C., 1930), 386; James C. Jackson to Gerrit Smith, September 1850, in Gerrit Smith Papers.
16. *Corydon Fuller Journal*, July 27, 1858; J. Fred Rippy, *The United States a Mexico* (New York, 1931), 173–74, 179; Olmsted, *Journey through Texas*, 106, 2! 323–27, 456, 502–503.

ediate emancipation. They would move plans beyond discussion
antislavery conventions by carrying them into the South. Al-
ough John Brown secretly developed his conspiracy, Lysander
ooner, a Boston lawyer, was less discreet. He published his plan
1858.

Spooner's analysis of southern class structure closely resembled
e one Hinton Rowan Helper of North Carolina recently had set
rth in his *The Impending Crisis of the South: How to Meet It.* Like
elper, Spooner depicted economic and social conflict between the
uth's slaveholders and nonslaveholders. Spooner's aim was to
tach small farmers from their long-standing alliance with the
anter class. He would launch military forces into the South at sev-
al points and appeal to nonslaveholding southerners as well as
aves to join them. "The state of slavery is a state of war," he de-
ared, echoing the new abolitionist orthodoxy. He urged nonslave-
lding whites to seize slaveowners and hold them as hostages for
e good treatment of slaves: "Man may rightfully be constrained to
justice," he explained. But he advised slaves to attempt no gen-
al insurrection until northern white armies "go down, to take part
it, in such numbers as to insure a certain and easy victory." [17]

Late in 1858, Spooner sent drafts of his plan to a few prominent
olitionists, inviting their endorsement and financial aid. Shortly
terward, it was published in the Boston *Courier* and by that means
me to southern attention. Almost no one who received his appeal
fered any encouragement at all. Wendell Phillips thought the
heme "a good one if it were only practicable," but cautioned that
o few would take part to save it "from being ridiculous" and
m being crushed by government forces. Francis Jackson, one of
arrison's closest associates, too polite to make light of the proj-
t, refused support on the ground he already had fully committed
s resources to other modes of abolitionism. Both Benjamin S.
edrick, recently discharged from the faculty of the University of
orth Carolina on account of his free-soil sympathies, and Helper
smissed the plan as absurd. "*Immature—impractical—impolitic*,"
rote Helper, adding that the abortive Lopez filibustering expe-
tion to Cuba would be ranked "a brilliant triumph compared
th the result your plan would have." Only Daniel Mann, a New
nglander temporarily living in Ohio, endorsed Spooner's proposal

17. The plan exists in several drafts in the Antislavery Collection, Boston Public
rary.

without reservation. It exactly met his desire for bold, coercive a
tion. "I want the bullies & desperadoes of slavery to be taug
that the champions of freedom are ready for the contest in ar
form, civil or savage," he wrote, and added, "My trust in God
stronger when I put some trust in myself, & keep my powd
dry."[18] But Mann's enthusiasm was not enough. Thoroughly r
buffed, Spooner made no effort to put his scheme into operatio
the essential element—northern white support—being absent. Jol
Brown suffered no such inhibitions.

Although it was Brown who moved beyond rhetoric in an ove
attempt to consummate the abolitionist-slave alliance, the ro;
he took to Harpers Ferry clearly had been prepared by othe
His association with certain militant blacks, among whom Hen
Highland Garnet and Frederick Douglass were the most prominer
and with radical white abolitionists, including Gerrit Smith ar
Thomas Wentworth Higginson, confirmed his determination to a
boldly rather than merely to pray and speak against slavery. F
many years, Brown had brooded on schemes to free slaves by e
larging operations of the Underground Railroad. His exploits duri
the guerrilla war in Kansas in the 1850s taught him military tec
niques that he believed might effectively further the emancipatio
ist cause.[19]

Brown gained the confidence of several prominent white abo
tionists who encouraged him and supplied financial aid witho
perhaps fully understanding exactly what he intended to do. He al;
conferred with northern blacks whose support he regarded as bei
crucial to his plan. It was they, or the men they could influenc
whom he expected to fill the ranks of his invading force and to he
fund it. "There are thousands of dollars in the Canadian Provinc
which are ready for the use of the insurrectionists," wrote one
Brown's confidants. At Chatham, Ontario, in the spring of 185
thirty-three blacks and twelve whites under Brown's leadership c

18. Boston *Courier*, January 28, 1859; New York *Tribune*, January 31, 1859; W(
dell Phillips to Lysander Spooner, July 16, 1858, Francis Jackson to Spooner, Dece
ber 3, 1858, Hinton Rowan Helper to Spooner, December, 1858, Daniel Mann
Spooner, January 16, 1859, all in Antislavery Collection, Boston Public Library. S
also Theodore Parker to Spooner, November 30, 1858, and Thomas Wentworth H
ginson to Spooner, November 30, 1858, *ibid*. A different interpretation of Philli
view is in James Brewer Stewart, *Wendell Phillips, Liberty's Hero* (Baton Rouge, 198
199–200.

19. Stephen B. Oates, *To Purge This Land with Blood: A Biography of John Bro*
(New York, 1970), 48–65, 126–228 *passim*.; James Redpath, *The Roving Editor;
Talks with Slaves in the Southern States* (New York, 1859), 286–87, 306.

ɪnized a provisional government whose main function would be
ɔ conduct guerrilla warfare in the South. Yet the rather fanciful
ʻoject Brown outlined seemed little more than playacting. When
onths passed and nothing more happened, support among the Ca-
ɪdian blacks faded away. Only one of the Chatham thirty-three fol-
ʻwed Brown to Harpers Ferry.[20]
Brown's efforts to organize support among blacks in the northern
nited States proved little more productive. Black leaders could
ɔt fail to sympathize with his goal, but few believed the time had
ʻme when his particular scheme could succeed. Such was the con-
ɪsion of Henry Highland Garnet, who a few years earlier had been
ʻ open in calling upon northern blacks to support slave revolt. In
ʻe summer of 1859, the Reverend Jarmain Loguen of Syracuse did
ʻhat he could to assist by organizing blacks in Canada into "Liberty
ʻagues," but he finally told Brown that these people lacked the
ʻancial means to travel to the intended base of operations on the
ɔrth-South border. Harriet Tubman, the black fugitive from Mary-
ɪnd who managed to lead scores of slaves out of the South, appar-
ʻtly favored Brown's plan and perhaps intended to join him at
ʻarpers Ferry, but at the last moment did not do so. Frederick
ʻɔuglass was in steady communication with Brown. Brown desper-
ʻely wanted support of such an able and effective leader and be-
ʻved he had it, but Douglass, too, finally declined Brown's appeal
ʻ join him in western Virginia, where his help was needed to "hive
ʻe swarming bees."[21]
Although Brown aimed at sharing his plans with only a very few
ɪsted friends, eastern abolitionists learned his intent, at least in a
ʻneral way, months before he attempted to put it into effect. In
ʻnuary, 1859, at a convention of the Massachusetts Anti-Slavery
ʻɔciety, Richard J. Hinton, a British-born newspaper correspondent
ʻ10 had visited Brown in Kansas, read to the delegates Brown's
ʻtter of greeting in which he proclaimed the start of a "new era in
ʻe Anti-Slavery movement." Hinton explained the pattern Brown
ʻw in recent events: "The rifle that laid low the first victim in Kan-
ʻs, has rung the death-knell of slavery on this continent." By at-
ʻcking free-state settlers, Hinton continued, southerners had inau-
ʻırated an intersectional war that would destroy slavery. Brown

20. Benjamin Quarles, *Allies for Freedom: Blacks and John Brown* (New York,
ʻ74), 43–51.
21. Benjamin Quarles (ed.), *Blacks on John Brown* (Urbana, Ill., 1972), 29–30;
ʻtes, *To Purge This Land*, 241, 247–48, 282–83.

viewed his own plans as an essential campaign in a war alreac under way.[22]

Hinton went on to advise the assembled Garrisonians, some whom still clung to nonresistance, that "the terrible Logic of Hi tory teaches plainly that no great wrong was ever cleansed witho blood." The lesson taught by guerrilla warfare in Kansas, he sai "was the mode and manner by which the most vulnerable point slavery, that of Insurrection may be reached. Kansas has done tl and it has also educated men for the work." Hinton presented ab litionists with scenes of carnage and the use of weapons that on recently they had believed their life's work was designed to avoi "For one, believing in the right of resistance for myself, I extend t' same to my African brother and stand ready at any time to aid the overthrow of slavery by any and all means—the rifle or revolv∢ the dagger or torch."

Thomas Wentworth Higginson, a romantic young preacher wl as befitted a confidant of Brown, long had talked of revolutic joined Hinton in advocating a scheme to promote slave revolt. doing so, he almost disclosed Brown's plan. Brown's recent raid ir Missouri to free slaves, Higginson explained, was "an indication what may come before long." Not long before, Higginson, like mc other abolitionists, looked to the Underground Railroad as the mc effective aid to slaves. He put that tactic behind him now. Slav∢ declared Higginson, desired "not as formerly to go to freedom b to have freedom come to them. And who knows how speedily morning may arise to show us that it has come?" The questi∢ hinted at impending events, for as Higginson knew, Brown alrea∢ had designated himself as the agent who would carry freedom the slaves.

Brown's plan coincided exactly with strategy outlined by Jan∢ Redpath, a Scottish-born reporter who, like Hinton, had spent sor time with Brown in Kansas. Redpath, then in his mid-twenties, w fascinated by revolution, particularly by black revolution. Slav he believed, were ready for the experience. Redpath claimed to ha interviewed numerous black people, slave and free, during extend∢ recent travels through Virginia, the Carolinas, Georgia, and A bama. Almost without exception he found them eager to free the∢ selves through insurrection. But they needed information, weapo∢ and—above all—assurance that northern whites would activ∢

22. Quarles, *Allies*, 72–80. The convention proceedings are in *Liberator*, F∢ ruary 4, 1859.

pport them in the attempt. Slaves, wrote Redpath, possessed an
nderground telegraph" that sped news the length and breadth of
e South. A northern-led strike for liberty at any point along the
uthern border would bring mass desertion by the slaves and,
obably, a violent servile uprising.[23]
On October 16, 1859, John Brown and his small band attacked the
1ited States arsenal at Harpers Ferry in western Virginia in a fu-
e attempt to start the rebellion that Redpath and a number of
her abolitionists desired and believed imminent. Brown displayed
tle skill as a tactician, and slaves did not respond as he had been
1 to expect. There was only a thin slave population in the imme-
ate area. At no time had Brown made any effort to acquaint even
ose few persons with his plan or what he expected of them. No
1ves fled their masters to join Brown's band. Neither did nonslave-
·lding white Virginians cooperate as Lysander Spooner, and prob-
·ly Brown too, had believed they would. The isolated conspirators
:re besieged and captured by government armed forces before
:dpath's "underground telegraph" could do its work.[24]
Despite the total failure of his undertaking, Brown and those who
ared his fascination with revolt made no error in their assessment
the slaves' desire for freedom. Events during the Civil War would
ove, too, that they were not mistaken in believing many slaves
uld welcome invaders who came to sweep away the dominion of
eir masters. But they were wrong when they assumed that slaves
uld blindly undertake rebellion at the behest of white radicals
1ose talent for the undertaking was untested and whose goals and
ethods remained for the most part unknown to them. Slaves
uld not heed appeals to trust whites and accept their leadership
nply because they lived in the North rather than the South. In the
:e summer of 1860, when "Mr. Ford" informed some slaves in
uth Carolina that "a man would come along between then &
1ristmas to set them free—with arms and would they fight," no
swer was forthcoming. The slaves politely put him off: "They told
m they would see about it."[25] Slaves had been in bondage for a

23. Redpath, *Roving Editor*, 286.
24. Oates, *To Purge This Land*, 290–306. Brown's plans may have embraced arm-
, whites in western Virginia. See Craig M. Simpson, *A Good Southerner: The Life of*
1ry A. Wise of Virginia (Chapel Hill, N.C., 1985), 208. For attitudes of white resi-
·ts of Harpers Ferry, see Scarborough (ed.), *Diary of Edmund Ruffin*, I, 373.
25. Slave Trial, October 11, 1860, Pendleton/Anderson District, Court of Magis-
·tes and Freeholders, Trial Papers, South Carolina Department of Archives and
story, Columbia.

long time. They were willing to wait awhile longer for deliveranc
They would judge matters for themselves and not let others det(
mine the time, the place, or the occasion for their casting off
slavery.

Slaves understood the great preponderance of power that lay w*
white southerners. Among the enslaved blacks were individuals
brave—and sometimes as cowardly—as members of other rac(
and as willing to take risks, but through generations of subjecti(
to force and terror, they had learned lessons in caution that wou
not be set aside casually. Experience and determination to survi
caused them to heed the same internal command that prompt
Garrison in 1859 to warn of the possible disastrous outcome of t
stampede toward violence. Garrison remained unconvinced that
would be better to end slavery in a holocaust than to see its contir
ance. He did not believe that southern blacks would be better (
dead than enslaved. "Where there is no life, there are no rights,"
said.[26] Blacks who had seen countless of their fellow slaves so,
maimed, hanged, and burned for resisting bondage would have u
derstood the wisdom of Garrison's words perhaps better than c
the northern reformers to whom he addressed them.

Free blacks in the North, like white abolitionists, welcom**
Brown into the lean ranks of the truly great as a martyr to the cau
of liberty. Since few slaves had known anything of Brown's plans,
is not strange that little evidence appears of their concern for I
fate. Yet impressions of his significance soon spread among the,
When the slave William Summers fled from Charleston in the spri
of 1862, he carried as one of his few treasures a picture of Jo*
Brown; some slaves in far-off Missouri knew of Brown's raid; and
Arkansas, Piomer Harshaw's mistress whipped her for singing
song about Brown.[27]

Although Brown's efforts brought almost no immediate slave *
ɔponɔe and were readily contained, his raid set new waves of fear
motion. It was easy to believe that this incident, itself trivial, h(
alded the doom of slavery. Papers found in Brown's possession su
gested that his plans for slave revolt were not limited to northwe
ern Virginia but extended even to South Carolina, Georgia, a
Florida.[28] Brown was dead, but others would follow, one might su

26. *Liberator*, February 4, 1859.
27. Blassingame (ed.), *Slave Testimony*, 700; Rawick *et al.* (eds.), *American Sl(*
Supplement, Series I, Vol. VI, p. 2, and Vol. XII, p. 170.
28. Steven A. Channing, *Crisis of Fear*, 19–20, 268n.

se, and with greater success. Harpers Ferry forecast the fate that
aited the South if abolitionists continued their agitation and if
e Republican party gained ascendancy. Abortive though it was,
own's raid made a large contribution to the crisis atmosphere
at enveloped the section in 1860, the year of the nation's most
teful presidential contest.

Abraham Lincoln's election brought dissolution of the Union, an
ent that some northerners had convinced themselves never would
ke place. Continued faith in the likelihood of slave insurrection
couraged some in the North to discount the possibility that the
uthern states would dare make good their oft-repeated threat to
cede. Abolitionists—or Republicans—might drive the South out
the Union, but rebellious slaves would force them to hurry back
for the sake of federal protection. Thomas Willis predicted that
uthern whites "would prove inadequate to defend themselves
om the knife, and the torch, and the poison in the hands of their
vn slaves, and would come back like the prodigal son, to be re-
mitted under the parental roof." Perhaps some southerners, too,
t misgivings as they considered the domestic consequences of session. "In case of a *separation* . . . we may have some fighting to
 at home," wrote Thomas H. Seymour just before he learned that
s home state of South Carolina finally had left the Union.[29]

Such qualms, though real enough, soon were set aside, for Lin-
ln's election convinced southerners that they faced an ultimate
isis. Particularly in South Carolina, for years the center of south-
n disaffection, and in Alabama and Mississippi, politicians ared that Republican electoral triumph made the Union untenable.
ith much reason, they equated Republicans with abolitionists.
r safety's sake, secession must come. It must come quickly, and
 must be carried through with little debate. Discussion "in field
d fireside," warned the Clayton (Alabama) *Banner* shortly before
ection day, "will only end in servile insurrections. Already the
ere Presidential canvass is provoking them everywhere. The direct
estion of Union or Division . . . will inevitably give them birth."[30]

Lincoln's election proved that the slave states had declined to the

---

29. Burton Alva Konkle, *The Life and Speeches of Thomas Williams . . . 1806–1872*
hiladelphia, 1905), II, 428; Thomas H. Seymour to Milledge Luke Bonham, Decem-
r 30, 1859, in Milledge Luke Bonham Collection. For doubts of the loyalty of poorer
ites, see Scarborough (ed.), *Diary of Edmund Ruffin*, II, 187–89.

30. Quoted in William L. Barney, *The Secessionist Impulse: Alabama and Missis-
pi in 1860* (Princeton, N.J., 1974), 206.

position of being a hopeless minority within the nation. Hencefor
they could not expect to set federal policy or to protect themselv
for long against hostile legislation. Under Republican control, t
Union no longer offered the South tangible advantage. On the co
trary, it now posed a threat more menacing than any yet encou
tered, for the young, aggressive Republican party might be expect
to extend its organization throughout the South. By use of the p
tronage, the Lincoln administration would create a Republica
party in the slave states. Who could doubt that the material for su
a structure lay readily at hand in the form of nonslaveholders w
would trade allegiance to the planters—and slavery—for office a
preferment? Behind the anxieties such a prospect generated lay t
slaves who could not be kept in subjection and at work once divisic
over fundamental issues erupted among the white population.[31]

Omens emerged during the presidential campaign. As the electi
of 1860 drew near, slaves, who long had followed the course of n
tional events, came to see their future at stake in the contest.
testimony given at Spartanburg, South Carolina, on October 1
1860, Robert Ott's slave Anderson was accused of "talking abo
being set free—said he expected the black people would have
fight and he would fight if he was obliged to." Ellis was still mo
eager; he "was going to get him a revolver and would be good f
six white men." Dave told John that "the North was going to set
the Negroes free, and seemed to feel certain of the fact."[32]

Republican victory appeared to heighten both slave expectatio
and white apprehensions. In the spring of 1861, a vigilance comm
tee in northern Alabama "ferretted out a most hellish insurrectio
ary plot among the slaves." By means of torture, authorities at Tri
extracted confessions leading them to conclude that slaves believ
"Lincoln is soon going to free them all, and they are everywhe
making preparations to aid him when he makes his appearance
Near Petersburg, Virginia, slaves assumed that the election of Li
coln was the equivalent of emancipation. Following his inaugur
tion, seventeen of them marched away from the plantation after a
nouncing to their master that they were free. They soon we
captured, however, and then sold out of the state.[33]

31. Eric Foner, "The Causes of the American Civil War: Recent Interpretations a
New Directions," *Civil War History,* XX (1974), 209–10.
32. Slave Trial, October 11, 1860, Pendleton/Anderson District, Court of Mag
trates and Freeholders, Trial Papers, South Carolina Department of Archives a
History.
33. Clement Eaton, *A History of the Southern Confederacy* (New York, 1954), 2
Liberator, May 24, 1861.

Southerners could not believe that slaves would hold such ideas
ithout artful indoctrination by outsiders. In 1860, at the height of
e presidential campaign, rumor sped through the South of aboli-
ɔnist agents infiltrating the section and inciting slaves to acts of
ɔngeance. Originating in Texas and spreading across the entire
ɔuth were reports of mounting slave discontent. To a dynamic
ɔoup of southerners confronting that menace and long bent on
volution, secession appeared the only recourse. Secession admit-
dly could not guarantee the slaves' docility or end subversion, but
could make abolitionists and slaveholders citizens of separate
tions, foreigners no longer bearing responsibility for the acts of
eir former countrymen. No longer would either group be subject
ɔ tyrannical imposition from the other.

Further, secession might offer a means to strengthen wavering
ctional loyalties. In particular, it might halt the apparent move-
ent of states in the upper South, most notably Kentucky and
aryland, into the ranks of the free states. The concern was not new.
; early as 1821, a Georgia editor noted what appeared to him to be
e lessening support for slavery in Virginia and Maryland. Will
ey not eventually "assume the tone of the northern states?" he
ked. Might they not "at some remote period, join in a general cru-
de against the South?" The apprehension continued. "How long
ill Maryland, western Virginia, Kentucky, Eastern Tennessee and
en the Western Part of North Carolina feel it their interest to re-
in slaves?" worried a South Carolinian in 1848. In 1859 a Missis-
ppi jurist explained that Georgia, Alabama, and Mississippi in the
rly 1830s had enacted laws regulating the interstate slave trade
cause "it was feared that if these border States were permitted to
ll us their slaves . . . *they too* would unite in the wild fanaticism of
e day, and render the institution . . . thus reduced to a few
ɔuthern States, an easy prey to its wicked spirit."[34] Secession
ould promote southern solidarity. By associating slavery with a
tion, southerners would restore to the institution the legitimacy
had lost throughout nearly all the western world. If separation
sked much, as some asserted, and solved no fundamental problem,
; others admitted, remaining in the Union offered only danger and
forced humility.

The course of the South toward secession was not in every in-

---

34. *Georgia Journal*, December 4, 1821, in Phillips (ed.), *Plantation and Frontier*, II,
*; David Johnson to John C. Calhoun, October 18, 1848, in Boucher and Brooks
ds.), *Correspondence Addressed to John C. Calhoun*, 482; Catterall (ed.), *Judicial
ses*, III, 361.

stance marked by such careful deliberation. The irrational note
the movement and evidence of its desperation can be discerned
emotion-distorted lines written by Representative Lawrence ℟
Keitt of South Carolina, whose brother recently had been murder₍
by the slaves on his Florida plantation: "If Lincoln is elected—wh₎
then? I am in earnest. I'd cut loose through fire and blood if nesc₍
sary [sic]—See—poison in the wells in Texas and fire for the Hous
in Alabama—Our Negroes are being enlisted in politics—with p₍
son and fire how can we stand it? I confess this new feature alarᵐ
me more than even everything in the past."[35] The prospect
a Republican-slave alliance was too much for Keitt and many oth
southerners to bear.

Countless rumors of slave plots and of actual revolts, presumab₎
in response to the Republican victory, did indeed disturb the Sou
in the weeks following the November election. A newspaper in t₎
Alabama black belt reported that "most" slaves in the area "hₐ
heard that Lincoln was elected, and took for granted that they we
to be free." The most venturesome among them were said to ha⁻
declared their intention to join "Lincoln's army" as soon as he se
it south. It was generally agreed, too, that slaves had measured t₎
fear sweeping the South and that even in tranquil neighborhoo₍
slaves believed insurrections elsewhere either were planned or ₐ
ready were taking place.[36]

President James Buchanan gave official stamp to this concern
his fourth annual message on December 3, 1860, when he declar₍
that "the increased and violent agitation of the slavery questioᵣ
had produced a "malign influence on the slaves and inspired the⁻
with vague notions of freedom. Hence a sense of security no long⁻
exists around the family altar. This feeling of peace at home hₐ
given place to apprehensions of servile insurrections."[37]

But the dreaded revolt did not come. In its place came interse⁻
tional war, with results fully as devastating to the South and i
institutions.

35. Lawrence M. Keitt to James H. Hammond, September 10, 1860, in Steven
Channing, Crisis of Fear, 269. On the murder of William J. Keitt, see C. Vann Woc
ward and Elisabeth Muhlenfeld (eds.), The Private Mary Chesnut: The Unpublish₎
Civil War Diaries (New York, 1984), 181, 182.
36. Barney, Secessionist Impulse, 210–11; Aptheker, American Negro Slave Revoℓ⁻
355–58; Steven A. Channing, Crisis of Fear, 272.
37. Richardson (ed.), Messages and Papers, VII, 3157–58.

12

❆❆❆❆❆❆❆❆❆❆❆❆❆❆❆❆❆❆❆❆❆❆❆❆❆❆❆❆❆❆❆❆

The War of the Rebellion
1861–1865

The war that began with the Confederate shelling of Fort Sumter
on April 12, 1861, was designated three days later by Abraham Lincoln as rebellion, and so by official usage it would be known. Union
authorities chose not to view the conflict as a civil war, a "war between the states," or a "war for southern independence." Instead,
according to them, it resulted from a combination of dissident individuals rebelling against the authority of the United States. But
despite official sanction, the name never caught on—even Lincoln
would speak of a "great civil war" in his Gettysburg Address of November 19, 1863. Yet "War of the Rebellion" acquires aptness extending beyond its origin in Lincoln's political theory when the conflict is viewed in its other, less familiar aspect. The war was not only
a rebellion of white southerners against the Union. It also was a
rebellion of slaves against masters or, more exactly, a rebellion of
slaves against bondage.

The war assumed the character of a slave uprising, not at all in
the horrific manner some had predicted, but gradually, with little
overt violence on the part of slaves, and with such inevitability as
rarely to provoke comment outside the Confederacy. Indeed, few in
the North equated the conduct of blacks during the Civil War with
insurrection. The lack of remark became the equivalent of popular
acceptance of a great folk movement that occurred spontaneously
without need for prompting or direction.

Slave revolt was more or less expected to follow withdrawal «
federal authority from the South, or if not at that moment, the
surely as soon as invading Union armies appeared. For obviou
prudential reasons, Confederate leaders chose not to dwell on th
danger but simply denied its possibility: "Of themselves—movir
by themselves—I say history does not chronicle a case of negr
insurrection," Jefferson Davis had told the United States Congres
on January 10, 1861. Northerners, however, and especially abol
tionists, made much of the perilous situation secessionists create
for themselves when they decided to dispense with federal prote
tion. "Well, the time has come to expect a slave insurrection ;
any moment," wrote Garrison, and he promised it his "warme
sympathies."[1]

No doubt Garrison envisioned secession as producing an up
heaval similar to the one that long ago had devastated Sain
Domingue. But Garrison would have trouble identifying slav
behavior during the Civil War with his notion of revolt, for n
blood-drenched uprising followed hard upon secession. From fir
to last, the slaves' response to war and invasion produced little «
the lurid drama and practically none of the insurrectionary horre
that for so long had been predicted.

Yet the conflict was hardly under way when slaves began to tak
advantage of the situation by shaking off white control and settir
themselves free. Some did not join the movement until late in tl
war, and as happens in all revolutions, some took no part at al
The process of self-emancipation was most evident wherever Unio
armies appeared; it was least evident far from military action. I
such places, slaves were likely to continue their usual routine a
most as though a revolutionary war was not under way. Many re
mained in their master's service until the very end (thus providir
basis for the "loyal Negro" tradition), while others, willingly or ur
der coercion, aided the Confederate war effort as military laborer
or in other capacities.[2] However much longed for, emancipatio
seemed to some an unreachable goal. "Us heard talk 'bout de wa
but us didn't pay no 'tention," one former slave remembered. "U

1. Dunbar Rowland (ed.), *Jefferson Davis, Constitutionalist: His Letters, Papers ar
Speeches* (Jackson, Miss., 1923), V, 30; *Liberator*, May 24, 1861.
2. For a comprehensive account, see Bell I. Wiley, *Southern Negroes, 1861–18€*
(New Haven, Conn., 1938). Pertinent documents appear in Ira Berlin *et al.* (eds.), *T*
Destruction of Slavery (New York, 1985); Vol. 1 of Berlin *et al.* (eds.), *Freedom: A Doc*
mentary History of Emancipation, 1861–1867, Series I, 2 vols. to date.

ever dreamed dat freedom would come."[3] The maintenance of traditional patterns of behavior while society crumbled and distant
armies decided their fate no doubt in some instances reflected ignorance as much as it did lethargy and unconcern. But except in
areas reached by the Union army, even slaves who desperately
wanted to be free and who understood the import of the war could
not easily find a practical alternative to remaining in bondage. Although gravely weakened by invasion, the same forces that maintained slavery in peacetime continued to operate in wartime.

As war began, southern state governments moved to lessen the
disruptive impact hostilities were expected to have on master-slave
relationships. Despite urgent requests from Confederate headquarters for additional men and arms, some state governors early in
1861 decided to retain a home guard and a store of arms and ammunition under their exclusive control for use within the state,
much as had been done during the Revolution and the War of 1812.
So extensive was this precautionary policy during the first months
of war that it produced shortages in the Confederate armies and
weakened their fighting capacity.[4]

Even though state officials probably understood the military consequence of their decision, they nevertheless had to balance local
exigencies with national needs. Pressure to yield to local concern
was hard to resist. Nervous citizens in Mississippi urged the governor not to allow Confederate authorities to remove militia or volunteers. In Georgia, citizens planned to request officials to leave
enough forces at home "as will be sufficient to keep our colored
population under supervision and control. . . . And also a force sufficient to give assurance and confidence of protection."[5] The same
considerations may have hindered recruitment as well. Confronted
by the dual threats of slave unrest and Yankee invasion, one Missis-

3. Rawick (ed.), *American Slave*, VI, 131. See also Rawick *et al.* (eds.), *American
Slave: Supplement, Series I*, Vol. X, pp. 2022–23, 2070.
4. Frank Lawrence Owsley, *State Rights in the Confederacy* (Chicago, 1925), 6;
Eaton, *History of the Southern Confederacy*, 263; Steven A. Channing, *Crisis of Fear*,
72. Armstead Robinson, "In the Shadow of Old John Brown: Insurrection Anxiety
and Confederate Mobilization, 1861–1863," *Journal of Negro History*, LXV (1980),
79–97.
5. Clement Eaton, *Freedom of Thought in the Old South* (Durham, N.C., 1940),
105–106; C. C. Jones to R. Q. Mallard, November 30, 1861, in Robert M. Myers (ed.),
Children of Pride: A True Story of Georgia and the Civil War (New Haven, Conn., 1972),
804. For the role of Georgia blacks in the war, see Clarence L. Mohr, *On the Threshold
of Freedom: Masters and Slaves in Civil War Georgia* (Athens, Ga., 1986).

sippi resident set "to thinking where I could be of the most servic
to my County *at home* or *in the army* you will see nothing but eterna
Vigilance will keep down the enemy at home as well as *at ou*
frontier."[6]

As white citizens became soldiers, civilians believed, slavery per
ceptibly changed. A warning reached the Mississippi governor from
Jackson in August, 1861, that if more men were taken from the
county, "we may as well give it to the negroes ... now we hav
to patrole every night to keep them down." Even patrols did no
always prove effective. In July, 1862, at Harrisonville, Georgia, cit
zens petitioned the governor to quarter soldiers in the count:
Fifty-one slaves—"traitors ... the worst of spies"—had run to the
Federals. The petitioners understood why: "The temptation of *chea*
goods, freedom, and paid labor cannot be withstood."[7]

Despite such disruption, means still were at hand in most place
for maintenance of the slave system. Especially during the first hal
of the war, soldiers sometimes remained temporarily in camp
within the state while they were being assembled prior to transfe
to the field. Since these men now were organized in military unit
and were armed, their capacity to maintain order was enhance
rather than diminished by their absence from home. While soldier
could not punish the slaves' ordinary day-to-day infractions, the
could be deployed as needed to crush any coordinated outbreak.[8]

Regular slave patrols for the most part ceased to function i
the summer of 1861, when the men who filled their ranks joine
the armies. Thus the principal force that always had impede
free movement of slaves disappeared, but the efforts of very youn
men and of men beyond military age partly made up the deficienc
In plantation regions such persons, organized as home guards
mounted pickets, and vigilance committees took the place of slav
patrols and helped prevent unauthorized movement and assembl
of slaves. While evidence was plentiful that slave dissidence in
creased, the white population generally succeeded in containing i
within manageable limits, even resorting to ruthless means to do sc

6. J. D. L. Davenport to Governor J. J. Pettus, May 14, 1861, quoted in Aptheke:
American Negro Slave Revolts, 364; Eaton, *Freedom of Thought*, 105–106.
7. Wiley, *Southern Negroes*, 36; C. C. Jones to C. C. Jones, Jr., July 10, 1862, i
Myers (ed.), *Children of Pride*, 929–30.
8. Bassett, *Slavery in the State of North Carolina*, 108–109; Eaton, *History of th*
Southern Confederacy, 245–46.

Brutal reprisals against defiant slaves continued as before the war, thereby restating the old lesson that white power was not to be flouted. "There is a great disposition among the Negroes to be insubordinate, and to run away and go to the federals," reported a Confederate official at Natchez in 1862. "Within the last 12 months we have had to hang some 40 for plotting an insurrection, and there has been about that number put in irons." A Louisiana planter wrote: "Things are just now beginning to work right—the negroes hated to go to work again. Several have been shot and probably more will have to be."[9] Those slaves had tested the planters' power and determination and found them still strong. Thus, except in places where the presence of Union armies effectively counterbalanced southern military power, slaves remained under coercion. They had little more chance of freeing themselves than before war began. Not until outside support appeared could revolt in the form of mass desertion occur.

The presence of a foreign foe always had provided the acid test of slavery, as southerners learned during the Revolution and again in the War of 1812. The effect of invasion proved no less severe in 1861. With the advance of Union armies, thousands of slaves, often in family units, deserted their owners to seek protection in the camps of the invaders, thereby becoming, in General Benjamin F. Butler's odd phrase, "contraband of war."[10] Distance from Union forces was a powerful obstacle to flight but not an insuperable one, as a slaveholder in the hills of northwestern Georgia revealed when he advertised for three runaways who he believed were heading west to join the Yankees at Corinth. Most slaves located so far from Union lines risked no such perilous journeys. Instead, they stayed where they were, though they still might manifest disloyalty by performing their prescribed duties reluctantly or not at all. Uncle Tom in Alabama provided an example of such behavior. When Union soldiers arrived at the plantation, he first led them to the horses and mules he had helped his master hide and then joined the soldiers in ran-

9. Herbert Aptheker, "Notes on Slave Conspiracies in Confederate Mississippi," *Journal of Negro History*, XXIX (1944), 76; John H. Ransdell to Governor Thomas O. Moore, May 26, 1863, in G. P. Whittington (ed.), "Concerning the Loyalty of Slaves in Northern Louisiana in 1863: Letters from John H. Ransdell to Governor Thomas O. Moore, Dated 1863," *Louisiana Historical Quarterly*, XIV (1931), 494.
10. On the origin of the term, see James G. Randall and David Donald, *The Civil War and Reconstruction* (2nd ed., rev.; Lexington, Mass., 1969), 371n.

sacking the plantation house. "He hadn't been much good to mass since de war commenced," a former slave remembered. "Lay off i de swamp mos' of de time."[11]

The mass flight of slaves from plantations to Union lines, an ac celeration of the folk movement that abolitionists and northern fre blacks had encouraged for years, was in itself rebellion, even thoug little violence accompanied it. Blacks in effect declared themselve free and, usually without raising a hand against their owner: simply walked away from slavery. The significance of this move ment—its equivalence to rebellion—was not lost on slaveholder: The Reverend Charles C. Jones in Georgia speculated on a possibl remedy in the form of harsh legal sanctions: "Could their overt re bellion in the way of casting off the authority of their masters b made by construction insurrection?" he asked.[12] Perhaps it was a Jones's urging that a committee in Liberty County, Georgia, re quested officials to extend martial law to runaway slaves. "The ne groes constitute a part of the body politic in fact," they reasonec "and should be made to know their duty; that they are perfectl aware that the act which they commit is one of rebellion against th power and authority of their owners and the Government unde which they live."[13] But such proposals were at best quixotic, for th time had nearly passed when law or even the threat of summar punishment could do much toward maintaining in blacks the att: tudes essential to slavery. Paternalism had had its day.

By their willingness to serve the invaders as guides, spies, in formers, laborers, and—as soon as Union policy allowed—soldiers the contrabands left no doubt about their rejection of their forme owners and their owners' government. By the third summer c war, southern white soldiers found themselves facing armed blacks most of them former slaves, wearing uniforms of the Union arm) At the moment northern blacks and southern contrabands took u; arms against the military forces of their former masters, the Civi War unquestionably assumed the character of controlled, blac insurrection.

All this happened, it must be noted, almost solely at the initiativ

11. Rome *Weekly Courier*, September 19, 1862, cited in Paul D. Escott, "The Con text of Freedom: Georgia's Slaves During the Civil War," *Georgia Historical Quarterly* LVIII (1974), 84; Rawick (ed.), *American Slave*, VI, 78.
12. Jones to C. C. Jones, Jr., July 21, 1862, in Myers (ed.), *Children of Pride*, 935.
13. *The War of the Rebellion: A Compilation of the Official Records of the Union an Confederate Armies* (130 vols.; Washington, D.C., 1880–1901), Ser. IV, Vol. II, p. 37.

f slaves themselves. The Union government designed no policies
imed at producing such a response. At the start of hostilities, Lin-
oln's administration had drawn no plan to deprive planters of their
ıbor and property, to incite social disorder within the South, or to
rm slaves. But by the summer of 1862, it found itself doing each of
hese things, if only by indirection.

Every earlier enemy—the French, the Spanish, the English—had
een quick to exploit slave discontent as a weapon to hamper and
mbarrass American military effort. Among all the foes American
laveholders ever faced, only the Union, as a matter of policy, de-
lined to do this. The self-denial appears the more remarkable be-
ause, of all the planters' enemies, the Union was the only one with
n antislavery reputation, the only one headed by the leader of an
ntislavery political party, the only one whose professed ideology
night have been expected to produce an emancipationist policy as
matter of course.

Contradictions early became apparent. The decades of intersec-
ional discord that preceded secession and war vested the northern
ıvaders with an ideological quality absent from the South's earlier
nemies. Southerners, black and white alike, viewed the Yankees as
ntislavery agents. But by no means did all Yankees view them-
elves that way. When Union commanders prepared to launch their
rst incursions into the Confederacy, Generals George B. McClellan
nd Robert Patterson undertook to remove any impression that they
ommanded armies of liberation. They issued proclamations assur-
ng slaveholding Unionists of their lack of revolutionary purpose
nd of their readiness to put down the revolt their presence might
ncourage. They renounced any plan to forge political and military
lliances with slaves, though the expediency of doing so must have
een obvious to them. When General Butler marched his army from
nnapolis to Washington in April, 1861, he, too, made his intent
nmistakably clear. He informed the governor of Maryland of his
eadiness to help suppress slave uprisings in the state.[14]

With no trace of gratitude, Governor Thomas Hicks reported him-
elf fully capable of controlling the situation without Yankee aid.
Butler's message to Hicks produced intense editorial controversy in
he North, thereby revealing support in some quarters for the insti-
ation of slave revolt. Predictably, Garrison preached his customary

14. *Ibid.*, Ser. I, Vol. II, pp. 47–48, 662; *Liberator*, May 17, 1861; *War of the Rebel-
ion*, Ser. I, Vol. II, p. 593.

editorial sermon in the *Liberator*—this time a reprimand—wit
Butler supplying the text. "General Butler supposes himself to b
better than a negro slave," wrote Garrison. "He is no better. He as
sumes to have a better right to freedom: he has none. . . . Men wh
glory in Bunker Hill and Yorktown must not deny to the oppresse
any of the means necessary to secure their freedom, whatever be
comes of their oppressors."[15]

Such statements, though consistent with abolitionist principle
ignored long-standing and widely shared dread of black insurrec
tion, but more important, they also ignored Lincoln's declared pur
pose in waging the War of the Rebellion. Lincoln had issued his ca
for seventy-five thousand volunteers to restore the Union, not to fre
the slaves or to ruin the planters. Although a dynamic element i
the North long had sought any opportunity to end slavery and elimi
nate planter influence from national affairs, only slowly did Lincol
come to share its revolutionary intent.[16]

Lincoln earlier had voiced a commitment to place slavery on th
road to ultimate extinction; yet the war he conducted bore in its firs
phase little relation to that end. War was an accident. It had bee
forced on the Union by the planters' rebellion and their subsequen
aggression. Union armies in 1861 drove into the South with no fur
ther political aim than to suppress white Rebels and thereby mak
the Union operable. Had slaves at that time misunderstood Unio
policy and managed to rise in open revolt, Union forces, it is pos
sible to believe, would have joined Confederates in restoring order
as Butler in fact had promised to do in Maryland. "The forlorn hop
of insurrection among the slaves may as well be abandoned," wrot
the northern black journalist Robert Hamilton in the summer o
1861. "They are too well informed and too *wise* to court destructio
at the hands of the combined Northern and Southern armies."[17]

The limited goal of political restoration could be achieved mor
quickly and at less cost, administration leaders supposed, if in th

15. *Liberator*, May 24, 1861. This issue contains commentary from other news
papers.
16. George M. Fredrickson, "A Man but Not a Brother: Abraham Lincoln and Ra
cial Equality," *Journal of Southern History*, XLI (1975), 39–58; Don E. Fehrenbacher
"Only His Stepchildren: Lincoln and the Negro," *Civil War History*, XX (1974)
293–310.
17. Quoted in James M. McPherson, *The Negro's Civil War: How American Negroe
Felt and Acted During the War for the Union* (New York, 1965), 42. For an instance o
Federal suppression of slave violence, see Louis S. Gerteis, *From Contraband to Freed
man: Federal Policy Toward Southern Blacks, 1861–1865*, (Westport, Conn., 1973)
114–15.

'ocess race relations were left undisturbed. In particular, slave-
)lding Unionists in border states—who had committed no politi-
il offense—should not be further alienated and perhaps driven to
in the secessionists. Lincoln hesitated for a long time to accept the
gic of the Union's position with respect to both planters and
aves. "What I do about slavery, and the colored race," he would
rite in 1862, "I do because it helps to save the Union; and what I
rbear, I forbear because I do *not* believe it would help to save the
nion."[18] Unacceptable as black and white abolitionists found that
atement, it accurately expressed the president's priorities and his
ssessment of political necessity.

A war against slavery was politically impossible in 1861. Lincoln
nderstood the complexities of public opinion better than did most
ntislavery radicals, who were prone to ignore or simplify them.
ecession drew a political line between the sections; yet the line
nperfectly demarked contrasting interests and ideologies. Lincoln
)uld never ignore the sizable body of states' rights, antiabolition-
t, anti-Negro thought that flourished in the North. Its presence
ust be taken into account when determining policy, and nothing
ust be done that might mobilize its influence against the war for
ie Union. Garrison, too, had grasped this fact well before the war
:gan, though he did not allow that insight to compromise his an-
slavery zeal. "If we fight with actual slaveholders in the South,"
: had written in January, 1859, "must we not also fight with pro-
avery priests, politicians, editors, merchants, in the North? Where
re we to begin?"[19] The Union's long delay in acknowledging eman-
pation as a war aim was the practical consequence flowing from
ie problem Garrison had identified.

With their hostility to slavery in no way compromised by political
ecessity, abolitionists held to a far different conception of the war
nd its revolutionary possibilities than did Lincoln. The slavehold-
·s' decision to dissolve the Union had added to their numbers and
etermination. "Lawyers and laymen who have never been willing
) own that they were abolitionists now publicly and privately avow
iemselves such and say slavery must die," observed an antislavery
ortherner shortly before hostilities began. Further, the North con-

18. Abraham Lincoln to Horace Greeley, August 22, 1862, in Basler *et al.* (eds.),
)llected Works of Abraham Lincoln, V, 388–89. LaWanda Cox, *Lincoln and Black
·eedom: A Study in Presidential Leadership* (Columbia, S.C., 1981), places Lincoln in
e vanguard of the movement for emancipation and equal rights for blacks.
   19. *Liberator*, February 4, 1859.

tained a dynamic element of persons, not self-defined as abolition
ists, who nevertheless agreed that the welfare and destiny of th
nation required destruction of the planters' power. The most direc
means to this end, they believed, was emancipation. A group withi
the Republican party, reflecting both antislavery idealism and ai
tiplanter bias, worked consistently toward that end. They joine
free blacks and abolitionists in directing merciless criticism again:
Lincoln for what they regarded as his narrow conception of the wε
and his hesitancy to exploit its opportunities.[20]

Military operations and the conduct of slaves themselves had tl
effect of supporting the critics' war aims rather than those of Li
coln, and in the end, his objections and reservations were swe
aside. Despite official rationale and political exigency, the Civil Wε
inevitably undermined slavery. But ideology and policy had less t
do with promoting this result than did slaves and the army itse
and the result would have been much the same even had Lincol
and the North not possessed an antislavery reputation well know
to many slaves.

Any "foreign" army operating on southern soil was certain to ur
settle master-slave relationships, for the masters' enemies, whoevε
they might be, were the slaves' friends. If invaders sought to "usε
slaves, slaves viewed invaders as instruments for accomplishir
their own purpose. But the Union army's disruptive effect and tl
use resistant slaves could make of it became greater on account ε
decisions made by some of its officers early in the war. In disregar
of Lincoln's hands-off policy toward slavery, a few military con
manders took a position far in advance of his. The most conspicuou
dissident was General John C. Fremont, the Republican party's fir:
presidential candidate, who then commanded the Western Depar
ment. On August 30, 1861, Fremont proclaimed martial law in Mi
souri and declared the slaves of every Rebel in the state free.[21] Tl
action accorded with Fremont's own antislavery convictions; it als
was appropriate to an invader bent on wounding the enemy by rε
sort to whatever weapon lay at hand. Lord Dunmore had acted sim

20. E. Andrus to the secretary, American Missionary Association, April 1, 1861,
American Missionary Association Archives; Kenneth M. Stampp, "And the W.
Came": The North and the Secession Crisis, 1860–1861 (Baton Rouge, 1950), traces tl
influence of these groups. For their later activity, see T. Harry Williams, Lincoln ar
the Radicals (Madison, Wis., 1965).
21. War of the Rebellion, Ser. I, Vol. III, pp. 466–67. For an assertion of the Unic
Army's central role in emancipation, see Dwight Lowell Dumond, America's Shar
and Redemption (Marquette, Mich., 1965), 47–48, 90–93.

rly when confronting slaveholding rebels in Virginia in 1775, but incoln declined to be Lord Dunmore. He modified Fremont's proc- imation in order to make it accord with Congress' First Confisca- on Act of August 6, which held that only Rebel-owned slaves ac- ually used in prosecution of the rebellion would be subject to onfiscation, though not necessarily freed. When in May, 1862, Gen- ral David Hunter, also acting well in advance of official policy, de- lared the slaves in South Carolina, Georgia, and Florida free, Lin- oln countermanded the order.[22]

Despite these early signs of reluctance, the Union moved inexo- ably toward an emancipationist policy. By terms of the Second onfiscation Act, July 17, 1862, Congress declared slaves of Rebel nasters "forever free" as soon as they entered Union lines, and on eptember 22, Lincoln issued his preliminary Emancipation Proc- amation, which announced that on January 1, 1863, all slaves in ne states still in rebellion would be "forever free."[23] Thus, gradu- lly and without show of enthusiasm, Lincoln adopted a position onsistent with his political role as head of a nation whose majority dhered to the principles of free soil, free labor, and free men. Yet o subsequent development quite removed the impression that the roclamation was primarily a political and military measure rather nan an ideological and humanitarian one. It did not, for instance, pply to the loyal border slave states—or even to some parts of the eceded ones—any more than Dunmore's proclamation of 1775 to laves in Virginia had applied to England's loyal slaveholding colo- ies in the West Indies.

Southern whites chose to interpret the Emancipation Proclama- ion as being a signal for slave insurrection.[24] Slaves, of course, did ot respond in such fashion, and it should go without saying that incoln did not intend that they should. On the contrary, he recog- ized and attempted to counter the proclamation's potential for cre- ting unmanageable servile unrest. Thus, included in the document

22. Abraham Lincoln to John C. Fremont, September 2, 1861, and September ll, 861, in Basler et al. (eds.), Collected Works of Abraham Lincoln, IV, 506–507, 517–18; Proclamation Revoking General Hunter's Order of Military Emancipation of May 9, 862," May 10, 1862, ibid., V, 222–23.
23. Ibid., V, 433–36. John Hope Franklin, The Emancipation Proclamation (Gar- en City, N.Y., 1963); Hans Trefousse, Lincoln's Decision for Emancipation (Phila- elphia, 1975).
24. Richmond Enquirer, October 1, 1862; James L. Roark, Masters Without Slaves: outhern Planters in the Civil War and Reconstruction (New York, 1977), 74–76; C. C. ones, Jr., to C. C. Jones, September 27, 1862, in Myers (ed.), Children of Pride, 967.

was counsel to slaves to refrain from violence "unless in necessar self-defense," as well as admonition to work faithfully if reasonabl wages were offered. By ruining the planters, emancipation woul constitute revolution, but Lincoln did not intend it to produce ar archy. Neither the planters nor the staple-crop economy was to b destroyed in a reign of terror (if slaves had any such inclination and emancipated slaves, it appeared, must work for others rathe than possess the soil.

By the time Lincoln issued the Emancipation Proclamation, thou sands of slaves already had stopped working on plantations and ha associated themselves with Union military forces, either as laborer or as soldiers, a development that would have considerable politica and military significance to both North and South. As soon as th war began, abolitionists and northern free blacks had called upo Congress to acknowledge the right of black men to enlist in th Union army. Blacks must take part, they argued, if the conflict wer to lead to popular acceptance of their freedom and expanded right "Every race has fought for Liberty and its own progress," explaine John A. Andrew, antislavery governor of Massachusetts. "If Sout ern slavery should fall by the crushing of the Rebellion, and colore men should have no hand and play no conspicuous part in the tas the result would leave the colored man a mere helot."[25] Arming o the blacks would recognize them as allies, if not equal partners, i war against the planters.

The cogency of the argument did not prevent objections. Critic pointed out especially the damaging effect black enlistment migh be expected to have on the morale of white soldiers, who were as sumed to be severely afflicted with racial prejudice, and they re peated allegations of the blacks' incapacity to fight. But looming a a large objection, too, was the prospect that their enlistment woul incite insurrection. Upon seeing fellow blacks in arms, slaves woul rise up in fury against the white population—so warned Senato Garrett Davis of Kentucky, who spoke of "insurrectionary war" a "a practical question." Blacks who in the 1850s commonly wer depicted by slaveowners as docile and unthreatening became, i Davis' exposition, fiends. Figures of savagery laced his rhetori He spoke of the black's cruelty and of the "latent tiger fiercenes

25. Quoted in James M. McPherson, *The Struggle for Equality: Abolitionists and th Negro in the Civil War and Reconstruction* (Princeton, N.J., 1964), 204.

h his heart ... when he becomes excited by a taste of blood he is demon."[26]

These were powerful arguments indeed, but Lincoln heeded them only to the extent of agreeing that enlistment of black troops would exploit southern fears and thus further damage Confederate morale. The bare sight of fifty thousand armed, and drilled black soldiers on the banks of the Mississippi, would end the rebellion at once," he wrote. Military necessity, as Lincoln's comment suggests, eventually overcame all other considerations, and on July 17, 1862, Congress authorized the enlistment of blacks as soldiers. A month later, General Rufus Saxton, commander of the Department of the South, received permission to recruit five black regiments in the South Carolina Sea Islands. In March, 1863, the secretary of war authorized Adjutant General Lorenzo Thomas to recruit black regiments in the lower Mississippi Valley, and in May the War Department established the Bureau of Colored Troops to supervise the raising of black regiments in every part of the country. "By arming the negro we have added a powerful ally," commented General Ulysses S. Grant.[27] It was equally true that Negroes found in the Union army a powerful ally in their incessant struggle against enslavement.

By the time Congress allowed free blacks in the North to enlist, their martial enthusiasm—as well as that of the whites—had declined. Free black men did not rush to join the Union armies. By the midsummer of 1862, the war had entered a costly phase and much of its romance had vanished. The Emancipation Proclamation had not yet been issued, and it was by no means certain that the Union intended to end slavery. Discrimination in pay and perhaps in treatment further discouraged black enlistment, as did the prospect of serving under white officers. The Confederate government's threat to treat captured black soldiers as traitors and insurrectionists rather than as prisoners of war was another deterrent. It is likely, too, that to former slaves, army discipline and plantation discipline

26. McPherson, *Negro's Civil War*, 163–64; *Congressional Globe*, 37th Cong., 2nd Sess., Pt. 4, p. 3204. Garrison described the blacks as "not of a savage nature, but remarkably docile, patient, slow to wrath, reluctant to shed blood, forbearing and forgiving to a wonderful degree." *Liberator*, May 24, 1861.

27. Abraham Lincoln to Andrew Johnson, March 26, 1863, in Basler *et al.* (eds.), *Collected Works of Abraham Lincoln*, VI, 149–50; Grant to Abraham Lincoln, August 23, 1863, in McPherson, *Negro's Civil War*, 191. On proposals for the Union's promoting actual slave rebellion, see Wiley, *Southern Negroes*, 83, and Mohr, *On the Threshold of Freedom*, 218.

appeared so similar as to evoke unpleasant memories. The Georgia born historian Ulrich Bonnell Phillips, while working at a United States Army camp in 1918, commented on the similarities of the life of blacks as soldiers and as slaves: "The negroes are not enslaved but drafted; they dwell not in cabins but in barracks; they shoulder the rifle, not the hoe."[28] There is every reason to suppose that blacks a half century or more before Phillips wrote also saw these resemblances, with resultant check to their martial fervor.

In the South, recruitment was more successful, for there in occupied territory Union commanders sometimes used their power to round up blacks and bring them into the army with little evidence of consent being required, a procedure that, according to General Saxton, produced "universal confusion and terror." Charlie Aarons in Mississippi remembered that he hid out in the swamp for fear of being impressed into the Union army.[29] Others, for much the same reason, may have decided to remain on the plantation and under their owner's control longer than they otherwise would have thought desirable.

After Congress instituted conscription in 1863, several northern state governments sent their own recruiting agents into the South in hopes of filling state troop quotas with blacks. The recruiters' successes were matched by their failures. Blacks sometimes showed little eagerness to accept the agents' offers. When an agent in Mississippi offered Berry Smith a chance to enlist, Smith remembered "I tol' 'em I wasn't no rabbit to live in de woods." An Illinois agent reported similar rebuffs: "'Oh sir,' say some, 'I would rather be a slave all my days than go to war. I cant shoot nor I don't want to shoot Any Buddy. I cant fight.'" General William Tecumseh Sherman viewed the state agents much as blacks did—"as the new master that threatens him with a new species of slavery." Yet of the 178,975 blacks who served in the Union army, 99,337 were recruited within the Confederacy.[30]

Enlistment of blacks was thought to serve an indispensable mili

28. McPherson, *Negro's Civil War*, 173–74; Phillips, *American Negro Slavery*, [ii].
29. Wiley, *Southern Negroes*, 309–10; Rufus Saxton to Edwin M. Stanton, December 30, 1864, in *War of the Rebellion*, Ser. III, Vol. IV, p. 1028; Rawick (ed.), *American Slave*, VI, p. 4; Gerteis, *From Contraband to Freedman*, 143.
30. Rawick *et al.* (eds.), *American Slave: Supplement, Series I*, Vol. X, p. 1981; John Hope Franklin (ed.), *Diary of James T. Ayres, Civil War Recruiter* (Springfield, Ill. 1947), 46; *War of the Rebellion*, Ser. I, Vol. XLVII, Pt. 2, p. 37; Frederick H. Dyer, *Compendium of the War of the Rebellion Compiled and Arranged from Official Records* ... (Des Moines, 1908), 11.

ary purpose. "All our increased military strength now comes from the negroes," wrote Gideon Welles, Lincoln's secretary of the navy, in January, 1863. Enlistment also lessened whatever possibility there was that the great numbers of blacks who had freed themselves or been freed from plantation discipline would become dangerously violent. Enrolling blacks in the army helped assure order by placing them again under white control.[31]

Most slaves, of course, experienced war as civilians, not as soldiers. War offered those not in the armies opportunity to gain advantage within the slave system, to escape from it, even to help destroy it, but in most instances the occasion for realizing these opportunities did not appear immediately. In early 1862, the slave Alek in South Carolina declared that "he was going to wait until all the men went away & he would do as he pleased." In large parts of the Confederacy, traditional authority persisted for a long time, a fact Alek evidently recognized, even as he felt the lessening of white-imposed pressure. When overseers and owners left for Confederate service, the absence of accustomed control invited a loosening of discipline. Slaves would not work without overseers, the governor of Florida warned Jefferson Davis: "The result will probably be insubordination and insurrection." The prediction was fulfilled in part, for though insurrection did not occur, the goals of production and profit, which had set the slaves' routine, receded from their lives. When white men rode away for the last time, slaves found it easier than before to conduct their daily affairs in ways pleasing to themselves. Common report held that under the supervision only of women, slaves worked less efficiently, became more insolent, and were harder to control. But male overseers, too, found their usual problems of exacting labor from unwilling bondsmen vastly greater than before.[32]

31. Howard K. Beale (ed.), *Diary of Gideon Welles, Secretary of the Navy Under Lincoln and Johnson* (New York, 1960), I, 324; Blassingame (ed.), *Slave Testimony*, 368; Berteis, *From Contraband to Freedman*, 5, 72, 96, 146, 164–66; William F. Messner, Black Violence and White Response: Louisiana, 1862," *Journal of Southern History*, XLVI (1975), 19–38.

32. Slave Trial, March 3, 1862, Pendleton/Anderson District, Court of Magistrates and Freeholders, Trial Papers, South Carolina Department of Archives and History; *War of the Rebellion*, Ser. IV, Vol. II, p. 401. The breakdown of plantation discipline is described in William Kauffman Scarborough, *The Overseer: Plantation Management in the Old South* (Baton Rouge, 1966), 138–57. See also Harvey Wish, "Slave Disloyalty Under the Confederacy," *Journal of Negro History*, XXIII (1938), 435–50, and Drew Gilpin Faust, *James Henry Hammond and the Old South: A Design for Mastery* (Baton Rouge, 1982), 368–70.

As a means of maintaining discipline and assuring crop produc
tion, the Confederate Congress on October 11, 1861, enacted legis
lation releasing and exempting from military service planters o
their overseers supervising twenty or more slaves, a number late
reduced to fifteen. The purpose, according to the act, was "to secur
the proper police of the country." Under its terms, some three thou
sand men received exemptions. The extent to which the measur
achieved its stated aim cannot be determined. What it certainly di
do, however, was to supply a slogan for political dissidents. As th
symbol of "a rich man's war and a poor man's fight," the exemp
tion law made operative the class divisions that had long trouble
persons aware of the necessity in a slaveholding society of maintain
ing white solidarity. The exemption law accompanied and justifie
faltering support for the Confederate cause.[33]

Even though the absence of white men from plantation areas en
couraged shirking and "insolence" among slaves, their loose behav
ior amounted to little more than intensification of customary resist
ance. It rarely erupted into overt rebellion. Slaves might becom
insubordinate, substituting their own values for those of the mas
ters, but until the Union army drew near, they could not easil
abandon their owners. "We heard about de Yankees was fighten' t
free us, but we didn't believe it until we heard about de fightin' a
Vicksburg," recalled one former Mississippi slave.[34]

During much of the war, slaves far from Union lines could do littl
to hasten the coming day of freedom except to meet together awa
from the eyes of the nearby whites and pray for deliverance. But a
earthly source of hope appeared in the form of news from the battle
field. Slaves took pleasure and encouragement from even smal
signs of Confederate difficulty and welcomed the South's reverses a
opportunity to improve their own circumstance. Rumors of Confed
erate losses and evidence of political disaffection among whites im
parted courage and thereby furthered slave resistance. In Lexingto
County, South Carolina, Confederates organized a "dog company,
which used bloodhounds to track down army deserters, much a
they tracked down fugitive slaves. The practice evidently wa
known to slaves in nearby Anderson County, where Alek was ac
cused of "making a plan to raise an insurrection." The Yankees wer
winning, he told his friends, and the Confederate army had starte

33. Eaton, History of the Southern Confederacy, 86. The standard treatment is Al
bert B. Moore, Conscription and Conflict in the Confederacy (New York, 1924).
34. Rawick et al. (eds.), American Slave: Supplement, Series I, Vol. X, p. 1986.

ite men schemed to evade military service, and "Dr. Hill" had

en obliged to beat the bushes for more recruits. Confederate au-

orities planned to "Handcuff all that would not go & take them to

lumbia . . . & take them to the army [and] they were going to give

man 100 lashes" if he failed to enlist. Alek thought that "if they

ere all gone they would see better times."[35] But whatever hopes

From one point of view, the Civil War experience confirmed the

at during war slavery would be even more secure than in periods

the Southern States is now constituted on a basis entirely mili-

ry," he told John Hay in November, 1863. "It would be easier

w than formerly to repress a rising of unarmed and uneducated

aves." But, he added, should peace be restored and secession prove

Vital to slavery was the slave's recognition of the superior coer-

thority, that too was gone. Yankee guns now ruled. Union military

rce stripped the master of both physical authority and the right to

mmand. He stood as naked before his enemy as the slave formerly

d stood before him. He was master no longer, and without mas-

rs there can be no slaves. No military or political power would

When Union soldiers arrived in a plantation area, slaves saw that

e ties that had bound them to their owners were severed. The

35. *Ibid.*, VI, 202, 249; Frank Wysor Klingberg, *The Southern Claims Commission*
rkeley, Calif., 1955), 104; Slave Trial, March 3, 1862, Pendleton/Anderson District,
urt of Magistrates and Freeholders, Trial Papers, South Carolina Department of
chives and History.
36. *Annals of Congress*, 12th Cong., 1st Sess., 480; Abraham Lincoln to John Hay,
vember 24, 1863, in Carl Sandburg, *Abraham Lincoln: The War Years* (New York,
39), II, 27.

revelation first became evident early in November, 1861, with tl
arrival of a Union fleet off the Sea Islands of South Carolina. Maste
slave relationships were immediately revolutionized in what ha
been one of the richest of all the South's plantation areas. The ma
ters fled the islands. The slaves who remained behind looted tl
houses of their former masters and destroyed the cotton gins. Tl
influence of that transformation extended beyond the area of actu;
Federal occupation to slaves in other parts of South Carolina an
into Georgia as well.[37]

Events in the lower Mississippi Valley in 1862 and 1863 likewi:
illustrate the electric effect of this change. In August, 1862, the ove
seer at Magnolia Plantation in Louisiana boasted that not eve
"Horace Greeley could get up an insurrection among the negro(
here." His confidence was short-lived. As soon as slaves learned th;
a Union army had occupied New Orleans and that another was a
vancing from the north, their former subservience gave way to wh;
the overseer called "insolence." They set a new labor routine f(
themselves. They would work in the fields for a few hours in tl
morning, then stop for the afternoon. On October 14, the women ;
Magnolia Plantation confronted the overseer with their decision t
do no more field work at all until he agreed to pay them ten dolla:
a month. A week later, the slaves built a gallows and gave "as a
excuse for it that they are told they must drive their master . . . an
Mr. Randall [the overseer] off the plantation, hang their master &
and that then they will be free." After slaves on a nearby plantatio
received arms from Union raiders, they drove the overseer away an
"immediately rose and destroyed everything . . . in the house."[38]

Southern Louisiana came under Union control early in 1862, bu
a Confederate army still protected the rich plantations that lay i
the central part of the state. These troops, together with an efficier
home guard, kept most slaves at work under their owners' contro
But when Union forces under General Nathaniel P. Banks reache
Alexandria on May 6, 1863, great numbers of slaves immediate
deserted the plantations and walked into town. Although the Unic
commanders accepted the fact of self-emancipation, they neverth
less set limits on acceptable behavior. Blacks might abandon the
owners and to some extent even were encouraged to do so. The
might appropriate property and—at least for a time—do as the
pleased. But a campaign of retaliation against white civilians, ha

37. Mohr, *On the Threshold of Freedom*, 68–70.
38. J. Carlyle Sitterson, "Magnolia Plantation, 1852–1862: A Decade of a Loui:
ana Sugar Estate," *Mississippi Valley Historical Review*, XXV (1938), 207–209.

ιe been projected, would not be tolerated. General Butler made
is clear in his response to a report that insurrection had broken
ιt near New Orleans and that white women had appealed to Union
ficers for protection. Attacks by blacks on white women and chil-
·en, he announced, would be severely punished. As Butler's or-
·r suggests, Union officers maintained order and decorum among
e black population, but their occasional attempts to bolster the
anters' authority were less likely to succeed. Butler returned the
acks who ran away from David Pugh's plantation, but not even a
·neral's command could make them slaves again. They refused to
ork and proceeded to assault both Pugh and his overseer.[39]
Such violent response was exceptional. White persons had little
ιuse to fear physical attack from slaves during the Civil War. Their
·sponse to liberation generally took place within well-defined lim-
·s that excluded violence against persons except when whites at-
·mpted to restrain or coerce them, which had been Pugh's error.[40]
.aves doubtless harbored deep resentments toward their owners
ιd perhaps toward other whites as well. Some evidently hated
ιeir oppressors, and in numerous instances bonds of interracial
·mpathy proved frail. Even trusted house servants whose owners
ιd imagined them affectionate and loyal fled without the least
ιow of regret and without saying good-bye. They were no respecter
· persons. In June, 1862, Jefferson Davis announced the arrival of
rs. Robert E. Lee in Richmond: "Her servants left her," he ex-
·ained, "and she found it uncomfortable to live without them."[41]
ιt the overriding motive among slaves was simply the desire to
·cape from slavery; few delayed their flight in order to inflict ven-
·ance on whites. Even the most abused appear to have been satis-
·d merely to witness their owners' distress as Yankee armies ap-
·oached. At last the tables were turned, and masters met a
ιallenge too strong to hurl back. Blacks need not take part in the
·tribution in order to welcome it and reap its consequence.

39. *War of the Rebellion*, Ser. I, Vol. XV, p. 172; Benjamin F. Butler to Edwin M.
·anton, August 2, 1862, in Benjamin F. Butler, *Private and Official Correspondence of
·njamin F. Butler During the Period of the Civil War* (Norwood, Mass., 1917), II, 142.
40. When whites resorted to violence to restore slavery, blacks sometimes retali-
·ed. See Blassingame (ed.), *Slave Testimony*, 359–60, and Gerteis, *From Contraband
· Freedman*, 112–13. See also Bell I. Wiley, *The Plain People of the Confederacy* (Baton
·uge, 1943), 82.
41. Jefferson Davis to Mrs. Davis, June 13, 1862, in Rowland (ed.), *Jefferson Davis*,
278. Note the bitter postwar comment of a South Carolina planter: "The negros
·d not care as much about us as we did about them." Theodore Rosengarten, *Tom-
·e: Portrait of a Cotton Planter, with the Journal of Thomas B. Chaplin 1822–1890*
·ew York, 1986), 348.

This does not mean that at the moment of liberation they cou
be counted on to remain stolid and, from the whites' point of vie·
well behaved. "The arrival of the advance of the Yankees aloï
turned the negroes crazy," wrote a Louisiana planter from south
Alexandria in 1863. "They became utterly demoralized at once ar
everything like subordination and restraint was at an end. All bus
ness was suspended and those that did not go on with the arm
remained at home to do *much worse*." What they did was not to tuï
on the whites who remained in the area, but rather to destroy tl
masters' property in the manner of primitive rebels, or else appr
priate it for their own use. They stripped the plantation houses
furnishings, killed cattle, sheep, and hogs. They declared a holidː
and wandered about the countryside. "No work was done and tl
place swarmed most of the time with negroes from other places
the Louisiana planter reported. Slaves on the rice plantations ·
South Carolina responded to Union invasion in virtually the sanᵐ
fashion.[42]

It would be a mistake to conclude from reports of such saturnal
that slaves always responded with jubilation or even approval ·
the Union presence. In an abstract sense, Yankee forces representᵉ
the idea of freedom and thus were the slaves' allies. Yet they camᵉ
as conquerors and despoilers. Slaves could not easily identify frᵉ
dom with the horsemen who rode through the countryside pillagiï
and violating their homes as well as great plantation houses. B
sides being slaves and eager to be free, most blacks also were isᵒ
lated rural people with strong attachment to place and propert
Accordingly, they were likely to dread northern soldiers as alieï
whose intentions they could not be certain of. Although they soc
learned that Yankees would not sell them to Cuba, as their masteᵣ
had warned, they still were slow to trust the invader. Northern mᵉ
might be liberators, but that did not always make them friends. Tk
soldiers' behavior sometimes did little to inspire confidence. Whᵉ
Union soldiers drove off the plantations' cows and horses an
cleared storehouses of food, they left slaves as well as masters ᵢ
want. They were as likely to appropriate the slaves' meager belonᵍ
ings as those of the masters. And Union soldiers sometimes abusᵉ
slaves as outrageously as abolitionists charged was customary ·
southern whites. They also could be guilty of acts of wanton crueᵗ

42. Whittington (ed.), "Concerning the Loyalty of Slaves," 487–502. For simil.
reactions by South Carolina slaves, see Charles W. Joyner, *Down by the Riverside:
South Carolina Slave Community* (Urbana, Ill., 1984), 228–29, and Easterby (edᵈ
South Carolina Rice Plantation, 211.

at, though perhaps in themselves trivial, offended slaves and left
a indelible impression on those who witnessed them. "When the
ldiers got to the big road the flock of geese were crossing," Smith
mmons remembered long afterward. "Them soldiers shot every
ose and left them there in the big road." Not even the passage of
venty years could blot out that sight.[43]
Violations of the blacks' sensibilities and autonomy were not al-
ays so haphazard, limited, and individualized as those mentioned.
'here are to be *no more bondsmen and no more whippings,*" was the
my's welcome message to blacks in Georgia at war's end, but the
nitations that hedged freedom soon were revealed. "A Yankee of-
er told the servants at the Creek this week," a planter's wife re-
orted, "that they were to stay at home and work harder than they
id ever done in their lives, and not run about and steal; that they
id come to see that they behaved themselves." This Yankee de-
and for devotion to calling too closely resembled their masters'
oscriptions to be received sympathetically. The blacks, Mrs. But-
lph continued, "were quite disgusted."[44]
As a matter of policy in some occupied regions, the army con-
olled the blacks' movement, confining them to plantations, forc-
g them to work, and punishing them for lapses of discipline, much
their former masters had done. Even in regions where official
licy did not embrace army-managed plantations, Federal au-
orities sometimes provided support for a system of forced labor
at closely resembled that of antebellum days. In Alabama, army
ficers and Freedmen's Bureau agents helped planters maintain or-
r, even on some occasions detailing soldiers to restrain and pun-
h recalcitrant laborers. When in the summer of 1865 Georgia plant-
s found their efforts to produce a cotton crop threatened by
estless" blacks, they informed Federal authorities of the problem.
my headquarters at Albany responded: "Two Federals, in blue
iiforms and armed, came out . . . and whipped every negro man
ported to them, and in some cases unmercifully. . . . Another party
sited Conquitt . . . and punished by suspending by the thumbs."

---

43. Franklin (ed.), *Diary of James T. Ayres*, 27; Charlotte Forten, "Life on the Sea
lands," *Atlantic Monthly*, XIII (May, 1864), 593; Joel Williamson, *After Slavery: The
gro in South Carolina During Reconstruction, 1861–1877* (Chapel Hill, N.C., 1965),
13; Rawick *et al.* (eds.), *American Slave: Supplement, Series I*, Vol. II, p. 181, and
l. X, pp. 1928, 2201; Escott, "The Context of Freedom," 92, 101; Bell I. Wiley, *The
fe of Billy Yank, the Common Soldier of the Union* (Indianapolis, 1952), 114–15;
awick *et al.* (eds.), *American Slave: Supplement, Series I*, Vol. X, p. 1940.
44. Laura E. Buttolph to Mary Jones, June 30, 1865, in Myers (ed.), *Children of
ide*, 1279.

The astounded blacks were heard to "whisper [that these were] on Southern men in blue clothes—that the true Yankee had not con yet." Doubtless both the disciplinary support given planters and t labor system Federal authorities established in some regions we designed to promote order and restore agricultural production, n primarily to repress blacks.[45] It also is true, however, that as means of accomplishing the primary goals, repression was assum to be both necessary and proper.

Impositions such as these destroyed neither the slaves' hopes f freedom nor their confidence in Lincoln as an emancipator. But hc their hopes and confidence were to be realized remained uncertai Blacks lived in terrible suspense throughout the war and Reco struction. They saw everything around them being transforme and with no more confidence than anyone else could they predi the form the new order would take. When the planters' world cc lapsed, so did that of the slaves. They simply did not know what expect. Union victory assuredly had brought freedom, but no on white or black, could say in 1865 exactly what that word meant

Few revolutions, as is well known, are all-embracing in their co sequence. The new order contains survivals of the old. These rer nants are modified and rearranged. Few altogether disappear. So would be in the aftermath of the Civil War. The groups thrown c top may have supposed that they had won the privilege of sortir out from Old South survivals those that were to be accepted as co sistent with the new order and those that were to be suppressed c allowed to die. But this was in large part illusion. Slavery had profoundly affected everyone involved with it that its effects wou endure well beyond the generation that saw its end. Thus the victo were not as free to mold the future immune from its influence : their triumph may have encouraged them to suppose. The freedme and women had not been so abjectly crushed by bondage as the detractors and the detractors of their owners sometimes claime but it surely would be a mistake to claim that slavery had left r scars or that these were of no future consequence. Although blac had cast off slavery, they had not managed to escape white don nation. The freedmen soon discovered the rigid limits set on fre

45. Gerteis, *From Contraband to Freedman*, 100; Peter Kolchin, *First Freedom: T Response of Alabama's Blacks to Emancipation and Reconstruction* (Westport, Con 1972), 33; John Jones to Mary Jones, July 26, 1865, and August 21, 1865, in My (ed.), *Children of Pride*, 1282–83, 1292; Gerteis, *From Contraband to Freedman*, 96.

46. Rawick *et al.* (eds.), *American Slave: Supplement*, Series I, Vol. VII, p. 515, a Vol. X, pp. 2022–23, 2070. For conditions in one Confederate state, see John Cin rich, *Slavery's End in Tennessee, 1861–1865* (University, Ala., 1985), 118–31.

)m. In rising against their masters, they became clients of north-
n whites. Their revolt, it appeared, had served to advance the
nion cause fully as much as it had advanced their own, and the
terests of the two, as it proved, were considerably less than iden-
:al. Slaves were free, but they were still dependents. The old plant-
s and others who thought like them had not been driven from the
)uth, nor, for the most part, were their lands confiscated. Neither
ere they deprived for long of political power. The freedmen must
1d their place in a new free-labor system. They did not own the
nd, and no political policy was adopted to help them acquire it.
To blacks belonged a large share of credit for the defeat of the
)nfederacy.[47] As abolitionists had anticipated, they proved an in-
spensable auxiliary to the Union war effort. Black soldiers and
ilitary laborers gave the Union army vital support, lacking which
e war almost certainly would have been prolonged and victory
tained only at the expense of still greater sacrifice. But that was
)t the whole of their contribution. Especially in the first months of
ar, concern for slave discipline led southern state authorities to
ithhold men and supplies that might have gone to strengthen Con-
derate forces in the field. Later, as an expedient designed to main-
in control over slaves, the Confederate congress exempted certain
hite men from military service, thereby weakening the Confed-
acy by antagonizing nonslaveholders and activating previously
tent class conflict.[48] Further, the wartime derangements under-
)ne by the slave system, and the common understanding by south-
n whites that restoration of the system was impossible, contrib-
:ed to their sense that continued resistance had no purpose.
Important as these developments were in hastening the Confed-
ate downfall, one might argue that they were more the conse-
1ence of the mere existence of slavery as an institution than of the
aves' will. But the calculated decisions of black men and women
kewise contributed—and in a devastating way—to Confederate
:feat. By rebelling against slavery and fleeing their owners, they
ippled agricultural production, shattered the social structure, and
:stroyed the principal purpose for which secession was under-
ken—the preservation of slavery and the status of slaveholders.

47. The themes presented in the next two paragraphs are developed fully in Arm-
2ad Robinson, "Day of Jubilo: Civil War and the Demise of Slavery in the Missis-
)pi Valley, 1861–1865" (Ph.D. dissertation, University of Rochester, 1976).
48. Georgia Lee Tatum, *Disloyalty in the Confederacy* (Chapel Hill, N.C., 1939), is a
ate-by-state survey of dissension. See also Michael K. Honey, "The War Within the
nfederacy: White Unionists of North Carolina," *Prologue*, XVIII (1986), 75–93.

With the disintegration of slavery white southerners had little th
was tangible left to fight for and little reason to continue to suppo
the Confederacy. Blacks thus contributed to the Confederacy's wea
ness while they added to the Union's strength.

But despite their essential contributions to Union victory, blac
were not in a position to make the choices that would shape the ne
regime. Northern whites would do that, and they had yet to decic
how much influence to accord abolitionist principles of freedom an
equality. One thing, however, soon became evident: The biracial a
liance forged in wartime would carry little weight in designing tl
postwar settlement.

The Union's antislavery reputation, which had been fostered b
white southerners as well as by abolitionists, led politically awa
freedmen to anticipate more from their liberators than the liber
tors were prepared to give. A national government whose principl
as well as facilities did not permit attempts at omnipotence cou
not carry out generous intentions through the vast expanse of tl
rural South. In the reconstructed South, as in antebellum days, rac
relations depended less on statutes than on private accommodatic
and the ability to coerce. Consequently, however generous and h
mane Republicans in Washington might wish to be, much that w
cruel and exploitative occurred beyond their view or remedy, ar
freedom in the new South, as in the old, was defined less as tl
freedmen desired than in terms congenial to the interests of the
white rulers. Given the aim, background, and power of the free
men's former masters, and the freedmen's own economic weakne
and political inexperience, and given the inadequacies of liberal id
ology and the eventual exhaustion of northern will, it could not hav
been otherwise.

Slaves had viewed the Union government and its armies as alli
in their generations-long war for freedom. White northerners, i
turn, and for their own purposes, had exploited the blacks' desire
be free and to humble their oppressors, but from beginning to en
they had set rigid limits on black revolt and had controlled its r
sults. They had made an alliance with the blacks, but no more tha
earlier enemies and invaders of the South had they recognized ther
as equal partners in the crusade that destroyed the system that e
slaved and exploited them.

Conclusion

Slavery served white Americans well for nearly 250 years. Enslaved blacks joined with whites to perform the labor that transformed the North American wilderness into one of the world's flourishing plantation regions. The crops they grew there not only enriched slaveowners, they also contributed mightily to the development of the entire American economy and the economy of Europe as well.

To those who visited them at any time before the Civil War, the South's slave-cultivated farms and plantations were likely to seem isolated and independent, and often they were so conceived by their prideful owners. But their autonomy was in fact an illusion, for however spatially remote the plantations might be, they were actually units in a far-flung system of capitalistic enterprise. Their economic fortune and, as it turned out, their fate were determined in large part by faraway economic and political developments over which their proprietors could exert scant control. Likewise the tensions and conflicts generated within the peculiar labor system that accounted for the plantations' importance were not concerns only of the men and women immediately involved with them, but were closely related to the acts and ambitions of people located far from the South.

Measured by its function as a labor system, slavery should be judged a success. It fulfilled its intended purpose of controlling

labor and allowing for its transfer while at the same time it pr
duced an abundance of valuable staples. But from first to las
these goals were accomplished only with pain and difficulty, an
ultimately the effort could not be sustained. In order to realize i
full potential as both an economic and social system, slavery need
to function as a nearly total institution. Slaves must be made
work like machines at tasks set for them by owners and overseer
Absolute discipline must be enforced, both for the sake of efficienc
of production and of protecting the authority and safety of the slav
holding class. That was the ideal, but like most ideals, it could t
achieved only in part. A problem was universally encountered. F
from being machines or acting like them, slaves turned out to t
human beings very like their owners, having wills and ambitio
and competencies that ill accorded with the goal of total subord
nation. Thus conflict, potentially severe, between owners and slav
always characterized southern labor relations. At the same time,
multitude of hostile influences originating outside the plantatio
also worked to impede the system. In the face of all of this, it is
tribute to the skill, determination, and ruthlessness of white Amer
cans that they were able to keep the blacks enslaved for as long
they did.

Only with great difficulty could the slaves' discontent and the
drive for autonomy be contained. Owners understood the signi
cance of that fact. They recognized the rapidly growing slave pop
lation as the country's most severe potential for internal subversio
From at least the early eighteenth century, white southerners frette
about the danger presented by so explosive a labor force. Before th
late antebellum period, when Romanticism and the "positive-goo
defense of slavery transformed the popular image of blacks int
meek, submissive beings, southern whites typically characterize
them as their "internal enemy."

That portrayal should come as no surprise, for slaves were co
stantly restive. Along with examples of faithful labor and unexcep
tional behavior went examples of sullenness and disobedience, co
spiracies, open revolt, and escapes. Instances of violence—assault
murder, and arson—were common enough to awaken apprehe
sions for the future. White southerners and their governments non
theless learned to cope with disorder, although its pervasivene
made the chief purpose of the slave system—profitable produ
tion—harder to achieve and generated suspicion that the resistanc
was encouraged if not induced by jealous or malevolent person
seeking the planters' ruin.

Slave discontent appeared to increase and its potential to be mag-
fied at those times when political discord divided white society, as
uring the Missouri controversy, or when internal stress became
·ident, as in Virginia during the constitutional debates of the late
320s and early 1830s. The appearance of alienation or disaffection
nong elements of the white population invited slave disorder.
hus nonslaveholders seldom were fully trusted; free blacks never
·ere. External threats—and these were constant in the colonial pe-
od—magnified the problem. An early goal of United States diplo-
·acy was the elimination of European powers from the continent,
·rtly to make possible the westward expansion of slave-cultivated
lantations and partly to stabilize slavery itself by removing a
imulus to discord. The goal was achieved, but only for a moment.
arly in the nineteenth century, the North replaced England,
·ance, and Spain as the South's major rival and enemy.
    The fundamental explanation for the sectional enmity that
arked antebellum decades doubtless lies in the contrasting lines
economic and social development then followed by North and
·uth, the differing values and interests these produced, and the
val political measures they engendered. But the agents who ar-
·ulated these differences (more often than not in the rhetoric of
·angelical Protestantism) and gave them their emotive power were
·e abolitionists, a dedicated group of black and white men and
·omen bent on destroying the South's labor system and on revolu-
·onizing American values. Slaves, too, played a critical role in the
·epening sectional conflict, influencing the actions of both aboli-
·onists and southern statesmen. It was widely recognized that
·aves were the subjects of hot debate. Less fully appreciated was
·e active part they took in driving the sections apart. The abolition-
·ts' crusade coincided with what was interpreted in both North and
·uth as increased slave unrest. Planters charged abolitionists with
·sponsibility for the vexing problems they experienced in their
·lds and quarters. Slaves who rebelled and slaves who ran away
·ay indeed have been encouraged to do so by northern antislavery
·tivity. But just as important, abolitionism was stimulated—and
·stified—by the slave unrest for which rebels and swelling num-
·rs of runaways supplied tangible evidence. Thus, slaves, planters,
·d abolitionists exercised reciprocal influence in the long process
·at moved the sections toward separation and war.
    Slaves and free blacks certainly were antislavery in attitude, and
·sofar as slaveholders represented the South, blacks also were an-
·southern. By fleeing to the North, slaves demonstrated their un-

derstanding that an antislavery, antisouthern North would offe them help and refuge exactly as the South's earlier enemies ha done. The motive for northerners to do these things may have bee humanitarian, or it may have been economic and political. Wha ever its source, its effect was the same: The slaves had found a ne ally, and slaveholders faced a new enemy.

When the abolitionists' program, or parts of it, became a force i electoral politics, as it manifestly had done by 1860, the slavehol ing South faced a threat for which much in its political theory bu nothing in its experience offered defense. The result was secessio and secession brought war. Civil War, with consequent military i vasion at many points, provided slaves with powerful support i their perpetual plantation struggles. The disruption that slaves an the Union armies then brought to the South ended slavery and wa the culmination of two and a half centuries of internal conflict.

Bibliography

I. Primary Sources

A. *Published Reports, Letters, Memoirs, and Other Contemporary Material*

lams, Charles Francis, ed. *Letters of Mrs. Adams* . . . . 4th ed. Boston, 1848.

——, ed. *Memoirs of John Quincy Adams Comprising Portions of His Diary from 1795 to 1848*. 12 vols. Philadelphia, 1874–77.

——, ed. *The Works of John Adams, Second President of the United States, with a Life of the Author*. 9 vols. Boston, 1856.

lams, John Quincy, and Lewis Condit. *Report of the Minority of the Committee on Manufactures, Submitted to the House of Representatives of the United States, February 28, 1833* (Boston, 1833).

ldress of the New England Anti-Slavery Convention to the Slaves of the United States with an Address to President Tyler, Faneuil Hall, May 31, 1843. Boston, 1843.

den, John R. "John Stuart Accuses William Bull." *William and Mary Quarterly*, 3rd ser., II (1945), 315–20.

nbler, Charles Henry, ed. *Correspondence of Robert M. T. Hunter, 1826– 1876*. Vol. II of American Historical Association, *Annual Report . . . for the Year 1916*. Washington, D.C., 1918.

nerican Anti-Slavery Society. *First Annual Report . . . 1834*. New York, 1834.

——. *Annual Reports for 1857 and 1858*. New York, 1858.

American Convention for Promoting the Abolition of Slavery. *Minutes of t. Proceedings of the Convention of Delegates . . . 1801*. Philadelphia, 180
———. *Minutes of the Proceedings of the Convention of Delegates . . . 180* Philadelphia, 1805.
American State Papers, Class VII: Post Office Department. 1834.
Andrews, Ethan Allen. *Slavery and the Domestic Slave Trade in the Unit. States*. Boston, 1836.
Annals of Congress. lst Cong., 2nd Sess.; 3rd Cong., 2nd Sess.; 6th Cong., 1 Sess.; 8th Cong., 1st Sess.; 9th Cong., 1st Sess., 2nd Sess.; 12th Cong., 1 Sess., 2nd Sess.; 13th Cong., 3rd Sess.; 14th Cong., 2nd Sess.; 15th Con: 1st Sess., 2nd Sess.; 16th Cong., 1st Sess.
Aptheker, Herbert, ed. *A Documentary History of the Negro People in t. United States*. 2 vols. New York, 1951.
Archives of Maryland: Proceedings and Acts of the General Assembly of Mar land, October 1678–March 1683. Baltimore, 1889.
[Ball, George]. *Fifty Years in Chains; or, The Life of an American Slave*. Ne York, 1858.
Barker, Eugene C., ed. *The Austin Papers*. Vol. II, Pt. 1 of American Historic Association, *Annual Report . . . for the Years 1919 and 1922*. Washingto. D.C., 1924–28.
———, ed. *The Austin Papers*. Vol. III. Austin, Texas, 1927.
Basler, Roy P., *et al.*, eds. *Collected Works of Abraham Lincoln*. 9 vols. Ne Brunswick, N.J., 1953–55.
Bassett, John Spencer, ed. *Correspondence of Andrew Jackson*. 7 vols. Was. ington, D.C., 1926–35.
———, ed. *The Southern Plantation Overseer as Revealed in His Letter* Northampton, Mass., 1925.
Beale, Howard K., ed. *Diary of Gideon Welles, Secretary of the Navy und. Lincoln and Johnson*. 3 vols. New York, 1960.
Berlin, Ira, ed. "After Nat Turner: A Letter from the North." *Journal of Neg. History*, LV (1970), 144–51.
Berlin, Ira, *et al.*, eds. *The Destruction of Slavery*. New York, 1985. Vol. I Berlin *et al.*, eds., *Freedom: A Documentary History of Emancipatio. 1861–1867, Series I*.
Billings, Warren, ed. *The Old Dominion in the Seventeenth Century. A Doc. mentary History of Virginia, 1606–1689*. Chapel Hill, N.C., 1975.
[Bishop, Abraham]. "Rights of Black Men." *American Museum*, XII (179: 299–300.
Blassingame, John W., ed. *Slave Testimony: Two Centuries of Letter. Speeches, Interviews, and Autobiography*. Baton Rouge, 1977.
Blodgett, Samuel. *Economica: A Statistical Manual for the United States. America*. Washington, D.C., 1806.
[Blunt, Joseph]. *An Examination of the Expediency and Constitutionality. Prohibiting Slavery in the State of Missouri*. New York, 1819.
Boucher, Chauncey S., and Robert P. Brooks, eds. *Correspondence Address.

to *John C. Calhoun, 1837–1849*. Vol. II of American Historical Association, *Annual Report . . . for the Year 1929*. Washington, D.C., 1930.

owers, Claude G., ed. *The Diary of Elbridge Gerry, Jr*. New York, 1927.

oyd, Julian P., ed. *The Papers of Thomas Jefferson*. 20 vols. to date. Princeton, N.J., 1950–.

ranagan, Thomas. *The Penitential Tyrant: A Juvenile Poem*. . . . Philadelphia, 1805.

———. *The Penitential Tyrant; or, Slave Trader Reformed*. . . . 2nd ed. New York, 1807.

rock, R. A., ed. *Official Records of Robert Dinwiddie, Lt. Gov. of the Colony of Virginia, 1751–1758*. 2 vols. Virginia Historical Society Collection, n.s., III and IV. Richmond, 1883–84.

3rown, John]. *Slave Life in Georgia: A Narrative of the Life, Sufferings, and Escape of John Brown, a Fugitive Slave, Now in England*. London, 1855.

runhouse, Robert L., ed. "David Ramsay, 1749–1815: Selections from His Writings." *Transactions of the American Philosophical Society*, n.s., LV, Pt. 4 (1965).

utler, Benjamin F. *Private and Official Correspondence of Benjamin F. Butler During the Period of the Civil War*. 5 vols. Norwood, Mass., 1917.

andler, Allen D., ed. *The Colonial Records of Georgia*. 26 vols. 1904; rpr. New York, 1970.

appon, Lester J., ed. *The Adams-Jefferson Letters: The Complete Correspondence Between Thomas Jefferson and Abigail and John Adams*. 2 vols. Chapel Hill, N.C., 1959.

arter, Clarence E., ed. *The Territory of Orleans, 1803–1812*. Washington, D.C., 1940. Vol. IX of Carter, ed. *The Territorial Papers of the United States*. 28 vols.

atterall, Helen T., ed. *Judicial Cases Concerning American Slavery and the Negro*. 5 vols. Washington, D.C., 1924–26.

hanning, William Ellery. *The Duty of the Free States; or, Remarks Suggested by the Case of the Creole*. Boston, 1842.

lark, Elmer T., *et al.*, eds. *The Journal and Letters of Francis Asbury*. 3 vols. London, 1958.

ongressional Globe, 37th Cong., 2nd Sess.

orrespondence of Mr. Ralph Izard of South Carolina, from the Year 1774 to 1804. New York, 1844.

ralle, Richard K., ed. *Speeches of John C. Calhoun*. . . . 6 vols. New York, 1853.

rummell, Alexander. *The Eulogy of Henry Highland Garnet, D.D., Presbyterian Minister*. . . . Washington, D.C., 1882.

avis, Edwin A., ed. *Plantation Life in the Florida Parishes of Louisiana, 1836–1846, as Reflected in the Diary of Bennet H. Barrow*. New York, 1943.

elany, Martin R. *Blake; or, The Huts of America*. Boston, 1970.

ew, Thomas R. *Review of the Debate in the Virginia Legislature of 1831 and 1832*. Richmond, 1832.

Donnan, Elizabeth, ed. *Papers of James A. Bayard, 1796–1815.* Vol. II
American Historical Association, *Annual Report . . . for the Year 191*
Washington, D.C., 1915.

Drayton, Daniel. *Personal Memoir of Daniel Drayton, for Four Years and Fo
Months a Prisoner (for Charity's Sake) in Washington Jail.* Boston, 1855.

Drew, Benjamin. *A North-Side View of Slavery: The Refugee; or, The Narr
tives of Free Slaves in Canada.* . . . Boston, 1856.

Dwight, Timothy. *An Oration Spoken Before the Connecticut Society for t◗
Promotion of Freedom and the Relief of Persons Unlawfully Holden in Bon
age.* Hartford, 1794.

Dyer, Frederick H. *A Compendium of the War of the Rebellion Compiled a◗
Arranged from Official Records.* . . . Des Moines, 1908.

[Earle, Thomas]. *Life, Travels, and Opinions of Benjamin Lundy.* Philad◗
phia, 1847.

Easterby, James Harold, ed. *The South Carolina Rice Plantation, as Reveal◗
in the Papers of Robert F. W. Allston.* Chicago, 1945.

Elliot, Jonathan, ed. *The Debates in the Several State Conventions, on t◗
Adoption of the Federal Constitution.* . . . 5 vols. Philadelphia, 1907.

Elliott, E. N. *Cotton Is King, and Pro-Slavery Arguments.* . . . Augusta, G◗
1860.

Evans, Emory G., ed. "A Question of Complexion: Documents Concerni◗
the Negro and the Franchise in Eighteenth-Century Virginia." *Virgi◗
Magazine of History and Biography,* LXXI (1963), 411–415.

Fawcett, Benjamin. *A Compassionate Address to the Christian Negroes in V◗
ginia.* London, 1756.

Fitzpatrick, John C., ed. *The Writings of George Washington.* 39 vols. Was◗
ington, D.C., 1931–44.

Foner, Eric. *Nat Turner.* Englewood Cliffs, N.J., 1971.

Foner, Philip S., ed. *The Life and Writings of Frederick Douglass.* 4 vols. Ne◗
York, 1950–55.

Foote, William Henry. *Sketches of Virginia, Historical and Biographical, 2◗
Series,* 2nd ed. Philadelphia, 1856.

Ford, Paul Leicester, ed. *The Writings of Thomas Jefferson.* 10 vols. Ne◗
York, 1892–99.

Ford, Worthington C., ed. *Letters of William Lee.* 3 vols. Brooklyn, N.Y., 189◗

Ford, Worthington C., *et al.,* eds. *Journals of the Continental Congre◗
1774–1789.* 34 vols. Washington, D.C., 1904–37.

Forten, Charlotte. "Life on the Sea Islands." *Atlantic Monthly,* XIII (Ma◗
1864), 587–96.

Franklin, John Hope, ed. *Diary of James T. Ayres, Civil War Recruiter.* Sprin◗
field, Ill., 1947.

Goodell, William. *Slavery and Anti-Slavery: A History of the Great Struggle
Both Hemispheres with a View of the Slavery Question in the United Stat◗
New York, 1852.

;reene, Jack P., ed. *The Diary of Colonel Landon Carter of Sabine Hall, 1752–1778.* 2 vols. Charlottesville, Va., 1965.

Iamer, Phillip M. *et al.*, eds. *The Papers of Henry Laurens.* 11 vols. to date. Columbia, S.C., 1968– .

Iamilton, J. G. de Roulhac, ed. *The Papers of Thomas Ruffin.* 4 vols. Raleigh, N.C., 1918–20.

Iamilton, Stanislaus, ed. *The Writings of James Monroe.* 7 vols. New York, 1893–1903.

Hammond, Jabez Delano]. *Life and Opinions of Julius Melbourne.* . . . Syracuse, N.Y., 1847.

Iarlan, Louis R., ed. *The Booker T. Washington Papers.* 13 vols. Urbana, Ill., 1972–84.

Iening, William Waller, comp. *The Statutes at Large, Being a Compilation of All the Laws of Virginia.* . . . 13 vols. Richmond, 1810–23.

Iigginbotham, Don, ed. *The Papers of James Iredell.* 2 vols. Raleigh, N.C., 1976.

Iildreth, Richard. *Despotism in America: An Inquiry into the Nature, Results, and Legal Basis of the Slave-Holding System in the United States.* Boston, 1854.

Iints for the Consideration of the Friends of Slavery, and Friends of Emancipation.* Lexington, Ky., 1803.

Iorsmanden, Daniel. *The New York Conspiracy; or, A History of the Negro Plot, with the Journal of the Proceedings Against the Conspirators at New York in the Years 1741–42.* . . . 2nd ed. New York, 1810.

Iurd, John Codman. *The Law of Freedom and Bondage in the United States.* 2 vols. Boston, 1858.

Iutchinson, William T., and William M. E. Rachal, eds. *The Papers of James Madison.* 16 vols. to date. Chicago, 1962– .

ameson, J. Franklin, ed. *Correspondence of John C. Calhoun.* Vol. II, Pt. 2 of American Historical Association, *Annual Report . . . for the Year 1899.* Washington, D.C., 1900.

anson, Charles William. *The Stranger in America, Containing Observations Made During a Long Residence in That Country.* . . . London, 1807.

Iillens, John Oliver, ed. *The Trial Record of Denmark Vesey.* Boston, 1970.

Iingburg, Susan M., ed. *Records of the Virginia Company of London.* 4 vols. Washington, D.C., 1906–35.

Ihe Lee Papers . . . 1754–1800.* 4 vols. New-York Historical Society Collections, 1871–1874. New York, 1872–75.

evering, Robert E. H. *The Kingdom of Slavery.* . . . Circleville, Ohio, 1844.

ipscomb, Andrew A., ed. *The Writings of Thomas Jefferson.* 20 vols. Washington, D.C., 1903–1904.

ovejoy, Joseph C. *Memoir of Rev. Charles T. Torrey, Who Died in the Penitentiary of Maryland, Where He Was Confined for Showing Mercy to the Poor.* New York, 1847.

Massachusetts Anti-Slavery Society. *Nineteenth Annual Report*. Boston 1851.

Merrill, Walter M., and Louis Ruchames, eds. *The Letters of William Lloy Garrison*. 6 vols. Cambridge, Mass., 1971–81.

Merriwether, Robert L., *et al.*, eds. *The Papers of John C. Calhoun*. 17 vol to date. Columbia, S.C., 1959–.

[Methodist Episcopal Church]. *The Address of the General Conference of the Methodist Episcopal Church, to All Their Brethren and Friends in the Unite States, Baltimore, May 23, 1800*. N.p., n.d.

Minutes of the National Convention of Colored Citizens Held at Buffalo on the 15th, 16th, 17th, 18th and 19th of August, 1843. . . . New York, 1843.

Monroe, Haskell M., Jr., and James T. McIntosh, eds. *The Papers of Jefferso Davis*. 5 vols. to date. Baton Rouge, 1971–.

Mullin, Michael, ed. *American Negro Slavery: A Documentary History*. Ne York, 1976.

Myers, Robert M., ed. *The Children of Pride: A True Story of Georgia and the Civil War*. New Haven, Conn., 1972.

Northup, Solomon. *Narrative of Solomon Northup: Twelve Years a Slave*. . Auburn, N.Y., 1853.

O'Kelley, James. *Essay on Negro Slavery*. Philadelphia, 1789.

Olmsted, Frederick Law. *A Journey in the Back Country*. New York, 1860.

———. *A Journey Through Texas; or, a Saddle-Trip on the Southwestern Fron tier*. New York, 1857.

Palmer, William, Sherwin McRae, and H. W. Flournoy, eds. *Calendar of Vi ginia State Papers and Other Manuscripts, 1652–1869, Preserved at the Capitol in Richmond*. 11 vols. Richmond, 1875–93.

Paul, Nathaniel. *An Address, Delivered on the Celebration of the Abolition of Slavery in the State of New York, July 5, 1827*. Albany, N.Y., 1827.

[Paulding, James K.]. *Letters from the South, Written During an Excursion i the Summer of 1816*. 2 vols. New York, 1817.

Pease, William H., and Jane H. Pease. "Walker's *Appeal* Comes to Charle ton: A Note and Documents." *Journal of Negro History*, LIX (1974 289–92.

"People of Colour." *Port Folio*, I (May 23, 1801), 163–64.

Phelps, Amos A. *Lectures on Slavery and Its Remedy*. Boston, 1834.

Phillips, Ulrich B., ed. *Correspondence of Robert Toombs, Alexander H. Ste phens, and Howell Cobb*. Vol. II of American Historical Association, An nual Report . . . for the Year 1911. Washington, D.C., 1913.

———, ed. *Plantation and Frontier, 1649–1863*. 2 vols. Cleveland, 1909.

Quarles, Benjamin, ed. *Blacks on John Brown*. Urbana, Ill., 1972.

Rankin, John. *Letters on American Slavery Addressed to Mr. Thomas Ran kin*. . . . Newburyport, Mass., 1837.

Rawick, George P., ed. *The American Slave: A Composite Autobiography*. 1 vols. Westport, Conn., 1972.

awick, George P., *et al.*, eds. *The American Slave: A Composite Autobiography: Supplement, Series I.* 12 vols. Westport, Conn., 1977.

edpath, James. *The Roving Editor; or, Talks with Slaves in the Southern States.* New York, 1859.

eview of *The Tenth Annual Report of the American Society for Colonizing the Free People of Colour.* . . . *Southern Review*, I (1828), 219–32.

ice, David. *Slavery Inconsistent with Justice and Good Policy.* . . . Philadelphia, 1792.

ichardson, James D., ed. *A Compilation of the Messages and Papers of the Presidents.* 20 vols. Washington, D.C., 1896.

ose, Willie Lee, ed. *A Documentary History of Slavery in North America.* New York, 1976.

owland, Dunbar, ed. *Jefferson Davis, Constitutionalist: His Letters, Papers and Speeches.* 10 vols. Jackson, Miss., 1923.

——, ed. *Official Letter-Books of W. C. C. Claiborne, 1801–1816.* 6 vols. Jackson, Miss., 1917.

uchames, Louis, ed. *The Abolitionists: A Collection of Their Writings.* New York, 1963.

carborough, William Kauffman, ed. *The Diary of Edmund Ruffin.* 3 vols. Baton Rouge, 1972–89.

eybert, Adam. *Statistical Annals: Embracing Views of the Population, Commerce, Navigation, Fisheries . . . of the United States of America.* . . . Philadelphia, 1818.

hea, Deborah, ed. "Spreading Terror and Devastation Wherever They Have Been: A Norfolk Woman's Account of the Southampton Slave Insurrection." *Virginia Magazine of History and Biography*, XCV (1987), 65–74.

illiman, Benjamin. "Some of the Causes of National Anxiety." *African Repository*, VIII (August, 1832), 161–87.

mith, Gerrit. *Speeches of Gerrit Smith in Congress.* New York, 1856.

mith, Margaret Bayard. *The First Forty Years of Washington Society.* New York, 1906.

parks, Edwin Earle, ed. *The Lincoln Douglas Debates of 1858.* Springfield, Ill., 1908.

pear, John M. *Twelve Discourses on Government; Purported to Have Been Delivered in Boston, Massachusetts, December, 1852, by Thomas Jefferson of the Spirit World.* Hopedale, Mass., 1853.

tarobin, Robert S., ed. *Blacks in Bondage: Letters of American Slaves.* New York, 1974.

Summary of Trial Proceedings of Those Accused of Participating in the Slave Uprising of January, 1811." *Louisiana History*, XVIII (1977), 472–73.

utcliff, Robert. *Travels in Some Parts of North America in the Years, 1804, 1805, and 1806.* Philadelphia, 1812.

aylor, John. *Arator; Being a Series of Agricultural Essays, Practical and Political.* 2nd ed. Georgetown, 1814.

Thompson, George. *Prison Life and Reflections.* . . . Hartford, 1854.
[Thompson, John]. *Life of John Thompson, a Fugitive Slave.* . . . Worcester Mass., 1856.
Thorndike, Rachel Sherman, ed. *The Sherman Letters.* New York, 1894.
Tragle, Henry Irving. *The Southampton Slave Revolt of 1831.* Amherst Mass., 1971.
[Tucker, St. George]. *A Letter to a Member of the General Assembly of Virginia on the Subject of the Late Conspiracy.* . . . Baltimore, 1801.
[Turnbull, Robert J.]. *The Crisis; or, Essays on the Usurpations of the Federal Government.* Charleston, S.C., 1827.
Turner, Frederick Jackson, ed. *Correspondence of the French Ministers to the United States, 1791–1797.* Vol. II of American Historical Association, *Annual Report . . . for the Year 1903.* Washington, D.C., 1904.
U.S. Bureau of the Census. *Historical Statistics of the United States, Colonial Times to 1970.* 2 vols. 1975.
———. *Negro Population, 1790–1915.* 1918.
U.S. Department of State. *State Papers and Correspondence Bearing upon the Purchase of the Territory of Louisiana.* 1903.
The War of the Rebellion: A Compilation of the Official Records of the Union and Confederate Armies. 130 vols. Washington, D.C., 1880–1901.
[Warner, Samuel]. *Authentic and Impartial Narrative of the Tragical Scene Which Was Witnessed in Southampton County (Virginia) on Monday the 22nd of August Last.* . . . [New York, 1831].
Whittier, John Greenleaf. *The Works of John Greenleaf Whittier.* 7 vols. New York, 1892.
Whittington, G. P., ed. "Concerning the Loyalty of Slaves in Northern Louisiana in 1863: Letters from John H. Ransdell to Governor Thomas O. Moore, Dated 1863." *Louisiana Historical Quarterly,* XIV (1931), 487–502
Windley, Lathan A., comp. *Runaway Slave Advertisements: A Documentary History from the 1730s to 1790.* 4 vols. Westport, Conn., 1983.
Winthrop Sargent to "Sir," November 16, 1800. Printed broadside. N.p. N.d. Ohio Historical Society.
Woodward, C. Vann, and Elisabeth Muhlenfeld, eds. *The Private Mary Chesnut: The Unpublished Civil War Diaries.* New York, 1984.

B. Newspapers

Abolition Intelligencer (Shelbyville, Ky.), 1822.
Boston *Courier,* January 28, 1859.
Boston *Daily Whig,* July 3 and 9, 1847.
Charleston *City Gazette and Daily Advertiser,* October 22, 1800, and September 27, 1822.
Cincinnati *Gazette,* April 29, 1852.
Colored *American* (New York), September 2, 1837.
Connecticut Courant (Hartford), December 12, 1796.

he Emancipator (Complete), Published by Elihu Embree, Jonesborough, Tennessee, 1820. Rpr. Nashville, 1932.
'reedom's Journal (New York), 1827–29.
;enius of Universal Emancipation (Mt. Pleasant, Ohio, and other cities), 1821–39.
;enius of Universal Emancipation and Baltimore Courier, 1825–26.
Iillsdale (Mich.) *Whig Standard,* September 15, 1846.
,iberator (Boston), 1831–65.
Jational Anti-Slavery Standard (New York), 1842 and 1850.
Jew York *Evening Post,* February 19 and 20, 1811.
Jew York *Tribune,* January 31, 1859.
Jiles' Weekly Register (Baltimore), I (1812)–LXVIII (1845).
Philanthropist (Cincinnati), 1841–42.
Richmond *Enquirer,* October–December, 1862.
;ignal of Liberty (Ann Arbor, Mich.), April 6, 1842.
Washington *Semi-Weekly Union,* September–October, 1845.

C. Manuscripts

Amistad Research Center, Tulane University, New Orleans
  American Home Missionary Society Papers.
  American Missionary Association Archives.
Boston Public Library, Boston
  Antislavery Collection.
Chicago Historical Society, Chicago
  Minutes of the Illinois State Anti-Slavery Society.
Cornell University Library, Ithaca, N.Y.
  Antislavery Collection.
Duke University Library, Durham, N.C.
  Enfield, Gertrude Dixon, ed. "Life and Letters of Christopher Houston."
  Typescript.
Georgia State Archives, Atlanta
  Executive Papers.
Historic New Orleans Collection, New Orleans
  Villeré, Jacques Philippe. Papers.
Historical Society of Pennsylvania, Philadelphia
  Pennsylvania Abolition Society Papers.
Manuscripts Division, Library of Congress, Washington, D.C.
  American Colonization Society Papers.
  Monroe, James. Papers (microfilm).
New-York Historical Society, New York, N.Y.
  Miscellaneous Manuscripts.
  Stewart, Alvan. Papers.
New York Public Library
  Peters Family Letters.

North Carolina Division of Archives and History, Raleigh
    Bertie County Slave Papers, 1800–1805.
    Gates County Slave Records, 1783–1867.
    Governors' Papers.
    Jacocks, Charles W. Papers.
    Legislative Papers. Petitions, 1800–59.
    Turner, James. Papers.
    Mordecai, Pattie. Collection.
    Onslow County Miscellaneous Records.
    Perquimans County Slave Papers, 1759–1864.
    Wayne County Records.
Ohio Historical Society, Columbus
    Giddings, Joshua. Papers.
    Sherman, William Tecumseh. Papers.
South Carolina Department of Archives and History, Columbia
    Governors' Messages, 1791–1800.
    Governors' Papers.
    Grand Jury Presentments.
    Legislative Papers, Slavery Petitions, 1800–30.
    Pendleton/Anderson District. Court of Magistrates and Freeholders. Trial
        Papers.
South Caroliniana Library, University of South Carolina, Columbia
    Aiken County Records.
    Ball Family Papers.
    Blanding, William. Papers.
    Bonham, Milledge Luke. Collection.
    Izard, Ralph. Papers.
    Manigault Family Papers.
    Pinckney, Charles. Papers.
    Read, Jacob. Papers.
Southern Historical Collection, University of North Carolina, Chapel Hill
    Kimberly, John. Papers.
    Mason, Nathaniel. Papers.
Syracuse University Library, Syracuse
    Smith, Gerrit. Papers.
Virginia State Library, Richmond
    Executive Papers.
William L. Clements Library, University of Michigan, Ann Arbor
    Fuller, Corydon. Journal.
    Van Deventer, Christopher. Papers.

II. Secondary Sources

Abzug, Robert H. "The Influence of Garrisonian Abolitionists' Fears of Slave
    Violence on the Antislavery Argument, 1829–1840." *Journal of Negro His-
    tory*, LV (1970), 14–28.

lden, John R. *The First South*. Baton Rouge, 1961.

mbler, Charles Henry. *Sectionalism in Virginia from 1776 to 1861*. Chicago, 1910.

mmon, Harry. *The Gênet Mission*. New York, 1973.

ptheker, Herbert. *American Negro Slave Revolts*. New York, 1943.

―――. *The American Revolution, 1763–1783*. New York, 1980.

―――. *Nat Turner's Slave Rebellion*. New York, 1966.

―――. "Notes on Slave Conspiracies in Confederate Mississippi." *Journal of Negro History*, XXIX (1944), 75–79.

―――. *"One Continual Cry": David Walker's "Appeal to the Colored Citizens of the World," 1829–1830, Its Setting, and Its Meaning*. New York, 1965.

allagh, James Curtis. *A History of Slavery in Virginia*. Baltimore, 1902.

anner, James M., Jr. *To the Hartford Convention: The Federalists and the Origins of Party Politics in Massachusetts, 1798–1818*. New York, 1970.

arker, Eugene C., "The Influence of Slavery in the Colonization of Texas." *Mississippi Valley Historical Review*, XI (1924), 3–36.

arney, William L. *The Secessionist Impulse: Alabama and Mississippi in 1860*. Princeton, N.J., 1974.

arnhart, John D. "Sources of Southern Migration into the Old Northwest." *Mississippi Valley Historical Review*, XXII (1935), 49–62.

assett, John Spencer. *Slavery in the State of North Carolina*. Baltimore, 1899.

ell, Howard H. "Expressions of Negro Militancy in the North, 1840–1860." *Journal of Negro History*, XLV (1960), 11–20.

erlin, Ira. *Slaves Without Masters: The Free Negro in the Antebellum South*. New York, 1974.

―――. "Time, Space, and the Evolution of Afro-American Society in British Mainland North America." *American Historical Review*, LXXXV (1980), 44–78.

etts, Albert Deems. *History of South Carolina Methodism*. Charleston, S.C., 1952.

lassingame, John W. *The Slave Community: Plantation Life in the Antebellum South*. Rev. ed. New York, 1979.

oles, John B. "Tension in a Slave Society: The Trial of the Reverend Jacob Gruber." *Southern Studies*, XVIII (1979), 179–97.

oney, F. N. *Southerners All*. Macon, Ga., 1984.

rackett, Jeffrey R. *The Negro in Maryland: A Study of the Institution of Slavery*. Baltimore, 1889.

reen, Timothy H. "A Changing Labor Force and Race Relations in Virginia, 1660–1710." *Journal of Social History*, VII (1973), 3–25.

retz, Julian P. "The Economic Background of the Liberty Party." *American Historical Review*, XXXIV (1929), 250–64.

rewer, James H. "Negro Property Owners in Seventeenth-Century Virginia." *William and Mary Quarterly*, 3rd ser., XII (1955), 575–80.

ruce, William Cabell. *John Randolph of Roanoke, 1773–1833*. 2 vols. New York, 1922.

Cassell, Frank A. "Slaves of the Chesapeake Bay Area and the War of 1812." *Journal of Negro History*, LVII (1972), 144–55.

Channing, Steven A. *Crisis of Fear: Secession in South Carolina*. New York, 1970.

Charlton, Walter G. "A Judge and a Grand Jury." In *Papers of the 31st Annual Session of the Georgia Bar Association . . . 1914*. Macon, Ga., 1914.

Childs, Frances S. *French Refugee Life in the United States, 1790–1800: An American Chapter of the French Revolution*. Baltimore, 1940.

Cimprich, John. *Slavery's End in Tennessee, 1861–1865*. University, Ala., 1985.

Connor, Seymour V., and Odie B. Faulk. *North America Divided: The Mexican War, 1846–1848*. New York, 1971.

Cooper, William J., Jr. *Liberty and Slavery: Southern Politics to 1860*. New York, 1983.

———. *The South and the Politics of Slavery, 1828–1856*. Baton Rouge, 1978.

Cox, LaWanda. *Lincoln and Black Freedom: A Study in Presidential Leadership*. Columbia, S.C., 1981.

Craven, Avery O. *The Coming of the Civil War*. New York, 1942.

———. "Poor Whites and Negroes in the Antebellum South." *Journal of Negro History*, XV (1930), 14–25.

Craven, Wesley Frank. "Twenty Negroes to Jamestown in 1619?" *Virginia Quarterly Review*, LVII (1971), 416–20.

———. *White, Red, and Black: The Seventeenth-Century Virginian*. Charlottesville, Va., 1971.

Crow, Jeffrey J. *The Black Experience in Revolutionary North Carolina*. Raleigh, N.C., 1973.

Davis, David Brion. *The Problem of Slavery in the Age of Revolution, 1770–1823*. Ithaca, N.Y., 1975.

———. *The Slave Power Conspiracy and the Paranoid Style*. Baton Rouge, 1969.

Davis, Thomas J. *A Rumor of Revolt: The "Great Negro Plot" in Colonial New York*. New York, 1985.

Dawidoff, Robert. *The Education of John Randolph*. New York, 1979.

De Conde, Alexander. *The Quasi-War: The Politics and Diplomacy of the Undeclared War with France, 1797–1801*. New York, 1966.

———. *This Affair of Louisiana*. New York, 1976.

Degler, Carl N. *The Other South: Southern Dissenters in the Nineteenth Century*. New York, 1974.

———. "Slavery and the Genesis of American Race Prejudice." *Comparative Studies in Society and History*, II (1959), 49–66.

Demos, John. "The Antislavery Movement and the Problem of Violent 'Means.'" *New England Quarterly*, XXXVII (1964), 501–26.

Dew, Charles B. "Black Ironworkers and the Slave Insurrection Panic of 1856." *Journal of Southern History*, LXI (1975), 321–38.

Dillon, Merton L. *The Abolitionists: The Growth of a Dissenting Minority*. DeKalb, Ill., 1974.

———. *Benjamin Lundy and the Struggle for Negro Freedom.* Urbana, Ill., 1966.

———. *Elijah P. Lovejoy, Abolitionist Editor.* Urbana, Ill., 1961.

———. "Three Southern Antislavery Editors: The Myth of the Southern Antislavery Movement." *East Tennessee Historical Society's Publications,* No. 42 (1970), 47–56.

orman, James H. "The Persistent Specter: Slave Rebellion in Territorial Louisiana." *Louisiana History,* XVIII (1977), 393–404.

rake, Thomas E. *Quakers and Slavery in America.* New Haven, Conn., 1950.

umond, Dwight Lowell. *America's Shame and Redemption.* Marquette, Mich., 1965.

aton, Clement. "A Dangerous Pamphlet in the Old South." *Journal of Southern History,* II (1936), 1–12.

———. *Freedom of Thought in the Old South.* Durham, 1940.

———. *A History of the Southern Confederacy.* New York, 1954.

scott, Paul D. "The Context of Freedom: Georgia's Slaves During the Civil War." *Georgia Historical Quarterly,* LVIII (1974), 79–104.

aust, Drew Gilpin. *James Henry Hammond and the Old South: A Design for Mastery.* Baton Rouge, 1982.

hrenbacher, Don E. "Only His Stepchildren: Lincoln and the Negro." *Civil War History,* XX (1974), 293–310.

eldstein, Stanley. *Once a Slave: The Slaves' View of Slavery.* New York, 1971.

adeland, Betty L. *James G. Birney: Slaveholder to Abolitionist.* Ithaca, N.Y., 1955.

———. *Men and Brothers: Anglo-American Antislavery Cooperation.* Urbana, Ill., 1972.

oner, Eric. "The Causes of the American Civil War: Recent Interpretations and New Directions." *Civil War History,* XX (1974), 197–214.

———. *Free Soil, Free Labor, Free Men: The Ideology of the Republican Party Before the Civil War.* New York, 1970.

oner, Philip S. *History of Black Americans.* 3 vols. Westport, Conn., 1975–83.

ordham, Monroe. "Nineteenth-Century Black Thought in the United States: Some Influences of the Santo Domingan Revolution." *Journal of Black Studies,* VI (1975), 115–26.

anklin, John Hope. *The Emancipation Proclamation.* Garden City, N.Y., 1963.

———. *The Free Negro in North Carolina, 1790–1860.* New York, 1969.

———. *The Militant South.* Cambridge, Mass., 1956.

edrickson, George M. *The Black Image in the White Mind: The Debate on Afro-American Character and Destiny, 1817–1914.* New York, 1971.

———. "A Man But Not a Brother: Abraham Lincoln and Racial Equality." *Journal of Southern History,* XLI (1975), 39–58.

eehling, Alison Goodyear. *Drift Toward Dissolution: The Virginia Slavery Debate of 1831–1832.* Baton Rouge, 1982.

eehling, William W. "The Editorial Revolution, Virginia and the Coming of the Civil War: A Review Essay." *Civil War History,* XVI (1970), 64–72.

————. "Denmark Vesey's Peculiar Reality." In *New Perspectives on Race an Slavery in America: Essays in Honor of Kenneth M. Stampp*, edited by Rob ert H. Abzug and Stephen E. Maizlish. Lexington, Ky., 1986.

————. *Prelude to Civil War: The Nullification Controversy in South Carolinc 1818–1836*. New York, 1966.

Frey, Sylvia R. "Between Slavery and Freedom: Virginia Blacks in th American Revolution." *Journal of Southern History*, XLIX (1983), 375–98

Galenson, David W. *White Servitude in Colonial America: An Economr Analysis*. Cambridge, Eng., 1981.

Gara, Larry. "Slavery and the Slave Power: A Crucial Distinction." *Civ War History*, XV (1969), 4–18.

Garrison, Wendell Phillips, and Francis Jackson Garrison. *William Lloy Garrison, 1805–1879*. 4 vols. Boston, 1885–89.

Gatell, Frank Otto. "Postmaster Huger and the Incendiary Publications. *South Carolina Historical Magazine*, LXIV (1963), 193–201.

Genovese, Eugene D. *From Rebellion to Revolution: Afro-American Slave R(volts in the Making of the Modern World*. Baton Rouge, 1979.

————. "'Rather Be a Nigger Than a Poor White Man': Slave Perceptions (Southern Yeomen and Poor Whites." In *Toward a New View of Americc Essays in Honor of Arthur C. Cole*, edited by Hans L. Trefousse. Ne York, 1977.

————. *Roll, Jordan, Roll: The World the Slaves Made*. New York, 1974.

————. "Yeoman Farmers in a Slaveholding Democracy." *Agricultural His tory*, XLIX (1975), 331–42.

Gerteis, Louis S. *From Contraband to Freedman: Federal Policy Toward Soutt ern Blacks, 1861–1865*. Westport, Conn., 1973.

Gewehr, Wesley M. *The Great Awakening in Virginia, 1740–1790*. Durhan N.C., 1930.

Greene, Lorenzo J. *The Negro in Colonial New England, 1620–1776*. Ne York, 1942.

Halasz, Nicholas. *The Rattling Chains: Slave Unrest and Rebellion in th Antebellum South*. New York, 1968.

Hamer, Phillip M. "Great Britain, the United States, and the Negro Seame Acts, 1822–1848." *Journal of Southern History*, I (1935), 3–28.

Harris, J. William. *Plain Folk and Gentry in a Slave Society: White Libert and Black Slavery in Augusta's Hinterlands*. Middletown, Conn., 1985.

Hoffman, Ronald. *A Spirit of Dissension: Economics, Politics, and the Reve lution in Maryland*. Baltimore, 1973.

Honey, Michael K. "The War Within the Confederacy: White Unionists (North Carolina." *Prologue*, XVIII (1986), 75–93.

Horton, James Oliver, and Lois E. Horton. *Black Bostonians: Family Life ar Community Struggle in the Antebellum North*. New York, 1979.

Hunt, Alfred N. *Haiti's Influence on Antebellum America: Slumbering Volcar in the Caribbean*. Baton Rouge, 1988.

Isaac, Rhys. "Evangelical Revolt: The Nature of the Baptists' Challenge the Traditional Order in Virginia, 1765–1773." *William and Mary Quarterly*, 3rd ser., XXXI (1974), 345–68.

acobs, Donald M. "David Walker, Boston Race Leader, 1825–1830." *Essex Institute Historical Collections*, CVII (January, 1971), 94–107.

ames, C. L. R. *The Black Jacobins: Toussaint L'Ouverture and the San Domingo Revolution*. Rev. ed. New York, 1963.

ohnson, Guion Griffis. *Ante-Bellum North Carolina: A Social History*. Chapel Hill, N.C., 1937.

ohnston, James Hugo. *Race Relations in Virginia and Miscegenation in the South, 1776–1860*. Amherst, Mass., 1970.

ones, Bobby Frank. "A Cultural Middle Passage: Slave Marriage and Family in the Ante-Bellum South." Ph.D. dissertation, University of North Carolina, Chapel Hill, 1965.

ones, Howard. *Mutiny on the Amistad: The Saga of a Slave Revolt and Its Impact on American Abolition, Law, and Diplomacy*. New York, 1986.

ordan, Winthrop D. *White over Black: American Attitudes Toward the Negro, 1550–1812*. Chapel Hill, N.C., 1968.

oyner, Charles W. *Down by the Riverside: A South Carolina Slave Community*. Urbana, Ill., 1984.

aplan, Sidney. "The 'Domestic Insurrections' of the Declaration of Independence." *Journal of Negro History*, LXI (1976), 243–55.

atz, Jonathan. *Resistance at Christiana: The Fugitive Slave Rebellion, Christiana, Pennsylvania, September 11, 1851*. New York, 1974.

erber, Linda. *Federalists in Dissent: Imagery and Ideology in Jeffersonian America*. Ithaca, N.Y., 1970.

lingberg, Frank Wysor. *The Southern Claims Commission*. Berkeley, Calif., 1955.

olchin, Peter. *First Freedom: The Response of Alabama's Blacks to Emancipation and Reconstruction*. Westport, Conn., 1972.

onkle, Burton Alva. *The Life and Speeches of Thomas Williams . . . 1806–1872*. 2 vols. Philadelphia, 1905.

ack, Paul D. "Slavery and the Texas Revolution." *Southwestern Historical Quarterly*, LXXXIX (1985), 181–202.

efebvre, Georges. *The Great Fear of 1789: Rural Panic in Revolutionary France*. New York, 1973.

emmon, Sarah McCulloh. *Frustrated Patriots: North Carolina and the War of 1812*. Chapel Hill, N.C., 1973.

ofton, John. *Insurrection in South Carolina: The Turbulent World of Denmark Vesey*. Yellow Springs, Ohio, 1964.

ogan, Rayford W. *The Diplomatic Relations of the United States with Haiti, 1776–1891*. Chapel Hill, N.C., 1941.

ynd, Staughton. *Class Conflict, Slavery, and the United States Constitution*. Indianapolis, 1967.

aier, Pauline. "The Charleston Mob and the Evolution of Popular Politics in Revolutionary South Carolina, 1765–1784." *Perspectives in American History*, IV (1970), 173–98.

Mathews, Donald G. "The Methodist Mission to the Slaves, 1829–1844.
Journal of American History, LI (1965), 615–31.
———. *The Methodists and Slavery: A Chapter in American Morality, 1780*
1845. Princeton, N.J., 1965.
———. *Religion in the Old South*. Chicago, 1977.
McColley, Robert. *Slavery and Jeffersonian Virginia*. Urbana, Ill., 1964.
———. "Slavery in Virginia, 1619–1660: A Reexamination." In *New Per*
spectives on Race and Slavery in America: Essays in Honor of Kenneth M
Stampp, edited by Robert H. Abzug and Stephen E. Maizlish. Lexington
Ky., 1986.
McLeod, Duncan. *Slavery, Race, and the American Revolution*. London, 1974
———. "Toward Caste." In *Slavery and Freedom in the Age of Revolution*
edited by Ira Berlin and Ronald Hoffman. Charlottesville, Va., 1983.
McManus, Edgar J. *A History of Negro Slavery in New York*. Syracuse
N.Y., 1966.
———. *Black Bondage in the North*. Syracuse, N.Y., 1973.
McMaster, John Bach. *A History of the People of the United States from the*
Revolution to the Civil War. 8 vols. New York, 1915.
McPherson, James M. *The Negro's Civil War: How American Negroes Felt an*
Acted During the War for the Union. New York, 1965.
———. *The Struggle for Equality: Abolitionists and the Negro in the Civil War*
and Reconstruction. Princeton, N.J., 1964.
Meriwether, Robert L. *The Expansion of South Carolina, 1729–1765*. Kings
port, Tenn., 1940.
Messner, William F. "Black Violence and White Response: Louisiana, 1862.
Journal of Southern History, XLVI (1975), 19–38.
Miles, Edwin A. "The Mississippi Slave Insurrection Scare of 1835." *Journal*
of Negro History, XLII (1957), 48–60.
Miller, John C. *The Wolf by the Ears*. New York, 1977.
Milligan, John D. "Slave Rebelliousness and the Florida Maroon." *Prologue*
VI (1974), 4–18.
Mohr, Clarence L. *On the Threshold of Freedom: Masters and Slaves in Civ*
War Georgia. Athens, Ga., 1986.
Moore, Albert B. *Conscription and Conflict in the Confederacy*. New York
1924.
Moore, George Henry. *Notes on the History of Slavery in Massachusetts*. New
York, 1866.
Moore, Glover. *The Missouri Controversy, 1819–1821*. Lexington, Ky., 195:
Morgan, Edmund S. *American Slavery, American Freedom: The Ordeal of Co*
lonial Virginia. New York, 1975.
Morgan, Philip D., and George D. Terry. "Slavery in Microcosm: A Con
spiracy Scare in Colonial South Carolina." *Southern Studies*, XXI (1982
121–45.
Morison, Samuel Eliot. *Life and Letters of Harrison Gray Otis, Federali*
1765–1848. 2 vols. Boston, 1913.

Morris, Thomas D. *Free Men All: The Personal Liberty Laws of the North, 1780–1861*. Baltimore, 1974.

Mullin, Gerald W. *Flight and Rebellion: Slave Resistance in Eighteenth-Century Virginia*. New York, 1972.

——. "Religion, Acculturation, and American Negro Slave Rebellions: Gabriel's Insurrection." In *American Slavery: The Question of Resistance*, edited by John H. Bracey, Jr., August Meier, and Elliott Rudwick. Belmont, Calif., 1971.

Mullin, Michael, ed. *American Negro Slavery: A Documentary History*. New York, 1976.

Mutersbaugh, Bert M. "The Background of Gabriel's Conspiracy." *Journal of Negro History*, LXVIII (1983), 209–11.

Nash, Gary B. *Forging Freedom: The Formation of Philadelphia's Black Community, 1720–1840*. Cambridge, Mass., 1988.

Norton, Mary Beth. "'What an Alarming Crisis Is This': Southern Women and the American Revolution." In *The Southern Experience in the American Revolution*, edited by Jeffrey J. Crow and Larry E. Tise. Chapel Hill, N.C., 1978.

Nye, Russell B. *Fettered Freedom: Civil Liberties and the Slavery Controversy, 1830–1860*. East Lansing, Mich., 1949.

Oakes, James. "The Political Significance of Slave Resistance." *History Workshop*, No. 22 (Autumn, 1986), 89–107.

——. *The Ruling Race: A History of American Slaveholders*. New York, 1982.

Oates, Stephen B. *The Fires of Jubilee: Nat Turner's Fierce Rebellion*. New York, 1975.

——. *To Purge This Land with Blood: A Biography of John Brown*. New York, 1970.

Ohline, Howard A. "Slavery, Economics, and Congressional Politics, 1790." *Journal of Southern History*, XLVI (1980), 335–60.

Olwell, Robert A., "'Domestick Enemies': Slavery and Political Independence in South Carolina, May 1775–March 1776." *Journal of Southern History*, LV (1989), 21–48.

Owens, Leslie Howard. *This Species of Property: Slave Life and Culture in the Old South*. New York, 1976.

Owsley, Frank Lawrence. *State Rights in the Confederacy*. Chicago, 1925.

Palmer, Paul C. "Servant into Slave: The Evolution of the Legal Servitude of the Negro Laborer in Colonial Virginia." *South Atlantic Quarterly*, LXV (1966), 355–70.

Pargellis, Stanley M. "Braddock's Defeat." *American Historical Review*, XLI (1936), 253–69.

Patrick, Rembert Wallace. *Florida Fiasco: Rampant Rebels on the Georgia-Florida Border, 1810–1815*. Athens, Ga., 1954.

Pease, William H., and Jane H. Pease. *They Who Would Be Free: Blacks' Search for Freedom, 1830–1861*. New York, 1974.

Phillips, Ulrich Bonnell. *American Negro Slavery: A Survey of the Supply,*

Employment and Control of Negro Labor as Determined by the Plantation Regime. New York, 1918.

Pletcher, David M. *The Diplomacy of Annexation: Texas, Oregon, and the Mexican War.* Columbia, Mo., 1973.

Porter, Kenneth Wiggins. "Negroes on the Southern Frontier, 1670–1763." *Journal of Negro History*, XXXIII (1948), 53–78.

Quarles, Benjamin. *Allies for Freedom: Blacks and John Brown.* New York, 1974.

———. "Lord Dunmore as Liberator." *William and Mary Quarterly*, 3rd ser., XV (1958), 494–507.

———. *The Negro in the American Revolution.* Chapel Hill, N.C., 1961.

Raboteau, Albert J. *Slave Religion: The "Invisible Institution" in the Antebellum South.* New York, 1978.

Rachleff, Marshall. "David Walker's Southern Agent." *Journal of Negro History*, LXII (1977), 100–103.

Randall, James G., and David Donald. *The Civil War and Reconstruction.* 2nd ed., rev. Lexington, Mass., 1969.

Rankin, Hugh F. *The North Carolina Continentals.* Chapel Hill, N.C., 1971.

Ratner, Lorman. *Powder Keg: Northern Opposition to the Antislavery Movement, 1831–1840.* New York, 1968.

Remini, Robert V. *Andrew Jackson and the Course of American Empire, 1763–1821.* New York, 1977.

Richards, Leonard L. *"Gentlemen of Property and Standing:" Anti-Abolitionist Mobs in Jacksonian America.* New York, 1970.

Rippy, J. Fred. *The United States and Mexico.* New York, 1931.

Roark, James L. *Masters Without Slaves: Southern Planters in the Civil War and Reconstruction.* New York, 1977.

Robert, Joseph C. *The Road from Monticello: A Study of the Virginia Slavery Debate of 1832.* Durham, N.C., 1941.

Robinson, Armstead. "Day of Jubilo: Civil War and the Demise of Slavery in the Mississippi Valley, 1861–1865." Ph.D. dissertation, University of Rochester, 1976.

———. "In the Shadow of Old John Brown: Insurrection Anxiety and Confederate Mobilization, 1861–1863." *Journal of Negro History*, LXV (1980), 279–97.

Robinson, Donald L. *Slavery in the Structure of American Politics, 1765–1820.* New York, 1971.

Rogers, George C., Jr. *Charleston in the Age of the Pinckneys.* Norman, Okla., 1969.

Rose, Willie Lee. *Slavery and Freedom.* New York, 1982.

Rosengarten, Theodore. *Tombee: Portrait of a Cotton Planter, with the Journal of Thomas B. Chaplin, 1822–1890.* New York, 1986.

Rothman, David. *The Discovery of the Asylum: Social Order and Disorder in the New Republic.* Boston, 1971.

Sandburg, Carl. *Abraham Lincoln: The War Years.* 4 vols. New York, 1939.

Sayre, Robert Duane. "The Evolution of Early American Abolitionism: The American Convention for the Abolition of Slavery and Improving the Condition of the African Race, 1794–1837." Ph.D. dissertation, Ohio State University, 1987.

Scarborough, William K. *The Overseer: Plantation Management in the Old South.* Baton Rouge, 1966.

Schaper, William A. "Sectionalism and Representation in South Carolina." In Vol. I of American Historical Association, *Annual Report . . . for the Year 1900.* Washington, D.C., 1901.

Schmidt, Fredrika Teute, and Barbara Ripel Wilhelm. "Early Proslavery Petitions in Virginia." *William and Mary Quarterly*, 3rd ser., XXX (1973), 133–46.

Schwarz, Philip J. "Gabriel's Challenge: Slaves and Crime in Late Eighteenth-Century Virginia." *Virginia Magazine of History and Biography*, XC (1982), 283–309.

Sellers, Charles Grier, Jr., ed. *The Southerner as American.* Chapel Hill, N.C., 1960.

Sewell, Richard H. *Ballots for Freedom: Antislavery Politics in the United States, 1837–1860.* New York, 1976.

Shore, Laurence. "Making Mississippi Safe for Slavery: The Insurrectionary Panic of 1835." In *Class, Conflict, and Consensus: Antebellum Community Studies*, edited by Orville Vernon Burton and Robert C. McMath, Jr. Westport, Conn., 1982.

Shortreed, Margaret. "The Antislavery Radicals: From Crusade to Revolution, 1840–1868." *Past and Present*, XVI (November, 1959), 65–87.

Simpson, Craig M. *A Good Southerner: The Life of Henry A. Wise of Virginia.* Chapel Hill, N.C., 1985.

Sitterson, J. Carlyle. "Magnolia Plantation, 1852–1862: A Decade of a Louisiana Sugar Estate." *Mississippi Valley Historical Review*, XXV (1938), 197–210.

Smith, Julia Floyd. *Slavery and Rice Culture in Low Country Georgia, 1750–1860.* Knoxville, Tenn., 1985.

Smith, Page. "Anxiety and Despair in American History." *William and Mary Quarterly*, 3rd ser., XXVI (1969), 416–24.

Stampp, Kenneth M. *"And the War Came": The North and the Secession Crisis, 1860–1861.* Baton Rouge, 1950.

Stegmaier, Mark J. "Maryland's Fear of Insurrection at the Time of Braddock's Defeat." *Maryland Magazine of History*, LXXVI (1976), 467–83.

Stewart, James Brewer. "Evangelicalism and the Radical Strain in Southern Antislavery Thought During the 1820s." *Journal of Southern History*, XXXIX (1973), 379–96.

———. *Wendell Phillips, Liberty's Hero.* Baton Rouge, 1986.

Stoddard, T. Lothrop. *The French Revolution in San Domingo.* Boston, 1914.

Strickland, John Scott. "The Great Revival and Insurrectionary Fears in North Carolina: An Examination of Antebellum Southern Society and

Slave Revolt Panics." In *Class, Conflict, and Consensus: Antebellum Southern Community Studies*, edited by Orville Vernon Burton and Robert C
  McMath, Jr. Westport, Conn., 1982.

Strickland, William P. *The Life of Jacob Gruber*. New York, 1860.

Szasz, Ferenc M. "The New York Slave Revolt of 1741: A Re-examination."
  New York History, XLVIII (1967), 215–30.

Tatum, Georgia Lee. *Disloyalty in the Confederacy*. Chapel Hill, N.C., 1939

Terry, George. "A Study of the Impact of the French Revolution and the
  Insurrection in Saint-Domingue upon South Carolina, 1790–1805." M.A
  thesis, University of South Carolina, 1975.

Thomas, John L. *The Liberator, William Lloyd Garrison: A Biography*. Boston, 1963.

Trefousse, Hans. *Lincoln's Decision for Emancipation*. Philadelphia, 1975

Trexler, Harrison A. *Slavery in Missouri, 1804–1865*. Baltimore, 1914.

Ver Steeg, Clarence L. *Origins of a Southern Mosaic: Studies of Early Carolina and Georgia*. Athens, Ga., 1975.

Wade, Richard C. "The Vesey Plot: A Reconsideration." *Journal of Southern
  History*, XXX (1964), 143–61.

Walker, James W. St. G. *The Black Loyalists: The Search for a Promised Land
  in Nova Scotia and Sierra Leone, 1783–1870*. London, 1975.

Webb, Stephen Saunders. *1676: The End of American Independence*. New
  York, 1984.

Webber, Thomas L. *Deep Like the Rivers: Education in the Slave Quarter
  Community, 1831–1865*. New York, 1978.

Whitfield, Theodore M. *Slavery Agitation in Virginia, 1829–1832*. Baltimore, 1930.

Wiecek, William M. "The Statutory Law of Slavery and Race in the Thirteen Mainland Colonies of British America." *William and Mary Quarterly*,
  3rd ser., XXXIV (1977), 258–80.

Wikramanayak, Marina. *A World in Shadow: The Free Black in Antebellum
  South Carolina*. Columbia, S.C., 1973.

Wiley, Bell I. *The Life of Billy Yank, the Common Soldier of the Union*. Indianapolis, 1952.

——. *The Plain People of the Confederacy*. Baton Rouge, 1943.

——. *Southern Negroes, 1861–1865*. New Haven, Conn., 1938.

Williams, George W. *History of the Negro Race in America from 1619 to 1880*.
  2 vols. New York, 1883.

Williams, T. Harry. *Lincoln and the Radicals*. Madison, Wisc., 1965.

Williamson, Joel. *After Slavery: The Negro in South Carolina During Reconstruction, 1861–1877*. Chapel Hill, N.C., 1965.

Willis, William S., Jr. "Anthropology and Negroes on the Southern Colonial
  Frontier." In *The Black Experience in America: Selected Essays*, edited by
  James C. Curtis and Lewis L. Gould. Austin, Texas, 1970.

——. "Divide and Rule: Red, White, and Black in the Southeast." *Journal
  of Negro History*, XLVIII (1963), 157–76.

ilson, Henry. *History of the Rise and Fall of the Slave Power in America.* 3 vols. Boston, 1872–77.

'ish, Harvey. "Slave Disloyalty Under the Confederacy." *Journal of Negro History,* XXIII (1938), 435–50.

ood, Peter H. *Black Majority: Blacks in Colonial South Carolina from 1670 Through the Stono Rebellion.* New York, 1974.

——. "Nat Turner: The Unknown Slave as Visionary Leader." In *Black Leaders of the Nineteenth Century,* edited by Leon Litwack and August Meier. Urbana, Ill., 1988.

yatt-Brown, Bertram. *Lewis Tappan and the Evangelical War Against Slavery.* Cleveland, 1969.

——. "William Lloyd Garrison and Antislavery Unity: A Reappraisal." *Civil War History,* XIII (March, 1967), 5–24.

oung, Tommy R., II. "The United States Army and the Institution of Slavery in Louisiana, 1803–1815." *Louisiana Studies,* XIII (1974), 201–22.

orn, Roman. "The New England Anti-Slavery Society: Pioneer Abolitionist Organization." *Journal of Negro History,* XLIII (1957), 157–76.

Index

67, 191; in upper South, 73; in South Carolina, 135–37; in North Carolina, 192; in Mississippi, 192; reprisals for, 193–95

laveholders: and state's rights, 43; vulnerability of, 54, 88, 136, 201; and Gabriel's conspiracy, 63; and abolitionism, 92, 164, 177, 181; and religion, 98, 100–101; and free blacks, 183–84; and poor whites, 197–98; and fugitive slaves, 207–208; and Republican party, 224–25

lave patrols: corruption in, 15; in South Carolina, 23, 35, 137; in Georgia, 35; increased, 56; deficiencies in, 63, 68; during War of 1812, p. 78; opposition to, 99, 160, 195–96; in Civil War, 245, 246

lave resistance: instigated by Spanish, 22; and politics, 50, 97; and antislavery, 114, 129, 199–200; and Missouri controversy, 124; prevalence of, 130–32, 134–35, 137, 144; in 1850s, 199

lave revolt: southern fears of, 20, 24, 199; in Louisiana, 73–74; in Florida, 85; as motive for antislavery, 114–16, 118–19; and diffusion argument, 126–27; as result of antislavery, 128–29, 165; and abolition, 170, 180–81, 202–203, 205, 212, 214–18, 228–29; and American Anti-Slavery Society, 172–74; and England, 221–22; and John Brown, 236–37; and Civil War, 243–44

laves: acculturation of, 13, 55, 56, 90, 149; and religion, 18–19, 68–69, 97–98; antislavery influences on, 19, 52, 140–41, 174–75, 186–88, 208–209, 237; in wartime, 20, 33–39, 72, 75–84, 132, 222, 244–45; and politics, 21, 55, 123, 130, 182, 187, 231, 242; control of, 56–57, 137–38, 152, 196–97; urban, 190–91

lave trade, 50, 72–73, 94, 184, 186

mith, George W., 75
mith, Gerrit, 206, 208–209, 234
mith, Margaret B., 78
mith, William, 128

outh America: revolutions in, 168
outhampton County, Va., 149, 158
outh Carolina: slave numbers in, 5; white immigration encouraged to, 6; fugitive slaves in, 14–15, 33; fears of slaves in, 17; revolt in, 24; and de-

fense of slavery, 24; in Revolution, 35, 52–54; and Saint-Domingue, 46–47; and Gabriel's conspiracy, 60; stability of slavery in, 69, 77–78, 128; slave religion in, 100; antislavery in, 101–102; Methodists in, 107–108; northern attitudes toward, 113; black militia in, 132; and upper South slaves, 184; murder of slaves in, 196–97; and election of 1860, pp. 239, 240

Spanish colonies, 22–24, 70, 81. See also Florida; South America
Spartanburg, S.C., 240
Spooner, Lysander, 233–34
Spotswood, Alexander, 17, 19
Stamp Act, 28
Stansbury, Tobias E., 80
Stark County, Ohio, 183
Stono rebellion, 6, 23–24, 24n
Suffrage, 143
Summers, George W., 160
Sumner, Charles, 225

Tallmadge, James, 123, 125, 126
Tallmadge Amendment, 127
Tangier Island, 79
Tappan, Arthur, 171, 171n
Tappan, Benjamin, 165
Tappan, Lewis, 203
Taylor, John, of Caroline, 90, 114
Texas, 86, 218, 219, 221, 222, 231
Texas Revolution, 219
Thom, John, 232
Thomas, Lorenzo, 255
Thomson, Charles, 39
Three-fifths compromise, 123, 182
Troy, N.Y., 215
Tubman, Harriet, 235
Tucker, George, 72
Tucker, Thomas, 50
Turner, Nat, 150, 152–53
Turner's rebellion. See Nat Turner's rebellion
Tyson, Elisha, 140

Union, the, 249, 252, 255, 256, 262, 263
United States Army, 74, 80, 252, 255, 256, 262, 263
United States Bank, 124n
Upper South, 56, 63–64, 105, 183–85, 231, 241
Upshur, Abel P., 185

Venable, Abraham B., 75
Vesey, Denmark, 133, 135–36